THE GEORGIANS

THE GEORGIANS

THE DEEDS AND MISDEEDS OF 18TH-CENTURY BRITAIN

PENELOPE J. CORFIELD

YALE UNIVERSITY PRESS
NEW HAVEN AND LONDON

For information about this and other Yale University Press publications, please contact:
U.S. Office: sales.press@yale.edu   yalebooks.com
Europe Office: sales@yaleup.co.uk   yalebooks.co.uk

Set in Adobe Caslon Pro by IDSUK (DataConnection) Ltd
Printed in Great Britain by TJ Books, Padstow, Cornwall

Library of Congress Control Number: 2021940107

ISBN 978-0-300-25357-3

A catalogue record for this book is available from the British Library.

10 9 8 7 6 5 4 3 2 1

CONTENTS

CONTENTS

ILLUSTRATIONS

In text

Part I: Detail from *The Coffee-House Politicians*, anonymous, *c.* 1733. © British Museum, Dept. of Prints and Drawings, no. 1868,0808.13254.

Part II: *A Cottage Interior: An Old Woman Preparing Tea*, William Redmore Bigg, 1793. © Victoria & Albert Museum, acc. no. 199–1885.

Part III: *Treason!!!*, Richard Newton, 1798. Library of Congress Prints and Photographs Division Washington, DC, 20540 USA, LC-USZC4-8788.

Part IV: Detail from *The Caricature Shop of Piercy Roberts*, anonymous, 1801. © The Metropolitan Museum, Fifth Avenue, The Elisha Whittelsey Collection (1953), no. 53.502.5.

Part V: *A Chemical Lecture at the Surrey Institution*, Thomas Rowlandson, 1809. Wellcome Collection, Attribution 4.0 International (CC BY 4.0).

Plates

1. *Self-portrait*, Henry Fuseli, *c.* 1780. Victoria and Albert Museum, London.
2. *Gin Lane*, William Hogarth, 1751. National Gallery of Art, Rosenwald Collection.
3. *Beer Street*, William Hogarth, 1751. National Gallery of Art, Rosenwald Collection.
4. *George I*, G.W. Lafontaine, *c.* 1720–7. Royal Collection Trust / © Her Majesty Queen Elizabeth II 2021.
5. Statue of Charles Edward Stuart, Bonnie Prince Charlie, on horseback, Full Street, Derby. travelib history / Alamy Stock Photo.
6. Detail from *Portrait of Dido Elizabeth Belle and Lady Elizabeth Murray*, David Martin, *c.* 1780. Courtesy of the Earl of Mansfield, Scone Palace, Perth.
7. Portrait of William Penn, *c.* 1690. Stock Montage / Getty Images.
8. *Gentle Measures or Voluntary Confessions*, Isaac Cruikshank, 1798. Trinity College Dublin, Digital Collections. Library of Congress Prints and Photographs Division Washington, DC, PC 1 – 9242.
9. Detail from *Westminster Election, 1796*, after Richard Dighton. Royal Collection Trust / © Her Majesty Queen Elizabeth II 2021.
10. *Warren Hastings with his Wife Marian in their Garden at Alipore*, Johann Zoffany, *c.* 1784. The Picture Art Collection / Alamy Stock Photo.
11. *Edmund Burke*, Sir Joshua Reynolds, *c.* 1769. © National Portrait Gallery, London.
12. *Samuel Johnson*, Sir Joshua Reynolds, 1775. © Courtesy of the Huntington Art Museum, San Marino, California.
13. Mary Somerville medallion. Metropolitan Museum of Art (Gift of Samuel P. Avery, 1898).

14. John Wesley statue, Bristol, 1932. Photo by Neil Phillips © John Wesley's New Room, Bristol.
15. David Hume statue, Edinburgh, 1997. Suddenfootloss / CC BY-SA 4.0.
16. *The Elopement*, Thomas Rowlandson, 1782. Yale Center for British Art, Paul Mellon Collection.
17. *The Rt. Honble. Lady Eleanor Butler & Miss Ponsonby "The Ladies of Llangollen"*, J.H. Lynch after Mary Parker (later Lady Leighton), 1828. Wellcome Collection.
18. *Peg Woffington*, John Lewis, 1753. © National Portrait Gallery, London.
19. *Kitty Fisher*, Nathaniel Hone, 1765. © National Portrait Gallery, London.
20. *The Woman Shopkeeper*, British School, c. 1790. People's Palace and Winter Gardens / CC BY-NC-ND.
21. Detail from inoculator cartoon. Library of Congress, Prints and Photographs Division, LC-USZC4-3147.
22. Tin Plate Workers Society banner, c. 1821. From the collection of People's History Museum.
23. Detail from *Progress of an Irishman*, Rich Newton. Published 8 April 1794, by William Holland, No. 50, Oxford Street. Courtesy of the Lewis Walpole Library, Yale University.
24. *Adam Smith*. © National Portrait Gallery, London.
25. *Thomas Paine*. © National Portrait Gallery, London.
26. *Mary Wollstonecraft*, John Opie, c. 1797. © National Portrait Gallery, London.
27. *Robert Owen*, Auguste Hervieu, 1829. © National Portrait Gallery, London.
28. Royal Navy plate, Liverpool, c. 1790. Musée de la Révolution française, MRF 1991-18.
29. The Zong Massacre. Author's personal collection.
30. *Inspection and Sale of a Negro*, 1854. Library of Congress Prints and Photographs Division, LC-USZ62-15392.

PREFACE

The eighteenth century is a period in British history which triggers strong responses – both admiring and censorious. Its architecture remains generally celebrated, as does its taste in furniture and garden design. Novelists as well as film and TV directors enjoy the period's reputation for steamy sex lives and the fashion for heaving bosoms in low-cut dresses. The hugely successful *Bridgerton* series, on screen and page, is a recent case in point. In addition, swashbuckling naval adventures set in the days of Horatio Nelson are perennial favourites. And readers of all ages can enjoy Georgian literary classics, from *Gulliver's Travels* to *Pride and Prejudice*. Together, the many key eighteenth-century legacies make a formidable list, including, not least, the successive Acts of Union which united the kingdoms of Great Britain and Ireland.

Yet the domestic political history of the era is often dismissed as parochial, and its industrial history as grimly utilitarian. One Victorian artist sweepingly claimed to find the entire period as boring as a wet Saturday afternoon. Meanwhile, there are big disputed issues which are not just matters of personal taste but are highly serious questions for society at large. The eighteenth century's scientific techno-culture has become enshrined as the ancestral basis of today's high-tech world, yet the intensive burning of fossil fuels inadvertently launched a process of global warming which is now generating total environmental crisis. Too much cultural optimism can lead to over-confidence, today as yesterday.

At the same time, moreover, eighteenth-century Britain's imperial expansion and its central participation in the international trade in enslaved Africans are developments that are nowadays viewed, at least by the huge majority of good-hearted people, as definitively on the 'wrong' side of history. The current disputes over public statues honouring eighteenth-century dignitaries whose reputations are compromised in the eyes of posterity make that point abundantly clear.

These complex links across time, complete with changing attitudes. are fundamental to the story of the Georgians' deeds and misdeeds. This book looks again at the direct evidence from the era, investigating individual lives and testimonies, and bypassing later myths and legends. In parallel, however, since the reputation of an epoch is also part of its long-term history, this book reconsiders how the actions and inactions of eighteenth-century Britain have been regarded by later generations. In that spirit, each chapter ends with a short coda entitled 'Time-Shift: Then and Now'. These offer brief interludes, with evidence for through-time contemplation, exploring how people today adopt, adapt, remember, forget, praise and blame the compound Georgian heritage. Further resources and links to special interest groups are also shared in website thegeorgiansdeedsandmisdeeds.com.

Of course, all these retrospective assessments raise central questions about which criteria of judgement can be validly adopted when judging the past. These major themes are debated throughout.

My personal interest in eighteenth-century life is long-standing. During my schooldays and undergraduate studies, however, this period of British history was skated through very rapidly. My move into the eighteenth century, as a postgraduate at the London School of Economics in the later 1960s, was thus a cheerful step into the unknown. The congenial company of other scholars on the same adventure was a great bonus, as was the abundance of accessible but under-studied sources. It is a particular pleasure to acknowledge my intellectual debts both to the meta-critical intellect of F.J. (Jack) Fisher, and equally to the creative power of E.P. (Edward) Thompson, no mean critic himself. Without agreeing totally with either scholar, it was a complete education to spend time in debate with such high-powered and generous minds.

A further point to mention is that my personal cultural roots stem from a distinctly secularised form of Protestant Dissent – particularly a secularised Quakerism. And it's also relevant that my outlook is temperamentally optimistic, although without believing that history constitutes an unalloyed march of 'progress'.

Given that this study has taken many years to complete, the roll-call of people who have helped is a lengthy one. The organisers and participants at London University's Long Eighteenth Century Seminar have delightfully informed, inspired, challenged, amused and sometimes even bored me into fresh thought. (I try to do the same in return.) Hearty thanks for shared intellectual camaraderie go also to all participants at the conferences of the British Society for Eighteenth-Century Studies (BSECS). And the same applies to the lively and ecumenical networks of the International Society for Eighteenth-Century Studies (ISECS/SIEDS). Invaluable support and stimulus have come too from colleagues and students at Royal Holloway, University of London; and from various institutions where I have held research fellowships, including Nuffield College, Oxford, All Souls College, Oxford, and Newcastle University.

Warm gratitude for sharing ideas and arguments goes also to: Junko Akamatsu, Lise Andries, Marc-André Bernier, Helen Berry, Margaret Bird, Jeremy Black, Gordon Bottomley, Ester Brot, Conrad Brunstrom, Michael Burden, Arthur Burns, Brycchan Carey, Philip Carter, Mary Clayton, David Clemis, Michèle Cohen, Linda Colley,

Joe Cozens, Sean Creighton, Adam Crymble, Stephen Boyd Davis, James Dixon, Jean-François Dunyach, Sutapa Dutta, Peter Earle, Chris Evans, Margot Finn, Edmund Green, Jeremy Gregory, Matthew Grenby, Leonie Hannan, Negley Harte, Charles Harvey, Karen Harvey, Farhat Hasan, David Hebb, Tony Henderson, Uriel Heyd, Tim Hitchcock, Stephen Hoare, Neil Howe, Eddie Hunt, Joanna Innes, Takashi Ito, Wen Jin, Serena Kelly, Mark Knights, Kazuhiko Kondo, Emi Konishi, Xabier Lamikiz, Sarah Lloyd, Matthew McCornack, Ichiro Michisige, Zeta Moore, Chris Mounsey, Takahashi Nakamura, Tadeshi Nakano, Desmond Newell, Frank O'Gorman, David Ormrod, Ivan Parvev, Julie Peakman, Nicola Phillips, Robert Poole, Steve Poole, Wilfrid Prest, Miranda Reading, Kate Retford, Giorgio Riello, Nicholas Rodger, Adrian Seville, Jill Shifrin, Akiko Shimbo, Heather Shore, Paul Slack, Carolyn Steedman, Anne Stott, Rosemary Sweet, Judith Thompson, Janice Turner, Tim Wales, Gina Luria Walker, John Walsh and Nuala Zahadieh.

Constructive criticism is always vital to bring a big project to completion. Cordial thanks are therefore due to: Peter Clark, Peter D'Sena, Beverley Duguid, Amanda Goodrich, Sally Holloway, Julian Hoppit, Liam Kennedy, Susan Whyman, Gillian Williamson and a set of rigorous anonymous readers.

Lastly, special thanks go to Amanda Vickery for her longtime exhortation to write this book; to Robert Baldock and Heather McCallum at Yale University Press for sage editorial advice; to my family for affectionate support, allied with quizzical scepticism; and, perennially, to my life partner and super-critic Tony Belton.

Battersea, London, 2021

PART I
The Georgians Debating an Age of Change

Sharing news, views and gossip, fuelled by word-of-mouth,
newspapers and caffeine.

❧ 1 ❧

Introducing the Georgians

The inhabitants of eighteenth-century Britain were great innova-
tors and travellers, both mentally and physically. New vistas
were opening. Needless to say, not everyone had the means or the
desire to travel far. While there was a notable diaspora of population
from all quarters of the British Isles, there were plenty of 'stayers' as
well as 'movers'. But even those who did not explore the world in
person could read – or have read aloud to them – the travel memoirs
and guides that were newly abundant in this period.

Moreover, all Britons were able to journey mentally up and down
the centuries. Looking backwards, they spoke of traditional ways,
dating from 'time immemorial'. They sang old and much-loved
songs, retold old fables and proverbs, used old folk remedies. And
they could potentially also study new specialist works of history,
a subject then gaining an increased cultural authority, which it
continued to wield in the following centuries.

Equally, looking ahead at the coming years, individual pioneers
helped in this period to develop future-projected actuarial calculations
of risk, as well as accurate astronomical predictions, and the new and

entertaining genre of science fiction. One example, published in 1733, was entitled *Memoirs of the Twentieth Century*, while another futuristic work, dating from 1763, imagined *The Reign of George VI, 1900–25*: it gave a good guess at the twentieth-century monarch's regnal name and number (though erring on the precise dates), whilst it also imagined a Britain still fighting naval wars around the world – and, reassuringly, still winning.[1]

Travel both mental and physical helped to sharpen people's sense of their own identities. Many shared a heightened cultural 'bullishness' about Britain's significance in the world; and an interest in how national destinies would play out over time. What would future generations think of them? An awareness of significant change encouraged both immediate optimism and a sense of transience in the longer term. Thus, in 1800, the politically astute Lady Holland wondered, in her private journal, how the imperial glory of Britain would be seen many millennia into the future. Being familiar with Gibbon's epic *Decline and Fall of the Roman Empire*, she imagined that the same fate might happen to Britain. Would some traveller in the far-distant future stumble upon the ruins of London, 'when this little island shall have fallen into its natural insignificancy', minus its colonial settlements and worldwide trade – and find nothing more than collapsed houses and piles of red-brick dust?[2]

In fact, the passage of time (in this case, not over many millennia but over the 300-plus years since 1700) has considerably changed many aspects of Britain's role. But, as will be seen, the resulting legacies – for both good and ill – are much more substantial than mere brick-dust.

Sharing Multiple National Identities

Eighteenth-century Britons were already aware of diversity in their own history. There were traditional differences between the ancient kingdoms of Ireland/Hibernia, Scotland/Caledonia, and England/Albion –

and certainly not forgetting the Principality of Wales/Cambria, tucked within the jurisdictional embrace of England. Furthermore, there were complex and continuing regional, social, political and religious divisions. Yet there were also unifying and bonding factors. One was the continuous movement of populations across the borders of the ancient kingdoms. Another, more intimate bonding factor, was the process of intermarriage – an important but under-studied social reality – between the inhabitants of all these historic jurisdictions.

Signals allowing the Georgians to decode traditional national differences were offered by cultural stereotypes in the form of songs, stories and jokes. In practice, these shorthand references were wildly oversimplified. Nonetheless, they offered starting-points. So, the Irish (in legend) were happy-go-lucky, superstitious, feckless, and famed for their 'gift of the gab'; the Scots (in legend) were puritanical, canny, money-conscious, and endowed with caustic wit; the Welsh (in legend) were loquacious, fiery and musical; and the English (still in legend) were calmly assertive but reserved, even melancholic, whilst possessing a quirky sense of humour.[3] One eighteenth-century handbook further added that the English constituted the psychological happy mean, being poised midway between (again in legend) the stereotypically dull Teutons and frivolous French.

However, this period also saw a key innovation. As the constitutional and (to an extent) the socio-economic and cultural relationships between the kingdoms were changing, a new concept of 'Britishness' emerged. This concept was not closely defined by past history, which gave it a useful flexibility. Following the dynastic 'union of the crowns' in 1603, Scotland and England in the Georgian period already shared the same monarchical head of state. A major transformation followed in 1707, not without controversy both then and subsequently: the Scottish and English Parliaments were merged, forming the legislative body of a new Kingdom of Great Britain. In heraldry, the Scottish unicorn was paired with the English lion. And a new flag, the Union Jack, was formed by superimposing Scotland's blue-and-white Saltire upon England's red-and-white Cross of St George.[4] Nonetheless, the merger was not pushed too far. Both countries kept their own legal systems: the Scots law, rooted in Roman civil law, contrasting with the empirically unfolding English common law. In addition, the constitutions of Scotland's traditional municipal burghs (boroughs) remained diversified until 1834, when they were standardised by Whig reformers. And, above all, each realm was left to acknowledge its own established Church: the English Episcopalian, the Scottish Presbyterian.

Despite these continuing differences, however, a new, personified embodiment of the Union in the form of 'Britannia' was gaining her own characteristics. Celebrated verses urging this proud lady to 'rule the waves' were penned in 1740 and then, set to music, became a popular song. Britannia also adopted England's regal lion, which became symbolically 'British' as well. And the term 'Briton' came into currency. So when the young George III sought to reassure MPs in 1760 that he had no 'tainted' German ancestry, he declared that: 'Born and educated in this Country, I glory in the Name of "Briton"'.[5]

Being 'British' did not carry the same nuanced historical baggage as did the much older labels of 'English', 'Irish', 'Scottish' or 'Welsh'. As time passed, however, the usage became more common and it acquired mythic associations of valour, coolness under fire, a degree of bellicosity (especially when confronting the French), an emotional reserve, a pointed wit, and a calm confidence when meeting people from other cultures around the world. (Again, in legend.)

'Britishness' could be attributed to people anywhere within the British Isles. The Scots were sometimes termed 'North Britons'. And Protestants in Ireland increasingly cultivated a 'British' identity.[6] However, the terms 'British' and 'English' were particularly close – and sometimes used interchangeably. Indeed, in a remarkable tribute to the power of tradition, the monarchical heads of the Union, defined legally post-1707 as 'Great Britain', continued to be described as kings and queens 'of England', as they are still to this day.

Incidentally, dynastic labels were slow to adapt in other areas too. Thus George III was proclaimed at his coronation as king of Great Britain, Ireland *and* France, invoking the old Plantagenet realms of Aquitaine and Calais. (He was, however, the last British monarch to be so saluted.) Similarly, the Bourbon kings of France and Spain played a reverse diplomatic game. For them, the Catholic heirs of the exiled Stuart King James II, who fled to France in 1688, were the true bloodline. Hence, after his father's death, James Francis Edward Stuart, the 'Old Pretender' (1688–1766), was theoretically James III of England and VIII of Scotland, whilst his son, Charles Edward Stuart, the 'Young Pretender' (1720–88), known as Bonnie Prince Charlie, succeeded him as Charles III.

Numerous eighteenth-century residents of the British Isles, particularly in Scotland and Ireland, initially maintained an attachment to the traditional dynasty. The numbers of active supporters, however, soon began to dwindle. After 1714, it was the new Hanoverian monarchs who had the magnetic power of incumbency. The first and comparatively large Jacobite rebellion (so named after the claimant's name James, Latinised as Jacobus) was defeated in 1715. It had gained significant support in Scotland and Ireland, but not enough to triumph. And the second Jacobite rebellion in 1745, which was smaller but still potentially redoubtable, ended in the bloody slaughter of the rebels at Culloden Moor, near Inverness, in April 1746. (Today this battlefield of many deaths is tended sensitively by the National Trust of Scotland.) The Young Pretender, who had arrived with high hopes, fled back into exile in France. There he styled himself Count of Albany, using the historic title of Scotland's dynastic heir. But after 1763, he had a new titular rival, when George III's second son was dubbed Duke of York *and* Albany.

Jacobitism thereafter dwindled as an active cause: the family's claim to the British throne is now purely notional, like that of the pre-Tudor Plantagenets. (A statue of Bonnie Prince Charlie in gallant pose stands today in Derby, where he turned to retreat northwards;

and a bronze image of the doughty Flora MacDonald, who aided his escape from the Scottish militia, stands outside Inverness Castle.)

Ireland meanwhile remained legally a separate realm throughout the eighteenth century. Nonetheless, in 1540 a new link had been forged. Henry VIII of England was also declared King of Ireland, while de facto English suzerainty was later enhanced, especially after tough military intervention and an extensive road-building programme under Oliver Cromwell. The big revolt which erupted in 1688–90 in support of the departing Catholic Stuart King James II met with military defeat at the hands of the incoming William III (the Protestants' 'King Billy'). The Battle of the Boyne (1690) ended the overt hostilities. Nonetheless, discontent continued to simmer among many, though not all, of the majority Catholic population. The English, 'who plume themselves on their own freedom', kept the Irish in 'abject Slavery and Dependence', complained a critic bitterly in 1743.[7] Catholics were subject to anti-Popish penal laws, variably enforced; and male Catholic property-owners were politically disenfranchised, without the right to vote in Ireland before 1793.

By contrast, most Irish Protestants, who constituted a substantial minority with their especial stronghold in the north, saw 'Hibernia' not as England's oldest colony but as a 'loyal, brave and free Nation', linked by shared kingship.[8] Indeed, the British monarchy's insignia in eighteenth-century Ireland featured not only the paired lion and unicorn but, between them, an Irish harp. It was an image of shared harmony. Yet Irish political opinion of all persuasions remained resistant to undue interference from Westminster. So a rumoured plan of 1759 to merge the British and Irish Parliaments met with great opposition. A riot in the streets of Dublin underlined the discontent.[9] In fact, however, the rumour was no more than that. And in 1782 the Irish Parliament was awarded extra powers. It took a major crisis in the later 1790s, when Ireland's Protestants feared a conjunction of both French invasion and an Irish Catholic rebellion, to prompt an abrupt change of policy. The old unfounded rumour was now turned into reality. A new Union was enacted in 1800, coming into force on 1 January 1801. It required legislation in both the Dublin and Westminster Parliaments, which were thereby merged, to form the legislative body of a new United Kingdom of Great Britain and Ireland.[10] The Union Jack was quickly redesigned. The flag then gained its current form with the addition of Ireland's red-and-white Cross of St Patrick (a design left unchanged even when in 1922 a majority of Irish counties seceded to form the Irish Republic).

During this upheaval, there were some dissenting voices, as there had been in Scotland in 1707. Yet the opposition was muted. A majority in both the Irish and the British Parliaments consented. The British prime minister William Pitt the Younger had proposed extending the franchise for the expanded Westminster Parliament to include Irish Catholic property-owners. It would have been an imaginative policy of real convergence. But the plan was rejected, leaving an unresolved issue which continued to trouble both nervous Protestants and resentful Catholics.

Few Britons worried on a day-to-day basis about the constitutional details. People identified as Irish, Scottish, Welsh and English, notwithstanding the extent of intermarriage and population mobility. Hence, just as there were Scots Societies in Georgian Newcastle, Norwich and London, linked by business and family contacts, so there were Hibernian Societies in Georgian Glasgow, Bristol, Birmingham and London.[11] These clubs provided social support and cultural familiarity. Yet in parallel a new identity was also evolving. Britain's expanding overseas possessions, initially described loosely as a 'commercial' empire, were becoming known as the 'British' (and not the 'English') empire. An early example of the usage, applied to the North American colonies, dates from 1708.[12] By the mid-century, the term was becoming commonplace.

People in this period, as later, were becoming accustomed to juggling multiple, overlapping and sometimes clashing identities, relating to both the traditional realms and to the British Unions of

1707 and 1801. Yet such daily identifications and interpretations did not depend upon strict constitutional law. Instead, they emerged from the entanglements of history and personal choices. And, as such, they are renewed – and also adapted – in every generation.

Defining the 'Long' Eighteenth Century

Historians these days often refer to the 'long' eighteenth century as a coherent and significant period for study.[13] Of course, there are many past 100-year slabs of history that merit attention.[14] Choosing one particular – and specifically extended – timespan does, however, focus attention upon a crucible period that was long enough not only for major and minor changes to become visible (as will be seen), but also for important continuities (not to be overlooked) to remain apparent. Broadly speaking, the core time span of this 'long' eighteenth century stretches for some 160 years, running through from approximately 1680 to around 1840 (with apologies to those literalists who like their eighteenth century to run precisely from 1700 to 1799, or from 1701 to 1800).

This 'long' era saw the emergence into the world of more than six successive generations of people (taking the demographers' standard of twenty-five years per generation). Or, putting the point another way, a retrospective gaze from the early twenty-first century looks back over the activities of some thirteen and a half generations to get back to the 1680s and to assess the unfolding long-term impact of eighteenth-century lives and legacies.

That span is still but a tiny chapter in the long history of humanity. In that spirit, the Irish poet Thomas Moore in his 1817 mock-Persian epic *Lalla Rookh* wrote plangently of the fleeting nature of temporality. The present moment in any era was but a fragment 'in Time's great wilderness/ This narrow isthmus 'twixt two boundless seas/ The past, the future, two Eternities!'[15] Nevertheless, people in the eighteenth century were becoming conscious of the chronological definition of their era. Precise datings were becoming much more widely adopted in routine usage. Biblical scholars had long originated a system based upon the calculation of Christ's birth at the start of Year 1, and then counting onwards and backwards from that date. Eventually, the year-count was further aggregated into a summary century-count. The first book in Britain to use that formula on its title-page appeared in 1756. Written by the clergyman-historian Ferdinando Warner, it covered *The Ecclesiastical History of England to the Eighteenth Century*.[16] The usage quickly spread. In 1800, for example, a poem entitled *The Last Dying Words of the Eighteenth Century* did not rise above doggerel.[17] Yet its title indicated that readers were expected to recognise their own due-date in history and to be interested in its passing.

A further anonymous salute to *The New Century* followed in 1801. It focused not upon death but upon renewal: 'Hail to the New Gigantic MASS of Years!'[18] The transition from one identifiable slab of time to the next also generated an earnest debate among clergymen and mathematicians. Was 1800 the last year of the old century or the first of the new? (Parallel arguments followed in 1899–1900 and, especially, at the millennium's end in December 1999 – or was it in December 2000?) The general point here was that educated contemporaries now placed their era into a known temporal sequence. So when historians refer to the 'long' eighteenth century, they are extending, for analytical purposes, a calendrical system that was familiar to those living through it.

Referencing time in numerical aggregates has one further advantage, of avoiding preset descriptive judgments. It was true that a number of eighteenth-century contemporaries believed that they were witnessing the birth of 'modern times'. Yet they strikingly disagreed about the meaning of such a momentous change. The author of *Thoughts on the Frequency of Divorces in Modern Times* (1800) was pessimistic.[19] No easy 'progress' for him. By contrast, *The Flowers of Modern History* (1789) offered a benign overview of social improvements since the time of the 'Goths' who had overthrown the Roman Empire.[20] This lack of consensus was apparent to contemporaries. The whimsical novelist and connoisseur Horace Walpole noted wryly in 1770 that 'The curse of modern times is that almost everything does create controversy'.[21] Accordingly, the concept of 'modernity' is taken, in the following chapters, not as a preset description of the era but as a matter for debate.

Much the same applies to would-be definitions of the eighteenth century as either an era of 'progress' or one of obtuse moral backwardness. Critics of eighteenth-century policies and behaviour can at times appear rather superior. They imply that earlier generations had more retrogressive values than have their 'enlightened' descendants; and that people then were often credulous and ignorant. Yet the historian E.P. Thompson long ago warned historians (and others) about the need to avoid the 'enormous condescension of posterity'. Later generations generally have their own moral black spots, for which they in turn will be criticised in years to come. As Thompson pertinently explained: 'After all, we [all the people of later times] are not at the end of social evolution ourselves'.[22]

Moreover, this warning also applies in reverse. For those who believe in catastrophist 'decline and fall' models of history, it is equally worth stressing that there was not one magical 'golden age' in the past, when sturdy upright individuals, all with uncorrupted values, lived in harmonious societies, in a manner that people in later epochs can never equal. The experience of historical change does not switch dramatically from pure good to pure evil, or vice versa.

There are, instead, multiple cross-linkages, trends and contrasts over time. Some are surprising. Twenty-first-century webtechnology provides an unexpected echo of an eighteenth-century satire upon human pride. In 1726, Jonathan Swift's *Gulliver's Travels* imagined a strange land ruled by noble and cultivated horses. These are the Houyhnhnms (Swift's clever evocation of a horse's whinny – try saying it aloud) and in their land the wild animals are a coarse, bestial tribe, known as 'yahoos': these are humans, and Gulliver is mortified by his kinship with them. Onwards to 1994, and the American creators of a new web service named it Yahoo.[23] Their jocular choice borrowed an American student slang term for an uncouth person, echoing Swift's original satire. Its application to a smart web domain is deeply ironic. Yet such outcomes spring from the creative processes of cultural cross-fertilisation. And, as will be seen, the remarkable eighteenth-century Britons have generated multiple legacies.

Naming the Georgians

At this point, it is helpful to find a summary term for the six generations who lived between the 1680s and the 1830s. It's cumbersome to repeat every time 'all who lived or originated in the British Isles during the long eighteenth century'. Collective naming is punchier, even if it depends on historical retrospection.

Dynastic surnames are often used to define past eras. Examples include 'Tudor England', 'Bourbon France' and 'Habsburg Spain'. And in eighteenth-century Britain, there was one monarchical dynasty for much of the period. After 1714, two leading Protestant powers of north-west Europe were intimately yoked. Five successive kings of Britain were simultaneously Electors (and, after 1814, kings) of Hanover. This link ended in 1837 through a combination of divergent constitutional rules and dynastic chance, when Victoria succeeded her uncle William IV to the British throne. As a woman, however, she was debarred from reigning in Hanover (the throne went instead to her uncle Ernest Augustus). The kingdoms were thus divided, the process being eased by the absence of an administrative union. One result was that, thirty years later, Victoria avoided a personal confrontation with Bismarck's Prussia, which in 1866 militarily annexed Hanover (despite some grumbling from its inhabitants) and deposed its ruler.

Before the divergence of the crowns, the link had appeared solid enough. It's true that it was initially controversial both with outright

Jacobites and with many backbench squires. In Henry Fielding's entertaining 1749 novel *Tom Jones*, Squire Western is depicted as a bluff country gentleman, who refers to royal courtiers and ministers as 'Hanover rats'.[24] Over time, however, the link became quietly accepted, fostering commercial, religious and diplomatic ties.[25]

Undoubtedly, however, the balance of power between Hanover and Britain in the eighteenth century was strongly tilted in favour of Europe's offshore islands, with their fast-growing populations and economic might. George I, who was fond of the Electorate, visited it regularly and was buried there. But, after 1760, his successors stayed away, apart from one trip made by George IV in 1821. Thus, it would be misleading to name their populations as 'Hanoverian Britons', although some experts write about Hanoverian Britain and Hanoverian Ireland.[26] There was no popular affiliation with the Electorate.

Another monarchical alternative, meanwhile, is more plausible. Describing the era as 'Georgian' and the population as 'Georgians' has no 'foreign' connotations. The terminology simply acknowledges the unusual sequence of four successive monarchs of the same name between 1714 and 1830. (There was an intervening Frederick, Prince of Wales, who might have disturbed the pattern, but he predeceased his father George II.) It is clearly a retrospective usage. But not by much: in 1832, shortly after George IV's death, a commentator saluted the previous century as the 'Georgian era'.[27] Applied loosely, not literally, it provides a familiar generic nomenclature.

More than one group are, of course, rightly known to the world as 'Georgians'. For identification purposes, however, context is all. So the inhabitants of the British Isles during the long eighteenth century can usually be distinguished easily enough from residents of the colony of Georgia in North America (founded 1732) and their successors in the US state after 1776. And all these people manifestly differ from the population of the Caucasian Republic of Georgia (founded as an independent state in 1991). It is also worth noting that many countries, cities and institutions also share a heraldic fealty to the chivalrous St George, legendary slayer of dragons. But the devotees of this patron saint, whose own mythologies are legion, embrace not his name but his flag.[28]

Naming the British population after a sequence of monarchs should not be taken to imply that Britons shared an excess of pro-royalist sentiment. On that question, there was a broad spectrum of opinion, which included a small but determined republican tradition. No doubt numerous Britons in the long eighteenth century would thus have stared in initial surprise – or even laughed aloud – at this collective name. After all, those living under the later Stuarts (in the 1690s and 1700s) had not encountered a real-life King George. Hence 'the Georgians' are so named, not literally, but elastically. And, for the avoidance of doubt, all references are intended ecumenically. 'Georgian Britons' here encompass all those either born or living in the archipelago of Great Britain and Ireland in the long eighteenth century, wherever they originated and wherever they moved. Hence, they include all whose legal status might have been uncertain (through earlier enslavement overseas) but whose human reality was not.

Referring to Georgian Britons has one big advantage, in that 'Georgian' has long become *the* descriptive term for British art, design, furniture, fittings, landscape gardening and, above all, architecture in the long eighteenth century.[29] Its prevalent design keynotes were neoclassical symmetry, harmony, elegance and a degree of restraint. The style also overlaps with the late seventeenth-century ornate 'English Baroque' associated with Christopher Wren, John Vanbrugh and Nicholas Hawksmoor. Their work was in practice quickly assimilated into the more restrained Palladian style. So they are often grouped as part of a dignified 'Georgian' neoclassicism, adapted from ancient Greece and Rome and adopted across the British Isles as well as in British overseas settlements, as in 'Canadian-Georgian' and 'Australian-Georgian' architecure.[30]

15

Today, its surviving output remains visible for all to see. 'Everyone loves a Georgian house,' ventures one commentator, adding with belated caution: well, 'nearly all of us'.[31] The era's greatest buildings are justly renowned. So the magnificent townscape of 'Georgian' Bath is listed by UNESCO as a World Heritage Site. Edinburgh's neoclassical New Town, complete with its scenic monuments on Calton Hill, was dubbed, at first teasingly and then in full seriousness, the 'Athens of the North'.[32] And 'Georgian' Dublin, awash with tensions and creativity, also impressed as a particular urban heartland which was seemingly universal – to paraphrase a later comment from James Joyce.[33]

Furthermore, there are notable eighteenth-century buildings in all corners of Britain and Ireland. Impressive Georgian concentrations are found in places as various as Birr (County Offaly), Blandford Forum, Buxton, Chepstow, Inveraray, Stamford, Tunbridge Wells and Westport (County Mayo). In addition, there are individual marvels, which deserve better fame: for example the freestone colonnaded piazza in Halifax, known as the Piece Hall (1779), which was built as a huge open-air textile exchange. Moreover, Georgian Palladianism spawned its own stylistic architectural alter ego in the form of neo-Gothicism.[34] Its best known exemplar remains the Houses of Parliament (rebuilt after the 1834 fire). Yet there are earlier Georgian neo-Gothic surprises, such as the towering brick observatory, known as Perrot's Folly (constructed 1758), in Edgbaston, Birmingham: its 96-foot height a possible inspiration for J.R.R. Tolkien, who lived nearby as a child, in imagining the impenetrable tower of Orthanc at Isengard.

Either way, these Georgian architectural legacies are an indelible part of the landscape. From 'simple' Palladianism to the alternative spice of decorative neo-Gothicism, they make a massive and distinctive heritage, well worth defending. Happily, the assiduous Georgian Group (founded 1937) does just that. In other words, history and architecture between them provide the inhabitants of the long eighteenth century with a familiar collective name.

Debating the Georgians

Long-eighteenth-century studies constitute an 'exploding galaxy' of ideas and arguments.[35] There is still much cosmic 'dark matter' relating to the period which awaits discovery. In particular, the current and prospective digitisation of many hitherto under-studied sources is starting new debates and revisiting old ones.

Aggrieved students often demand: 'Why don't the experts argue things out once and for all, and then tell us the right answer?' But historical studies don't work like that. Over time, they do provide a much strengthened evidential base. They also rule out some entirely unsubstantiated cases. And they can develop a broad consensus view. Nevertheless, historians cannot close down debates for all time. Nor do they seek to do so. The subject thrives upon argument and assessment, because people in past eras as well as those writing later histories often have differing perspectives, rival interests and competing values.[36] And it's right that multiple viewpoints be aired. Human experiences, being complex, demand complex evaluations.

The full extent of disagreement among the Georgians themselves is explored in later chapters. Here, however, the point is underlined by two contrasting views of Britain's fortunes. The first verdict, in 1728, from a pioneering British map-maker named Ephraim Chambers, was radiant. He highlighted the country's growing maritime and colonial strength. Hence he assured the new king, George II, that it would soon be Britain's turn at the top:

The Time seems at hand when we are no longer to envy Rome her AUGUSTUS and AUGUSTAN AGE, but Rome in her turn shall envy ours. There is a Time reserv'd in Fate for every Nation to arrive at its Height; and the uppermost Place on the Terrestrial Ball is held successively by several States. May not the numerous Presages, which usher in Your Majesty's Reign, give us Room to expect that *our Turn is next?*[37]

Apparent success, however, holds the seeds of later failure, warned another observer thirty years later. He was a melancholic clergyman named John Brown. His *Estimate of the Manners and Principles of the Times* (1758) assumed that historical stages followed in inexorable sequence.[38] So when Britain was doing badly at the start of the Seven Years' War (1757–63), Brown's fears reached fever-pitch. For him, the nation had already passed its best and doom was nigh: nations develop through stages, he wrote, which are 'rude; simple; civilised; polished; effeminate; corrupt; profligate; [leading] to . . . final DECLENSION and RUIN'. Hence, in the case of Britain, 'We are rolling to the Brink of a Precipice that must destroy us'.[39]

Both utter triumph and utter disaster were thus detected within a generation by two eminently serious commentators. Such disagreements mean that historians cannot find just one contemporary verdict and declare it to be conclusive. Disputing the trends of history was characteristic of the Georgian Britons, when Edward Gibbon and others were first establishing its professional study – and debating history remains one of their many cultural legacies too.

ᥜ Time-Shift: Then and Now ᥣ

Here are three long-surviving eighteenth-century songs to hear or sing to mark musical sharing and adaptation over time.

1. 'Sally in Our Alley'
Written by Henry Carey in 1725, rendered into a twentieth-century musical (1902) and three films (1916, 1927 and 1937), and sung to memorable effect in the last of these by the Lancastrian entertainer and comedienne Gracie Fields (1898–1979), whose swooping theme tune it then became.

2. 'Amazing Grace'
A Christian hymn (written 1772; published 1779) by the poet-clergyman John Newton (1725–1807), with a message of

divine forgiveness and redemption; originally chanted or sung, it was set to instantly recognisable music in 1835 by the American Baptist hymn-writer William Walker (1809–75), becoming an acclaimed folk spiritual. There is a riveting 1995 performance by Jessye Norman in concert in New York on YouTube.

3. 'Auld Lang Syne'

Written in 1788 by Robert Burns (1759–96) and sung to a traditional Scottish folk tune. Translated into at least forty-one languages, it is the world's most ubiquitous song, associated with ceremonies of farewell and remembrance, especially at graduations, military passing-out parades, the finale of dances and New Year's Eve festivities. There are many versions to access on YouTube, from an instrumental version for bagpipes and violin, arranged by Amy Lee, to ones with full lyrics, including some in multi-lingual translations, and one that sends a strong vocal and emotional message from an American community choir in Birmingham, Alabama, singing farewell to the turbulent year 2020.

2

Locating the Georgians at
Home and Abroad

'If I was to entitle ages, I would call this *the Century of Crowds,*' decided Horace Walpole in September 1761.[1] This snappy verdict came from a keen chronicler of his own times, and was an apt one. After a mid-seventeenth-century pause associated with the civil wars and demographic turbulence, Britain's population was newly launching into prolonged growth, forming part of a global pattern which continues, with regional variations, to this day.[2] The 'madding crowd' (in Thomas Gray's famous phrase from 1759) was becoming an iconic image of the era – even if not all agreed with Gray on the need to escape 'far from [its] ignoble strife'.

A visitor to eighteenth-century Britain would detect that the Georgians were comparatively short in stature by the standards of today, with men standing on average 5 feet 5 inches, and women 5 feet 1 inch; people of higher social rank tending, again on average, to be comparatively healthier and taller. The staple food of the poor in England and Wales was bread and cheese; in Scotland, oatcakes and porridge; and in Ireland, oatcakes and potatoes.

People at all social levels were at risk of itchy skins and lousy bodies. However, during this period, the expanding production of soap began to encourage a more thorough bodily cleanliness. So did the growing use of easily washed linen shirts and shifts. Those were replacing traditional undergarments of 'sordid and filthy woollen, long worn next to the skin', as was noted in 1789.[3]

Yet health hazards abounded. The most ferocious of many chronic infectious diseases was smallpox. It killed many, especially babies, and left survivors scarred and pock-marked. Typhus and other fevers were also endemic, especially in towns. Those who suffered from then-rampant venereal infections experienced intimate pains and penalties, while patients taking the favoured mercury treatment for syphilis risked being poisoned by the 'cure'. Similarly, those who drank medicinal cordials risked addiction to laudanum (a tincture of opium), which was a common ingredient in such preparations. It happened, famously, to the Lakeland poet Samuel Taylor Coleridge. He soothed a bad toothache with a local cure-all, named the Kendal Black-Drop, whose opium base boosted his drift into addiction.[4]

Coleridge was not alone in having dental problems. The importation of cheap cane sugar from the West Indian plantations was soaring – with dire effects on standards of dentition. Blackened and rotting teeth were ever more common. (Portraits showing people with full teeth-baring smiles were accordingly rare, as artists liked to show their sitters looking calm and composed – and without manifest signs of dental decay.) It was a reminder, if one were needed, that cheap consumer goods are not automatically problem-free, either for consumers or for those who produce them – in this case, the enslaved Africans on the plantations. In 1791, a leading anti-slavery campaigner dramatised this last point starkly: 'in every pound of sugar used ... we may be considered as consuming two ounces of human flesh'.[5] Such exhortations did have some effect, as will be seen below (p. 237). Yet the popular taste for sugar, backed by a powerful international trading lobby, was not easily changed.

Numbering the Georgians

During the eighteenth century, the number of people living in the British Isles continued to rise. Their precise numbers, however, remained unknown. In 1752, a fledgling plan for a national census was proposed – but rejected: the House of Commons feared that a house-by-house survey, organised by the central state, would undermine individual liberty. Those objections were overcome only in 1801, when Britain, struggling in prolonged warfare against France, urgently needed accurate manpower information.

Before then, all population data are best-estimates, based upon contemporary reports and historians' assessments. Those for England and Wales in the 1690s, based upon calculations by the pioneering statistician Gregory King, are considered tolerably accurate. Then the human population constituted some 5.2 million people, who were, incidentally, outnumbered by the country's 11 million sheep and lambs.[6] Meanwhile, the totals for Scotland and Ireland *c.* 1700 are more conjectural. Both were less populous than England. Scotland had probably under 1 million residents, after its 'lean years' and local famines in the 1690s; and Ireland had about 2 million (perhaps more).

Then all three kingdoms began to share in a major demographic shift. The mean age of first marriage began to fall, causing birth rates and fertility rates per female to rise (as did interest in contraception). Moreover, the previously steep mortality rates were also beginning to decline, although there was still a huge death toll of children aged under five. By the 1750s, Scotland had some 1.3 million residents, compared with *c.* 6.1 million across England and Wales. The combined total of 7.4 million within Great Britain was a milestone. It surpassed the previous peak, estimated at *c.* 6.5 million in the early fourteenth century (before the Black Death of 1348–49 and the ensuing sequence of lesser plagues, which continued in Britain until the later seventeenth century).[7]

Ireland, meanwhile, was launching into one of the greatest surges in population to be found anywhere across eighteenth-century

Europe. As is well known, its inhabitants were sustained by the cheap and nutritious potato, planted abundantly in the newly drained Irish peat bogs. By the 1750s Ireland was home to some 3 million people, indicating a much faster net growth rate than was the case in Scotland.[8] Even so, the collective demographic clout of all three kingdoms at the mid-century was no match for the might of France, with its population of *c.* 22 million. They were all ruled from the magnificent palace of Versailles by the absolute Bourbon kings, who were viewed from Britain with edgy suspicion. Hence military victories over France were particularly appreciated as morale-boosters. After Britain's success at the 1708 Battle of Oudenarde, for example, British patriots could give hearty renderings of an enjoyable new song, entitled 'Jack Frenchman's Lamentation', explaining how the French king, named as 'Old Bully', was rudely awakened from his 'dream of success'.[9]

Fluctuations in population size meanwhile were constantly affected by political and socio-economic factors. In the case of Scotland, thousands of displaced Gaelic-speaking crofters and their families moved from the Highlands either to Lowland Scotland or, predominantly, to North America.[10] This outflow was prompted by the agricultural 'clearances', accelerating after the Jacobite defeat at Culloden in 1746. The old clan system, based upon trust between laird and tenant, was fast eroding. Aristocratic landowners were evicting crofters in order to switch from labour-intensive crop farming to labour-minimalist sheep-rearing. The process was anguishing; and the Highlanders' memories of displacement were expressed in haunting songs, many still potent within the ballad repertoire.

Gradually, however, accelerating growth in the Lowlands began to offset losses in the north. At the first census in 1801, Scotland's population had risen to 1.6 million, while numbers in England and Wales had comparatively drawn ahead to 8.9 million. And that pattern continued. By 1851, the resident population in Scotland had risen to 2.9 million, while that in England and Wales had multiplied to 17.9 million (definitively exceeding for the first time the number of sheep and lambs). Both realms saw considerable emigration, both voluntary and involuntary. And Scotland in particular sent many young men to Britain's expanding overseas territories and into its armies.[11] One such who undertook medical service in India was the Perthshire physician Francis Buchanan-Hamilton. He not only organised major geological and historical surveys of Bengal, but also worked with Indian artists to record botanical collections.[12] In addition, just to demonstrate the diversity of these transnational connections, his surname was taken for the scientific naming of the Asian freshwater black pond turtle: *Geoclemys hamiltonii*.[13]

Contrasting with those experiences was Ireland's dramatic parabola of runaway growth followed by prolonged decline. Its population in 1801 has been estimated at over 5 million, more than double the figure in 1700.[14] This boom was based upon the potato economy, as ever more land was taken into cultivation (with regional variations), and as poor tenants subdivided their rented plots, generating ever larger households. The result was an under-employed rural workforce, and substantial Irish migration into the towns of west-coast Britain and into the rank-and-file of the British Army.

One or two commentators did express prescient fears. An Irishman from County Tyrone returned from military service in 1818 to tour the country. He saw it as 'a sleeping volcano, in which the fire of ages is pent up'. He feared that fevers, famine, emigration or warfare could devastate the land, 'sufficient to erase half the actual generation from the earth'.[15] Given that Ireland's aggregate population in the early twenty-first century has not yet surpassed the level reached before the 1845–52 Famine, this prophesy had a melancholy point. However, most contemporaries were unaware of the dangers of over-reliance upon a mono-crop, as local shortages in one county, which did occur, were commonly remedied by supplies of food from others.

After a long eighteenth century of apparently unstoppable growth, however, demographic catastrophe struck. No one had expected year-on-year crop failures, caused by potato blight, in all regions simultaneously. But that's what happened in the Great Famine. Schemes were introduced for the provision of soup-kitchens and sundry make-work projects. But the Westminster government, Irish officialdom and local landowners were all badly out of their depth, as well as hampered by an official belief that free markets would provide a solution. There followed a huge loss of population, caused by famine-related deaths, by population dispersal to mainland Britain and, especially, by emigration to the USA. The Irish population, which peaked in 1841 at 8.2 million, fell in every decade thereafter until the 1930s, which it flat-lined until the 1970s.[16] The Great Famine thus constitutes one of the worst such natural catastrophes, exacerbated by human mismanagement, in recorded history.

Demographic boom in many areas of Great Britain tended to encourage in growth areas a sense of optimism and buoyancy. Populations were youthful, labour abundant, with many opportunities for geographical mobility, especially for young men. Food supplies from home and overseas were expanding and diversifying; harbours and markets were typically vivid, bustling places. For most of this period, all three kingdoms were experiencing prolonged urbanisation (see below, pp. 360–2). The traditional capital cities more than retained their importance – and eighteenth-century London had become a world-giant in terms of population and impact.[17] Yet new growth elsewhere was also striking. On the British mainland, new industrial technologies, plus the rise of the Atlantic economy, generated urban expansion in south Wales, Bristol, the Midlands, Lancashire, Yorkshire, the north-east, and Lowland Scotland. Equally, in pre-Famine Ireland, Dublin was joined by the emergent 'Linenopolis' of Belfast and by mercantile Cork, hymned in song as 'the beautiful city'.[18]

Nevertheless, eventually the stark demographic divergence between mainland Britain and Ireland carried the warning that 'growth' was (and is) not invariably well sustained and unstoppable. In fact, there were various inventive make-work projects in response to food crises in eighteenth- as well as nineteenth-century Ireland. The toweringly ornate obelisk (erected 1740) at Celbridge near Maynooth, County Kildare (now owned by the Irish Georgian Society), was one example of philanthropic endeavour to offset distress, while in the 1840s there were several official road-building schemes.[19] Nonetheless, the desperate Irish population needed not temporary relief but regular livelihoods in a well-functioning economy.[20] Georgian demographic expansion had thus left Ireland vulnerable to natural disaster, with which officialdom was ill-equipped to deal (relief agencies still struggle today to reboot entire failing economies). In the absence of new solutions, meanwhile, many Irish families took the empirical option of emigration, motivated by a combination of grief and determination.

Georgian Immigrants

Europe's offshore islands had a long, long history of population mobility, both inwards and outwards. The novelist and journalist Daniel Defoe amused readers in 1701 by lampooning the mongrel heritage of *The True-Born Englishman*: 'The Scot, Pict, Britain, Roman, Dane, submit;/ And with the English-Saxon all Unite.'[21] (Norman French invaders followed in 1066, and Dutch and Walloon religious refugees in the sixteenth century.) Moreover, Britain's long aversion to national identity papers made it hard for the authorities to track such migrations. Many foreign newcomers in the eighteenth century quietly anglicised their names and settled quickly. They faced no special regulations – unlike, for example, non-Islamic newcomers in the Ottoman Empire, who were required, in theory at least, to wear distinctive dress, featuring specifically coloured turbans to indicate their religious or ethnic origins.[22]

Throughout the Georgian era in Britain, there were, notably, no large-scale anti-immigrant riots or violent demonstrations – in contrast to experiences in both earlier and later times. Given that

Britons were prone to take direct action, their inaction on this particular issue indicates a rough-and-ready acceptance of immigration, if no more than that.

Much the greatest single foreign influx in this era arrived in the later seventeenth and early eighteenth centuries. Some 40,000–50,000 French Protestant religious refugees, known as Huguenots, settled in England, chiefly in Norwich, Canterbury and London's Spitalfields. Smaller but not insignificant numbers also moved to Ireland, especially to Belfast, Dublin and Cork. And a few hundred such households settled in Edinburgh. The first generation continued to speak French at home. Yet their commercial, industrial and financial skills helped them to prosper and to assimilate quickly.[23] Many intermarried with the host population. The quintessentially 'English' eighteenth-century actor, playwright and theatre manager David Garrick had a Huguenot father and grandfather, while his mother's family came from Lichfield. Some wealthy benefactors among the immigrant communities funded separate schools and relief systems. One surviving example is Westminster's French Protestant School Foundation, formerly the French Protestant School (1747–1924), which to this day provides educational grants for needy applicants of Huguenot descent. Such charities, by providing fall-back insurance for individuals, aided the process of assimilation.

Migrants often settled near others from similar ethnic backgrounds, seeking companionship and linguistic familiarity. But not all prospered. In 1761, Theodore Gardelle, a French enamel-painter living in London, was charged with the murder of his Soho landlady. On trial at the Old Bailey, he petitioned that half the jury be foreign-born, like him. His request was granted. Even so, Gardelle was convicted.[24] Nonetheless, his request from the dock indicated that, despite being a relative outsider, he did not view himself as being entirely alone.

Recruits from the eighteenth-century tessellation of German states were notably plentiful, encouraged by the Hanoverian connection.

Indeed, the four queens of the first four Georges were all German-born. Others, less eminent, arrived to trade or to avoid religious persecution, as did an influx of Protestants from the Palatinate in 1708. By the mid-century, an area in London's Whitechapel was known as 'Little Germany' and services in St George's German Lutheran Church were given, at least for some years, in German. A common Protestantism aided the process of assimilation. Indeed, the most famous of all German migrants became a naturalised British subject. He was the Saxon-born composer Georg-Friedrich Händel (Anglicised simply as Handel), who was, at his death in 1759, buried in Westminster Abbey.

Also from Europe came a smaller number of Jewish families, chiefly traders and financiers, many of whom were escaping religious persecution or harassment. In 1753, new legislation entitled them to become British citizens.[25] However, the Whig government, which took this liberal step, did not enjoy enough support to withstand a noisy clamour of opposition, and the new law was suddenly repealed in 1754. Such abrupt reversals in attitudes are not unknown in relationships between native-born Britons and immigrants. In this case, however, the legislative volte-face did not stem the flow. At the mid-eighteenth century, the leading figure in Britain among the Sephardic Jews from Portugal was the opulent banker Sampson Gideon (1699–1762). Born within the City of London, he married an Englishwoman and saw his son elevated to a barony.[26] As a practising Jew, however, Gideon was denied a peerage in his own right, although his loans to the British government were always welcomed.

There were a few cases of outright conversion. Thus in Exeter an Italian Jewish immigrant named Joseph Ottolenghi caused shock by switching to Christianity.[27] In general, however, Jewish communities in Britain remained bonded by their separate observances. They formed their first Board of Deputies in 1760, to act as a mutual forum and a lobby group. Discreet synagogues were built, as at Plymouth (1762) and Exeter (1763). After that, a new wave of Ashkenazi Jews from Germany and eastern Europe settled in

London's East End. By 1800, they numbered perhaps 20,000. Many were relatively poor, being engaged in the clothing trades and in small-time moneylending. Their heavily accented English made them easy targets for caricature. Yet responses were not uniform. Richard Cumberland's play *The Jew* (1794), featuring a benevolent Jewish moneylender, had a big success, before being recycled into both a rapid patter song (a precursor of rap music) and a novel.[28] Liberal acceptance contended with tensions and envy.

Mingled hostility and welcome were also experienced by other migrants from further afield. In these years, the flow of people coming from India was relatively small.[29] But the numbers from both the West Indies and from Africa's west coast were much greater. They included the princely figure of the Ghanaian William Ansa Sessarakoo, who was in 1748 'in fashion at all [the London] assemblies'. He had been betrayed and sold into slavery before being freed and fêted.[30] Many reported tough experiences. The celebrated African Ignatius Sancho, who had been born on a slave-ship in the mid-Atlantic, complained that people in Britain stared at and followed him, sometimes uttering abuse. He felt unaccepted, even after many years. Such direct testimony records the psychological impact of being seen always as a 'stranger'. Grittily, however, Sancho prospered in a varied career as a manservant, composer, City of Westminster shopkeeper and, finally, trenchant author.[31]

Most other Africans and Caribbean migrants similarly found jobs in the commercial and service sectors. They defined themselves – and were defined – in variegated styles. Thus one Nottingham entrepreneur, George Africanus, who ran a successful servants' Registry (employment exchange) in the 1790s, was indicated as 'African' by his surname. The dignified author and lecturer Olaudah Equiano published as Gustavus Vassa but joined a London society known as the 'Sons of Africa'. (Today Equiano is honoured in his family homeland of Nigeria, while his precise birthplace is disputed.)[32] In Bristol, by contrast, an acrobat advertised in 1752 as a 'Negro' and a music teacher in 1773 was styled as a 'Black'. Yet again sometimes all ethnic identifications were omitted. In Bristol in 1728, for example, two 'Blacks' were registered as marrying one another in St Augustine's Church. However, the baptisms of their four daughters appeared in the following years without any mention of the children's appearance or heritage.

Britain had no tradition of confining migrants into anything like enclosed ghettoes. Georgian prints and drawings of urban scenes frequently show people with dark faces mingling freely among the crowds. There were also far more successful black writers in Georgian Britain than has hitherto been realised, writing on a wide array of topical themes.[33] At the same time, the poorest African and West Indian newcomers tended to congregate in dockland areas, especially in Liverpool, Bristol and London, where lodgings were cheap and plentiful. By 1800, members of these communities numbered at least 15,000, and possibly twice that.[34] Similarly, African and Caribbean migrants in Ireland gravitated to dockland areas in Limerick, Cork and Dublin.[35]

The richly diverse contribution of immigrants to Georgian Britain is now being rightly commemorated.[36] However, numbers are hard to calculate over time because of the frequency of intermarriage between migrants and host communities. In the second and subsequent generations, there were many people of 'mixed' genetic ancestry – some of them looking 'mixed', with others looking much less so, or not at all. This spontaneous mingling over time remains part of the evolutionary adaptability of humans, as geneticists constantly demonstrate.

Georgian Emigrants

Counter-flows of emigrants, meanwhile, generated a massive long eighteenth- and nineteenth-century global diaspora of British and Irish people. This process was part of a European-wide 'outward dynamic'. Russians were marching eastwards, across the Siberian steppes. Spain and Portugal already had established settlements in South America, while Holland, Britain and France were looking not only across the Atlantic but also to Africa and the Far East.[37] The theme of population wanderings resonates throughout Georgian literature.

It was once believed that some entire regions, like Wales[38] or England's north-east, were excluded from Britain's colonial and commercial expansion. But that view is mistaken. The links were everywhere, and were known to eighteenth-century contemporaries. In Wales, one Georgian antiquary even claimed that the European discovery of North America was first made by an adventurous Welsh prince named Madoc ab Owen Gwynedd. He had, allegedly, arrived long before Columbus and Amerigo Vespucci. Hence the New World should properly be renamed 'Madocia'.[39] But, alas for the enthusiastic antiquary, the Americans were not listening.

Generally, emigration from eighteenth-century Britain was voluntary, fuelled by individual decisions, even if triggered by severe economic blight, as in the case of emigrants from the Scottish Highlands and from Ireland, as discussed above (pp. 23–6). The great exception was the transportation of criminals (discussed below, pp. 215–16). So there was no express intention of gaining anything as formalised as an overseas empire, and no Hanoverian monarch claimed the title of emperor. (Only in 1876 was Victoria made Empress of India – and British MPs then prevented the title being extended either to Britain and Ireland or to the overseas possessions as a whole.) Instead, most Georgian commentators stressed the role of trade in raising Britain's overseas profile. 'To the instrumentality of Commerce *alone*, the Britannic empire is most particularly indebted,' asserted one analyst in 1764.[40]

Nonetheless, Britain's army and navy were essential for consoli-dating and defending overseas territories and trading interests. Successive British governments found themselves fighting against both France and Spain in North America and in the Caribbean. In

India, too, Britain's surrogate, the East India Company, fought, with discreet support from the British state, against many established rulers as well as against France.[41]

At the mid-eighteenth century, there were some 80,000 sailors in the Royal Navy – a poet fancifully imagined in 1762 that each ship had a British lion roaring at its masthead – plus an equal number of mariners in the merchant fleet.[42] Numbers rose in periods of warfare and were cut back in peacetime. By 1800 there were some 120,000 sailors in the Royal Navy under Nelson. The number of soldiers also varied sharply, rising in war and shrinking abruptly with peacetime demobilisation. Thus in 1800, when Britain was locked in battle with France, British generals commanded some 250,000 men, of whom a number were foreign mercenaries, including Hanoverians and French Royalists. In addition, there was a 'shadow' army of female camp followers. They catered, laundered, looked after the sick and helped with the logistics of transport.

Of those who left to fight, some did return. The Highlander Sir Hector Munro was one example. Serving in the East India Company Army in 1781, his greatest success was capturing the Dutch-controlled port of Negapatam (today Nagapattinam) in Tamil Nadu. Upon returning the following year to his estate at Fyrish in Easter Ross, Munro ordered the construction of a giant stone monument as a project to provide work for unemployed locals. It was not enough to reboot the economy. Yet the Fyrish Monument, echoing the design of the Negapatam Gate, still stands in lone hilltop grandeur as a monument to Georgian population mobility and cultural exchange, having now easily outlasted Britain's Indian interests, for which Sir Hector was fighting.

Facilitating these worldwide travels was a significant technological invention. In 1761, the H4 marine chronometer, developed by the self-educated Yorkshire clock-maker John Harrison, won a special state-sponsored contest to measure accurately longitude at sea. (Today it is one of the most cherished exhibits at the UK's

National Maritime Museum in Greenwich.) In fact, Harrison had to wait for years to get the promised prize money.[43] Nonetheless, his feat boosted Britain's precision instrument-making, as well as aiding the art of navigation and accurate cartography. The round-the-world seafaring feats of Captain Cook, which followed between 1768 and 1779, relied heavily upon Harrison's new precision technology. An additional aid to effective navigation and to naval warfare was devised in 1805. The Irish-born rear admiral Francis Beaufort then created a standard chart for measuring wind speeds – used and known today as the Beaufort scale.[44] Prosaic, but, once invented, invaluable.

For the first three quarters of the eighteenth century the most admired of Britain's overseas possessions were its North American settlements. These ranged from charter colonies (like Massachusetts), run by independent corporations, to crown colonies (like Virginia and Georgia), under the authority of a governor and commission appointed by the king. Their economic expansion and distinctive cultures attracted many new recruits. Specifically, too, Nonconformists went to the Puritan colonies of New England, and Quakers to the Quaker-founded Pennsylvania from the 1680s. However, by the end of the eighteenth century, the British and Irish diaspora had also spread to South America, the West Indies, south and west Africa, India, the East Indies, and Australia and New Zealand, once those latter territories were 'discovered' by Captain Cook.[45] Notably, these flows of population were not attracted solely to territories under direct British control. So today many descendants of Scottish emigrants celebrate an annual Tartan Day (in a pleasant ritual dating from the 1980s) in Argentina as well as in Canada, Australia and New Zealand. (It's part of life's quirkiness that these festivals are not all held on the same date.)[46]

Another intriguing indication of the British diaspora was visible in the heraldic use of the Union Jack. At various times, this emblematic design appeared in the flags of over twenty-five former British colonies, including the first flag of the independent USA. Today it still appears in the state flag of Hawaii and the city flag of Coquimbo in Chile. In neither case does its use record formal constitutional links. For the Hawaiians, the heraldic device records on-off encounters with British explorers dating back to the 1790s. And for Coquimbo, it acknowledges key economic contacts going back to the 1810s, with the recruitment of British commercial, mining and naval help.[47]

By the later eighteenth century, British emigrants were also looking eastwards to India. They did not all stay for long. Some were discouraged by illness. Others returned home to enjoy their booty. But very wealthy returnees from India were often met with suspicion. Known as 'nabobs', they were criticised for getting rich by corrupt means – and for importing corruption into British society.[48] However, over time the most swashbuckling phase of Britain's role in India was changing into a more orderly system, though still underpinned by military force as well as by princely alliances.[49] Bengal became home to a settled administration, located initially in Kolkata. It was there that the East India Company, which from 1757 to 1858 organised Britain's role in India, had its headquarters. Dalhousie Square (now Benoy-Badal-Dinesh Bagh, in tribute to three Indian freedom fighters) was a key focus. Its majestic architecture accordingly grouped together civic, religious and ceremonial functions in the form of the Writers' Building (which began as the East India Company's first administrative HQ, and then in 1800 became Fort William College), the soberly stylish Anglican St John's Church (built 1784), the Presbyterian St Andrew's Church (built 1815–18), and, especially, the lavish Government House (built 1799–1803).[50]

Under the shelter of Britain's growing power, a small phalanx of British families came to stay. Some British men found Indian wives or mistresses.[51] One long-term result was the presence of numerous people with 'mixed' Eurasian ancestry.[52] They contributed to India's de facto pluralism, although later, when British rule was attacked and then ended, they faced difficult times.

Around the globe, different terrains offered different challenges. In settled territories, the British acquired toehold ports as trading and victualling stations. So in 1819 Stamford Raffles founded Singapore as a successful commercial station.[53] Later, in 1841, Hong Kong was first leased by Britain, as a gateway to China. In the very different case of the 'unknown' continent of Australia, the first approach was to circumnavigate and map its contours. That task was undertaken in a series of voyages (1801–3) led by Matthew Flinders. He was a surgeon's son who went to sea, against the advice of his family and friends, after being inspired by reading *Robinson Crusoe*.[54] And Flinders had crucial help from Bungaree, an indigenous Australian, who became his guide. He in turn was a leading figure among the local population living near Sydney. However, despite the personal cooperation of Flinders and Bungaree, no wider meeting of minds and cultures ensued. The Britons were expanding into what they considered to be vacant territory; and the indigenous peoples were pushed to the margins. Bungaree himself remained a popular figure in Sydney, where he greeted newcomers with a flourish. He was treated respectfully and viewed as a local 'king'.[55]

It was the British immigrants, however, who held all the cards. Their numbers surged rapidly from 1788 onwards, initially in the Sydney area. Many newcomers were free settlers. Others, controversially, came under duress, as convicts. After 1776, Britain could no longer transport declared malefactors to North America. The apparently 'vacant' Australia appeared to be the perfect alternative. Numbers of transported convicts rose, particularly as opinion in Britain turned against the death penalty for minor crimes. A rapid process of colony-building followed under Lachlan MacQuarie, a Scottish soldier-turned-administrator. As governor of New South Wales from 1810 to 1821, he introduced town planning, a settled currency and a legal system. Forced to resign after a series of disputes, he remains widely commemorated. (And today, on Scotland's Isle of Mull, MacQuarie's family mausoleum, inscribed to 'the Father of Australia', is maintained by Australia's National Trust.)[56]

Frictions between free settlers and ex-convicts long continued. So did those between Australians of European origin and the indigenous peoples. Similar tensions also arose in New Zealand. The interests of explorers, traders and settlers increasingly clashed with those of the indigenous people. As in Australia, their way of life was 'unsettled' by maltreatment, imported diseases, population loss and culture shock, even while they struggled (and, later, campaigned vigorously) to sustain their own identity.[57] The 1840 Treaty of Waitangi, signed between representatives of the British state and various Maori chiefs, was in practice circumvented.[58] Most newcomers, cocooned by their own cultural blinkers, were preoccupied with their own needs. By 1850 there were some 400,000 inhabitants of Australia, the great majority being of British origin, and a further 22,000 Britons in New Zealand. These settlers were becoming a distinctive cohort within the massive and sustained global diaspora.[59]

Individual decisions, as well as the actions – and inactions – of governments and armies collectively made for an epic history. Furthermore, the effects of these population movements have ricocheted through time, gaining additional gravity over the years as their full ramifications have become clear.

Georgians as Global Consumers

Global connections were meanwhile promoting incremental changes to the daily lifestyles of Georgian Britons. Houses, built in local stone or kiln-fired bricks, were topped out with roofing materials ranging from Welsh slate to the popular red pantiles from Holland. Interior décor featured traditional oaken wares, alongside (from the 1720s onwards) modish furniture in high-sheen mahogany, imported from the West Indies. The most coveted items were produced by Thomas Chippendale (1718–79), from a wood-working family in Otley, Yorkshire. His name remains synonymous with elegance, and some of his specially commissioned furniture and interior designs can still be viewed in the houses for which they were created. (In Otley today, both a fine statue and the Chippendale Society HQ commemorate his work.)[60]

Many Georgian houses were warmed by fires of British coal – the 'black gold' that underpinned the thriving coastal trade of Newcastle upon Tyne – but a pungent smoke of another kind was emitted by smokers of West Indian tobacco leaf, processed by great tobacco refineries in Glasgow and Bristol. Smaller snuff mills also produced fine powdered snuff to tempt fashionable Georgian men and women, including George III's Queen Charlotte.

Other imported luxuries included fine-quality printed cottons, silks and brandy from France, and tea from China. Smugglers promptly tried to undercut the market by bringing in clandestine supplies. Britain's long, indented coastline was ideal for night-time operations by the 'owlers', as they were termed. Public opinion was ambivalent. Many people were happy to avoid paying custom duties. James Woodforde, a law-abiding Norfolk clergyman, noted calmly in his diary for March 1777 regular visits from 'Andrews the smug-gler', who supplied a fine China green tea.[61] On the other hand, violence between rival gangs, or between smugglers and customs officials, was not appreciated. A dramatic confrontation in 1747 between the feared Hawkhurst Gang and the villagers of Goudhurst in Kent indicated that local tolerance had ended.[62] Smuggling, which never entirely disappeared, was gradually cut down to size, partly by increased surveillance by excise collectors and partly by reduced tolerance from coastal communities.

Alcoholic drinking cultures meanwhile centred around a range of both domestic and foreign beverages. Homemade products were always popular: whisky in Scotland, poteen or 'moonshine' in Ireland, ales and porters in England. In fact, a number of today's great distilleries and breweries date from this very era. In addition, England's gin-dealers profited from low grain prices in the 1730s and 1740s to flood the market with ultra-cheap gin. This 'craze', which had drastic social effects, caused sufficient alarm that regulation was introduced in 1751, curbing, although not ending, gin-drinking.[63] At the same time, affluent consumers also drank imported French clarets and brandies, as well as port from England's strong naval ally Portugal. A further new alcoholic staple, rum, was distilled from West Indian sugar.[64] Rum punches, served from big punch bowls, became popular festive fare. And, best known of all, sailors in the Royal Navy were given a daily tot of rum (a practice which survived from c. 1740 until 1970). The drink was watered down to make the classic naval 'grog', jovially consumed by all ranks.

Non-alcoholic drinking habits were equally transformed by two new imported products. Coffee's big success dated from the later seventeenth century onwards, with bulk imports from Turkey. There were early complaints at its bitter taste, yet palates quickly adjusted. Coffee houses became modish meeting places, especially for men-about-town who enjoyed news-mongering and caffeine-fuelled conversation.[65] Before long, these venues became urban staples. Moreover, a few such meeting places acquired special roles. In particular, Lloyd's Coffee House (opened 1688) evolved into an insurance business, now world-renowned as Lloyds of London.

Black China tea, meanwhile, soon came to rival coffee in its transformation of British drinking habits. Between 1720 and 1750, imports more than quadrupled; and they continued to rise, especially after import duties were slashed in 1785. Porcelain manufacturers in Chelsea (the first being founded in 1743) and later in the Potteries made dedicated tea-sets. Purveyors of fine tea flourished; and one London business, Twinings (founded 1706), does so still. Women were notably avid consumers. Yet tea won devotees among every sex, age-group, region and class.[66] Earl Grey, of parliamentary reform fame, was an aristocratic fan, whose name remains synonymous with his favourite bergamot-flavoured blend.

New foodstuffs were being imported from around the world – and from Britain's overseas settlements.[67] Lesiurely dinners often featured exotic fruits and elaborate puddings. At the same time, fast food for busy consumers was also being popularised by the inventive Georgians. It was an eating style which suited both travellers and townspeople, who were characteristically 'on the go'. The pairing of bread and cheese, commonplace in the diet of the poor, was updated and diversified for all social classes. A serving of salt beef between two bread slices was named after one keen snacker, John Montagu, 4th Earl of Sandwich (1718–92). He was a rake in his youth and, later, became a dutiful first lord of the Admiralty.[68] Now his abbreviated title is everywhere much better known than he is. Today the Georgian sandwich, made with a wonderfully versatile range of ingredients, is a global staple.

✑ Time-Shift: Then and Now ✑

Three markers of global mobility can be visited physically or virtually: these venues are chosen, out of many possibilities, to indicate the processes of Georgian immigration, emigration and global consumerism.

1. The Plymouth Synagogue (1762)
This synagogue is the oldest surviving of all places of worship built by Ashkenazi (Central European) Jews in the English-speaking world. It is one of many notable British eighteenth-century edifices that are associated with immigrants, who, while settling into a new society, generally remained loyal to their traditional religions. Plymouth's discreet synagogue is set in an unobtrusive location. Its wooden interior is also plain, hence focusing the congregation's full attention upon its elaborately baroque Ark of the Covenant.

2. The Emigrants Monument (2007) at Helmsdale, Sutherland
This site hosts one of an increasing number of evocative memorials to mass migrations, undertaken in times of hardship. The

Monument, sculpted by Gerald Laing, shows a family group of four who evoke the mixture of determination and regret felt by Scottish emigrants during the Highland Clearances. A bronze replica of the Monument has since been erected in Winnipeg, Canada, near to where many Scots landed in 1814; and similar replicas are contemplated elsewhere.

3. Two eighteenth-century snuff mills (built 1750 and 1830) at Morden Hall Park, Surrey

These snuff mills provide evidence of new consumer habits (of which there were many), based upon international trade. Dried tobacco leaves were ground between large millstones, powered by the River Wandle, and the resultant powder, kept in decorated snuff boxes, was inhaled by snuff-takers seeking an instant nicotine buzz. Production at the Morden Hall site was relatively small-scale, but rendered profitable by the low costs of the raw materials, imported from American slave plantations, and by quick access to the huge nearby market of London. From the mid-nineteenth century onwards, however, the Georgian habit of snuff-taking began to fall out of favour, and it has today fallen almost to the point of disappearance – prefiguring the future fate of smoking tobacco in pipes, cigars and cigarettes.

✑ 3 ✑

Georgian Voices of Gloom

The Georgian era was an acutely time-conscious one; and people in growing numbers began to produce brisk summary verdicts upon their own era. In fact, it is often tricky to identify the full trends of the times whilst living through them. (Try helping future historians by writing a pithy summary of the early twenty-first century in the form of a diary, blog or tweet.) But defining the times remains a popular form of instant journalism. Books published in 2000, for example, pronounced upon the current 'Age of Globalisation', 'Age of Virtual Reality', 'Age of Uncertainty' (a perennial favourite) or, more starkly, this 'World of Lies, Hype and Spin'.[1] Authors who make such generalisations are not under oath. There's nothing to stop them from adopting extreme views to make a point and then later changing their minds. These same qualifications applied to the Georgians who named the long eighteenth century. Nonetheless, their summary verdicts provide historians with a good starting point.

Over 200 pithy Georgian dicta about 'the age', 'the times' or, more rarely, 'the century' have to date been identified. (There are always more to find.) They come from commentators from literate and tolerably educated backgrounds. Among them were many clergymen and minor literary figures, as well as professional journalists from the eighteenth century's notorious Grub Street. That specific location in London's Moorfields was first associated in the early 1730 with the gutter press[2] – and the attribution has stuck, even when the trade became more widespread. By the early nineteenth century, the practice of age-naming was commonplace. For the young philosopher John Stuart Mill in 1831, it was especially characteristic of a society in transition: 'The idea of comparing one's own age with former ages, or with our notion of those which are yet to come, had occurred to philosophers; but it never before was itself the dominant idea of any age'.[3]

In fact, the age-naming process had begun much earlier than Mill imagined. Yet his general point was a good one. Georgian commentators were characteristically aware of change, whether they approved or disapproved, and were keen to convey their views to others. About half the Georgian age-namings expressed shades of woe and despair. Some were apoplectic; others mildly nostalgic. Their cultural negativism was, for the young Samuel Taylor Coleridge in 1794, metaphorically located 'a thousand fathoms deep in the dead sea of pessimism'.[4] This particular abstract noun was at that date a novelty. Yet attitudes of woe, gloom and deep despair were not.

Grumbling is, after all, a human reflex, especially among the ill and embittered. In 1769, one commentator announced (without proof) that: 'We are almost *universally* unhappy'.[5] Farmers who were subject to the vagaries of the weather were particularly famous complainers. The touring missionary John Wesley noted that characteristic in 1766. Observing the country farmers, he remarked that: 'In general, their life is supremely dull, and it is usually unhappy too'.[6] Yet townspeople were also vociferous in complaining. 'Gloom and misanthropy have become the characteristics of the age in which we live,' mourned Shelley in 1817, temporarily downcast by the weakness of reform campaigns.[7] Getting into the market for pessimism, a poet in 1840 versified eloquently about the current *Age of Lead*, declaiming: 'What doleful days! what *drivelling* times are these!'[8]

Some degree of stylised grumbling was customary. Taxes were too high; prospects for trade too uncertain; governments too 'corrupt'; weather too fickle. As a result, a character in a 1758 drama announced chirpily that: 'The people of England are never so happy as when you tell 'em they are ruined'.[9] And in 1810 an American visitor, Louis Simond, commented that: 'These people are well broken to taxation – they complain indeed; but it is just as they complain of their climate, from habit'.[10] Georgian voices of pessimism must therefore be interpreted with a pinch of salt – and the same applies to Georgian voices of optimism (discussed in the next chapter). Yet it's still highly instructive to know what issues were causing concern and what complaints were expected to trigger a sympathetic response.

Fears of National Degeneration

Approximately half the Georgian age-namings were critical or pessimistic; and, of those, approximately half focused upon national danger. Complaints were couched in generalised terms, sometimes with the addition of phrases – 'as everyone knows', for example – intended to supply proof. Sources of danger were manifold. Moral decay was a perennial favourite. Thus in 1690 it was claimed that 'the great Corruption of the Manners of the People . . . has tainted them (to say nothing here of other Immoralities) with Unfaithfulness, Greediness of Gains, and narrow-soul'd Selfishness . . . contrary to the true *English Genius*'.[11] It was 'a dull Censorious uncharitable Age', argued another tract in 1699.[12] Or it was a 'Cheating Age', according to a pamphleteer, denouncing in 1705 the 'Vast sums of Money' spent on fighting France.[13] Joining the pessimistic chorus, a balladeer called it 'the Age of Mad-Folks' in 1710.[14] And the High Church Anglican preacher Henry Sacheverell caused a public sensation with his sermons, diagnosing 'a Church and Kingdom debauch'd in Principles, and corrupted in Manners, and . . . given over to all Licentiousness . . . all Sensuality, Hypocrisy, Lewdness, and Atheism'.[15]

Accusations were emphatic, if not always specific. Readers of a guidebook to *The Present State of Great Britain and Ireland* in 1716 learned that they lived in 'a depraved Age', although the author conceded that 'Virtue is not yet banish'd out of the Land'.[16] Others were not so hesitant. Particularly during the long premiership of Robert Walpole in the 1720s and 1730s there were searing attacks upon political corruption and the arts of patronage: it was a 'very depraved and corrupt age' (1726).[17] And in 1727, one poet lamented: 'Well – we have reach'd the Precipice at last;/ The present Age of Vice obscures the past'.[18] This rhetoric implied a crisis of unheralded proportions. And the target of complaint? It was the new fashion for masked balls, which were said to be encouraging sexual debauchery and an undue mingling of 'incognito' revellers from different social ranks.[19]

Women were specifically to blame, in the view of several commentators. 'So vain and wicked is our Age', claimed *Several Discourses . . . Addressed to the Ladies of the Age* in 1689: the 'fair ones' were too becoming bold and saucy.[20] That accusation was a grumbler's favourite, often appearing in satirical prints and reproachful sermons. Yet men, alas, were fallible too. Another poet in 1727 criticised the *Luxury and Effeminacy of the Age*. Young men should cease to act like coxcombs. Effeminacy would ruin the nation.[21] A later jeremiad in *The Times: A Poem* (1764) feared specifically that too many men were being tempted into sexual relations with their own sex, warning wryly that: 'Woman is out of date, a thing thrown by/ As having lost its use'.[22]

'Luxury' was often attacked too. It was becoming a codeword not just for economic growth but for moral rot, consequent upon new wealth. A tract entitled *Luxury, Pride and Vanity: The Bane of the British Nation* (1736) asserted that: 'Nothing of the present Pride and Vanity, or but very little of it, was seen in former Times'.[23] In similar vein, *The Reigning Vanities of the Age* (1754) itemised an eclectic list of moral faults, including duelling, gaming, wantonness, drunkenness, gluttony and luxury.[24] It was 'an age of affectation' (1753); an 'age of hypocrisy' (1773); a 'relaxed and indolent age' – not intended as a compliment (1791); 'this age of slander and detraction' (1785); an 'age of vice and dissipation' (1794).[25] An unfettered quest for money created new problems. 'Low-thoughted Commerce! heart-corrupting trade!/ To blast pure morals and true Virtue made', sighed an anonymous poet in 1773.[26] Oliver Goldsmith's *Deserted Village* (1770) had already decried the impact of agrarian change upon the rural poor. 'Ill fares the land, to hast'ning ills a prey,/ Where wealth accumulates and men decay.'[27] Resonant criticism, ripe for borrowing.[28]

Problems were especially highlighted when consumers favoured extravagant fashions, copied from 'a vain neighbouring nation' – meaning the frivolous French. That complaint came from a tract against *The Reigning Vanities of the Age* in 1754.[29] A letter in *The Gazetteer* in the same year concurred that luxury in clothing was blurring social distinctions, so that: 'by their dress, the clerk, apprentice, or shopman are not distinguishable from their master; nor the servant-maid, even the cook-wench, from her mistress'.[30] Complaints on that point were not confined to this era in history. Certainly, however, they were often made by the Georgians, both jocularly and seriously. 'It requires no ordinary capacity to distinguish the mistress from the maid by their dress', claimed a comedy of 1805 entitled *The Days We Live In*.[31] (In a later era, similar jokes were recycled about the difficulties of telling men from women, when trendy youngsters wore flowers in their long hair.)

Military crises meanwhile propelled the disaster literature into overdrive. Failures in battle were feared as signals of divine wrath. After the 1745 Jacobite rebellion, James Burgh, a moderate reformer, chastised the familiar faults of luxury, idleness, irreligion and sensuality. Such vices had destroyed great empires in the past, and could easily do so again.[32] John Brown's warning in 1758 has already been cited above (p. 18): 'We are rolling to the Brink of a Precipice that must destroy us'.[33] And the confrontation with the America colonies provoked further woe. A Nonconformist minister in Nottingham agonised in 1778: 'Our Country bleeds at its heart; our vices have risen to their crisis; ... and Britain, the envied among nations, the seat of glorious liberty, and science, and law, the refuge of the oppressed, the friend of mankind, is sinking into ruin.'[34]

Admittedly, that preacher did concede that Britain had a lofty reputation, at least among friends. Yet that very fact, for patriots, made things worse. In December 1781, the ever-excitable Horace Walpole wrote of 'the crisis of our total ruin'.[35] Meanwhile, a French visitor, the comte de Mirabeau, who resided in England for several months in 1784, was wryly amused. To him, the country seemed rich and prosperous. Yet he observed that there were enough tracts on Britain's national decline to fill a huge library.[36] However, just as rich people don't generally become rich by squandering money, so the acquisitive Britons did not amass extensive overseas interests by losing prime colonial territories cheerfully.

Disaster literature hit the absolute heights in the 1790s, as the French Revolution unfolded and warfare with France followed. Many viewed the conflict in religious terms, as will be seen (below, p. 50). Yet some pointed to secular trends. 'The age of chivalry is gone,' pronounced the political philosopher Edmund Burke, famously, in 1790. Instead, a harsh new world of 'sophisters [debaters], economists, and calculators' had arrived.[37] Martial valour was failing. A middling-status Witham grocer named Jacob Pattisson waxed sardonic in a private letter dated January 1794: 'Formerly One Englishman was said to be the equal to Three Frenchmen, But now the degenerate Brood cannot stand their ground against the scum of that rising nation of Men, their *Sans Culottes*'.[38]

Traditional ways were sapped by 'Modern Infidelity' and 'Modern Philosophy', added the conservative propagandist John Bowles in 1800. 'Never was the world in so calamitous or so perilous state as at this moment.'[39] Somewhat incongruously, Bowles again found fashionable women to be most at fault: their 'indecent modes of dress' in the latest modish thin drapery were not just lewd and unhealthy but socially calamitous. 'Female modesty is the last barrier of civilised society.' Hence, he asked in anguish: 'When *that* is removed, what remains to stem the torrent of licentiousness and profligacy?'[40]

Warnings came from all points on the ideological spectrum. A bluestocking lady with liberal views warned of the costs and dangers of warfare. 'Ruin, as with an earthquake shock, is here,' declaimed Anna Laetitia Barbauld's poem, 'Eighteen Hundred and Eleven'. 'Arts, arms and wealth destroy the fruits they bring;/ Commerce, like beauty, enjoys no second spring.'[41] However, it was not straightforward to be a Cassandra. Barbauld was roundly criticised as being unpatriotic – her denunciations of the war being considered untimely.

After triumphing at Waterloo in 1815, meanwhile, Britain no longer feared military invasion. The public mood changed and optimists had freer rein (as shown in the next chapter). Yet pessimists still had domestic gripes. 'Was there ever a period at which the vigorous hand of a satirist was more necessary?' demanded a Tory anti-reform newspaper, the *Spirit of the Age*, in 1829. This diatribe attacked all those 'rogues, swindlers, idiots, buffoons', who sought constitutional reform.[42] By contrast, John Wade's polemical *Black Book: Or, Corruption Unmasked* (1820–23) argued that the stupidity was all the other way. Aristocratic factionalism was reducing a potentially rich and great country to 'a woeful spectacle of want, misery, embarrassment, and degradation'.[43]

Economic growth, meanwhile, was no simple panacea. One ballad (*c.* 1830) sang ironically of pollution in the thriving 'cottonopolis' of Manchester: children were choking in the dense plumes of factory smoke: 'so black, so thick, so nourishing/ . . . It makes me mad to hear folk, really,/ Cry *Manchester's improving daily*'.[44] Environmental damage stalked outward success stories.

Anguish at Religious Infidelity

Matching the anxiety directed at secular targets, other urgent concerns focused upon religion. Traditional Christian piety was seen as fading, both in terms of church attendance and in everyday behaviour. 'Wherever God erects a house of prayer,/ The devil always builds a chapel there', as Daniel Defoe rhymed in *The True-born Englishman* (1701); adding sharply that the devil got the largest congregations as 'he rules us by our own consent'.[45]

Traditionally, the churches had well-established roles. They were sources of ethical and spiritual teaching; and their meetings provided occasions for communal worship, education, news-sharing and solidarity – or sometimes friction.[46] For the first time, however, no church had an official monopoly. Three Acts of Toleration in England and Wales (1689), Scotland (1712) and Ireland (1719), allowed some consumer choice in church attendance to all Protestant Christians (as further discussed below, p. 134).[47]

These legal changes were enacted to end conflict, not to encourage irreligion. However, soon there were warnings that the policy was backfiring. Without a system of compulsion, people were either failing to attend church or, despite continuing to attend, were taking Christian precepts too lightly. A tract of 1707 accordingly urged the 'careless world' to take religion more seriously.[48] And in 1710 the combative High Church Anglican cleric Henry Sacheverell used his dramatic sermons to magnify conservative fears. His powerful slogan was 'Church in Danger'. Unwisely, his political opponents tried to impeach Sacheverell, making him a martyr for the Anglican cause. His supporters rioted, attacking the new meeting-houses which were being built by Protestant Dissenters. Mutual suspicions were heightened.[49]

Meanwhile, all churches were being challenged, not just by rival denominations but by a wider mood of scepticism. A tract of 1734, entitled *Some Observations upon the Present State of Religion in England*, thus remarked matter-of-factly: 'That there is a spirit of *Irreligion* very common here, is obvious to everyone.'[50] And this development was happening within a nation theoretically dedicated to Christianity, as many observers noted sharply. Hence *The Sacred Outcry upon a View of the Principal Errors and Vices of Christendom in the Eighteenth Century* (1788) was scathing about the moral back-slidings of 'modern Christians'.[51] And another observer agreed in 1801: 'There is but little genuine Christianity, even among those who profess to be *Christians* – they have the name indeed, but not the reality'.[52]

'Infidelity' became the eighteenth-century's term-of-art for the weakening of traditional religious unity and for a perceived diversity in moral values.[53] ('Conjugal infidelity', meanwhile, meant adultery.) Anxious tracts warned that the nation was slipping collectively into an 'Age of Infidelity'. These jeremiads were often written in times of national crisis. This was not, however, invariably the case. The learned Anglican bishop William Warburton preached against 'this Age of Infidelity' in 1738 (a quiet year). He took it to be a commonplace observation.[54] At least fifteen different tracts, all referencing *The Age of Infidelity* in their titles or prefaces, appeared in print between 1675 and 1800.[55] Then a new block-buster appeared. Robert Hall's *Modern Infidelity Considered* began as a sermon to his Baptist congregation in Cambridge. Launched into print in 1800, it was reprinted nine times by 1858, and a Welsh-language edition appeared in 1840.[56]

To an extent, complaints at the 'wicked world' were exaggerated in order to alarm public opinion and to encourage better behaviour. It was impossible to prove (or disprove) changes in people's inner religious faith. Nonetheless, frequent references to the 'Age of Infidelity' and religious laxity indicated that these issues were touching an exposed nerve. The process of religious toleration had (as its critics feared) weakened the sense of universal adhesion to one faith, one set of morals, and one form of worship.

Lamentations notably peaked at times of military crisis. A few examples serve to indicate the tone. In 1780, when Britain was struggling against the rebellious American colonies, an Anglican curate in Yorkshire warned of the spread of 'Atheism and Deism (so prevalent among us)'. Lesser failings included: scoffing at religion, swearing, drunkenness, lewdness, lying and cheating.[57] Another clergyman, also in 1780, preached against the prevalent 'spirit of infidelity', adding in exasperation: 'An enlightened age we called it? ... Alas! it was a corrupted one.'[58] And anxieties reached fever-pitch in the 1790s. One observer foamed in 1798: 'Do not adultery, gaming, Sabbath-breaking, neglect of public worship, and, above all, lukewarmness and indifference about Religion itself, prevail, to a degree unknown in any former age?' He feared the imminent 'eradicating [of] Christianity in this Quarter of the World'.[59] And, not to be outdone, an Anglican dean, also in 1798, fretted that enemy forces were poised to eliminate Christianity not just in Europe but worldwide.[60] Indeed, the wartime years constituted a prime time for even more generalised end-of-the-world predictions. The world's many sinners were doomed, as proclaimed by prophets such as Richard Brothers, Joanna Southcott and Lady Hester Stanhope.[61] The apocalypse seemed a logical consequence, following upon the collapse of morals and the decay of faith.

Interestingly, too, the anxiety literature often canvassed the causes of changing attitudes towards religion. Disputes between rival churches – and sometimes within congregations – were alienating to the lay public, it was noted in 1747.[62] Other critics blamed boring sermons. An evangelical reformer in 1788 mourned: 'We have dexterously preached the people into downright infidelity.'[63] But even good sermons could be off-putting. In 1721, a witty tract, attributed to Dean Jonathan Swift, warned that an alarmist style could prove counter-productive. Too many sermons focused upon 'preaching against *Atheism, Deism, Free-thinking*, and the like, as young Divines are particularly fond of doing'. Real non-believers, however, rarely attended church and so did not hear such denunciations, whilst pious church-goers resented being chastised for sins which they were not committing.[64] One antidote to the scolding style accordingly offered in 1794 a consciously bright summons to *Religion without Gloom*.[65]

Clerical lifestyles were also criticised. If they were too rich and worldly, then parsons were attacked as indolent and complacent. On the other hand, if they were poor curates on small stipends, they were too penny-pinched and harassed to do their jobs well.[66] Either way, they were failing to set a good example. Clergymen of the established Anglican Church were particularly assailed if they held more than one living at once (known as pluralism), or if they failed to live within their allocated parish (known as non-residence) – and some were deemed guilty of both. On top of all that, the customary parish tax on agricultural produce, known as the tithe, was much resented, especially by poor country parishioners. Hostile cartoons therefore depicted plump parsons feasting on their plump 'tithe pigs' while emaciated parishioners gazed on in envy. One Anglican clergyman in 1785 accordingly noted that his flock were too preoccupied with 'earthly things' and regretted the decline in status of his office. When he offered to attend upon the dying, he reported that the common response, even from those seriously unwell, was: 'I hope, I am not yet so bad'.[67]

Strikingly, indeed, one tract in 1732 tried to deter young men of independent minds from undertaking a clerical career. They were warned that their scope for doing good was too limited in such 'libertine' and 'corrupted' times.[68] By this era, the clergy were no longer the chief group of literate men in key positions of social authority. Instead, they were becoming matched by many others such as lawyers, doctors, teachers, even journalists.

Automatic reverence for men of the cloth was receding.[69] *An Inquiry into the Causes of the Infidelity and Scepticism of the Times*, published in 1783, was one of a number of tracts to report upon the readiness of people to scoff at the clergy and the Scriptures.[70] Already by the 1690s, some feared that critical Bible scholarship might inadvertently foster an overly casual attitude.[71] John Vanbrugh's play *The Provok'd Wife* (1697) imagined the result. When Lady Brute is reminded of the biblical adage that good must be returned for evil, she replies pertly: 'That may be a mistake in the Translation'. At which, her husband snorts: ' 'Tis a damned Atheistical Age, Wife'.[72] The joke worked by pressing upon live social fears.

Pointedly, no eighteenth-century witnesses have been found who named their age as an 'age of faith' or an 'age of piety'. Instead, all the known commentators indicated their anguished fears of the corrosion or even outright loss of the Christian faith. There was no statistical proof of trends in church attendance. (Britain only ever held one religious census, in 1851, and its results remain contentious to this day.) But in 1761 one minister warned explicitly of the 'Decline of Religion': 'That religion is decayed, hath, for a long time, been the general complaint'.[73] And two further clerics in 1819 and 1821 agreed, using the exact same phrase to define the trend.[74] What they saw as the 'decline of religion' constituted a long-term process of secularisation, entailing nothing so dramatic as the ending of religious faith but its compartmentalisation (a change which is further explored in Chapter 8).[75]

Pessimism as Depressant or Goad?

Deep-dyed pessimism was a satisfying reflex in times of anxiety. In 1758, the middling-status shopkeeper in the small village of East Hoathly in Sussex, Thomas Turner, reacted in his diary to a local episode of arson with unstinting woe: 'Oh what a continuing proof is this of the predominancy of vice and wickedness in *this irreligious age*'.[76] However, two days later his mood had changed entirely. Turner was intent upon self-improvement, confiding to his diary: 'Oh what an unspeakable pleasure it is to be busied in one's trade and at a leisure hour to unbend one's mind by reading!'

Pessimism was thus a variable attitude – as were its outcomes. It could promote despondency and inertia. In a few extreme cases, the deepest gloom could even lead to self-destruction. The cleric John Brown, who was subject to melancholia and whose diatribe on the *Manners and Principles of the Times* (1758) has been quoted above (p. 18), ended his life in 1766 by committing suicide. (Needless to say, plenty of people announced national ruin without going that far.)

On the other hand, in some circumstances a reasoned pessimism could be advantageous. Philosophers advise that, when in genuine difficulty, it is wise to be realistic – thus avoiding false hopes and a facile Micawberism, hoping vaguely that 'something will turn up'.[77] In the mid-twentieth century, the indomitable Italian communist Antonio Gramsci counselled precisely such a combination of a negative analysis with positive activism: 'pessimism of the intellect; but optimism of the will'.[78]

Many Georgian religious reformers were inspired by their gloom at the nation's morals. The blacker the state of the world, the more urgent the need for redress. Hence the eighteenth century saw numerous powerful campaigns of religious revivalism (as discussed below, pp. 144–6). Practical responses had better chances of success if the levers of action were within the reformers' control. Thus in 1818 the polemicist John Bowdler, who had earlier feared that Christianity was disappearing, founded the Anglican Church Building Society (today part of the National Churches Trust), drawing upon funds from wealthy donors. By contrast, his brother Thomas Bowdler had a different project, which tried to refine behaviour. Worried that bawdy language was corrupting morals, he undertook a literary purge. His sexually 'purified' *Family Shakespeare* (1818) initially had good sales.[79] Yet the public was resistant. Bowdler became mocked for his prudery. And the verb 'to bowdlerise' has become synonymous with stuffy, prurient censorship.

Demographic (Malthusian) Pessimism

Initially prompted by the prevalent atmosphere of anxiety in the 1790s, one potent intellectual expression of pessimism proved to be more than a passing polemic. It came from the parson Thomas Malthus in 1798. While his personality was cheerful, his intellect was not. He feared for the future of humanity in this world. Prolonged population growth was liable, he calculated, to multiply people well ahead of the available resources. The outcome would be impoverishment, disease, famine and eventual demographic disaster. Already in Britain's large towns, he warned that too many families were 'crowded together in close and unwholesome rooms'.[80] Here pessimism was focused upon a genuinely testing development, in the form of runaway population growth.

Malthus's own suggestion for averting calamity was the wider adoption of sexual abstinence – an idea which did not prove popular. However, his warnings did help to encourage interest in birth control options. In 1823 John Stuart Mill (then aged seventeen) became an active member of a London society which distributed free pamphlets on contraception to working-class women. Alas for Mill, he was well ahead of conventional public opinion. He was prosecuted and briefly imprisoned for circulating material considered 'obscene'.[81]

However, in the long run, Malthus has proved to be, if not accurate in all his predictions or popular in all his solutions, then prescient in identifying the risks of long-term demographic and environmental challenges. These questions have become even more urgent today. Hence climate-change activists face a similar challenge as that faced by Georgian pessimists, struggling to alert people to danger – without depressing them into despondency and fatalism.

⁓ Time-Shift: Then and Now ⁓

Art also lasts through time, both perpetuating stereotypes but also allowing scope for reassessment over time. One pessimistic image shows the iconic power of a negative vision.

William Hogarth's satirical print *Gin Lane* (1751) (Plate 2) is the most brilliant and shocking work of the Georgian artist's huge output. The print's demonic dynamism features (centrally) a lackadaisical mother, ragged and diseased, who is taking snuff, and allowing her infant to fall, probably fatally. Other chaotic details show: the distant spire of St George's Bloomsbury, identifying the area as the notorious St Giles's rookery; crumbling houses; an out-of-work tailor in an upstairs room who has committed suicide by hanging himself; a corpse being put into a coffin; a drunkard being wheeled home, still being served with gin; one woman dosing her child with gin; a poor man and dog fighting over a bone; and a pawnbroker taking in goods from ragged and desperate customers. At front right, there appears a cadaverous ballad-seller, who clutches his glass and a demijohn of gin; and at front left a ginshop, which promises customers that they can be 'Drunk for penny; dead drunk for two pence'.

The original copperplate version can be viewed in the Metropolitan Museum, New York, and it is widely reproduced, as in S. Shesgreen (ed.), *Engravings by Hogarth* (New York, 1973), plate 76.

4

Georgian Voices of Optimism

Very notably, optimistic Georgians were as determined in their optimism as were the pessimists in their gloom. William Hogarth, aware of this cultural dualism, contrasted his demonic *Gin Lane* with a plumply prosperous *Beer Street* (the two prints were published together in 1751), although the 'sunny' version, lacking the shock-horror factor, never won the same fame as its 'dark' rival. Nevertheless, half of those Georgian commentators who gave names to their era found things to praise. They saw the proverbial glass as half full – and, for some, it was overflowing. The major topics that prompted their enthusiasm tended to be domestic developments, which were close at hand and apparent. Very few boasted about British colonial possessions.

Laughter and joking were certainly not the same as happiness – but they did counter-balance the grumblings. A guide-book in 1717 proclaimed that: 'England is most certainly, all Things considered, the happiest Kingdom in the known World, and so confess'd by Travellers'.[1] A popular song from the 1680s urged: '*Begone, Dull Care!*'[2] And Milton's sonnet *L'Allegro*, with its rousing command

'Hence loathèd Melancholy', was a Georgian favourite.[3] So when Handel set the poem to music, with its dark counterpart, *Il Penseroso* ('Hence vain deluding Joys!'), a sanguine librettist in 1740 added a new cheerful finale, quoting Shakespeare: 'As steals the morn upon the night/ And melts the shades away'.

Georgian culture was celebrated for its wit and satire, both visual and literary.[4] Stage comedies were popular, including instant classics like Congreve's *Way of the World* (1700), Farquhar's *Recruiting Officer* (1706), Goldsmith's *She Stoops to Conquer* (1773) and Sheridan's genial *School for Scandal* (1777).[5] Old jokes and new quips, many derived from Jonathan Swift without acknowledgement, were widely circulated as sayings and in print. A supposed traveller from Turkey reported in 1710 that the English 'are a People that take great delight in Puns, Quibbles, and Conundrums'.[6] *The Caledonian Jester* (1806) later savoured Scottish humour; *The Welsh Jester* followed in 1820; and women had earlier been offered *The Female Jester: Or, Wit for the Ladies* (*c.* 1780).[7]

At times, indeed, the public mood seemed too frivolous. The essayist Soame Jenyns mused in 1757 that his philosophical meditations were insufficiently heeded 'in this age of levity and ridicule'.[8] Others used similar phrasing. Laurence Sterne's comic masterpiece *Tristram Shandy* (1759) contributed to what Sterne too defined as 'this age of levity'.[9]

Merriment, of course, has its masks. Songs, comedy and satire did, however, offer a set of resources for communal cheer, including consolation for sorrows. So, while there were plenty of expressions of pessimism, those were offset by counter-declarations of joy and optimism, which – furthermore – began over time to gain cultural predominance.

Praise for National Prosperity

Expanding towns, trade and, later, industry were regularly cited as proof of national prosperity. Daniel Defoe, who toured Britain in the early 1720s, found it the 'most flourishing and opulent country in the

World'. Its inhabitants had some faults, he agreed. Yet 'where-ever we come, and which way so-ever we look, we see something new, something significant, something well worth the traveller's stay, and the writer's care'.[10] And his *Tour* became a publishing hit, going through many later editions.

'Luxury', which had dark connotations for pessimists, was interpreted positively by optimists. For them, the concept signalled economic growth and prosperity.[11] Defoe in 1722 defined the times as a 'luxuriant age'.[12] Henry Fielding, the novelist and JP, referred, almost bemusedly, to 'the vast Torrent of Luxury' that was showering upon Britain.[13] The nation had 'arrived at a degree of prosperity none ever knew before', agreed another observer in 1757, who did, however, worry that wealth would foster moral degeneracy.[14] Mirabeau, whose stay in England has already been noted, admired the 'luxurious profusion of the age'. And he scoffed at British fears of national ruin.[15] Positive references became almost a cliché. Hence yet another dictum in 1793 noted that: 'We live, it is true, in an age of luxury'.[16]

Praise for commerce was particularly widespread. It fostered national greatness, stated David Hume in 1742.[17] Yes: commerce promoted wealth, innovation and liberty, agreed one Dr John Harris in 1744.[18] And William Hutton, himself a Birmingham businessman, was sure that: 'Civility and humanity are ever the companions of trade; ... a barbarous and commercial people is a contradiction'.[19] Associated words of praise were 'refinement', indicating elegance of style, and 'politeness', meaning cultivated good manners. There were many permutations. It was an age of 'high refinement and opulence' for Scotland's pioneering social scientist Adam Ferguson in 1767.[20] He also called it 'an age of politeness', using a phrase recently popular with historians.[21] In 1778 an anonymous lady detected an 'age of refinement and luxury', whilst warning piously against living for pleasure alone.[22] And another author in 1800 also lauded British scientific advances in this 'enlightened age', whilst warning that national rise might precede a fall.[23]

Social changes were invoked, generally in admiration. 'This is an age of Gallantry and Gaiety', wrote Defoe in 1726.[24] For James Burgh, a Nonconformist veering between optimism and distaste, it was a 'gay and voluptuous age' (1746).[25] London's open-air pleasure gardens symbolised change. The epoch was 'an age of pleasure and luxury, of Vauxhalls and Ranelaghs' (1756).[26] But that remark was unusually precise. Many stuck to generalisations. 'The present time is distinguished as the age of Pleasure,' agreed the reformer Jonas Hanway in 1775.[27] Already in 1754 the extent of social transformation was becoming a source of amazed commentary: 'Were the same persons who made the full tour of *England* thirty years ago, to make a fresh one now, and a third some years hence, they would fancy themselves in a land of enchantment. *England* is no more like to what *England* was, than it resembles *Borneo* or *Madagascar*.'[28] And, yet more sweepingly, another author in 1761 praised 'the high degree of perfection, to which the world has been advanced in our days'.[29]

All metallic associations, for optimists, were glittering. It was an 'age of gold': variously in the countryside (1747); throughout Britain (1756); across England, but satirically so (1822–23); and in the world of ideas, this time according to Coleridge in 1830.[30] The newly expanding professions were also saluted. In 1712, the physician and wit John Arbuthnot wrote wryly that: 'I have read of your golden age, your silver age . . . One might justly call this the *Age of the Lawyers*.'[31] By contrast, in 1753 the sage Dr Samuel Johnson offered an alternative: 'The present Age, if we consider chiefly the state of our own country, may be styled, with great propriety *The Age of Authors*'. They included many women, dubbed by Johnson somewhat sardonically as a new 'generation of Amazons of the pen'.[32] It was a good time to write, confirmed William Green in 1768, 'in such a scribbling age'.[33] 'Ours is a studious literary age;/ Ours is a land of books', a poetic guide to *The Age of Frivolity* added sonorously in 1806.[34] Yet, alas, the author noted that very few new works were actually original (ouch).

Other optimistic buzz words were 'invention', 'innovation' and 'improvement'. Such claims emerged in the mid-seventeenth-century ferment of ideas – and multiplied under the Georgians. Dean Josiah Tucker of Gloucester, a cleric turned economic pundit, admired the spread of labour-saving mechanical inventions. England's industrial regions in the north and Midlands 'exhibit a Specimen of practical Mechanics scarce to be paralleled in any Part of the World'.[35] A 1769 guidebook reported that 'the traces of the busy hand of improvement, guided by genius, and supported by industry, are visible in every corner of this flourishing Island'.[36] It was 'an age of experiments', concurred the trans-Atlantic polymath Benjamin Franklin, who practised what he enunciated.[37] Another endorsement of change-for-the-better came from the architect James Stuart in 1771: 'A general spirit prevails for correcting ancient errors and establishing new improvements.[38] Dr Johnson agreed, though less enthusiastically. 'Sir, the age is running mad after innovation,' he growled in 1783.[39]

Admittedly, some new products were mundane. According to a bullish advertisement in 1795, the times constituted 'an era of inventions, improvement, and taste'. The chosen example was, however, no more than a 'new, improved' razor strop.[40] Nonetheless, such copy showed how even humdrum utensils were hyped as part of a progressive picture. The role of the press was accordingly identified in 1785: 'This is the Advertising Age'.[41]

By the later eighteenth and early nineteenth centuries, praise for inventions and innovations had become far too ubiquitous to quote every instance. One example, from Exeter in 1798 was euphoric: 'The present age is still in a rapid state of improvement, although already in possession of discoveries [of] which past times could not entertain the most distant ideas'.[42] Where would it all end? In 1824 the *Preston Chronicle* marvelled that: 'If the nineteenth century shall carry on at the speed we have already gone, imagination itself cannot say where we shall be at the close'.[43]

Optimistic generalisations tended to gloss over short-term problems, just as pessimistic declarations of gloom tended to magnify the immediate crisis. But it is significant that Georgian commentators were aware not only of the culture of innovation but specifically of the advent of steam power, with its eventually monumental consequences both for the globe's economy and climate. One poetic encomium in 1806 was rhapsodic: 'O, rare invention! To thy skill we owe,/ Refinements, our rough fathers did not know'.[44] And in 1805 the poet Robert Southey gave a bold and perceptive summary. The advent of the steam engine was, he declared, 'almost as great an *epocha* [epoch-marker] as the invention of printing'. It was generating an entirely new 'manufacturing system'.

Other great changes were simultaneously happening in commerce, towns and transport. Southey argued that England had undergone since the 1760s a peaceful but fundamental transformation: 'The alternation extends to the minutest things, even to the dress and manners of every rank of society'.[45] A generation later, Thomas Carlyle, the Scottish-born 'sage of Chelsea', was even more emphatic. Not all would have agreed with his verdict in 1829 yet it would not have caused surprise: 'Were we required to characterise this age of ours by any single epithet, we should be tempted to call it, not an Heroical, Devotional, Philosophical, or Moral Age, but, above all others, the Mechanical Age. It is the Age of Machinery, in every outward and inward sense of that word.'[46]

Belief in Cultural Progress

Positive code-words for Georgian optimists included 'philosophy', 'science', 'reason', 'liberality', the 'march of mind' and, above all, 'light' or 'enlightenment'. There were many variants. It was 'an *Age* of the greatest Light and Knowledge that has been for above these twelve hundred Years' (1746); a 'happy aera [*sic*] of experimental philosophy' (1748); an age of 'civilisation and refinement' (1771); 'an age, wherein every part of Science is advancing to perfection' (1772); 'an age of light and liberality' as well as one of 'science and free enquiry', for the reformer John Cartwright (1782); an age of 'science and philosophy' in a 'free and civilised' country, for the historian Edward Gibbon (*c.* 1789); 'this enlightened age' for the experimental chemist Joseph Priestley (1790); and an 'advanced Age of reason and science' for an anonymous woman in 1796.[47]

Claims of cultural betterment were widespread in liberal educated circles across western Europe.[48] An anonymous author in 1760 scolded critics of the times. In fact, he claimed, humankind was '*wiser, happier* and *better*' than it had ever been, whilst scientific know-how was in a 'state of much higher perfection' than ever before.[49] People in this era were more 'enlightened and informed' than their forebears, another added in 1777.[50] The spread of ideas proved 'the liberal-mindedness of the present age', as a contributor to the *Gentleman's Magazine* claimed in 1783, asking someone to provide a simple definition of 'liberal' for all readers.[51] And the mantra was repeated in 1793. Every 'liberal and manly spirit' must be pleased at the spread of philosophical enquiry and the dispersal of 'so many clouds of prejudice and error'.[52] But 'illumination' was not always a code-word for science. A poem to *The Age of Light* (1818), by an anonymous 'Cornish Tinner', praised the divine light emanating from the 'Grand Creator of all Things'.[53] Nonetheless, secular faith in the growth of knowledge was simultaneously using phrases redolent of biblical conversion.

Declarations of confidence in experimentation began to multiply from the mid-seventeenth century. It was a 'learned and inquisitive age', stated a 1667 report on the formation of the Royal Society. A broad base of membership was sought. Hence their meetings should 'resemble the *Cities* themselves: which are compounded of all sorts of men, of the *Gown*, of the *Sword*, of the *Shop*, of the *Field*, of the *Court*, of the *Sea*; all mutually assisting each other'.[54] Scientific knowledge was to be shared, not hoarded. It is a motto sustained by the Royal Society to this day. Pooling and debating knowledge would enhance its quality. Bold claims to that effect were legion. So a commentator in 1748 lauded the patient transmission of ideas from generation to generation: 'By proceeding with due care, every age will add to the common stock of knowledge; the mysteries that still lie concealed in nature may be gradually opened, arts will flourish and increase, mankind will improve, and appear more worthy of their situation in the universe, as they approach towards a perfect knowledge of nature.'[55]

Rationalist philosophy gave the cerebral philosopher Jeremy Bentham similar cause for optimism: 'The age we live in is a busy age; in which knowledge is rapidly advancing towards perfection'.[56] And the radical politician Thomas Paine in 1791 was a true optimist's optimist. He considered the spread of learning to be irreversible: 'It has never yet been discovered, how to make man *unknow* his knowledge, or *unthink* his thoughts'.[57] Even Parson Malthus prefaced his pessimistic demographic warnings in 1798 with a relatively fulsome compliment. He denounced hopes of endless betterment as 'silly speculations'. Yet he accepted that remarkable changes were occurring in science and general knowledge.[58]

Women as well as men were active contributors to the ferment of ideas. It was an 'age of ingenious and learned ladies', wrote a contributor to the *Monthly Review* in 1798, refuting traditional allegations of innate female intellectual inferiority.[59] The pioneering feminist Mary Wollstonecraft was also positive. 'This spirit of enquiry is the characteristic of the present century,' she explained in 1796, 'from which the succeeding [century] will, I am persuaded, receive a great accumulation of knowledge.' It would eventually promote 'the grand causes which combine to carry mankind forward, and diminish the sum of human misery'.[60] Learned ladies like Wollstonecraft were often denounced by critics (both male and female) for being outspoken and indecorous. Nonetheless, creative women had their supporters too. A group portrait, entitled *Characters of the Muses in the Temple of Apollo* (1778), updated classical imagery to praise contemporary female achievers. They were famed, respectively, as a poet, linguist, novelist, dramatist, historian, religious writer, singer, painter and society hostess, who headed a famous 'Blue Stocking' salon.[61] The painting, exhibited at the Royal Academy, did not have a runaway success; but the point was made.

Opponents of female (and indeed male) literacy and learning were themselves becoming figures of fun. 'Madam, a circulating library in a town is as an ever-green tree of diabolical knowledge!' huffs the irascible Sir Anthony Absolute in Sheridan's joyous play *The Rivals* (1775).[62] But audiences were expected to laugh (they still do) at his old-fogeyish attitude. Indeed, the term 'old fogey' itself dates from the 1780s.

Advocates of learning were themselves confident in the trend of the time. The 'bad old days' were dismissed as boringly 'Gothic'.[63] The adjective, derived from pre-Renaissance architecture, was applied to a remarkable range of targets. Art connoisseurs were urged to shed their '*Gothick* rust' in 1719.[64] The 'backwoods' country Squire Western in Fielding's *Tom Jones* (1749) was decried by his fashionable sister with the words: '*O more than Gothic ignorance!*'[65] (The same phrase resurfaced in a 1762 comedy by Samuel Foote).[66] Anything old-fashioned qualified. So in 1757 the economist Josiah Tucker defined levying tolls on inland trade as an 'ancient, *Gothic,* barbarous Custom'.[67] Duelling was denounced in 1773 as both '*Gothic*' and 'absurd'.[68] And in 1780 a nervous London citizen criticised the Gordon rioters (see below, pp. 189–90) as '*Gothic* incendiaries'.[69] The hostile meaning was clear. This anti-Gothic rhetoric started to abate only when the culturally positive Gothic revival began among patrons and architects in the later eighteenth century.[70]

For those looking onwards, 'reason' became a particular buzz word. That concept was enhanced, for many rationalist Christians, by John Locke's *Reasonableness of Christianity* (1695). By the late eighteenth century, 'the Age of Reason' had become a cliché, as some critics complained. The most notorious application of the phrase came from Thomas Paine. His *Age of Reason* (1794) was a deistic tract, challenging belief in all forms of religion based upon divine revelation.[71]

It caused an immense scandal and the government tried to suppress the book. Nonetheless, the catchphrase survived (albeit without Paine's specific meaning), whilst 'magical' beliefs in wizardry, fairies and ghosts were dwindling into minority attitudes, increasingly deemed 'quaint'.[72]

Above all, the eighteenth century nurtured an even mightier watchword for benevolent change. 'Progress' as a term was brisk and punchy.[73] And as a concept, it was redolent of inevitability. Instead of the pessimistic 'Decline and Fall', the optimistic alternative was 'Rise and Progress'. An early use of the progressive terminology launched a popular classic. John Bunyan's *Pilgrim's Progress* (1678) recounted the pilgrim's spiritual journey from sin to redemption.[74] The storyline also lent itself to satirical reversal. Hogarth did that wittily with, firstly, his series of engravings *A Harlot's Progress* (1732) and then the insouciant *Rake's Progress* (1735).[75] Yet the progressive usage predominated. There were far too many to cite every example. But alert readers could study the *Rise and Progress* of a great range of themes, from the history of Glasgow (1736) to that of geometry (1745), and on to a poem enthusing about *The Rise and Progress of the Present Taste in Planting Parks, Pleasure Grounds, Gardens, etc.* (1767).[76]

True optimists saw improvements across the board. Thus Joseph Priestley envisaged 'an endless progress in our investigations ... a prospect truly sublime and glorious'. The masses would come to participate not only in learning and industry but eventually in government. Hence, he warned, despots should rightly 'tremble even at an air-pump or an electrical machine'. Not only that, the human species would itself advance towards perfection. And the outcome would be unimaginable: 'As men a few centuries ago could have no idea of what their posterity are at this day, we are probably much less able to form an idea of what our posterity will attain to as many centuries hence.'[77]

'Revolution' was also, for a while, another favoured concept for drastic change. The youthful William Wordsworth famously exalted the fall of the Bastille: 'Bliss was it in that dawn to be alive/ But to be young was very heaven'.[78] Thomas Paine added gleefully in 1790 that: 'The Revolution in France is certainly a Fore runner to other Revolutions in Europe', and within a year amplified his confidence: 'It is an Age of Revolutions, in which everything may be looked for'.[79] Similarly, the Dissenting clergyman Richard Price in 1789 urged his fellow optimists: 'Be encouraged, all ye Friends of Freedom. The Times are auspicious'.[80]

From the mid-1790s onwards, however, 'revolution' became in Britain a hotly contested term. As events in France became bloody and unpredictable, majority opinion turned against the French and their armies. A tract of 1799 entitled *A Fig for the Invasion!* assured the English, Welsh, Scots and Irish that, if they pulled together, they 'could beat the world'.[81] Evolutionary change seemed preferable to unpredictable revolutions.

And a heady cultural euphoria revived a thousandfold after Trafalgar in 1805, and especially after Waterloo in 1815. Britain's glory had no equivalent in the history of the world, announced the editor of the *Gentleman's Magazine,* reviewing the events of 1805: 'our hearts expand with confidence and hope'. Years of prosperity and happiness were bound to follow.[82] 'Hail BRITAIN, EMPRESS of the SEA/ And GUARDIAN GENIUS of the WESTERN WORLD', concluded Elizabeth Cobbold's *Ode on the Victory of Waterloo* (1815).[83] No sales came from underplaying success.

Thereafter declarations of national and cultural confidence continued, not unchallenged, but unabated. Quite which historical trends would turn out ultimately to be positive and which negative remained open to debate. Yet the simple (not to say simplistic) mantra 'You can't stop progress' was becoming a catchphrase that circulates to this day.

Optimism as Smugness or Spur?

One possible response to optimistic views of history can, however, be complacency. Why take action, when inexorable trends are already doing the job? It can also lead to a degree of heartlessness towards individual suffering. If the times are seen as progressive, then people falling by the wayside may be personally blamed for their misfortunes, or at least thought of as 'minor' problems within a benevolent trend.

Most political activists with optimistic outlooks, however, generally avoided any such smugness. On the contrary, they were enthused by working with what they interpreted as the grain of history. In that context, interim defeats were no more than temporary setbacks. And larger disasters required a dogged determination to await the long term. 'Truth and Liberty, in an age so enlightened as the present, must be Invincible and Omnipotent', ran a 1794 resolution from the London Constitutional Society, backing the vote for all adult males.[84] The 'sublime grandeur of Freedom' was imminent, agreed the activist Henry Redhead Yorke in the same year.[85] Yet their immediate campaign was thwarted.

So the indomitable John Thelwall offered the consolation that long-term change would eventually promote a new democratic politics. 'Every large workshop and manufactory is a sort of political society,' he wrote in 1796, 'which no act of parliament can silence, and no magistrate disperse.'[86] In reality, however, it is worth noting that – whether for good or ill – not every failed campaign does recover for later triumph. The Jacobites, after all, fought for one eighteenth-century 'great cause' which was lost, and which remained lost.

Another contrasting alternative to taking control of central government was therefore to institute local reforms on a small scale. A practical example came from the Welsh reformer and manufacturer Robert Owen (1771–1858). In 1799 he took over some existing cotton mills, founded in 1785 at New Lanark on the Clyde, 25 miles south-east of Glasgow, and sought to establish around them a model community based upon co-operative principles. 'It is confidently expected that the period is at hand, when man, through ignorance, shall not much longer inflict unnecessary misery upon man,' wrote Owen.[87] Moreover, this ambitious project was replicated in other

Owenite settlements in Britain and then in the USA. Their economic basis, however, was not strong enough for long-term viability. So these settlements, though not the cooperative ideal, eventually failed.[88]

Otherwise, advocates for change focused upon specific campaigns. In the later eighteenth century, the greatest of the liberal 'good causes' was opposition to the slave trade and then to slavery as an institution. Supporters were both encouraged and scolded into action. One abolitionist tract in 1791 was reproachful: 'We, in an enlightened age, have greatly surpassed in brutality and injustice the most ignorant and barbarous ages: and while we are pretending to the finest feelings of humanity, are exercising unprecedented cruelty.'[89] People should live up to their times. That argument was made, emolliently, by the African abolitionist Olaudah Equiano, a former slave. Freedom for 'the sable people', he declared in 1789, was essential in this era of 'light, liberty, and science'.[90]

Abolitionism was thus depicted as part of an inevitable trend. Having banned the trade in captive workers, the next campaign was to ban all forms of enslavement itself. William Roscoe's *Manifesto against African Slavery* (1830) accordingly urged that 'a great era is opening upon the earth'. Such a golden age would have to preclude one group of humans holding others in permanent bondage.[91] His hope was infectious; but again the ending of personal enslavement was not bound to triumph automatically in that or any age.

Enlightenment Optimism

Gradually, the view that the world was still young and was likely to survive for many millennia was gaining intellectual credibility. New specialist studies were emerging, dealing with the very long term. Astronomy and geology were two such fields. Comparative linguistics was yet another, as was the study of the long swathes of human history. The rhetoric of 'modernity', although disputed between optimists and pessimists, implied a timescale which allowed room for change. Georgian Britons were thereby encouraged to see their own era as part of an epic process, in which successive eras were not just 'more of the same'.

'Light' became a particularly significant symbol of desirable change. It was invoked as a metaphor for the cultivation of reason – and for the growth of education and science. Moreover, light was literally becoming more incandescent thanks to oil-fired lamps in the eighteenth century and, from the 1820s onwards, new gas lamps. These had been pioneered in England in the 1790s, and within a generation were being used to light townscapes across Britain and Ireland. The visual impact of applied technology encouraged a favourable view of the human powers of invention. The literal spread of 'enlightenment', the banishment of 'darkness', seemed to be turning metaphors into reality.

A linear view of 'Rise and Progress' thus began to predominate over the old-style model of perennial cycles. Not everyone remained convinced. Indeed, a number of eminent early twentieth-century thinkers in the West, notably Oswald Spengler and Arnold Toynbee, offered strong reinterpretations of cyclical history. However, they were reacting to a long period when majority opinion had tilted the other way. In eighteenth- and nineteenth-century Britain, a belief in linear 'progress' was slowly winning the battle of ideas (though the unfolding disaster of the Irish Famine in the 1840s was a huge blow to concepts of universal betterment).

This gradualist model of incremental change matched the scientific ethos of trial-and-error and a step-by-step reformist approach to political change. And, when 'progress' appeared to be boosted by national and imperial dominance, particularly after Waterloo in 1815, British confidence in the apparent trends of history was much strengthened.

Of course, the debates never stopped. Wars, conflicts, exploitation, hunger and disasters did not end. Moreover, the triumphs of industrialisation have generated unanticipated environmental problems on a global scale. Thus Malthusian pessimism still battles against techno-optimism to this day.

✑ Time-Shift: Then and Now ✑

One optimistic image is worth examining as an attempt to rebut pessimism, even if it also shows how 'good' visions may lack the demonic power of their disaster counterparts.

William Hogarth's *Beer Street* (1751) (Plate 3), featuring placid urban prosperity and good cheer, was produced as a sunny contrast to the demonic *Gin Lane*. This genial presentation of happy citizens in an orderly, peaceful city includes images of: roof repairs being undertaken by cheery workers aloft on scaffolding; a flourishing inn (middle back) showing the sign of the Sun; a thin, impoverished artist painting a rival sign of gin (left); plump beer-drinking craftsmen, one waving a hearty joint of meat; an amorous man kissing a pretty wench, who holds a large key, symbolising plenty; many brimming tankards of beer, including one tankard being handed through a peephole in the door of the only dilapidated house, which belongs to the now-failing pawnbroker.

The original copperplate version can be viewed in the Metropolitan Museum, New York, and it is widely reproduced, as in S. Shesgreen (ed.), *Engravings by Hogarth* (New York, 1973), plate 75.

PART II
The Georgians Experiencing Change in Daily Life

Enjoyed by rich and poor alike, the fast-growing daily taste
for imported China tea and cheap West Indian sugar also
triggered urgent calls from campaigners to abolish the slave
trade, which transported captive Africans to work in the
West Indian sugar plantations.

5

Sharing Family Lives between Private and Public Worlds

A s many contemporary witnesses focused upon manners and morals in daily life – up close and personal – the discussion now moves to investigate shared daily experiences. This chapter accordingly focuses upon Georgian home life; and the next chapter upon Georgian sexualities. While there was a brisk market in dashing accounts of outlaws, pirates and highwaymen (preferably far away), everyday life was generally much more mundane.

At home, the Georgians lived in separate households, with live-in servants in the case of the well-to-do. Each domestic grouping resided either in a separate dwelling or in a portion of a house or tenement block. In these years, the status of the Georgian domicile was rising. Their sturdy houses were better warmed than in earlier eras (though not universally), and were seen as places to enjoy and to decorate in personal style. As part of that trend, living areas were becoming ever more separated from work-places, as old-style domestic industries slowly disappeared.

'Hame's hame, be it never so hamely,' rhapsodised John Arbuthnot in rich demotic Scots in 1712.[1] No matter how dilapidated, home terrain had the appeal of familiarity. The Georgians were cultivating the concept of a stable family sanctum, to be displayed, at least in part, to others, yet simultaneously defended as personal space. A classic dictum, much cited in the eighteenth century, likened an Englishman's home to a private castle. Intrusive passers-by, peering through keyholes or the new glass windows, were deplored. In Thomas Rowlandson's print entitled *Curiosity Cured* (*c.* 1780), a nosey neighbour is doused from an upstairs window with the contents of a chamber pot. Two gleeful neighbours (and an urban dog) are ready to help in chastising her. Conventions of privacy may be flouted, as they always can be, but they are also monitored by communal expectations. The poorest Britons, who slept rough in barns or flitted between cheap rented rooms, might rightly scoff. Yet the ideal 'home' was gaining allure.

Legal convention was also important. It upheld the sanctity of all private residences, whether of rich or poor. That position was reaffirmed in a much-quoted parliamentary speech, delivered with great authority by William Pitt the Elder in March 1763: 'The poorest man may in his cottage bid defiance to all the forces of the crown. It may be frail – its roof may shake – the wind may blow through it – the storm may enter – the rain may enter – but the King of England cannot enter! — all his force dares not cross the threshold of the ruined tenement!'[2] In practice, to be sure, there were legal exceptions. Customs and excise officers had the right to enter premises without a warrant when searching for unlicensed liquor.[3] It was that unpopular task which in the 1790s disillusioned the merry Dumfries exciseman and poet Robert Burns.[4] Nonetheless, the taxmen were monitored carefully, because Pitt's attitude was widely shared. Each front door, whether ornate or plain, marked both a legal and a sociocultural boundary.

One multi-occupied house or one block of tenements, as famously found in Edinburgh's Old Town, might contain several distinct households, living cheek by jowl. Yet each unit had its own front doorway, even if it did not open onto the street. The average Georgian household contained 4.75 people. That figure was relatively low, when compared with earlier times, but still high in comparison with the British mean of 2.3 in 2011.[5] Chief among the factors promoting the long-term shrinking in household size were the continuing fall in numbers of live-in apprentices, the provision of increased residential workhouse care for the elderly, and the acceleration of urban-commercial growth, which aided young couples to set up on their own. (It was only much later, however, post-1945, that the numbers of live-in domestic servants declined sharply.)

Living in relatively small households heightened the emotional focus upon the nuclear family. Most Georgian households contained no more than one conjugal unit of parents plus children. That pattern was already prevalent across western Europe by the sixteenth century, making multi-generational family life unusual.[6] Traditionally, each household was headed by a venerated father figure.[7] Yet there was no timeless 'patriarchy' in operation. The status of men was changing; and a sizeable number of Georgian households were headed by women, often, but not invariably, widows. Household variety was commonplace. And the rhetoric of 'family' was used very diversely, often referring just to the close conjugal unit but at other times embracing a wider tribe of relatives, servants and apprentices as well.

Singletons and Couples

Single people living on their own were early pioneers in the trend towards the atomisation of living arrangements, which has become marked in the twenty-first century. For some Georgian bachelors, it was a stage in the life cycle, before marriage and independent household formation. Arrangements were typically flexible. Thus, in 1762, when James Boswell (aged twenty-two and unmarried) first came from Scotland to stay in London, he 'took a lodging up two pair of stairs, with the use of a handsome parlour all the forenoon'. He catered for himself, but could, if he wished, dine with his Scottish landlord, paying an extra shilling per meal.[8] Incidentally, their shared house was located in Whitehall's Downing Street, then an open thoroughfare – as it remained until 1989.

For a few men, solitary living was a lifetime choice. John Fransham, who dwelt alone in a garret room in Norwich, supporting himself by weaving and writing, was viewed by his neighbours as an amiable eccentric and freethinker.[9] More oddly, the 2nd Baron Rokeby, at one stage MP for Canterbury, withdrew from company to indulge his passion for prolonged daily immersion in his private swimming pool (unheated). Occasionally, he emerged, with his long beard, which put observers in mind of an authentic Neptune.[10] His sister sniffed unkindly that this venerable style gave Rokeby an air of wisdom, but without the reality. Odder still in the Georgian roster of eccentrics, John Tallis stayed in bed for over thirty years before his death in 1755. He claimed that a curse would fall upon him if he encountered fresh air. Consequently Tallis lay, swathed in coverings, with a peg on his nose, in a darkened, draught-proof room in a Worcestershire country inn, seeing no one but his servants, who changed his bed annually.[11] (His story may have inspired Wordsworth's later ballad on the ever-frozen and frozen-hearted Harry Gill.)

However, the Georgians' most famous loner was a more romantic figure. The forger-poet Thomas Chatterton left Bristol to reside in an attic in London's Holborn, hoping to launch his literary career.[12] Disappointed, he committed suicide in 1770, aged seventeen. Before long, however, he became a legend. Romantic poets enthused over the lost 'marvellous boy' and his precocious literary skills, even if misapplied to faking works by an imaginary fifteenth-century poet.[13] Chatterton also became the hero of a play (1835) and an opera (1876). And his lonely death was commemorated in a much-admired Victorian genre painting. Chatterton thus became an icon of solitary and misunderstood genius.

Most single young women, by contrast, lived with families or friends.[14] It was not unusual, however, for widows to head their own households. Many settled in the growing spas and resorts, where low-cost lodgings were plentiful. In Jane Austen's *Persuasion* (1817), the protagonist Anne Elliott meets in Bath an old school-friend, Mrs Smith. She is an impoverished, disabled widow, living alone in two rooms and 'unable even to afford herself the comfort of a servant'. Nonetheless, although not in smart society, Mrs Smith gets all its news 'through the short cut of a laundress and a waiter'.[15] That specification was an adroit touch from Austen, an expert on both gossip networks and genteel poverty.

Overwhelmingly, however, Georgian society and literature focused upon the challenges of finding a marriage partner and then making the union work. Both tasks were hazardous. Harsh or heedless husbands featured regularly in the complaint literature as did licentious or shrewish wives. Law reports on titillating cases of adultery, known as 'Crim. Con' (criminal conversation), became best-sellers.[16] However, in this era it was increasingly expected that the route to successful matrimony would be facilitated by a positive choice, made by both partners. In practice, Britain had no long tradition of formally 'arranged' marriage. And a growing trend rejected absolute parental direction in matters matrimonial – although youngsters from rich and titled backgrounds often experienced considerable cultural pressures as well as family input to encourage them into financially beneficial unions.

An ideal of a freely chosen companionate marriage fused older Christian and especially Puritan teachings of marital partnership, with a fresh stress upon freedom of choice.[17] From the 1720s onwards, this ambition was encouraged by the concept of individual 'sensibility'. And hopes were also boosted by the language of romantic love, which was in full flower by the later eighteenth century.[18] It was too prosaic to be married as a 'mere Smithfield bargain', like a deal in London's premier cattle market. So Lydia Languish complains in Sheridan's courtship comedy *The Rivals*.[19] Wedlock without affection could prove disastrous. Hogarth's print sequence *Marriage-à-la-Mode*

(1743) satirised a mercenary match between a poor nobleman's son and a rich alderman's daughter, which quickly degenerated. (In 1999, the Portuguese artist Paula Rego updated this work with further stern warnings against any parental meddling.)

Georgian weddings were relatively low-key events. Three weeks before the date, the couple posted the banns (or, more rarely, obtained a license) as a public declaration of intent. Ceremonies were simple, with few people in attendance, and couples wore smart but not as yet standardised wedding finery.[20] In the early eighteenth century, moreover, one effect of increased personal choice was seen in the spread of clandestine marriages. Official opinion became alarmed. A new Marriage Act (known as Hardwicke's Act) was passed in 1753 to tighten regulations in England and Wales.[21] Thereafter, couples were required to be married in church by an Anglican clergyman, although Jewish and Quaker nuptials were exempted – and royalty remained subject to special rules. Family scrutiny of wedlock seemed to be enhanced. But an immediate counter-effect was the increase in English couples eloping to Scotland to take advantage of its looser regulations. There a purely spoken contract before witnesses was acceptable.[22] Gretna Green, just across the Anglo-Scottish border, became the destination of choice for couples seeking to evade family disapproval. And quietly, too, many others lived together in irregular common-law unions, outside wedlock.

A lawful wedding, which was the stock happy ending, could in practice go wrong. Mary Ellen Bowes, a North Country heiress dubbed the 'Unhappy Countess', ran through three high-profile partnerships.[23] Her first marriage gave her a noble title and five children. She then had an affair with a nabob, who had made (and lost) a fortune in India. But Bowes declined to marry him and aborted their embryonic child. She next wed an Anglo-Irish adventurer, who maltreated and kidnapped her. After escaping with help from her maids, Bowes sued him for divorce. This saga highlighted the capacity of high-born society figures to flout conventional morality, their resort to both self-help and litigation, and the usefulness of loyal servants. Moreover, Bowes's social eminence was not permanently eroded by these misadventures. After a respectable old age, she was buried in Westminster Abbey, where 150 years later, her direct descendant (via the Bowes-Lyon family) was crowned as Queen Elizabeth II.

Within the family, it was conventionally expected that husbands would control the purse-strings, unless the wife had an independent fortune.[24] Women meanwhile ran the household, managed the servants, and organised or undertook childcare. But there was much variation between different couples; and some big tasks were frequently shared – such as ordering furniture, in an era when affluent consumers often chose designs and commissioned bespoke items.[25]

Under common law, power was ultimately vested in the husband. He was allowed to chastise his wife physically (albeit within the limit of 'reasonableness'). In reality, again, practice varied. Thus in 1753 it was stated, sarcastically: 'How fortunate for them [wives], that the men, either through affection or indolence, have given up their legal rights; and have, by custom, placed all the power in the wife!'[26] Yet domestic tyranny remained a genuine hazard. Legal cases suggest that the commonest responses were to flee or to shout loudly for help. In one instance from Lincolnshire in 1690, a frightened servant raised the alarm, whereupon a neighbour climbed into an upstairs room and barred the door against the husband until the battered wife and child had escaped down a ladder.[27] No unassailable Englishman's castle there. In another case in 1774, it was the husband, a draper in Coltishall, Norfolk (8 miles north-east of Norwich), who injured himself by jumping from an upstairs window, fearing that his wife was about to kill him.[28] Overall, public opinion was turning against the use of substantial physical violence against the weak and relatively powerless, such as women, children and animals. But daily behaviour remained hard to monitor and attitudes towards lighter smacks and cuffs were more permissive.[29]

Furthermore, most married women had only limited property rights (before legal changes in 1870).[30] Only a relatively few wives were protected by pre-nuptial agreements, giving them control of their own finances. It was that mechanism which gave leverage to Mary Bowes, who was the heiress of a great Durham coal-mining fortune. The cards were thus stacked in favour of husbands, but with varying effects according to circumstances.

Throughout this era, legal divorce was very hard to obtain; and, if achieved, was harsh on the 'guilty' party.[31] Plenty of Georgian couples did, however, litigate with one another. Husbands sued over their wives' failure to fulfil their sexual and domestic responsibilities, while wives counter-claimed with evidence of their husbands' cruelties or negligence.[32] In particular, suits for the 'restitution of conjugal rights' were used either to force an absconding partner to return or, by wives, to seek alimony for separation, short of divorce. Such agreements, however, were costly, difficult and slow to obtain. If couples obtained a legal separation, moreover, fathers usually gained custody of their offspring. Only after 1839 were mothers permitted to seek custody of children under seven and access to their elder siblings, as one step in the campaign to improve the rights of married women.[33] A particularly harsh case occurred in 1778. Elizabeth, the first wife of Henry Dundas, Scotland's political supremo, confessed to a brief adulterous affair. He promptly divorced her, while retaining her estate, which provided him with the title of Lord Melville. And for the rest of her long life (she died in 1847 at the age of ninety-seven), the divorced wife was forbidden to see her children.

It was not the case, however, that adultery was always punished. Rich and powerful men got away with it, often very publicly. In the 1780s, the 5th Duke of Devonshire lived in a publicly known *ménage à trois* with his wife Georgiana and his mistress, later his second wife, Lady Elizabeth Foster. Adding to the complications, the duchess reared her husband's illegitimate daughter and herself had a child by the leading Whig politician, Earl Grey. All parties thus flouted conventional morality. The men faced no penalties. The duchess retained her celebrity role, which survives in legend and film, although her extra-marital child was sent away to be reared by Earl Grey's family.[34]

Another famous Georgian *ménage à trois* was that of Emma Hamilton, her husband Sir William Hamilton, and Admiral Horatio Nelson. Again, society was dazzled rather than censorious. After her husband's death, she and Nelson continued to live publicly together, out of wedlock, since Nelson was already married. Only after his demise in 1805 was Lady Hamilton in effect 'dropped' by smart society.

Many kings and aristocrats, meanwhile, kept known mistresses. Some fathered illegitimate children. And in 1769, one of George II's grandsons was sued in court for adultery. Little wonder that the clergy and moralists expressed concern. Yet no political support was forthcoming in 1779 when the Bishop of Llandaff introduced a bill 'for the preventing of adultery'. Enforcing Christian morality was thought best left to the churches rather than the state.[35]

Evidently, the balance of power within a Georgian marriage lay with the men. It was, however, untrue (although often repeated) that the law regarded married women as mere 'chattels' (property), who were thus 'owned' by their husbands. Instead, a wedded couple was legally deemed to constitute one person at law. The wife thus shared the couple's possessions and liabilities jointly with the husband. It was true that it was generally he who acted in their name. Yet it was equally the case that numerous Georgian businesswomen, including not only widows, who inherited from their dead husbands, but also spinsters and married women, ran businesses on their own behalf (see below, pp. 273–4). So it was not true that the status of wives was literally equivalent to enslavement, as is sometimes claimed. They were partners (if often junior partners), not property. Moreover, individuals could often find ways around the traditional legal position; and many did, although reformers later and rightly sought to establish systematic safeguards for all married women.

Two fascinating and semi-clandestine traditions showed a further degree of popular monitoring of matrimonial behaviour, without recourse to either the law or church courts. The raucous Skimmington Ride entailed the communal pillorying in effigy of individuals who had provoked social criticism.[36] Targets included 'unmanly' husbands who were henpecked by their wives, or scandalous adulterers (as later retold in 1886 by Thomas Hardy in *The Mayor of Casterbridge*).[37] In practice, such events were rare. They occurred chiefly within small and close-knit communities. Yet such communal rebukes indicated that Georgian domestic life, whilst private, was not beyond public scrutiny.

Another popular ritual was the 'wife sale', which was a form of ad hoc and definitely illegal divorce.[38] (Again, Hardy's *Mayor of Casterbridge* provides a later literary exemplar.) Such exchanges were often collusively pre-agreed between a husband and a lover, with a small sum of money changing hands in ratification. The custom, with the wife wearing a loose halter around her neck, was demeaning to the woman, even if the exchange freed a couple from an unhappy union. Yet the transaction was not the equivalent of a commercial deal in a slave market. If the witnessing crowds disapproved, the 'sale' was void, as happened upon occasion. The number of such wife exchanges remained tiny. And official disapproval remained total. Nonetheless, these informal transactions indicated how individuals exercised choices, whilst seeking public approbation for their domestic resettlement in the form of de facto divorces.

Servants and Employers

Major witnesses to all the vagaries of Georgian family life were the ubiquitous domestic servants. They constituted a crucial cross-class social link, as many young adults from poor families lived and worked in affluent households. Apprentices had in earlier eras also played a big domestic role.[39] By this period, however, they were decreasingly common as household members. And lodgers, who included visitors to town for business or leisure purposes, were often short-stay residents, managing independently in rented rooms.[40] Domestic servants were thus key social intermediaries. Their role gave people from different social backgrounds, both rich and poor, at least some knowledge of 'how the other half lives' (a phrase dating from 1752), although the amount of social mixing – and servant turnover – tended to be greater in the towns than in the countryside.

Live-in domestic servants, though not always loved, were viewed as part of the 'family'. They were 'insiders'. Even families on modest incomes might employ at least one maid-of-all-work. And in 1771 the Duke of Bedford, bolstered by his wealth and title, engaged the services of as many as forty-two servants in his town house in London's Bloomsbury.[41] (Even that total, however, was small compared with the great retinues of feudal magnates in pre-Tudor times.)

Servants and employers daily negotiated the subtleties of their relationships within a framework of law and custom. In the grandest Georgian households, considerable formality prevailed. Menservants on duty wore special liveries and maids were stylish, often wearing their mistresses' cast-off dresses.[42] Consequently, one stock eighteenth-century joke laughed at the country bumpkin, new in town, who bowed to the footman, taking him for the master, and made sexual advances to the lady of the house, taking her for the maid.

Menservants remained in demand, working as butlers, footmen and coachmen. The artist William Hogarth, who c. 1750 painted an affectionate group portrait of his household staff, employed three women, two mature men and a young lad, probably an errand-boy. One dignified post was that of the Georgian 'gentleman's gentleman', or personal valet. The memoirs of one such valet, John Macdonald, revealed his pride in the job, alongside an anxiety to assert his personal status. (For good measure, he stressed his own attractiveness to maidservants and, at times, to elite ladies.)[43] Another specialist male occupation was the post of 'man cook'. In the 1810s, some 300–400 of the wealthiest families across Britain kept a male chef – the most highly paid being recruited from France.[44] Over the long term, however, domestic service was becoming the preserve of women, and especially of young women. The 'feminisation' of the household workforce was a slow process (historians differ over the precise timetable), but an inexorable one. In Britain's expanding economy, men found plentiful other forms of employment, allowing household chores to become redefined as women's work.

Turnover of all domestic staff was routinely high, causing frequent anxiety for employers. Servants were caricatured as selfish and self-indulgent. In 1751 one commentator alleged (sweepingly) that *'Tippling* [is the] bane of *London Servants*, and I am afraid of many of a more elevated Station, especially among the *Female Sex'*.[45] Another complaint was the prevalence of gossip. Servants itemised their employers' faults 'with saucy Railings', as one footman-poet agreed in 1732.[46] Moreover, a popular farce entitled *High Life below Stairs* (1759) depicted the servants making merry on the house as soon as their masters left home.[47] To keep order, employers relied upon their social status and financial clout. At times, too, they cuffed or beat their staff in anger. But as already noted, direct physical action was increasingly seen as unacceptable. Instead, faulty workers were punished by deductions from wages or dismissal, while minor offences were reprimanded.

From the servants' point of view, domestic service provided remuneration, an informal apprenticeship in household management, access to news and an element of informal cross-class education.[48] Furthermore, servant-halls could function as multi-ethnic meeting-places. In the mid-eighteenth century, there was a fashion among the wealthy for employing African page-boys.[49] A number of Indian women also came to Britain as servants to returning nabob families. And plenty of people from the West Indies found jobs in service too. The best-known case was that of the Jamaican-born Francis Barber. He had a sequence of jobs on land and at sea, before settling as the trusted factotum of Dr Johnson, whose will made Barber his residuary legatee. (Sadly for the faithful servant, there was very little left, once all the other Johnsonian bequests were paid.)[50]

From the employers' point of view, live-in servants provided immediate assistance for basic household chores. But they required constant supervision. And it could be difficult to find and train good staff. Take the case of Mary Hardy, wife of a brewer and farmer in Letheringsett in north Norfolk. In May 1797, she left her maid Hannah Daglass in charge of the house. But Daglass absented herself, leaving the back-door unlocked for the chimney-sweep. Being rebuked for negligence, she was then 'saucy'. Hardy dismissed Daglass on the spot. Yet the local labour market offered unlimited choice neither to employers nor employees. Hannah Daglass was rehired in 1799 and she worked for another two years in the Hardy household.[51]

Secrets were also hard to keep from servants with sharp ears and eyes. Many legal cases turned upon their witness testimonies.[52] Sometimes employers found it constraining to live under constant surveillance. Hence some purchased a new item of furniture (available from the 1730s) known as the 'dumb-waiter'. Employers and their guests could then serve themselves from sideboards or from tables with circulating centre-pieces. Gentlemen drinking deeply after dinner could equally avoid intrusive witnesses while pouring large libations.[53] Servants, conversely, disliked their silent competitor, which curbed their access to news and scandal – or so Christopher Smart's 1755 poem by a fictional Abigail, or lady's maid, alleged.[54] (The term 'dumb-waiter' was later extended to refer to a mechanical service lift, which is its most common usage today.)

Shared domesticity fostered intimacy, but not equality. In 1763 the blunt Dr Johnson teased the republican historian Catharine Macaulay. He reportedly urged: 'Here is a very sensible, civil, well-behaved fellow-citizen, your footman; I desire that he may be allowed to sit down and dine with us'. Macaulay rejected the suggestion, causing Johnson to add: 'She has never liked me since'.[55] Of course, this anecdote comes from Johnson, without any correction from Macaulay. It indicates, however, that shared households were not communes.

Wages were paid yearly, supplemented by ad hoc perquisites. Gifts of clothing were common, plus a special gift or 'box' on Boxing Day. However, in the long run the master–servant relationship was becoming more commercialised and more impersonal. One sign was apparent in the declining custom of guests in grand mansions tipping the liveried staff. Rejection of this practice began in Glasgow in 1759 and mushroomed. The change was opposed by the liveried footmen, who earned most from such tips (known as 'vails'). However, angry demonstrations – and even riots – failed to stem the tide.[56] Tipping for services rendered within private households began to disappear relatively rapidly, although the custom still remains today a matter for negotiation within commercial residences like hotels.

Privacy remained a matter of general concern. In this period, individuals habitually kept a solid wooden chest, secured by a stout key, to store personal treasures.[57] And, significantly, sleeping arrangements were becoming more segregated. Formerly, maidservants slept on makeshift beds in the corners of their employers' bedrooms. In Georgian households, by contrast, menservants had truckle (moveable) beds in corridors or workrooms, while maidservants either shared with the children or, increasingly, with other female servants in garrets or sculleries. (In the long term, bed-sharing among unmarried people in all social classes has continued to decline, except in the very poorest households.)

The Chelsea household of the historian-philosopher Thomas Carlyle provides an example of this change. In the early nineteenth century, he and his wife habitually employed a maid-of-all-work. She slept in the kitchen and was expected to wait outside whenever the sage wished to smoke there.[58] Unsurprisingly, the Carlyles had an exceptionally high staff turnover, employing thirty-four maids in thirty-two years.

Trickiest were the hazards of transgressive sexual encounters in small households where family and servants lived at close quarters. From time to time, there were dramatic consequences. In 1810 the Duchess of Manchester (a married mother of eight children) eloped with her footman.[59] But this outcome, which the ducal family tried to conceal, was unusual. Generally, female servants were the most vulnerable.[60] Samuel Richardson's epistolary novel *Pamela* (1740) highlighted that scenario, causing a literary sensation. His story allowed the virtuous maidservant to manoeuvre her gentleman would-be seducer into marriage.[61] Moreover, some real-life encounters did lead to that outcome. In 1720 Sir John Rudd, a sixteen-year-old-baronet, wed a friend's maidservant. (His family, however, found legal grounds to dissolve the union.)[62] And in 1825, an eccentric landowner, Sir Harry Fetherstonhaugh of Uppark in Sussex, married, at the age of seventy, his young dairymaid, to much social ridicule.[63] In their case, the union was a success, and she inherited the house and estate.

Commonly, however, servant seductions risked leading not to wedlock but to illegitimate children, on an unquantifiable scale. And sometimes to disaster. Hence the observation that 'The typical infanticidal mother [in the Georgian era] was an unmarried servant girl'.[64] Events inside households had manifest ramifications outside as well, as all concerned were often aware.

Parents and Children

Simultaneously, liberal attitudes to child-rearing – with a stress upon gentler, child-focused educational styles – were also being strengthened, though with undoubted limitations as to how widely these were implemented.[65] In 1693, the traditional tight swaddling of very young babies was tellingly criticised by the liberal philosopher John Locke and then by many Georgian doctors.[66] Harsh discipline, with excess physical chastisement, was also decried. Children were decreasingly seen as 'imps of Satan' needing punishment, but rather as valued individuals, deserving encouragement. Teasingly, in 1802 the poet William Wordsworth offered a famous paradox: 'The Child is father of the Man'.[67]

Rote learning was by no means abandoned everywhere but was criticised as old-fashioned and ineffective. Children were to be nurtured with the aid of special toys, games and clothing.[68] *Robinson Crusoe* and *Gulliver's Travels* were quickly abridged and retold for the young; and new books were written specifically for this flourishing market.[69] One popular example came from Sarah Trimmer, a liberal Anglican. Her *Story of the Robins* (1786) showed wildlife and humans living happily together. (Intriguingly, Trimmer's humanised birds, Dicksy, Pecksy, Flapsy and Robin, prefigure Beatrix Potter's rabbits, Flopsy, Mopsy, Cottontail and Peter, in Potter's 1901 *Tale of Peter Rabbit*.)[70] So the Georgians launched what became a long line of imaginative children's classics.

Styles of address were also changing. Traditionally, a son, once past infancy, would bare his head before his father and address him as 'Sir'. Yet some sought a more intimate and affectionate style. In 1781, the twenty-year-old Jacob Pattisson, a medical student in Edinburgh, wrote to his tradesman father: 'If you think the word "Sir" at present necessary from yourself to me, I cannot object to it – but it appears cold, & seems to place one at an uncomfortable distance'.[71] The parental reply has not survived and this son died young. Nonetheless, a decade later Jacob's younger brother William Pattisson wrote sometimes to 'My Dear Sir' but, increasingly, to 'My Dear Father'. The stylistic shift was slow and patchy, as such changes in behaviour usually are. The remote, authoritarian Victorian paterfamilias remained a cultural type, against which later generations of sons and daughters rebelled. Yet there was also a liberal style emergent alongside.

Coping with illegitimate children was an edgy problem, which affected many families high and low. The number of births to mothers outside wedlock was growing, in the context of rising migration from countryside to town and of weakened supervision by the churches.[72]

At law, such 'bastards' had no right to inherit titles or any share of parental goods, and were ostracised in traditional devout circles. Yet many Georgians were socially flexible.[73] The prime minister Sir Robert Walpole gained royal consent for a title for his illegitimate daughter, Maria Walpole. She then married the MP Charles Churchill, the illegitimate son of the senior Charles Churchill (also an MP), who was himself an illegitimate nephew of the 1st Duke of Marlborough. The young couple were accepted everywhere, and Maria Churchill gained a post in the royal household.

Similar moral nonchalance was displayed in the 1780s by a high-profile Georgian lawyer. No less a man than the Lord Chancellor, John Thurlow (whose brother was a bishop), had three 'natural' daughters who kept house for him. None were legitimised. Yet two married well, one to a Scottish peer, the other to an English baronet.[74] As Jane Austen observed sharply in 1816, high family status, especially when backed by great wealth, usually proved sufficient to bleach the 'stain' of illegitimacy.[75]

Problems, however, were acute in cases of poverty. Then social disdain and financial need put pressure on desperate mothers; and the early eighteenth century saw a crescendo of horror stories about abandoned babies.[76] In 1741 a dedicated Foundling Hospital was opened in London by a group of philanthropists, led by the merchant Thomas Coram. Initially, the institution accepted all deserted children. However, the policy was soon made more restrictive, since the numbers needing care was so great.[77] Often the parents left with their babies various small identifying tokens, including trinkets, fabrics, marked coins, messages and verses.[78] And in a few cases, one or both parents returned to reclaim their offspring. Yet most proved unable to do so. So the foundlings were farmed out to rural wet-nurses and, if surviving to the age of sixteen (many didn't), were sent into domestic service or apprenticeship.

Contrasts between the ideal of a nurturing education for every child and the reality remained stark. Nonetheless, there was an unsystematic safety-net of sorts, based on parochial and charitable relief. Cases of infanticide in Georgian Britain were thus comparatively rare.[79] And the activities of philanthropic reformers began to highlight the need for community intervention. Jonas Hanway, the son of a Portsmouth victualler, was another Georgian activist. In 1756 he founded the Marine Society to get unemployed or orphaned boys into the navy; he supported the London Foundling Hospital, of which he became governor in 1758, and vice president in 1772; he launched the first Magdalen Hospital in 1758, to provide training for 'fallen' women; and from 1773 onwards he campaigned to help young chimney-sweeps.[80] Their work was risky, poorly paid and physically stunting. (In 1775 testicular cancer was first identified as a specific occupational hazard associated with their working conditions.) Hanway agonised about Britain's travails, diagnosing 'the decay of our morals and national piety'. Yet he offset despair by calls for remedial action, urging that: 'Children are *our greatest wealth*'.[81]

Discrepancies between the shining ideal and the actualities of working-class childhood began to cause public anxiety, but only slowly. There was considerable deference to the rights of parents to make decisions about their offspring. Many youngsters were sent out to work from the age of ten, or even younger. In Britain's industrial-ising regions from the mid-eighteenth century onwards, their tasks included repetitive and often dangerous work in mines and facto-ries.[82] And their lack of schooling was only very partially remedied by access to Sunday schools, when children were often too weary and mind-numbed to learn.[83]

Eventually, Parliament agreed to overrule the unfettered powers of both the market and parents. In 1819 the Cotton Mills and Factories Act banned children under the age of nine from factory labour, even while allowing those from nine to sixteen to work up to twelve hours per day.[84] It was a modest step but it did not open the floodgates. Regulation was adopted only slowly. The Mines Act did not follow until 1842, and later still the Ten Hours (Factory) Act of

1847 provided protection for women and youngsters aged between thirteen and eighteen.[85]

Eradicating child poverty (which is inextricably linked with adult poverty) is proving to be a long-term task, not easily resolved even in democratic societies which officially desire that outcome. Having generated the high ideal of a nurturing childhood and the concept of state intervention, the Georgian legacy remained a challenging one to implement successfully.

Family Life between Private and Public Worlds

Home life for the Georgians fell between private and public worlds. This verdict conflicts with one notable interpretation, from the German social philosopher Jürgen Habermas. He posited a clear demarcation between the private world of the home and the public sphere of politics, sociability and community action.[86] For him, 'indoors' remained a female domain, while men predominated 'outdoors'.

However, Georgian life was not so simply stratified.[87] As noted above (p. 79), some male household heads, including bachelors living alone, played active roles 'indoors'; and, equally, numerous Georgian women participated in social, cultural and economic life 'outdoors' and (to a lesser extent) in politics. There were gender stereotypes, but also many de facto alternatives to the culturally expected norms.[88] In mid-Victorian times, some commentaries encouraged a positive cult of woman as the 'Angel in the House'. That attitude was not, however, a response to the perennial state of cloistered female domesticity. Instead, it marked a conservative cultural resistance to a long-emerging trend of liberal sharing between companionate partners.

Equally, the physical home in Georgian times was not seen or experienced purely as 'private' space. Some rooms (bedrooms, closets) were relatively more secluded, while others (parlours, halls, kitchens) were half public, half private. Friends and sundry visitors were welcomed. Sometimes excisemen entered in pursuit of unlicensed liquor. Thieves crept in uninvited. Servants went everywhere. And nosey neighbours peered through windows and spread domestic gossip.

Overall, consumer spending in the home was undertaken by both men and women, not only for personal pleasure but also to impress friends and visitors. Interior walls were being clad not with heavy tapestries but with light, bright patterned wallpapers.[89] Decorative plasterwork to create wall panels and ornamental ceilings was ordered from skilled craftsmen, many of them Italian.[90] Spoons and forks were deployed at table, alongside the ubiquitous knives. Clocks, pictures and ornaments were put on display, as were kettles and prized tea-services. Elegant new furniture was ordered, as was, from the later eighteenth century, the latest status-symbol – a piano.[91]

Clearly, people's capacities to participate in consumerism and to invite guests into their homes to witness ther choices were constrained by their incomes and inclinations. Yet the role of the home as both private refuge and semi-public social showcase was here to stay.

✎ Time-Shift: Then and Now ✎

Performances of classic plays demonstrate how interpretations are liable to change over the generations, ranging from (sometimes) substantial rewritings of the basic text to (at other times) a careful quest for period 'authenticity'.

For contested Georgian views of love and marriage, plus some insights into the ubiquitous presence of servants in the Georgian household, see Richard Brinsley Sheridan's effervescent comedy *The Rivals*. Three contrasting love affairs highlight the hazards of romance. The lead story features a dreamy young heroine hoping to marry for love; a subplot involves an older woman seeking a beau; and the third couple showcases a doubting young lover who makes his own troubles. All meet in the great spa city of Bath, where urban gossip and scandal provide the essential backdrop.

Notable details include: family tensions between the Absolutes, father and son, especially on the subject of marriage; changing attitudes to duelling; the active role of servants; a conventional satire of a country bumpkin (Bob Acres); and a very stereotyped satire of an Irish adventurer, Sir Lucius O'Trigger; as well as the comic creation of Mrs Malaprop, who mangles her pretentious vocabulary to humorous effect, and whose name is the origin of 'malapropism', or misspeaking (see also Chapter 7, below).

By the way, note that – particularly in an era when the text of the play was not widely known, and in which there was no technology enabling instant replays – the jokes get a lot of repetition to assist audience reception.

Ideally, attend a live performance; but otherwise view the impeccable 1970 production starring Donald Sinden, Sheila Hancock, Patrick Rycart, Amanda Redman, Ronald Pickup, Michael Maloney and others; remastered for BBC Two's *Theatre Night* series (dir. J. Spoczynski, 1985), available on YouTube.

❦ 6 ❦

Exploring Sexualities

In the Georgian era, strong human passions and emotions were struggling to emerge from the constraints of an older set of laws and conventions pertaining to sexualities and love – which are not the same thing, though often linked. The result was a prolonged sexualisation of British social life and culture, with a greater freedom of discussion, liberalisation of behaviour, and openness (within limits) to exploring alternative sexualities.[1] These changes, which were far from friction-free, were encouraged by the freeing of the press after the licensing laws were allowed to lapse in 1695. And the weakening of the traditional moral surveillance exercised by the Anglican Church courts decreased anxiety about penalties for sexual 'irregularities'.[2] One effect of this experimentation was to challenge the Georgians with pointed questions about consent and coercion.

There was not just one eighteenth-century moment of revolutionary change in sexual matters, contrary to some claims.[3] It is very rare for the intimacies of personal life to change all of a sudden, across an entire society. Even the much touted 'sexual revolution' in the West in the 1960s concealed a lot of continuing tradition.[4]

Moreover, Georgian generalisations about the extent of 'immorality' were often exaggerated. Private sexual behaviour was expected to remain private, so that accurate evidence is lacking.

However, within a generation after 1695 there were perceptible changes in public manifestations of the human sex drive; and there-after the sexualisation of British society and culture continued. Gossip, bawdy songs and rumour, those traditional standbys, were augmented by an abundant written and visual record. Ideas and information were canvassed, not only on practicalities like concep-tion and giving birth, but also on controversial topics such as contra-ception, abortion, erotica and pornography, libertinism, masturbation, sexually transmitted diseases, and prostitution – as well as cross-dressing, male same-sex relations and (mutedly) lesbianism.

Titillating tracts soon publicly celebrated *The London-Libertine: Or, the Lusty Gallant[s] New Ingenious Way of Living* (1700); and his female counterpart in *Clarinda: Or, the Fair Libertine* (1729). Moreover, the advantage was not always given to the men: readers could laugh knowingly at *A Nuptial Dialogue between a Pert Young Lady and an Old Fumbling Libertine* (1735).

Indeed, the Georgians' open preoccupation with sexual matters was sufficiently distinctive that it later prompted a degree of middle-class backlash from the mid-nineteenth century under pressure from evangelists and moralists.[5] But what is termed 'Victorian' prudery did not halt the sexualisation of either behaviour or public discus-sions. There were certainly oscillations in long-term trends and many attendant anxieties. Yet slow-moving changes were afoot.

Lovers

A loving courtship was a semi-public process, encouraged by the sale of visible tokens, such as rings, lockets and (from the 1780s) printed cards for Valentine's Day.[6] (The oldest surviving example dates from 1797 and can be seen in York Castle Museum.) But sexual activity usually took place in seclusion. Bedrooms were habitual locations. Nonetheless, since homes were crowded, people found other venues, such as hired rooms in taverns and in bathhouses, known as bagnios. Couples also resorted to fields, parks, riverbanks and urban alleyways, although in popular places they were often bothered by peeping toms. The amorous young James Boswell, who enjoyed alfresco encounters in London, tried many locations. In May 1763, he noted in his diary that he had sex with a street-walker ('a strong jolly young damsel') on Westminster Bridge: 'The whim of doing it there, with the Thames rolling below us, amused me much'.[7]

Collectively, those Georgians who were able, interested and in tolerable health were having more penetrative sex, in aggregate, than were their ancestors. That trend was produced by the shift from rural to urban living, which offered a greater range of work opportunities and choice of partners. Evidence for the age of first sexual activity is extremely hard to find. So historians use the age of first marriage (documented in parish registers) not as the same thing but as a proxy for active sexual maturity. In the sixteenth and seventeenth centuries, that average was twenty-two years for women, twenty-five for men; but, during the long eighteenth century, those figures were slowly coming down, especially in the towns.[8] Even more notably, there was a steep fall in the proportion of adults never marrying. In 1701 bachelors and spinsters together constituted about 25 per cent of the population. By 1801, their proportionate number had fallen to 7 per cent.[9]

Accompanying those changes was a related shift in attitudes to pre-marital sexual intimacy. The old rural custom of 'bundling' was disappearing. This practice allowed courting couples to spend the night together, with heavy petting but no more.[10] Yet, as this semi-supervised style of courtship was gradually side-lined, the number of couples having premarital sex before marriage rose. A considerable proportion (perhaps as many as one third) of eighteenth-century brides were pregnant at their weddings.[11] They had flouted conventional religious teachings about pre-marital sex while conforming to social expectations in marrying.

Chief 'winners' from these liberalised sexual relationships were men, especially if wealthy and well connected. The leading 'losers' were poor women with illegitimate children, along with many of those illegitimate children themselves. Nonetheless, it was not the case that all changes were intrinsically female-unfriendly. Determined Georgian women with rank and money had tolerable chances of exercising choice in love and sex.

Moreover, affluent males did not have everything their own way. The essayist William Hazlitt confessed as much in his *Liber Amoris* ('Book of Love') in 1823, which related his thwarted passion for the daughter of his tailor landlord.[12] None of the protagonists in this saga appear to great advantage. Yet it was clearly not unimaginable for a young dowerless woman to toy with – but then reject – the advances of an older, wealthier and utterly respectable gentleman.

Mutuality of choice did entail the risk of rejection. But some assertive women did not take kindly to being jilted. Numerous breach-of-promise cases began to appear in the law courts from 1787 onwards.[13] The jilted would-be brides stressed not only their sufferings from blighted affection but also the financial costs of wasted wedding preparations. (Shades of Dickens's Miss Havisham.) And, interestingly, the judges were often favourable to such pleas.

Social attitudes, however, remained censorious when older ladies, even of great respectability, showed an interest in sex. Widows who got remarried to younger men were particularly ridiculed as 'old hags'. Nevertheless, with funds and willpower, the deed could be done. The literary hostess Hester Thrale braved the wrath of family and friends in 1784. At the age of forty-three, and three years a widow, she chose as her second husband one Gabriele Piozzi, a young music teacher, who was Italian and Catholic to boot. They defied convention successfully. But they did retire from London to live in a specially built Palladian villa, Brynbella, on her family estate in north Wales.[14]

Elopement cases also signalled female determination to choose their own partners, although some would-be brides may have been pressurised by their suitors. In 1782, the banker Robert Child tested that theory by pursuing his eighteen-year-old daughter to halt her runaway marriage to John Fane, 10th Earl of Westmorland. Yet even when the irate father caught the couple and shot their lead carriage horse, they continued to Gretna Green and tied the knot. Elopements were particularly risky for women, if the motives of their lovers were suspect. A law-suit in 1794 tested whether a fourteen-year-old heiress, Clementina Clerke, had willingly left with Richard Perry, a Bristol apothecary, or whether she had been abducted by a fortune-hunter. In this case, Clerke stood by her husband, and the marriage was upheld. But if the eloping male was seeking to marry for money or, treacherously, not to marry at all, social disaster could easily follow.

Making choices was challenging, as couples tested the boundaries between love and lust, between courtship and fortune-hunting. These tensions added a frisson of excitement at the Georgians' informal 'marriage marts', in the form of fairs, festivals, balls, masquerades, assemblies, pleasure gardens and race-meetings.

Among the themes getting newly frank literary coverage was the role of female desire. Georgian Britain's dream female sex-object, the eponymous protagonist of John Cleland's *Fanny Hill* (1748), gets an extended education in sexual techniques. But while the book may have titillated male readers, they are advised throughout of the importance of Fanny's enjoyment too. Her games of dominance and subjugation are shown as being undertaken for erotic arousal, unlike brutal instances of real-life sexual violence and assault. However, the book's frankness created such a scandal that it was withdrawn and circulated thereafter only in pirate editions. (When the ban on *Fanny Hill* was lifted in 1963, its reappearance prompted the novelist Brigid Brophy's enthusiastic remark that 'the two most fascinating subjects in the universe are sex and the eighteenth century'.)[15]

One Georgian metaphor for sexual desire was being 'on fire'.[16] The unconventional Mary Wollstonecraft, advocate of the *Rights of Woman* (1792), faced the world boldly, despite having an unhappy liaison with a married man, plus an illegitimate daughter. She then married the philosopher William Godwin and, after a sexy night together, wrote joyously to tell him that: 'I have seldom seen so much live fire running about my features as this morning'.[17] Interestingly, that metaphor was given a techno-update by the apothecary Richard Perry, who had scandalously eloped with Clementina Clerke. Explaining their mutual attraction, he claimed that, when their eyes first met: 'a kind of electrical fire shook them to their souls'.[18] Desire thus gained a quasi-scientific rationale.

Very unusually, too, one playwright confronted openly the potential fragility of male virility. In Oliver Goldsmith's comedy *She Stoops to Conquer* (1773), the bashful young hero of good breeding can relax sexually only with women who are his social 'inferiors'. With the squire's daughter he is tongue-tied and can hardly look her in the eye. Accordingly, the heroine 'stoops' to act as a maidservant to win the hero's attention and then affection. The gradual sparking of love and social ease between the two principals is well conveyed by Goldsmith. And this play, which touches sensitively on a sensitive theme, has lasted in the repertoire, even if recent revivals tend to overshadow the blossoming romance amidst exaggerated romping from the 'rustics'.[19]

Freedom of choice and behaviour was manifestly not limitless. Individuals faced all sorts of religious, social and financial constraints. However, there was enough sense of laxity to generate acute social anxiety, as voiced by gloomy Georgian commentators. In that vein, a critic of the spread of prostitution and adultery agonised in 1792: 'If the present age be arrived to such a pitch of depravity in this part of morals, how frightful must be the prospect with respect to that age which is to succeed?'

Georgian smart society was tolerant about deviations from strict morality, at least up to a point. One glamorous beauty, famed for wearing a see-through dress, was Elizabeth Chudleigh, a 'lowly' lieutenant's daughter. In the 1760s, she lived openly with one peer of the realm, having already secretly married another. Yet her conviction for bigamy in 1776 was a step too far. She fled abroad to avoid losing her acquired fortune, joining Europe's overseas demi-monde.

Otherwise, sexual liaisons in high society were tacitly accepted. Royal mistresses were publicly known (though George III had none), as were those of many politicians, peers and generals. The illicit relationship between Horatio Nelson and Emma Hamilton has been noted above (p. 89).[20] It was widely condoned as long as he lived. Hamilton, who was the ill-educated daughter of a poor Cheshire blacksmith, prospered via her shrewd intelligence, sexual charisma and charm. After Nelson's death, however, things changed. State honours and a title were conferred upon his blood family but not upon her. She died in Calais in 1815, aged fifty-nine, poor and out of fashion. Only recently has a monument to her been erected there. Again, sexual adventuring and transgressive love went only so far.

Libertines

Particularly notable in the early Georgian era was the visibility of a number of male libertines, who could afford financially to gratify their sexual tastes and socially to defy conventions. (Female libertines, discussed below, pp. 313–14, played a different role.) Whereas in earlier times, such behaviour, when occurring, was usually confined within aristocratic or court circles, these Georgian libertines became more overt, more socially variegated, and more consciously out to shock.

Best known of all were the men who described themselves as members of the Order of the Friars of St Francis, also dubbed the Monks of Medmenham. In the 1750s they frequented the notorious Hell-Fire Club. It was not the first of that name (there was an earlier one run by the Duke of Wharton from 1719 to 1721). Nor is it the last: in 2013, Hell-Fire Clubs were advertised online in Dublin, Glasgow, greater London, Manchester, Melbourne and Sydney. Nonetheless, though they keep the spicy name, none have achieved the scandalous notoriety of the original Medmenham prototype. The Club's rakish organiser was Sir Francis Dashwood, a landowner and politician.[21] He and his fellow Monks met in the Medmenham caves near West Wycombe, in Buckinghamshire. There they feasted and indulged in unconventional sex, spiced with blasphemous ritual and pagan symbolism.[22] Their parody of religion added to the shock caused to respectable opinion. No legal or clerical action, however, was taken against the private club. Nor did its members face social ostracism.

Morally the most debauched of the Monks, according to contemporary gossip, was one Thomas Potter, the affluent second son of an archbishop. He may have been the true author of the pornographic *Essay on Woman*, for which the radical John Wilkes (discussed below, pp. 196–7) was convicted of obscenity in 1763. Indeed, the Hell-Fire Club's libertarian motto *'Fais ce que tu voudras'* ('Do what thou wilt') matched with Wilkes's later campaigns for free speech: Publish what you dare.[23] Yet these rakes mocked religion rather than crusaded against it.

Many similar men's clubs, whether organised to suit heterosexual or same-sex tastes, also flourished.[24] They were usually much more discreet than were the flamboyant Monks. One example was the Beggar's Benison. This club, based in the small Scottish coastal town of Anstruther in Fife, survived from the early 1730s until 1836.[25] Its membership included landowners, civic officials and a professor of civil history at St Andrews University. They talked of sex, with readings from *Fanny Hill*, and lectures on anatomy. And they enjoyed rituals of obscene songs, lewd toasts, and shared masturbation ceremonies.

Featuring among the Beggar's Club recreations was the live viewing of naked or near-naked young women. This pastime was an up-market version of the human peepshow, which was commonly available, for a small fee, in a side-tent at fair-grounds. These lucrative live exhibitions were part titillating and part educational. One example in 1810 became famously controversial. The black South African Sarah Baartman, billed as 'the Hottentot Venus', attracted both fascinated and prurient attention. But anti-slavery activists asked whether she was acting freely or under coercion from her manager. In the event, Baartman, whose case is further discussed below (p. 382), declined their help. Her career, however, indicated that the line between sexual freedom and exploitation is easily blurred.

Information about sexual options and opportunities was readily circulated. Erotic prints and books played upon allusion, knowingness and a sly suggestiveness.[26] By contrast, pornographic writing and songs favoured a bawdy openness and ribald frankness.[27] Both genres revelled in wit and innuendo. And much of this material, while implicitly directed at men in the first instance, was potentially available to women, though ordinary usage is hard to document.

Sexual techniques expounded in *Fanny Hill* included erotic flagellation. This practice was reportedly a special interest of Englishmen: '*le vice anglais*'.[28] Yet one early tract on 'the use of flogging as a provocative to the pleasures of love' (1718) was translated from a German medical text.[29] Fragmentary evidence certainly confirms that consensual sado-masochism was not unknown. A divorce case from Norwich in 1707–8 yielded evidence of group sex, voyeurism and bisexual spanking among a group of artisans.[30] And in early nineteenth-century London, a dominatrix named Mrs Theresa Berkley prospered by employing a retinue of female helpers to flagellate wealthy customers.[31]

Additionally, there was a (small) minority interest in the dangerous sexual art of auto-asphyxiation. One case concerned the Czech musician František Kočžwara, who in September 1791 paid a London prostitute named Susannah Hill to procure ropes and to help him hang himself, as an extreme measure of sexual stimulation. The plan went disastrously wrong. Koczwara died, and Hill found herself on trial for murder (she was acquitted). Interestingly, public attitudes to the incident thereupon diverged. The law court took steps to suppress all details of the case, which was omitted from the popular published record, sold as the *Old Bailey Sessions Papers*. By contrast, however, a number of London and provincial newspapers printed full details – sure that they would find an eager readership.[32]

Voyeurism was another theme given public airing. In one dramatic legal dispute, it was a husband who brokered the practice. When in 1782 Sir Richard Worsley sued one of his wife's lovers for adultery, the injured husband won only a shilling in damages, after his estranged wife testified that he had aided the defendant to spy upon her, unbeknown, while she was bathing.[33] A satirical print of the unconventional domestic incident was promptly circulated by James Gillray, who lampooned the husband as 'Sir Richard Worse-than-Sly'.

Such openness about sexual behaviour was accompanied, in this era, by the growing visibility of female prostitution as an urban service industry.[34] Prime locations were the larger towns, resorts, garrison towns and international ports. In particular, armies and navies, recruiting young men far from home, were noted for providing clients. Alarmist accounts produced exaggerated figures of sex-workers, both full- and part-time. Reformers debated the relative merits of either regulating or banning prostitution; and whether to help or to punish the women involved. In 1724, the hard-headed Bernard de Mandeville had already argued that the best response was by regulation. He favoured the provision of public brothels, in order to stop men from 'private whoring' and debauchery.[35] However, the British state lacked either the will or power to attempt such a drastic measure.

High-class Georgian courtesans with upper-crust lovers also made it difficult simply to ban all who made a living from their sexual allure. In the later seventeenth and eighteenth centuries, there were many literary examples of witty and independent female libertines.[36] And over time the number of real-life exemplars was multiplying. One sexual celebrity was Fanny Murray, whose lovers included the rakish 4th Earl of Sandwich. She was the dedicatee of the obscene *Essay on Woman* (*c.* 1755) and may have part inspired Cleland's *Fanny Hill*.[37]

Even more famous courtesans were the actor-poet Mary 'Perdita' Robinson, publicly known for her dalliance with the Prince of Wales (later George IV); and Harriette Wilson, whose aristocratic admirers included the 1st Duke of Wellington.[38] It was he who famously refused to be blackmailed by her threats. When telling her to '*publish and be damned*', he was confident that, as the victor of Waterloo, a past affair could not ruin him. Wilson did then publish in 1825, inventing the new genre of scandal memoirs. Meanwhile, Mary Robinson turned from sexual adventurism to public advocacy of feminism. In her *Letter to the Women of England* (1799), she denounced female subordination and declared unequivocally that women 'are not the mere appendages of domestic life, but the partners, the equal associates of man'.[39]

Opinion was becoming critical of unfettered male dominance or undue violence within all sexual relationships.[40] Partner-beating, as opposed to amorous flagellation, was deplored, as noted above (p. 79), although shifting attitudes did not make the practice disappear. And sexual abuse of underage children generally caused public revulsion. Legally, boys under fourteen could not consent to sexual activity or marriage; for girls the relevant ages were ten (sexual intercourse) and twelve (marriage). A number of cases did come to court, almost invariably brought by the mother of the abused child. Such litigation can be interpreted as an attempt to shame the perpetrators, since it was hard to get legally watertight evidence.

This changing context helps to explain why male libertinism, which did not disappear, was tending by the 1830s to become more discreet. The shift is sometimes seen as a simple case of 'middle-class' morality overtaking an older libidinous aristocratic one. Yet it did not necessarily halt the cultural expression of sexual diversity. Instead it marked an attempt at social re-balancing between unfettered libido and care for sexual partners. It could be called a quest for companionate sexuality, to go with the Georgians' growing stress upon companionate marriage.

Same-Sex Relationships

Most dramatic of all these changes was the emergence into social visibility of previously covert forms of sexual behaviour. This cultural change considerably preceded changes in the law, which came only slowly. A range of overt Georgian terminologies emerged for same-sex relationships between men, ranging from the biblical 'sodomites' to teasing talk of 'mollies' for notably 'effeminate' men; from the demotic wit of 'back-gammon players' (according to a 1785 *Dictionary of the Vulgar Tongue*) to classically erudite 'catamites' and 'Ganymedes'.[41]

Officially, the 'detestable and most shocking' act of sodomy remained both sinful and illegal.[42] Men caught in compromising circumstances with other men were at risk of being executed. And some were. The last two to suffer this fate, despite appeals for clemency from their families, were John Smith (aged forty), a labourer, and James Pratt (aged thirty), a groom. They were hanged in front of Newgate Prison in November 1835.[43] An older man, William Bonhill (aged sixty-eight), who allowed them to use his rented room, was convicted as an accessory and transported for fourteen years.

Yet these men were exceptionally unfortunate. In practice, a degree of toleration, sometimes grudging, was apparent, long before the death penalty for sodomy was abolished in England and Wales in 1861. Only a small minority of homosexual encounters ever came to trial; and court procedures demanded hard-to-obtain eye-witness evidence of both penetration and ejaculation. Nonetheless, it took more than a further long century before homosexuality was decriminalised in England and Wales (1967), Scotland (1980) and Northern

Ireland (1982). Thus there was no easy progression from traditional moral condemnation to muted cultural acceptance and then, later still, to legal reform.[44] Instead, the random nature of law enforcement, before decriminalisation, added to the sense of injustice and victimhood among those brought to court.

Unofficially, there were numerous private venues and public parks or gardens where men went to meet male sexual partners. In the Georgian metropolis, two open spaces known for their rendezvous were Moorfields (just north of the City) and St James's Park (adjoining Whitehall). In addition, there were specialist indoor venues – often in taverns or private rooms – for this clientele. These places were known genially as 'molly-houses'. However, they always remained at risk from hostile policing. In February 1726, Margaret Clap's molly-house in London's Holborn was suddenly raided.[45] As a result, three men – a wool-comber, an upholsterer and a milkman – were tried and hung for sodomy, while 'Mother' Clap was sent to the pillory for public shaming.

Relatively high social status was one safeguard. In the early eighteenth century, the bisexual John Hervey, 2nd Baron Hervey, second son of the Earl of Bristol, pursued passionate love affairs with both men and women.[46] And while he was lampooned, he was never charged with any offence. The worst that befell him was a witty denunciation from Alexander Pope, who nicknamed Hervey 'Sporus', after a male partner of the Emperor Nero: 'His Wit all see-saw between *that* and *this*,/ Now high, now low, now Master up, now Miss,/ And he himself one vile Antithesis'.[47]

Conventional moralists continued to denounce all cases of sodomy as on a par with blasphemy and atheism.[48] Men sexually interested in other men were not only 'unnatural', but they were rendering women 'out of date' for anything other than breeding.[49] By contrast, a daring study by Thomas Cannon, entitled *Ancient and Modern Pederasty* (1749), did defend the 'naturalness' of same-sex love. He affirmed stoutly that 'Unnatural Desire is a Contradiction in Terms'.[50] But this work was quickly suppressed: no copies survive. Unsurprisingly in those circumstances, Jeremy Bentham a generation later decided not to publish his 1785 tract defending homosexuality.[51] Britain was not ready to emulate revolutionary France, where in 1791 sodomy between consenting adults was declared no longer a crime. Instead, caution continued to prevail. If caught, respectable men stressed the non-sexual nature of their friendships, and, if feeling seriously endangered, moved discreetly abroad.

An intricate legal case in 1772 revealed the complexities. Captain Robert Jones, a lieutenant in the army's artillery corps and an expert on both fireworks and figure-skating, was convicted for sodomising a child, but then pardoned. This outcome outraged popular opinion in London. Crowds gathered in Islington to hang the effigy of a sodomite, and dispersed only after the Riot Act was read. Whether these Londoners were more offended by Jones's sexuality or by his abuse of a child remains a moot point. Their response, however, showed that social disapproval could still remain a penalty, notwithstanding a legal pardon.[52]

Dread of scandal in such circumstances remained potent. In 1822, the suicide of Foreign Secretary Castlereagh was triggered, among many factors, by his fears of being blackmailed over (probably false) accusations of homosexuality.[53] But such anxieties were not unjustified: the Anglican Bishop of Clogher in Ireland had earlier that year been caught *in flagrante* with a Grenadier guardsman and was dismissed from his see, becoming a figure of public fun.[54] Same-sex amatory culture thus remained both semi-known and semi-secret.

Lesbianism was then even more discreet as a sexual practice and cultural preference.[55] Female lovers of other women wanted to avoid scandal – and to elude male voyeurism, which prompted numerous pornographic accounts of lesbian sex.[56] Such activities were not in themselves illegal, although a woman passing as a man, who 'married' another woman, could be tried for fraud. Georgian dictionaries did not include 'lesbianism' as an abstract noun. However, the terms 'lesbian' (1732) and 'sapphick' (1773), derived from the classical poet Sappho of Lesbos, were known and used.[57] And references were also made to 'female husbands'; in slang, to 'flats'; and, in the later eighteenth century, to 'tommies'. Other terms were 'tribades' and 'rubsters'. Thus, while it was once, perhaps semi-jokingly, claimed that 'lesbianism' did not exist before 1870, when the abstract noun was coined, such linguistic literalism is misleading.

Women who sidestepped normative expectations by cross-dressing as men did so for sundry motives.[58] When, however, they deceived others for financial gain, they were liable to prosecution. Mary Hamilton, 'the female husband', was convicted of fraud in 1746, having allegedly 'married' fourteen different women. She was sentenced to public whipping in four market towns of south-west England. The novelist and magistrate Henry Fielding thereupon wrote a fictionalised tract about Hamilton's adventures, entitled *The Female Husband* (1746).[59] It was part warning; part erotic curiosity. Another case in 1777 brought Anne Marrow to the pillory at London's Charing Cross. Like Hamilton, she had been convicted of impersonating a man and defrauding her 'wives' of their assets. In the pillory, Marrow faced a hostile crowd, who pelted her with sufficient violence to blind her.[60] By contrast, an unknown number of women may have switched their gender identities but without public discovery. In nineteenth-century Dublin, Patrick M'Cormack (born *c.* 1820) lived as a man but was discovered, after death, to have a female physique.[61] He had successfully lived his choice, his secrecy winning for him security from prying eyes and social ostracism.

During the long eighteenth century, meanwhile, there were several Georgian women who had intense semi-public same-sex relationships, which may or may not have been sexually consummated. Queen Anne herself had a turbulent friendship with Sarah Churchill, Duchess of Marlborough (privately 'Mrs Freeman' to Queen Anne's 'Mrs Morley'); and then a more soothing one with Abigail Masham.[62] In 1778 one Anne Damer, from an aristocratic family background, dressed in male attire and was satirised for her rampant sapphism, having 'Kissed every female's lovely mouth'.[63] However, Damer, a sculptor who moved in artistic circles, outfaced the innuendoes. Not only that, but she inherited from her relative Horace Walpole a life interest in his valuable estate at Strawberry Hill. Similarly, in the 1820s Anne Lister, a Yorkshire landowner, traveller and lover of women, braved disapproval from neighbours, who dubbed her 'Gentleman Jack'. Undaunted, Lister persisted in enjoying with her women lovers 'something more tender still than friendship'.[64]

Most significantly for lesbian history, two upper-class Irish women managed to conduct their life-long romantic companionship in the public eye. Known as 'the Ladies of Llangollen', Eleanor Butler and Sarah Ponsonby braved initial family displeasure to co-reside for fifty years, from 1780 until Butler's death in 1829. Throughout they shared a double bed, whilst keeping their sexual activities (if any) to themselves. In fact, numerous Georgian women co-resided with other women in female-headed households. Yet Butler and Ponsonby did not hesitate to declare their loving partnership; and their many visitors from smart society in effect condoned their relationship. Today the Llangollen Ladies have become admired exemplars for same-sex civil partnerships and marriages between women: their Gothicised house at Plas Newydd in Denbighshire (now a museum) testifies to their mutual devotion.[65]

Fluid gender identities were becoming subjects for debate, although individual cases were usually regarded as curiosities. In 1750 a Parisian 'boy-girl' hermaphrodite named Michel-Anne Drouart was displayed in London to interested medical men, prompting discussion of his/her anatomy.[66] Cross-dressing men and women were reported from time to time. In the early 1730s, one John Cooper found male lovers at Vauxhall Gardens while dressed as 'Princess Seraphina'. And in the 1770s, most famously, the androgynous chevalier d'Éon, a French diplomat-cum-spy, lived at different times as a man and as a woman, in a career which moved between

France, Russia and England.[67] People debated his/her 'true' gender identity. But d'Éon maintained his/her right to privacy. So it's fitting that the Beaumont Society (founded 1966) adopted the chevalier's family name to define its role as a transgender, transvestite and transsexual support group.[68]

Sexual Experts

Medical advice and sexual counselling became Georgian growth industries. The sexologist James Graham was one such pioneer. Having already made his name with a Temple of Health devoted to therapeutic medicine, he launched in 1781 a new Temple of Hymen, complete with a special 'celestial bed'. This canopied couch was designed to assist conception and to cure impotence, using music, fragrances, flowers, mirrors and electrical displays to achieve arousal.[69] For those who could afford the fees, it must have been fun. Graham eventually went bankrupt in the economic downturn of the mid-1780s. He was, however, a portent of a new industry of professional counsellors and 'sexperts', updating and replacing traditional advice from friends, 'wise women' and proverbial maxims.

Both real and imaginary sexual maladies attracted much media attention. Urgent tracts warned of the ills of masturbation, known as 'onanism' in biblical reference to the sin of Onan, who 'spilled his seed on the ground' rather than engaging in reproductive sex.[70] This 'solitary vice' was said to harm both mental and physical health. The anonymously authored *Onania* (1756), which warned against 'self-pollution', became a best-seller. Such didactic works – even if often ignored in practice, like the laws against swearing – marked a growing rationalist stress upon self-control, plus anxiety at unchecked sexual self-indulgence.

Above all, doctors in Britain, like those across continental Europe, struggled to treat sexually transmitted diseases, which were major scourges. Sufferers from syphilis were subjected to toxic mercury 'cures', before, in the early nineteenth century, William Wallace produced a milder iodine therapy.[71] But all these diseases remained rampant. For those who could afford it, one protective measure was the use of contraceptives. Georgian condoms were made of sheep's gut, and secured in place by a ribbon. Shops in mid-eighteenth-century London sold them as 'implements of safety'. However, these devices were clumsy in operation.[72] James Boswell noted that problem in March 1783 after engaging with a prostitute 'in armour'. And on that occasion, he recorded some rare, if limited, sympathy for his partner: 'Poor being, she has a sad time of it'.[73]

Eighteenth-century women, meanwhile, were targeted by advertisements for pills and powders to resolve 'female complaints'.[74] Some medicines offered to promote the conception of children, others to halt it.[75] In a number of cases, desperate women took direct action to procure abortions or even (comparatively rarely) to kill unwanted children.[76] In fact, the legal penalties for abortion were tightened in 1803, albeit without halting the practice. In response, birth control enthusiasts, influenced by Malthusian ideas, began to campaign for safer and better alternatives. As noted above (p. 54), they circulated free pamphlets about contraception (advising the use of vaginal douches) to working-class women and maid-servants.

Future debates beckoned on how best to allow polymorphous human sexuality to flourish, whilst simultaneously preventing exploitation and harm. The Georgians opened for all comers a veritable Pandora's box. Different individuals at different times provided examples of sexual liberation and experimentation, while others strove to establish unconventional but loving partnerships and respectful non-exploitation. These pioneers did not seek or achieve an entire 'sexual revolution'. Nor did they agree in their aims and aspirations. Yet, collectively, they ushered in an openly sexualised culture which flourishes still despite tensions and ambiguities, not to mention occasional backlashes, and which still debates the socially just boundaries between liberation and exploitation.

﹏ Time-Shift: Then and Now ﹏

Three films which demonstrate how recent film-makers have drawn inspiration from themes of love, lust and sexuality in Georgian Britain use the format of costume drama as a means of startling viewers into fresh thought about issues which are at once historical and timeless.

The directors of these films are confident that Georgian themes of love, quest and sexual experimentation have a timeless appeal. Close attention is paid to period dress and ambience, although some anachronisms are allowed – such as the pearly whiteness of the actors' teeth – in the interests of visual acceptability to today's audiences.

1. *The Favourite* (dir. Y. Lanthimos; starring Olivia Colman, Rachel Weisz and Emma Stone; 2018)
Based upon a triangular contest over love and politics between three women, including the queen, at the court of Queen Anne (ruled 1702–14). The rival emotions are based upon documentedly intense friendships between these women, although the sexual details are invented.

The screenplay delivers an over-the-top sexual romp, which is very good on the complex mingling of amatory and political rivalries at court, plus the scheming life of the backstairs, without striving for undue historical accuracy. Its shock value and high-camp acting have divided viewers, with some being impressed, others shocked, and yet others reduced to sceptical laughter.

2. *The Duchess* (dir. S. Dibb; starring Keira Knightley and Ralph Fiennes; 2008)
Based on the life of Georgiana, Duchess of Devonshire (1774–1806), the screenplay is good on the famous matrimonial

triangle between duke, duchess and his lover, her best friend, with interesting reflections upon the treatment of illegitimate children. However, it does feature one glaring anachronism, when the duchess makes a political stump speech before a crowd of male voters (long before women were accepted either as voters or as front-line political activists).

3. *Pride and Prejudice* (dir. S. Langton; starring Colin Firth, Jennifer Ehle, Alison Steadman and Benjamin Whitrow; 1995)
There are many good films of this classic 1813 novel by Jane Austen, but this TV adaptation has become iconic, chiefly for the sparks between the two romantic leads, and the scene (not in the novel) when Colin Firth, as Fitzwilliam Darcy, dives into a pool and emerges with a clinging, dripping shirt − looking sexy, but also symbolic of his psychological rebirth.

All the characters face important, timeless questions: how do people establish and maintain their social position? How can they decide who is trustworthy and who is not? How much should they value social rank and money? What qualities or assets make a person desirable? Who is truly worthy of being loved? What are the best auguries for a good marriage? And how can families succeed (or fail) to promote favourable outcomes for all who may be open to offers in the marriage 'market'?

7

Gaining Literacy and Numeracy

The Georgian era saw the numbers of both men and women who were literate and numerate decisively overtake – for the first time in Britain's history – the numbers of the illiterate and innumerate. This change happened without state prompting. It was slow in unfolding. But it was seismic in its impact, encouraging optimists in their bright hopes for the future. Moreover, the shift from mass illiteracy to collective literacy and numeracy has so far proved to be one of those historical macro-changes which has (to date anyway) proved irreversible.[1]

Printed books, which had been invented long before, began to wield a new cultural hegemony in Britain with the ending of rigorous press censorship in 1695.[2] The older oral culture was not forgotten, but embraced by the new medium. There was much crossover.[3] Books and papers were read aloud, not just in families but also in semi-public places like taverns, work-rooms and coffee houses. In addition, ideas, jokes and news items were circulated in songs, to tunes both old and new – creating the daily soundtrack provided by radio broadcasting in later eras. There was also a rich world of travelling musicians – singers, harpists, fiddlers – who performed locally and regionally.[4] Thus the illiterate and semi-literate did not live in mental isolation from the rest of society.

All the same, the power of writing and print culture was becoming steadily more predominant. It was true that newspapers and cheap books were often ephemeral. Pages were torn out to line pie-dishes, to wrap goods, or to serve as lavatory paper in the privy. (That familiar fate was wryly noted by a pamphleteer in 1747.)

Nevertheless, many written words appearing in books and pamphlets have lasted. The eighteenth century was a brilliant period in British poetry, as older oral traditions of verse were transformed into print.[5] The same was true of British prose, as older oral traditions of storytelling were transmuted into the birth of the novel.[6] Many Georgian masterpieces of fiction remain in print, and many are also adapted for later theatre, film and TV, in tribute to this foundational era.[7] All publications, furthermore, had a high multiplier potential as copies were circulated, lent, read aloud and sometimes reprinted; the most successful have an enduring impact.

Print not only stored the accumulating stock of global knowledge, it also encouraged the eighteenth century's notable codification of rules, whether applied to grammar, to mathematics, to sports or to popular games. Thus Edmond Hoyle's *Treatise on the Game of Whist* (1742) was much reprinted, with later editions also elucidating the rules of backgammon, quadrille, piquet and chess.[8] Equally, print aided the conservation of traditional songs and music. After the great Belfast Harp Festival of 1792 – attended by ten Irish harpists and one from Wales – a keen apprentice, Edward Bunting, collated and published his seminal *General Collection of the Ancient Music of Ireland* (1796).[9] So, while the Georgians gained much cultural stimulus from fresh discoveries and contacts overseas, they were simultaneously galvanised by the mixing of new creativity and traditional know-how via spreading literacy and numeracy.

Writing

Alexander Pope, that waspish critic of his fellow sages, cheerfully warned that 'A *little Learning* is a dang'rous Thing!' His solution: people should either 'Drink deep' from the fountains of knowledge – or not at all.[10] In this period, optimistic contemporaries favoured deep learning – and they saw its diffusion as integral to the spirit of the age. Merchants and traders wanted literate and numerate assistants, as did scientists and engineers. Parents, including those who were illiterate themselves, saw the advantages of such skills for their children. And clergymen, especially Protestant Dissenters and Anglican evangelicals, urged the spiritual as well as the social value of reading, so that all could study the Bible for themselves.

In that context, Georgian Britain became a world leader in rising literacy rates, along with the Protestant Dutch and the Nonconformist colonies (later states) in North America.[11] The process was demand-led, not organised by the state. (Free compulsory schooling for all British children was not enacted until 1870.) Instead, public, private and charitable schools multiplied – as did the number of private tutors, self-help groups, printed educational guides and, from the 1740s onwards, school-books designed especially for the young.[12] One path-breaking conversational primer was Laetitia Barbauld's *Lessons for Children* (1778). She stressed the huge mental growth potential of the young, hoping that her book would thus provide 'the first stone of a noble building'.[13] And she conveyed the moral and commercial value of education with an assured calm.

Illiterate people survived within this burgeoning print culture, by gleaning information by word-of-mouth and by listening to books and newspapers being read aloud. Moreover, if they needed to send a letter or petition, they could get help in letter-writing from professional scribes, such as the 'pettifogging attornies [*sic*]', who characteristically clustered around the law courts and debtors prisons.[14]

Conservative opposition to the spread of learning did exist, but was cumulatively pushed onto the defensive. Too much education, it was feared, would spoil poor children (and Britain's colonial subjects) for their adult lives of drudgery. Concerns were also expressed that tender female brains would be taxed by rigorous schooling, and that young women in particular would be distracted from their maternal duties by reading novels. Such views were lampooned in Sheridan's comedy *The Rivals*. The heroine's aunt denounces female brain-power, with the dictum that: 'Thought does not become a young woman'.[15] (Cue: audience laughter.) Sheridan furthermore made the aunt, Mrs Malaprop, into a famous mangler of words, thus launching a new English term 'malapropism' (from the French *mal à propos*). So the lady needed more, not less education.

Sheridan's jovial fencing indicated that the debates were still live. In the 1790s, the government worried that political lectures for lower-class audiences were potentially seditious; and tried to clamp down on them. And in the countryside, some landowners opposed educating labourers above their 'station'. Thus in Somerset in the same decade, the schools founded by the religious reformer Hannah More were greeted with great hostility.[16] Yet not all landowners took that view.[17] And some educationalists with conservative social views pressed the positive case for literacy. Thus the High Church Anglican Sarah Trimmer – a controversial figure for later feminists – declared access to education to be a God-given right. She ran her own schools in Brentford to showcase the best child-centred teaching, in lieu of rote learning. She also wrote popular spelling books and plentiful classroom readers for children.[18] Trimmer's liberal-conservative advocacy helped to calm traditionalist fears, even though opposition to educational expansion, particularly to higher education for women, took a long time to die.

Within the trend towards rising literacy rates, there were variations over time, between regions, between different religious groups, and between families. In general, urban literacy rates rose more rapidly than did rural ones. Yet a rapid influx of illiterate migrants from the countryside could produce a short-term fall in skills in specific localities. Such a fluctuation, which no doubt happened in many places, was documented in early nineteenth-century Halifax in West Yorkshire. Notably, however, the dip was reversed within a generation.[19]

Identifying literacy by the ability to sign one's name (not a perfect test, but one for which historical data survives) yields historically impressive figures. By 1801, all upper- and middle-class men in England and Wales were literate, as were a good proportion of lower-class men. For instance, across the diocese of Gloucester and arch-deaconry of Oxford almost 50 per cent of male labourers and servants could sign their names.[20] Literacy levels among women were lower but also increasing from c. 1750 onwards.[21] All were no doubt encouraged by expanding job opportunities for those who could read and write. However, the extent of literacy by 1801 was much greater than that required for the basic functioning of the economy. Gaining skills was thus a socio-cultural as well as utilitarian asset.

By 1840, when comparative data for all three traditional kingdoms is first available, two-thirds (66 per cent) of adult males in England and Wales were literate, as were half of all women: that is, including large numbers with working-class backgrounds. In Scotland, levels were higher still. In 1840, over 80 per cent of adult men could sign their names, although some could do little more than that, and urban–rural variations remained marked.[22] Oral traditions of Gaelic in the Highlands, meanwhile, provided an older form of cultural continuity. Even there, however, print culture was starting to encroach. The first Gaelic New Testament appeared in 1767, with a complete Gaelic Bible following in 1801.[23]

Meanwhile, change was slowest to arrive in the Catholic areas of rural Ireland, where the acquisition of literacy was a nineteenth-century process.[24] Everywhere, however, the communal acquisition of reading and writing skills had a collective ratchet effect. Hence working-class letters, diaries and autobiographies, which began as a trickle, were soon contributing to these growing genres of personal writings.[25]

Learning to write was viewed as a key step towards gaining a set of communication skills. In Georgian Britain, numerous people became literate as young adults, learning from multiple sources, including from other adults and self-help groups as well as from educational literature. The already mentioned philanthropist Thomas Coram, of Foundling Hospital fame (see above, p. 90), had no formal schooling and was sent to sea at the age of eleven. In the course of his seafaring and business life, however, he trained himself to write, often using phonetic spellings.[26] Many others similarly learned 'on the job'. Winning through as an unschooled mature autodidact could confer great confidence on those who managed the feat. One who did just that was the Birmingham businessman William Hutton, who celebrated by writing a stream of poetry, travelogues, histories, antiquarian studies and guides to local government, as well as an autobiography.[27]

As literacy rates rose, however, it was increasingly expected that the alphabet should be introduced to children at a young age. Moreover, more formal tuition was becoming more widely available. Newspapers were full of advertisements for private tutors, on a wide range of subjects. Countless educational establishments were founded, many run by clergy. Across Presbyterian Scotland, there were ubiquitous parish schools, giving that country its noted reputation for inculcating basic skills widely.

Characteristically, across England and Wales and much of Ireland, the situation remained distinctly ad hoc. Basic teaching was often provided for poor children at local 'dame schools', which were female-headed private organisations. Some offered little more than community child-minding. However, one in Lichfield famously taught the alphabet to the boy who later became the great lexicographer Dr Johnson. There were also substantial philanthropic efforts to found charity schools.[28] These had no power to enforce attendance, relying instead upon parental interest in getting an education for their children. Of course, not all adults were keen and not all children were willing. Yet there was certainly enough support in the early nineteenth century to provide custom for the growing number of Ragged Schools and Sunday Schools for children of poor families.[29]

Generally, the era was one of educational innovation, though also one of wildly varying standards between rival institutions. Most high-powered were the new Dissenting Academies with ultra up-to-date curricula, including science and modern languages, for young men.[30] Meanwhile the old-established urban grammar schools were slowly changing their educational remit. Some still continued to offer free tuition for poor children, while many were switching to become wholly or partially fee-paying. From their ranks, a number were morphing into what became Britain's classic public schools, so named as they were 'public' to all who could pay. Leading establishments became famous for providing recruits for the domestic and imperial civil service. But it's a later myth that Victorian public schoolboys were all sons of aristocrats. Many, in fact, came from middle-class families, especially in the professional sector.[31] The Georgians thus left a strong legacy of educational institutions, but nothing like a universal system, hence leaving plenty to fall through the net.

Nonetheless, one impressive indicator of the era's widespread diffusion of literacy was the great range of Georgians from different social backgrounds who penned private letters. Such missives became a prime resource, in the days before telegrams, telephones, emails, tweets or Facebook entries, for maintaining personal contact between people at a distance.[32] Travellers overseas particularly valued personal letters as a way of keeping contact with friends and family 'back home'.[33] The whole process was underpinned – and further encouraged – by the early development of a national postal service from the 1660s onwards. In addition, plentiful advice manuals, like *The Complete Letter-Writer: Or, New and Polite Secretary* (1755), offered practical guidance. Needless to say, in practice, many of their more conservative nuggets of wisdom were ignored – such as advice to women not to write to men outside their immediate family circle.[34] Yet these advice manuals, repetitive as they often were, provided reassurance about the quotidian normalcy of letter-writing.

Practical support also came from the many Georgian printed guides to grammar and spelling. Leading the field was Dr Johnson's *Dictionary of the English Tongue* (1755). This magisterial work did not in fact invent the genre, as is often (wrongly) stated. But it established Johnson's literary fame, and became the British standard dictionary for the next 150 years. Such authoritative reference works further helped to raise the status of the language. At home, law Latin was dropped in 1733 as the required terminology for legal business. And English was notably squeezing the older Gaelic tongues in Scotland, Ireland and Wales.[35] Abroad, French long remained the chosen language for diplomacy. Yet English was becoming the language most apt for 'Business and Dispatch', as one writer enthused in 1770.[36] Its hybrid ancestry, with Teutonic roots and French-Latinate infusions, gave it great linguistic flexibility. And in this period, with the expansion of Georgian trade and travel, it continued to acquire new terms, accents and idioms, slowly gestating the varieties of 'Global English', which in the twenty-first century constitutes the world's lingua franca.[37]

Reading

Reading was the close counterpart of writing skills. The two went integrally together. Very few readers could not undertake some basic writing – although from time to time traditionalists expressed the hope that such skills could be separated. And, just as the status of writing was rising, so was that of reading. A Georgian cultural guru like Richard Steele was sure of its key role. 'Reading is to the mind what exercise is to the body,' he urged in the *Tatler* in 1709.[38]

Often, the exercise was undertaken alone. But in this period it was common for both printed books and letters to be read aloud.[39] In that way, news and views were widely shared. For quick-witted listeners, it could be exasperating to hear a slow, drawling delivery of a written text, with frequent pauses and fumbling over tricky words. (Alexander Pope was characteristically sardonic on that point.) But reading aloud should be regarded as a proxy for radio broadcasts of later eras: sometimes to be ignored or half-attended to, but readily available.

Solitary reading was equally recognised as a great personal pleasure, available to both men and women. Many chose private moments, and, if they could, favoured locations.[40] So Dr Johnson, a great bibliophile, expressed a preference for easily portable 'books that you may carry to the fire, and hold readily in your hand'.[41] However, a law-case in November 1688 showed that private reading might trigger matrimonial friction. Anne Dormer, the wife of Robert Dormer, an Oxfordshire landowner, habitually retreated into her closet to read and write in seclusion. But her husband objected. On one occasion she reported that Robert broke down the closet door 'and made it flie across the roome, when he fancied I was there – but I was not'.[42] Shades of Virginia Woolf's later dictum about a woman's need for 'a room of one's own' (1929). This particular example came from an already troubled marriage. Nonetheless, it demonstrates that private reading could be viewed as exclusive, as well as 'improving'.

Sharing was one way of resolving disputes. Reading could be incorporated into daily routines. Once the printed newspaper was invented – with the *Norwich Post* (1701) leading the way – Georgian plays soon began to show stage families at the breakfast table, scanning through the papers and handing them around. Clearly, such a scene had verisimilitude.[43] Another standard venue for scanning the press was the coffee house, where reading the available newspapers was interspersed with conversation. Another special venue for reading was the library. It was both a repository and a place for study. Throughout the long eighteenth century, a significant number of private libraries were built in grand town and country mansions. A room full of books was taken as a signal mark of culture, even if some displays were amassed chiefly for decorative purposes.[44] Many of these private collections were later disbanded, though some were acquired by institutional libraries.[45]

There were also notable university initiatives. In Scotland, many new libraries were added to those already existing. One was the Advocates Library in Edinburgh, which began as a resource for lawyers (built 1689; rebuilt 1830) and evolved to become a national resource. Meanwhile, the University of Cambridge gained the harmonious Wren Library at Trinity College (built 1695), and Oxford, the stately Codrington Library (All Souls, built 1716–51), with nearby the free-standing Radcliffe Camera (built 1737–49), constructed to house a special scientific collection. More imposing still, the Old Library at Trinity College, Dublin (built 1712–32) housed the magnificent Long Room, which, as expanded in 1860, now houses 200,000 volumes. Collectively, these book-temples were among the most spectacular creations by Georgian architects.[46]

Towns were another magnet for eighteenth-century readers. A few urban centres, like Norwich, maintained their own city libraries, while many others saw the advent of commercially funded circulating libraries (Norwich had both).[47] Later these organisations were augmented by subscription libraries, where readers clubbed together to buy books 'for our mutual improvement', as one Scottish group specified in 1742.[48] It could be costly to join, although fees varied. The net effect was to encourage an expectation that the presence of a library, as well as special Assembly Rooms and a theatre, was a quintessential mark of civic status. Shared access to books facilitated both individual education and social bonding. It was therefore no surprise that the English traders and settlers in Bengal were also quick to establish libraries there.[49]

Among so many readers, furthermore, there were also a few serious book collectors. It was a passion which could lead to madness.

Or so the Rev. Thomas Frognall Dibdin declared in *Bibliomania* (1809).[50] Indeed, he admitted that he suffered from this affliction himself. One outstanding bibliophile was King George III (though his madness had other roots). His collection ran eventually to over 65,000 volumes. It was later donated to the nation by George IV, forming the basis of the British Library. In 1998 its impressive new building was built around a special glassed tower, designed specifically to display the original Georgian collection.

Catering for the growing book trade was an additional world of printers, publishers, journal editors, translators, type-setters, paper manufacturers, street-vendors and booksellers.[51] For the most part, they operated behind the scenes. Publishers, however, were visible figures, linking between authors and readers.[52] One such was the senior Jacob Tonson, founder in the early eighteenth century of a celebrated literary group, known as the Kit-Cat Club.[53] A century later, John Murray II was another hegemonic figure. A celebrated spotter of literary talent, he turned his family business (founded 1786) into a flagship publication house, which survives to this day (post 2002, as part of a conglomerate).[54]

Moreover, at the other end of the market, but equally successfully, Thomas Tegg published popular classics in cheap editions, with satirical illustrations by the likes of Thomas Rowlandson.[55] His early nineteenth-century business was much less prestigious. Yet Tegg and others like him helped to diffuse a shared literary and artistic culture between elite and working-class readers.

Booksellers similarly greased the wheels of literary commerce. One influential figure was James Lackington. From his vast London emporium, named 'The Temple of the Muses', he sold new books at economical prices for ready money. He also bought up remaindered works to sell off cheaply. Putting his business onto something akin to a mass scale fuelled his personal rise from poverty to wealth, including a landed estate in Gloucestershire.[56] And his success, like that of Tegg, showed the value of cultivating the cheaper end of the market.

By contrast, another bookseller-publisher named James Hutton managed by cornering a special market. He supported the small Protestant Moravian sect, originating in Germany, which favoured devotional simplicity. And he focused upon helping religious reform groups with similar values. Thus Hutton specialised in publishing hymnals, catechisms and devotional works by the Methodist preachers Wesley and Whitefield, sending them regular supplies.[57]

Reviewing books and news items was a strikingly new Georgian literary art form, which provided extra work for struggling authors. Periodicals, full of brief essays and reviews, offered a midway option between newspaper snippets and lengthy tomes. The *Tatler* and the *Spectator* led the way in 1709 and 1711: both with great titles (both still current, though under much changed management). Their editors, Richard Steele and Joseph Addison, advised readers, with urbane good humour, on news, gossip, manners and contemporary issues. The monthly *Gentleman's Magazine* followed in 1731, from the bookseller Edward Cave. It ran until 1907, blending news digests with topical information and lively letters to the editor. His 'gentlemanly' audience was aimed at a broad readership of wealthy and middling families.[58]

Literary reviews also became the special focus of the *Monthly Review* (founded 1749) and its rival *Critical Review* (founded 1756), edited by Tobias Smollett. But most powerful of all the literary 'Bloodhounds', as Byron indignantly termed them, were those writing for the *Edinburgh Review* (founded in 1802 – the third journal of that name).[59] While authors often writhed, readers generally found the reviews useful and the controversies stimulating.

One further delight was to attempt the unmasking of authors who published anonymously or under a pseudonym.[60] This stratagem was widely used in the long eighteenth century, favoured particularly by cautious women publishing their first books. Hence Jane Austen appeared as 'A Lady', just as, a century earlier, one Catherine Trotter had used the title of 'A Young Lady'. Readers' avid interest in the identity of authors was a form of detective skill, leading (if the author was unmasked) to fictive friendship. Well-loved novelists, as well as their most successfully realised characters, often seemed 'known' to their fans. Certainly that has happened to Jane Austen, as her literary star continues to ascend.[61] After her death in 1817 at the age of forty-one, her range was considered (by some) as too restricted, her irony missed, and her prose sentimentalised in translations. Yet more than 200 years later, she has both critical and popular fame. Austen Societies flourish across Europe, America and Australasia. And her literary ghost both haunts and inspires the ever-expanding genre of Regency novels and rom-coms.

Numeracy

Numeracy, defined as the capacity for quantitative thought and expression, was the quieter and much less glamorous counterpart to Georgian literacy. (It has been much less studied by historians too.) Generally, there was little serious opposition to teaching children the rudiments, since basic arithmetical skills were accepted as practically useful.[62] People were also expected to have a grasp of the changing times of day. The passing hours were marked by chiming church bells and by many ingenious sundials and official public clocks – as well as by the private fob-watches which proved so tempting to Georgian pickpockets.

To be sure, the general awareness of the passing years was often imprecise; and many unlettered people were hazy about their exact ages and birth dates. But there were cheap almanacs and calendars which could be consulted or interpreted by others, when required. As a result, there was a common numerical framework and sense of communal timetabling. Moreover, historians have discovered that the myth of popular riots against calendar reform in 1752 was exactly that – a myth.[63] The allegedly ignorant masses were not as gormless and hostile to calendrical adjustment as later commentators imagined.

Hence grassroots numeracy levels (as opposed to a capacity for higher mathematics) were almost certainly higher than basic literacy levels at all times throughout the long eighteenth century in Britain. As more people learned to read and write, the number undertaking simple calculations was pushed upwards also. Many, perhaps most, adults would recognise written numbers, as well as the chalked tallies that tracked running accounts in taverns.[64] In grand households, menservants understood the value of tips, or 'vails'; cooks and kitchen staff managed quantities and costings; street-sellers operated scales and handled coins; and sporting enthusiasts knew how to calculate the betting odds.[65] Furthermore, it only needed one numerate person in a group to act as intermediary for others who were innumerate. So when the Loanhead colliery in early eighteenth-century Midlothian established a 'stock-purse' or insurance plan for its miners, the scheme incorporated a regular review so that the miners could keep a check. In other words, the process assumed that at least one among their number would understand the accounts sufficiently to audit the balance.[66]

Self-help was one important route to numeracy. There were handy publications like John Ward's *Young Mathematician's Guide* (1707), which went into many editions.[67] So did *Cocker's Arithmetic* (first published in 1677; updated in 1751). This work launched the Georgian phrase 'according to Cocker', meaning 'absolutely correct and by the rules'.[68] Such handbooks commonly set exercises for their readers. And a surviving maths notebook from 1704, belonging to the twelve-year-old James Stenning (possibly a farmer's son), who lived in the village of Ockley in Surrey, recorded his workings and answer to a question set by Cocker, about calculating the price of Virginia tobacco.[69]

Friends sometimes provided informal mentoring. Occasionally, too, groups were organised for mutual support. In London's Spitalfields, a Mathematical Society was founded in 1717, and similar bodies appeared in Manchester (1718) and Northampton

(1721). Special-interest clubs like these were characteristic of Georgian society, and they testified to local commitment.[70] Certainly, an interest in mental skills was assumed to be widespread enough in 1808 to provide audiences for a touring entertainer, billed as the 'Caledonian Conjuror'. He offered to surprise his Nottingham audiences with a display of 'philosophical experiments, mathematical operations [probably feats of mental arithmetic] and magical deceptions'.[71]

Growing numbers of pupils, however, were gaining formal instruction from freelance tutors or, increasingly, from schools. Thus the grandfather of the inventor James Watt taught mathematics to local pupils in late seventeenth-century Greenock. Indeed, Scotland had an impressive record of new academies, led by Perth (1696), many with 'modernising' curricula. Not to teach mathematics and the developing sciences began to be seen as distinctly old-fashioned. So a traditional institution, like Newcastle Grammar School, decided in the later eighteenth century to get outside help. It sent its boys for classes at the nearby mathematical school, which was a private academy, founded in 1760 by Charles Hutton. He was a colliery supervisor's son who wrote the popular *Schoolmaster's Guide* (1764), en route to his appointment as professor at the Royal Military Academy, Woolwich. Eventually, he was lauded as the leading mathematician of his generation.[72]

Hutton, moreover, was sure that his subject would intrigue both sexes. Appointed editor in 1773 of the *Ladies Diary: Or, Women's Almanack* (founded 1704), he continued to provide mathematical puzzles for its readers.[73] And the journal's avoidance of gender stereotypes helped its sales to rise to over 30,000 copies per annum by the later 1830s. Hutton also supported a pioneering teacher named Margaret Bryan, whose schools in London and Margate successfully taught mathematics and astronomy to 'young ladies'.[74]

Women were beginning to infiltrate in some numbers into the world of mathematics and astronomy, where the labour was intellectual, not physical. In the case of Mary Somerville, a Scottish admiral's daughter, she first gleaned instruction by listening to her brother's tutor. Her advanced studies then won European-wide fame and (later still, in 1879) the tribute of having an Oxford college named after her.[75] Somerville in turn mentored the young Ada Lovelace, the daughter of Lord Byron.[76] Her forte was what she termed the 'Poetical Science' of numbers. It was Lovelace's techno-partnership with the mathematician Charles Babbage which led to the building of the world's first mechanical computer, the Analytic Engine (1835–37). (A late twentieth-century replica works perfectly.) The exact extent of Lovelace's originality or otherwise remains disputed, but her name is commemorated in the high-level programming language ADA, first devised in the years 1977–83.

Building the Analytic Engine was an utterly epic development, fusing advances in micro-engineering with developments in theoretical and applied mathematics. Eighteenth-century Britain was already known for one great contribution to the subject. Isaac Newton's calculus, devised in the 1670s, was first published in 1707 and initially jostled with claims for its independent invention by the German polymath Gottfried Leibniz – the dispute being fomented by their rival supporters.[77] However, in the long term, the importance of the mathematics took centre stage, as it was adopted as *the* internationally shared language of science.

Aided by that basic development, British inventors in the Georgian era were enabled to contribute a stream of major innovations in engineering, technology, mining and armaments. And the self-renewing capacity of this 'inventing' culture was notable. While the first break-through in harnessing new forms of mechanised power in the 1770s was based on steam, experimenters like Benjamin Franklin in Philadelphia and Joseph Priestley in Birmingham were already experimenting with steam's equally remarkable successor power: electricity.

Fusing Skills and Knowledge

Spreading literacy and numeracy does not automatically guarantee a pathway to sustained economic transformation.[78] There is no one formula for perennial growth – and clearly no easy guarantee that growth will always be beneficial. Other critical factors in the socio-economic circumstances of eighteenth-century Britain included: the global availability of suitable physical resources and raw materials; abundant capital; a set of conducive socio-cultural attitudes; a favourable political-legal framework; an array of scientific and technological knowledge; and an economic system which gave enough people a positive stake in promoting innovation.

Specifically, however, the availability of abundant supplies of labour, providing not only straightforward muscle-power but capable of fusing skills with knowledge, was also key. It was both a necessary precondition and a contributory factor to growth, if not the sole cause. As more people in Georgian Britain learned to read, write and calculate, society became turbo-charged. Via the relatively unfettered output of the press (subject to the laws of libel and slander), people had potential access to the entire stock of human knowledge, as created by 'the collective labour of a thousand intellects', in the words of Dr Johnson.[79] In 1840, Thomas Carlyle waxed similarly lyrical: 'All that Mankind has done, thought, gained, or been: it is lying, as in magic preservation, in the pages of Books'.[80]

True, knowledge was best when skills were applied with common sense. In his satirical novel *Crotchet Castle* (1831), Thomas Love Peacock lampooned the Steam Intellect Society, its modish name implying its vaporous nature. Its leaflets distracted the cook, who then burned the dinner. So much for book-learning![81] Yet many were genuinely interested in keeping up-to-date with new ideas. Responding to that demand, the eminent scientist Michael Faraday worked to spread public awareness of science, by launching in 1825 the (still-continuing) series of Christmas Lectures for Young People at the Royal Institution.[82] Logically, too, he warned his fellow citizens to shun bogus spiritualists and fake soothsayers.

Gaining skills was both a private and a public process. It promoted the ferment of ideas – and Britain's experimental culture. The *March of Intellect* (1829) seemed to offer boundless prospects of new inventions. The satirical print of that name imagined those to include: a steam-powered horse-carriage, named Velocity; a range of mechanically driven conveyances by land and air; a pleasure-boat pulled by dolphins; a huge vacuum tube sending passengers instantaneously to India; an iron suspension bridge; and ironic gadgets for relieving current social pressures, such as a cannon to shoot unwanted immigrants into the sky, away from Britain.[83] Some of these jesting proposals proved to be smart anticipations of later developments; others did not. Nevertheless, ideas like these were 'in the air'.

Not everyone approved. 'The Age of Chivalry is gone,' mourned Edmund Burke in 1790, in his already cited classic lament. And what would replace chivalric deference? A new age of 'sophisters [debaters], economists and calculators has succeeded'. Yet Burke's shrewd prophecy, which filled him with gloom, was simultaneously for others a beacon.

৵ Time-Shift: Then and Now ৵

Three places to visit in person or virtually in celebration of eighteenth-century literacy and numeracy, providing a chance to re-imagine the effect upon society when the masses first learned the skills of reading, writing and 'rithmatic.

1. Bluecoat: Liverpool Centre for the Contemporary Arts
This building, now an arts centre, was erected in 1716–25 as a residential charity school for poor children. (Such institutions were supported by benefactors, motivated by religious and utilitarian concerns, who sought to impove the life chances of the

poor by giving them access to education.) The Liverpool Blue Coat School – one of some twenty such Georgian foundations, and so named for its pupils' distinctive uniforms – remained in use until 1906, when it was moved out of town.

2. The Old Library, Trinity College Dublin

In the eighteenth century, Trinity College's library, founded in 1602, commissioned a new building (constructed 1712–32; expanded to incorporate an extra storey 1860). Known as the Old Library, with its celebrated Long Room, it now houses some 200,000 of the university's oldest and rarest books, plus a rare surviving medieval Gaelic harp – an Irish national symbol. As the most imposing of the many magnificent libraries constructed in the Georgian era, this venue is now a tourist as well as academic attraction.

3. The Enginuity Museum

This venue constitutes an interactive design and technology museum, with the genial motto 'Serious just got fun. And vice versa!' The whole place challenges visitors, especially children, to play and learn – with an admirable Enlightenment aim of demystifying science and technology, and spreading awareness of scientific skills. It is appropriately located within the Coalbrookdale Museums Complex at Ironbridge Gorge, where the world's first iron bridge (1781) stands amidst this World Heritage Site.

$\mathcal{C}\mathcal{P}$ 8 $\mathcal{C}\mathcal{P}$

Redefining Religion and Irreligion

One significant impact of long-term literacy was the cultural decentring of the clergy. That is, these men (and a few bold women field-preachers) were losing the old clerical monopoly of access to the written word. The churches remained visibly prominent everywhere. Each of the three traditional realms had one majority religion, plus a plurality of other groups. So there was no undisputed monopoly; but no complete fragmentation either. New churches were being built, and old ones refurbished. Throughout, British culture remained deeply influenced by Christian beliefs and morality. Moreover, the weekly cycle of six working days and a seventh day of rest provided an unchanging template of community life, as did the yearly cycle of religious festivals.

Nonetheless, the churches' role was slowly becoming adapted to suit a changing society. Within a pluralist system, people had choices between different faiths and non-faith. So religion and irreligion were slowly redefined. Anxious Georgian commentators named the trend as the spread of 'infidelity'. But historians use the neutral term 'secularisation' (and disagree over its timing).[1] Secularisation signifies not the death of religion, contrary to wild claims, but its specialisation into optional modes of worship-plus-morality. The mindset of society was becoming more this-worldly – in a word, more 'secular'.

Books and newspapers were augmenting, and eventually superseding, church services as key or sole sources of news and views. And, while the Bible remained revered for its spiritual power, it was decreasingly expected to explain the world's physical operation, let alone its entire biology, geology and history. Literalist interpretations of the Scriptures were on the retreat (though they did not disappear – and have not, to this day). These trends were acknowledged by many Georgian religious revivalists, who sought not just to combat irreligion but also to provide a more direct and personalised 'religion of the heart'.

The deep context for these developments was the spread of literacy, as already chronicled; plus a growing acceptance of religious toleration. Different churches were learning to live peaceably, side by side. Before 1689, successive monarchs attempted to enforce religious uniformity. But thereafter official policy switched. Three Acts of Toleration, in England and Wales (1689), Scotland (1712) and Ireland (1719), did not accept every variant of belief and – certainly not – unbelief.[2] Hence they were not 'tolerant' in the full sense of the word. They did, however, enact a political compromise which allowed a limited freedom of worship, which enabled many separate Protestant groups to emerge.

Furthermore, Catholicism, which was initially subject to strict legal penalties, became relatively accepted, long before the big push for Catholic emancipation in 1829. And, it should be recalled, Jewish synagogues were being built openly from the 1760s onwards. In other words, the Toleration Acts led to a much wider cultural tolerance than was initially envisaged. Consumer choice between rival religions was arriving. And, as that happened, irreligion was also being redefined – not without great angst and controversy – as its status slowly changed from 'demonic possession' into another lifestyle option.

Personalised Religion

Personal attitudes to faith may well have varied over an individual's lifetime. If the consolations of religion were needed at times of illness or bereavement, then scoffing was possible in bold or merry moments. The extent of such inner fluctuations remains unknowable. However, one outward sign was attendance at church services. Soon after the first Toleration Act (1689), fears were expressed that absenteeism was on the rise. In response, both clergymen and lay moralists tried hard, in the new pluralist world, to strengthen people's inner faith rather than their mere outward social conformism. It was a good challenge, which took many forms, without automatically producing the expected outcome.

Singing hymns throughout the Georgian era became an increasingly popular practice, in which both the literate and illiterate could join. It began first among the Protestant Dissenters, albeit excluding the silent Quakers. Yet by the early nineteenth century, hymns were included in even the most traditionalist Anglican services. One pioneer hymnodist was the Nonconformist Isaac Watt. His simple ballad-like verses conveyed great emotional force, and were adopted by many churches. Indeed, in 1780 the Anglican citadel of Westminster Abbey erected its own memorial to the Nonconformist Watt in tribute to his work.[3]

Hymns helped to intensify people's personal experience of religion; and in this period of transformation, some enduring songs of great power were created. The gospel staple 'Amazing Grace' (1779) has already been mentioned. It drew upon the conversion experience of the Anglican cleric John Newton; and gained its memorable music from an American composer in 1835. Another great community chant, which infallibly shakes the rafters, was 'Cwm Rhondda / Guide Me, O Thou Great Redeemer', also known as 'Bread of Heaven'. It was written in 1762 by a Methodist evangelist, William Williams Pantycelyn, and acquired its most famous tune later, in 1905.

Other impressive Georgian hymnodists were William Cowper and the brothers John and Charles Wesley. New hymns for children were also promoted.[4] And many famous Christmas carols were newly penned, including 'While Shepherds Watched' (1703) and 'Hark the Herald Angels Sing' (1739). Individuals could thus participate directly in church services – or simply enjoy the songs on their own account.

Another direct experience, for the literate, was reading religious works and commentaries. The King James Bible was the eighteenth century's most frequently reprinted book, and Dr Benjamin Blayney's Oxford edition (1769) set a new standard.[5] Similarly available was the Anglican Prayer Book, plus devotions for specific occasions.[6] These encouraged personal understanding and introspection, as did, for example, a handbook like *The Daily Self-Examinant* (1720).[7] Such works encouraged a confident lay piety, without a need for constant recourse to the clergy. Three notable Georgian women who wrote influential works of moral instruction – Hannah More, Anna Laetitia Barbauld and Sarah Trimmer – themselves exemplified that trend.

A particularly expressive genre of Protestant writing was that of the spiritual autobiography. John Bunyan's confessional *Grace Abounding* (1666) was a key contribution, later transmuted into the classic fable of spiritual testing in *The Pilgrim's Progress* (1678).[8] A number of Georgian evangelists added their own conversion narratives: from the hell of doubts to the inner fire of personal belief. William Cowper's *Light Shining Out of Darkness* (1779) was frank about his struggle with illness and depression.[9] Such exploratory writings not only influenced accounts of people's inner consciousness in Georgian novels.[10] They also anticipated the much later secular-confessional genre of 'misery lit'.

Sermons also provided their own variegated fare.[11] True, congregations could be inattentive. When commenting 'On Sleeping in Church' (1744), Jonathan Swift sniped at parishioners who divided their time 'between God and their bellies, when, after a gluttonous meal, their senses dozed and stupified, they retire to God's house to sleep out the afternoon'.[12] Nonetheless, powerful preachers at times had a great impact. One incandescent example was the High Church Anglican Henry Sacheverell. As noted above (p. 48), his dire warnings of an '[Anglican] Church in Danger' fuelled riots in 1710. By contrast, Bishop Joseph Butler's *Fifteen Sermons Preached at the Rolls Chapel* in 1726 were quite unfrenzied. He mused on the power of the 'still, small voice' of conscience, in an approach which greatly influenced later psychoanalytical studies.[13] Many sermons were circulated in print format to gain a longer life. There was clearly a thriving market, consisting not only of lazy clerics who borrowed ideas from others, but also of an interested public.

Cogitating on matters of faith could, of course, lead people away as well as towards orthodoxy. Some people were theologically restive. One Charles Lloyd was a Unitarian minister in 1788, before becoming a Baptist minister in 1790, joining an independent breakaway Welsh chapel in 1801, followed by a return to Unitarianism by 1803. Eventually, he moved in 1811 to become a schoolmaster in London. Lloyd's autobiography revealed, unsurprisingly, that he had not enjoyed his clerical career.[14] Other questing individuals lost their faith entirely, though it was easier to announce publicly a recovery of belief than its loss.

Lectures, meanwhile, were becoming a successful new Georgian medium for communicating and debating new ideas. Specialist venues, like the Rotunda at London's Blackfriars, provided a large auditorium for the equivalent of secular sermons.[15] In the early nineteenth century, various freethinkers spoke openly there to challenge all forms of religion. Two bold women who did so were the Scot Frances (Fanny) Wright, before she left for an energetic public career in the USA, and the Lancastrian feminist Eliza Sharples.[16]

Over time, therefore, clerical sermons were competing in crowded markets, just as the clergymen's advisory roles, within families and communities, were becoming shared with new professional authority figures. Already by 1700, there were as many lawyers as clergymen in England and Wales. Thereafter, both groups grew in numbers, being rapidly joined by the emergent medical profession.[17] So whereas, in earlier times, clergymen often gave medical advice and sometimes dosed their parishioners, in this period that role was being transferred to the doctors. The clergy were redefining their own profession too, heightening their focus upon spiritual, pastoral and educational roles.[18] And if they failed at their high calling, they became top targets of Georgian satire.[19]

Appeals to a personalised lay piety thus helped to renew people's religious commitments; but also redefined faith into a matter of personal choice as well as community adherence. That shift in turn carried a risk of reducing theological precision and increasing unorthodoxy or outright disbelief (as discussed below, pp. 146–9). A literate and reflective public needed not coercion but wooing.

The Multiplication of Churches

Clerical responses to these changes, to which many were themselves contributing, ranged from inertia from the notorious 'dumb dogs' (as inarticulate preachers were traditionally dubbed) to impressive campaigns for renewal made by evangelical reformers. It was never the case that the 'gentlemen of the *Long-Petticoat* tribe' spoke with one voice. There were too many arguments between churches and within them too. Indeed, the catchphrase *odium theologicum* ('theological hatred') was current in the 1730s to refer precisely to the rancour and bitterness generated by theological disputes.[20] By contrast, a few thinkers did appeal for pan-Christian church unity; but without success.[21]

Large and long-established institutions drew strength from their traditional ceremonial, political and administrative roles. They also benefited from familiarity, as many enjoyed community worship with agreed norms and rituals. By contrast, the ever-changing number of micro-churches had their own special messages, sometimes thrillingly sustained in semi-secrecy. Yet enthusiasm was prone to fade; and disputes to grow. As a result, all churches, particularly within the fissiparous and argumentative Protestant tradition, were prone to splits – whether on points of administrative practice or on points of doctrine.

Tradition, familiarity and respectability provided ballast for the established (Anglican) Church of England.[22] It was headed by the monarch; and it was enmeshed within the constitution, its twenty-six bishops sitting *ex officio* in the House of Lords. In addition, Anglicans had a monopoly (before 1828) of senior posts in the civil service, army and universities, although under the Indemnity Acts from 1727 onwards the legal situation for non-compliant individuals was blurred.[23] With its churches spread across both town and countryside, Anglicanism thus embraced all but those who withdrew to attend rival congregations. Such breadth gave it resilience. So one admirer in 1719 was happy to praise it as '(so far as I am able to judge) *the Best National Church in the World*'.[24]

Moreover, despite many contemporary criticisms – Edward Gibbon's sardonic reference to Anglicanism's 'fat slumbers' being best known[25] – there were plenty of diligent clergymen. Some were theological die-hards, who opposed all change; but there was also a substantial liberal wing. Hence Anglican advice on matters relating to sexuality was by no means always punitive.[26] At times, too, active bishops worked hard to organise their dioceses effectively.[27] Interestingly, there had been a secession of senior Anglican clergy in 1689, following disputes over taking oaths of loyalty to the new monarchs, William and Mary. Their small breakaway group, known as the Non-Jurors (non-oath-takers), survived as a separate church for many years, but eventually collapsed in 1779.[28]

Such schisms, while challenging, could not destroy Anglicanism's well-entrenched national role. More tricky, however, were its endemic organisational problems. Its finances relied upon tithes (church dues), which were unpopular, especially with those who did not attend Anglican services. The incomes attached to its different livings were very variable, with some being very poorly remunerated indeed. As a result, the quality of its ministers was equally variable. A lurid tract like *The Crimes of the Clergy* (1823), written by the Nonconformist radical William Benbow, paraded by name numerous clerical sinners for public shaming.[29] Furthermore, too many parishes lacked a resident incumbent (*c.* 58 per cent across England and Wales in 1827). And a large number of clerical appointments remained, for historic reasons, in the hands of lay patrons, who were usually local landowners.[30] Their choices were not always animated by the highest religious zeal. On the other hand, this system did give many landowners a vested interest in sustaining the church.

It took organisation, enthusiasm and funding to found a new religious body. When done successfully, it indicated the force of demand for change. In Scotland, the predominant Presbyterian Kirk focused upon its preaching power. Yet its congregations, who provided the funds, were demanding; and there were frequent splits. The Cameronians or Society-Men left in 1690. A new Secession Church, led by Ebenezer Erskine, departed in 1737 (with its own later splits), as did the Relief Church in 1761. And all these changes occurred long before the great schism of 1843. Then more than one third of the Presbyterian Kirk's ministers and parishioners left to found the evangelical Free Church (known as the 'Wee Frees'). A fissile Presbyterianism thus left plenty of options for parishioners to choose between rival preachers and preaching styles.

Across England and Wales and the northern counties of Ireland, too, there were similar pressures for religious variety. Emerging from the legal shadows post 1689, separate churches of Presbyterians, Congregationalists, Baptists and Quakers hastened to establish themselves. They constructed their plainly elegant meeting-houses, which remain everywhere visible: the earliest being smaller and located in side streets; the later ones, grander and in public thoroughfares.[31] These Nonconformists, also known as Dissenters, focused upon providing good preachers, while the Quakers offered an egalitarian alternative. They had no ministers but allowed their members to speak freely 'as the spirit moved them'.

All non-established churches had their own voluntaryist systems of governance and fund-raising, run by their members. These typically included independent-minded tradesmen, artisans and professionals.[32] Running their own affairs and often choosing their own ministers gave them considerable civic experience. Hence in Dissenting strongholds, like Norwich and Birmingham, prominent Dissenters were leading lights in their urban communities. There was also an unusual financial expedient, first adopted by the government of Robert Walpole in 1722 (and continuing to 1851). A semi-secret Treasury grant, called the *regium donum*, was made annually to various leading Presbyterian, Congregationalist and Baptist churches.[33] It constituted, in effect, a limited but practical state recognition that England's Dissenting interest had come to stay.

These known and publicly visible congregations were also supplemented by micro-churches of varying size and tenacity. Some groups relied upon the appeal of an esoteric message, imparted only to the few. The Muggletonians provide one remarkable example. They saw themselves as the biblical 'Last Witnesses' at the end of the world, whilst all others were damned. Recruiting purely by word of mouth among poor artisan families from 1652 onwards, they survived as a small cause, holding on tenaciously until 1979.[34] A different appeal was seen in the case of the Glasites, who followed a special lifestyle. At some stage in the 1730s, a group of followers gathered around a fervent Scottish preacher, John Glas. They lived simply, sharing their goods. And from the 1760s onwards further small groups of communal-sharers were founded in London, northern England and North America by Glas's son-in-law Robert Sandeman.[35]

Often, the call to found a new group came from a powerful preacher. In the case of the New Church of Jerusalem (founded

1789), however, the impulse came from the mystical writings of the Swedish visionary Emanuel Swedenborg, who died in London in 1772. A dedicated group followed his rejection of Trinitarian orthodoxy. Instead, they sought 'oneness' with Christ.[36] The young artist-poet William Blake was among their number, at first joyously. However, disputes followed. Blake found the New Church to be too restrictive, especially in sexual matters. His poem *The Garden of Love* (1794) accordingly mourned: 'And the gates of this Chapel were shut/ And *Thou Shalt Not* writ over the Door!'[37] Blake's membership lapsed, though not his love of visionary thinking.

Rarely, too, charismatic women with a special message emerged as church founders. The most sensational was Joanna Southcott, a Devonshire farmer's daughter who had worked as a dairymaid and later went into service. In 1814, however, drama ensued. She announced that she was, at the age of sixty-four, pregnant with the new Messiah. Several reputable doctors promptly certified that she was with child. Millenarian hopes (and fears) that the end of the world was nigh reached fever pitch.[38] Southcott launched a new church, with a male minister to conduct services. And she personally issued signed tokens, guaranteeing salvation in the next life to named individuals, termed the 'Elect Precious'. Her personal story ended in a sad anticlimax. She died of a stomach tumour, without any sign of the celestial child. Most supporters were disillusioned. Yet, as can happen, a few followers remained faithful. A tiny Southcottian church, plagued with splits, survived into the twenty-first century.[39] The volatility of religious fervour was revealed, but also its potential tenacity, once turned into a cult. Southcott's career also marks the tolerance of officialdom, as she faced no legal or religious penalties.

Given such permutations, the importance of public responses to the churches and their messages remained crucial. In Georgian Britain and Ireland, the strong survival of Catholicism, or what Protestants termed the 'Old Religion', depended upon cultural tenacity. It was excluded from the Toleration Acts, and Catholics were subject to strict legal penalties, designed to exclude them from civic participation and from various forms of property-ownership. Nonetheless, the law on its own could not extirpate a faith. In England, where Catholicism had waned long before 1689, it survived as a minority commitment among a few staunch landowning families.[40] They braved an intermittent but well-entrenched strand of British anti-Catholicism. And the old faith flourished across Ireland. The Catholic priesthood was revitalised by recruits trained in European seminaries. And discreet mass-houses were built, without outward religious insignia. Gaelic-speaking, Irish and Catholic identities were strongly welded together, bonding the great majority of the population against Ireland's Protestant Ascendancy.

Eventually, however, the situation became more fluid. By the 1760s a number of private 'papist' chapels were established, including in London. Various legal changes began to ameliorate the status of individual Catholics, both reflecting and encouraging a degree of rapprochement.[41] A number of Catholics converted (at least nominally) to improve their legal rights.[42] Some couples from different faiths intermarried – as did the Catholic mother and Protestant father of the political thinker Edmund Burke. Yet, while such unions could smooth divisions, they generated frictions too. Wealthy Protestants worried that their heiress daughters were at risk of abduction by impoverished Catholic suitors. Such dramas were actually rare, but fears persisted.[43]

Daring plans for pan-religious political unity were expounded in the 1790s by a radical group, organised as the Society of United Irishmen. Religious fault-lines were not, however, easily bridged. There were tensions among Irish Nonconformists, who had their own splits. There were tensions too between them and the Church of Ireland, which was the established church in law but which represented a minority in terms of numbers. There was further friction between all Irish Protestants and Irish Catholics.[44] And, adding to these complications, there was tensions within Catholicism itself, as an impoverished peasantry often baulked at paying special dues to fund the priesthood.[45] Remarkably, however, in 1795 Britain's Protestant government realised the political advantages of a religion devoted to duty and obedience. It began abruptly to provide funds for a new Irish Catholic training seminary at Maynooth, outside Dublin.[46] It was a dramatic switch in policy. But it still took major campaigns to achieve full Catholic emancipation in 1829.[47]

Choices, which people made in the context of the law and their own social positions, included options of non-attendance and religious indifference. It was specifically to combat such responses that a number of extraordinary Georgian evangelists took action. Their movement of religious revival, known as the Great Awakening, spread from the 1730s onwards across Protestant Europe and North America.[48] How could backsliders recover religious zeal? William Hole, a concerned Anglican archdeacon, fretted that Protestant churches were too plain and visually unexciting to attract the crowds.[49] Leading charismatic preachers solved that problem by going out to the people directly. Preaching an emotionally urgent 'religion of the heart', they toured the country speaking to crowds at big open-air meetings as well as smaller indoor ones. Critics found the style too emotive. Sometimes, there were hostile riots by locals resisting change.[50] But the evangelists' aim was to appeal to each individual's conscience.

John Wesley, son of an Anglican clergyman and grandson of a Dissenting minister, devoted his life as in itinerant preacher to inculcate 'plain old Bible Christianity'. Rapt audiences, caught in his searching gaze, felt that he was addressing them individually.[51] He went especially to areas where the Anglican parochial system was weakest. In that spirit, he preached to the 'wild' colliers in the poor industrial parish of Kingswood, outside Bristol, and in 1748 founded a school for their children (now an esteemed Methodist public school).

Furthermore, Wesley's powerful appeal was matched by that of another hypnotic field orator, George Whitefield, famed for his sonorous, positively bell-like tones. He was a not-very-affluent inn-keeper's son who in his youth experienced an inner conversion. After that emotional crisis, he became an evangelist, particularly to poor and outcast communities in Britain and North America. Other rousing itinerant preachers included men like Howell Harris, Daniel Rowland and the hymnodist William Williams Pantycelyn, as well as a few highly determined women.[52]

Before long, the followers of these evangelists became known as 'Methodists'.[53] The term sprang from Wesley's system of setting locally organised classes to engage in Bible study and stringent moral audit. Believers were asked not merely to conform outwardly but to have an active inner faith. Regular attenders were issued with membership tickets. Early Methodism also incorporated other group festivals, such as 'love feasts' with (non-alcoholic) drinks and song. By organising their own 'parachurches', these evangelists were creating networks of chapels-within-a-church; and eventually they struck out on their own. In 1741 Whitefield founded his Tabernacle and launched his strand of strict Calvinistic Methodism. Under his aegis, the widowed Selina, Countess of Huntingdon, organised her own 'Connection', which developed a strong missionary calling to Africa.[54] Other Calvinistic Methodist networks followed in Wales, where the Anglican parochial system was organisationally weak.

The largest of all these networks were the Arminian Methodists, inspired by John Wesley. For many decades, they remained loosely within the Church of England, even though in 1784 Wesley, unauthorised, began to ordain his own Methodist ministers. After his death in 1791, however, his followers soon split to form the Wesleyan Methodist Connection. The movement also began to shed its social radicalism. For example, in 1803, the Wesleyan Methodists banned women from preaching in anything other than all-female gatherings (a ban which survived until 1910). Various splits followed, including the emergence of Primitive Methodism in 1811, seeking a return to old-style revivalism.[55]

Self-organisation was the key that allowed some of these preaching campaigns to transmute into settled churches. By the mid-nineteenth century, Methodism or 'New Dissent' had regular support from over 10 per cent of the population of England and Wales, having collectively overtaken Old Dissent, supported by just over 8 per cent.[56] Moreover, all these Protestant Nonconformists had a cultural impact that spread well beyond their numbers. In particular, they played a big role in overseas evangelism. Nonetheless, the Methodist saga reveals both the power of a dynamic 'religion of the heart' and the difficulty of sustaining mass levels of personal commitment at fever pitch.

Public Declarations of Scepticism and Irreligion

Britain had no equivalent of an Inquisition to root out heresy. Before 1688, both Charles I and James II had tried to exert control via a crown-appointed Court of High Commission.[57] But the existence of such a body, or anything like it, was declared 'illegal and pernicious' by Parliament in 1689. Thereupon the absence of repressively close invigilation – and the Georgian cultural flowering – opened the floodgates to explorations not only of religion but of irreligion too.

Blasphemy did certainly remain a serious public offence throughout this period. In 1697, one unfortunate twenty-year-old Scottish student, named Thomas Aikenhead, transgressed within the hearing of plentiful witnesses. He was accused of ridiculing the Scriptures, rejecting the Trinity and declaring a preference for Muhammad over Christ. Forthwith found guilty, he was hung as a blasphemer at Edinburgh's Tollbooth, despite many appeals for clemency and his expressed contrition.[58] Yet this death was the last. The penalty was then reduced to imprisonment, intermittently enforced; it has not been applied since 1843. Officialdom had hoped to use Aikenhead's punishment as a grim warning. However, his death had no noticeable effect in halting the debates – making him an unsung martyr for the cause of freedom of expression.

Tides of thought in European intellectual circles meanwhile were promoting confidence in human 'rationalism'.[59] The eminent thinker

John Locke made the case for religion by appealing to God-given Reason, as the title of his influential tract on *The Reasonableness of Christianity* (1695) explained.[60] Excess zeal was dismissed as fanatical and socially dangerous. One tract accordingly appeared with the brisk title *A Discourse Proving that the Apostles Were No Enthusiasts* (1730).[61] Revivalist preachers like John Wesley did not fully agree. He was certainly an enthusiast for enthusiasm, yet he still warned his followers to respect human Reason: 'Never more declaim in that wild, loose, ranting manner, against this precious gift of God. Acknowledge "the candle of the Lord".'[62]

Cultural scepticism was turning against supernatural beliefs in 'magic', miracles and devils.[63] In Britain, the old laws against witchcraft were repealed in 1736. Thenceforth penalties applied only to those 'pretending' to have witch-like powers. Gradually, a literal belief in wicked supernatural spirits, along with their benevolent counterparts, elves, fairies and sprites, was dwindling into a 'quaint' folk tradition.[64] In 1762, reports of strange noises and ghosts haunting a house in London's Cock Lane attracted curious crowds and controversy. The spectre, however, was declared to be a fraud and the perpetrators punished.[65]

Ideas about hell-fire were equally in transition. Old concepts of the burning fiery pit, where sinners are endlessly tormented, were being reinterpreted more symbolically.[66] The devil too was becoming more of a metaphorical danger than a serious demonic tempter in daily life. So William Combe's poem *The Diaboliad* (1777), jauntily dedicated 'to the Worst Man in his Majesty's Dominions', turned out to be a critique of vice in smart society.[67] Intellectual sceptics like David Hume, who directed his philosophical criticism at claims for supernatural miracles, faced much controversy.[68] Yet his work boosted a cultural shift against belief in Christian 'relics' with allegedly magical powers. It was an attitude which augmented the known Protestant disapproval of wearing religious tokens (rendering anachronistic later costume dramas of Georgian Britain, which at times show Catholic crucifixes on the 'heaving bosoms' of Protestant ladies).

Intellectual scepticism was meanwhile prone to tip into more radical freethinking. An old Christian heresy, variously known as Arianism, Socinianism or Unitarianism, favoured not the conventional Trinity but instead one divine spirit. Officially, this belief was deemed blasphemous. But in these years supporters of Arianism were growing in numbers. One was the admired physicist Isaac Newton, who prudently kept to himself his doubts about the Trinity.[69] Another was an erudite theologian, Dr Samuel Clarke of Norwich. His career as an Anglican divine began well but then stalled. Voltaire then mischievously reported that Clarke's potential appointment as Archbishop of Canterbury was blocked because 'he was not a Christian'.[70]

Yet greater unorthodoxies were also voiced by a few bold thinkers.[71] The republican Irishman John Toland caused a storm with his *Christianity Not Mysterious* (1696). His book (but not he himself) was deemed blasphemous and publicly burned in Dublin.[72] Undeterred, Toland declared himself a 'pantheist', saluting a universal divine spirit. He invented a new humanist service, published initially in Latin as his *Pantheisticon* (1730; anglicised, 1751). A fellow innovator was Anthony Collins. His *Discourse on Freethinking* (1713) gave deists such as himself their familiar eighteenth-century name.[73] And Matthew Tindal, the questing son of an Anglican cleric, offered a new 'religion of nature', with a rationalist prayer beginning: 'O First Mover! O Cause of Causes!'[74]

An intellectual Unitarianism, rationally accepting the power of the Christian deity but discarding any belief in a miraculous Trinity, gained considerable adherence among later eighteenth-century English Presbyterians. Joseph Priestley, another ever-questing intellectual, took that view. Accordingly, he proposed to simplify Christian services, which he believed should be educational and participatory.[75] And an example of that religious ethos can be seen to this day in Norwich's Octagon Chapel (built 1756). Its neo-Palladian octagonal frame encloses a circular meeting room, focused upon a central lectern. There is no high altar. The ambience is coolly rational, not mystic.[76]

Deistic freethinking was furthermore opening doors to even more radical expressions of disbelief. The term 'agnostic' was not coined until 1869, so Georgian doubters did not use that name.[77] But a few boldly accepted the label of 'philosophical unbeliever'. One anonymous author did just that in 1782.[78] He was replying to a challenge from Priestley, who was himself (wrongly) criticised as a God-denying atheist. Standing out against the Christian norms of society was not easy. But in 1776 the philosopher David Hume was the first heavyweight intellectual to die whilst publicly refusing to allow a clergyman to attend his deathbed. His friends, like James Boswell, expostulated, but to no avail. Hume, who may have endorsed a form of deism, kept his own counsel as to his private beliefs but rejected all forms of conventional piety.[79]

No such hesitation troubled two doughty polemicists in the 1790s: Thomas Paine's *Age of Reason* (1794) and John Hollis's *Apology for the Disbelief of Revealed Religion* (1799) rejected both the theory and practice of revealed religion. Surviving fierce controversy themselves, they also paved the way for others. So when in 1811 the young student Percy Shelley published *The Necessity of Atheism*, he did so with cool confidence. 'No degree of criminality is attachable to disbelief,' he wrote. 'God is an hypothesis, and, as such, stands in need of proof.'[80] Unlike the unfortunate Aikenhead in 1697, Shelley was not hung for blasphemy but sent down from his Oxford college instead.

There was nothing as organised or systematic as an 'apostolic succession' from deism to atheism or to agnosticism. Nonetheless, by the 1790s, there were networks of sceptics – radical freethinkers being keen to maintain contacts across mainland Europe and the USA. Before 1844, however, there was no British Anti-State-Church Association (later renamed as the Society for the Liberation of Religion from State Patronage). Equally, before 1866, there was no National Secular Society, and before 1896, no British Humanists Association (now Humanists UK).

Georgian society was, however, generating opportunities for individuals to explore alternatives to traditional religion and morality. When Robert Owen, manufacturer-cum-utopian socialist, announced in 1817 that all faiths are false, he urged communities to generate their own cooperative values. (Later, Owen switched to spiritualism, seeking to channel spirits of earlier reformers to save the world – a fan later announcing the Owenite Seven Principles of Spiritualism.)[81]

'Blasphemy' was slowly mutating into multiple explorations of irreligion and alternative values. Declarations of irreligion still had the power to shock. Yet they were neither unthinkable nor unsayable. Self-declared atheists even began to proselytise. In 1819 the republican Richard Carlile, with his common-law partner, the freethinker Eliza Sharples, travelled the country in an 'infidel missionary tour'. (In later life, however, Carlile returned to Christianity.)[82] The varieties of scepticism and irreligion were characteristically disorganised. Yet in Georgian Britain such views were being voiced publicly and with some frequency, whilst the unfortunate Aikenhead in 1697 remained the last religious sceptic in the UK to be put to death for blasphemy.

Religious and Irreligious Pluralism

An awareness of religious options at an individual level can be seen in one example from 1777. Harry Dunnell, an Anglican parishioner in Weston Longueville, 12 miles outside Norwich, wanted a private baptism for his second child. He was much aggrieved when his request was refused. The parson, James Woodforde, recorded their dispute in his diary: Dunnell 'had the Impudence to tell me that he would send [the baby] to some [Nonconformist] Meeting House to be named – *very saucy indeed*'.[83] In the event, they avoided a prolonged rift. Woodforde continued to employ Dunnell occasionally as a handyman, while Dunnell's third child was baptised in the parish church and the fourth privately. Evidently, parishioner allegiance was not to be taken for granted and, upon occasion, parsons had discreetly to give way.

Without statistics before 1851, when Britain's first and only religious census was held, the distribution of churches cannot be identified with precision. Nonetheless, the mid-nineteenth-century evidence throws light upon long-unfolding developments since 1689. In England, every one of the 576 census registration districts had churches belonging to more than one denomination, and many had more.[84] Dissenters constituted a relatively high proportion of those actually attending church. But absenteeism was also apparent every-where. In Scotland, Presbyterianism remained very dominant, but was structurally divided into many rival churches. And in Ireland (where the census returns have survived only patchily), Catholicism was the majority faith, with Irish Presbyterianism strong in the north, and a persistent strand of Irish Anglicanism.

Collectively, the increasingly literate Georgians, with their urban-ising, commercialising and industrialising economy, were nurturing a secularised and comparatively tolerant society. Such a correlation is by no means automatic. But in this case, it was so. The French philo-sopher Voltaire was a witness. After living in England between 1726 and 1729, he argued that a degree of religious variety was the best shield against either a monopolistic despotism or a total fragmenta-tion leading to civil war: 'As there are such a multitude [of churches], they all live happy and in peace'.[85]

In truth, contentment was very far from universal. But the Georgians provided de facto cultural space for those who were simply indifferent to religion, even while their numbers remain completely unknown (particularly as people's views may have oscillated over a lifetime).

Collectively, then, to recapitulate: a huge majority of the Georgians, if questioned, would no doubt have called themselves Christians, even if their church attendance was not very regular. This period also saw strong evangelical campaigns to promote a personalised 'religion of the heart'. Far from the entire population was galvanised. Yet the effect was to sustain and renew Christianity, various splits and heated disagreements among the evangelists notwithstanding. At the same time, the Georgians also came to accept, if often grudgingly, the existence of multiple churches side by side. And, even more strikingly, they witnessed public expressions of many forms of scepticism and outright unbelief. Yet those who were 'infidels' in the eyes of the orthodox were not (after 1697) put to death for their views. They were left free to explore an ethical secularism, without recourse to divine sanctions. Such a shift to consumer choice in religion – and in irreligion – was truly epic.

∽ Time-Shift: Then and Now ∾

Two statues commemorating eighteenth-century religion and scepticism can be viewed personally or virtually. Long-term trends are the work of many people but these two individuals not only personified but also propelled the advance of personalised faith and of rational scepticism.

1. Equestrian statue to the Methodist Evangelist John Wesley (1703–91)
This iconic monument, designed in 1933 by Arthur George Walker, is located outside the New Room, Horsefair, Bristol – a landmark chapel opened by Wesley in 1739. The design catches his mixture of eager determination and itinerant restlessness, as he rode tirelessly around the country, a book always in his hand, in pursuit of his personal motto: 'You have one business on earth – to save souls'. A replica also stands in the grounds of the Wesley Theological Seminary, Washington, DC.

2. Civic memorial to the philosopher and historian David Hume (1711–76)

This statue, designed by Edinburgh-born sculptor Alexander Stoddart and unveiled outside the High Court on Edinburgh's Royal Mile in 1995, shows Hume as a classical Greek philosopher, complete with robes and laurel wreath. It attracts numerous visitors, many of whom rub his protruding right big toe 'for luck'. That playfully superstitious homage is a tribute to his still rising status as a cultural guru, even though it is at odds with Hume's own rationalist credo, which stated that: 'In all the events of life, we ought still to preserve our scepticism'.

PART III
The Georgians Ruling and Resisting

A plebeian John Bull farts mightily at a poster of King
George III, while Prime Minister William Pitt gasps in
horror, lampooning tensions between radical street politics
and successive government clampdowns.

ॐ 9 ॐ

Negotiating Political Power 'Indoors'

The Georgian political world had two faces: one, in full view, was stately, powerful and dignified; the other, behind the scenes, was disputatious, tetchy and reliant upon negotiation rather than force. Elements of that dichotomy apply in most ruling systems, even the most tyrannical. Yet the British monarchy post-1689 notably lacked the power to tax, legislate or maintain a standing army without Parliament's consent; and it was banned from reviving the old prerogative (royal) courts like Star Chamber.[1]

So the Georgian political world relied crucially upon negotiation. Power lines in Westminster ran between the royal court at St James, the prime minister's office at 10 Downing Street (from the 1720s onwards), the Houses of Parliament, and the growing institutions of the civil service (that term being first coined in 1785). Simultaneously strings of connection linked central government with local centres of power throughout the three traditional realms, and with the constellations of overseas territories under British rule. Constant negotiation gave that intricate spider's web considerable flexibility, provided that rulers were ready to listen and to adapt, as well as to lead. (Sometimes they were not.)

Many Georgians were deeply hostile to ideological conflict and civil strife. They did not want a return to the bloodshed of the mid-seventeenth-century civil wars.[2] 'For Forms of Government, let fools contest;/ Whate'er is best administer'd is best', ran a melodious couplet from Alexander Pope.[3] It was an irenic dictum from a Catholic outsider. Incremental change would deliver where conflict would backfire. In 1785 Archdeacon Paley offered a soothing account of Britain's constitution: 'It resembles one of those old mansions, which, instead of being built all at once . . . has been reared in different ages of the art, has been altered from time to time, and has been continually receiving additions and repairs suited to the taste, fortune, or conveniency, of its successive proprietors'.[4]

Given its pluralist networks, the Georgian political world is best defined as one of an emergent constitutionalism. It was not an absolutist *ancien regime* on a par with Spain or France.[5] It had an army but was not a militarised state on a par with eighteenth-century Prussia. It was ruled by an oligarchy, meaning the rule of the few (as opposed to either an absolute monarchy or a full participatory democracy), but this oligarchy was broad-based and economically diversified, not a narrow group of landowners, as is sometimes incorrectly assumed.

There was an increasingly prevalent culture of individual 'rights', claimed by a wide, if ill-defined, sector of the adult male population, including (in England) the right to participate in the jury system.[6] Specific policies adopted by the broad-based ruling oligarchy veered between liberal and conservative, while critics outside Parliament pressed for radical change. The unsystematic system was full of tensions and never static, but it was developing a tradition of political due process and 'reason' rather than all-out or even covert civil war.

Heading the Constitution

One achievement of the Georgian political world was the entrenchment of constitutional monarchy, with an increasingly ceremonial role. After the death of Queen Anne – the last ruling Stuart from the old dynasty – no monarch dared to halt laws which were passed by both Houses of Parliament. The royal veto, last used in 1708, remains a purely dormant power. Furthermore, Anne was the last monarch to 'touch' invalids to cure them of the 'king's evil' (scrofula). The Hanoverians, recruited to the throne by Parliament rather than by strict hereditary right, simply discontinued the practice. By 1734 a robust commentator dismissed the special claims of the royal touch as nothing other than a 'childish delusion' or 'pious fraud'.[7]

A traditional kingly role, which was becoming purely ceremonial, was heading the armed forces. William III led troops into battle (successfully, if for some controversially, at the River Boyne in 1690). But the last British king to appear in the field was George II at Dettingen in Bavaria in 1743. He was aged sixty, and his horse bolted – but the battle was won. After him, two royal princes had active military careers. But the Duke of Cumberland at Culloden in 1746 gained an unenvied reputation as 'Butcher' George.[8] And the 'Noble' Duke of York, in hasty retreat after military defeat in northern France in 1794, was pilloried in an enjoyable children's rhyme – still used as a marching song.[9] Thereafter, British royalty transposed its titular leadership into military and naval ceremonial, and into sponsoring military and naval charities. Fighting was left to the much admired professionals. And outstanding Georgian naval and military commanders, headed by Marlborough, Wolfe, Nelson and Wellington, remain widely memorialised in monuments, statues, pub names, festive dinners and flag-flying rituals to this day.

Also significant for Georgian political stability were the two big defeats of the Catholic Jacobite claimants in 1715 and 1745–46. The Hanoverian monarchs were Protestants, married to Protestants, as required by the 1701 Settlement Act. Furthermore, by the later eighteenth century, George III's large family ensured that his dynasty had no lack of heirs. By contrast, the last credible Jacobite claimant, Cardinal Henry Stuart, was a celibate Roman Catholic cardinal.[10]

He died childless in 1807, propelling Jacobitism into romantic myth and literature.

Meanwhile, at the British court, a strict etiquette sustained the status of royalty. Reputations of individual monarchs wax and wane over time.[11] But the early Hanoverians worked hard at their role. Their courts functioned as political sounding-boards; and attendance there was a social accolade.[12] Each monarch also had a regular retinue of ladies- and gentlemen-in-waiting. Yet their numbers were kept relatively low, unlike in France, where the titular nobility was required to spend some months every year at Versailles, staying in the palace's extensive residential facilities – and remaining under the monarch's watchful eye. The relative simplicity of British royal style was also evident in the absence of any formal royal progresses around the country, other than George IV's choreographed visit to Scotland in 1822.[13] Thus his father George III's summer trips were informal ones to Weymouth, where he was given a friendly welcome as 'Farmer George'.

Nonetheless, there were limits to the social mingling. When George III's youngest daughter Princess Amelia sought to marry a court equerry, who was a 'mere' younger son of a baron, her father refused his consent, using his power under the Royal Marriages Act (1772). Princess Amelia remained a spinster, dying young and thwarted in 1810.[14] (There are some interesting, if inexact, parallels with the later saga of Princess Margaret in the 1950s, although the earlier drama was not conducted in the columns of the popular press.)

Amelia's sacrifice to convention contrasted with her eldest brother's flamboyant rule-breaking. Prince George (regent in 1811; king in 1820) had sensational love affairs and then a conflicted marriage with his cousin Caroline of Brunswick. In 1820, she was put on public trial for adultery. Radical opinion was noisily on her side. When her husband was crowned king in 1821, Queen Caroline was denied access to Westminster Abbey, whereupon she stood outside, beating upon its closed doors.[15] The unseemly scandal ended only with her sudden death a few weeks later. Large crowds paid tribute to Caroline's funeral cortege, in effect rebuking George IV, but without going any further.

With the consolidation of constitutional monarchy, British republicanism was transmuted into a sleeping tradition: not defunct but often quiescent. Unsurprisingly, it was relatively active in the 1820s under the spendthrift George IV – in fact reaching its post-1650s all-time peak.[16] Thereafter, however, the pressures of relentless public inspection have meant that the royal family remains aware of the need not only for constitutional propriety but also for personal respectability.[17]

Ministers Pulling the Political Strings

Alongside the ceremonialisation of the monarchy, the parallel trend was the normalisation of day-to-day rule by the king's ministers. They made policy, pulled the practical strings, and either used – or advised on the use of – the remaining monarchical prerogatives (discretionary powers). As the de facto heads of the executive, they were secret 'kings', below the throne but actually heading the government.

These leading ministers were not elected directly by Parliament. They were selected by the monarchs. Yet there were practical constraints. Ministers were key links between crown and Parliament. So appointees who lacked sufficient support in the legislative branch, and specifically in the House of Commons, were liable to face problems. That outcome followed the elevation of the Earl of Bute, the chosen adviser of the young George III, to become First Lord of the Treasury in May 1762. But royal support only went so far. Bute, who had actually lived most of his life in England, was pilloried for his alleged 'Scottishness', as well as fiercely attacked for his policies. Politically friendless, he resigned in April 1763, after an inauspicious premiership of less than a year.[18]

Generally, however, there were many long and stable governments during this era. Those included the three longest unbroken premierships in British history: that of Robert Walpole (just short of twenty-one years – 1721–42); that of Robert Jenkinson, Lord Liverpool (just short of fifteen years – 1812–27); and that of Lord North (just over twelve years – 1770–82).[19] Among them, it was Walpole who crystallised the role. He was the first to be known as 'prime' minister – a phrase originally used in satire. He was also the first to operate from 10 Downing Street. And, when George II offered him the freehold of the terrace house in 1735, Walpole accepted as First Lord of the Treasury, ensuring that the conveniently sited residence became tied to the job.[20] Moreover, when in 1742 Walpole realised that a majority of his colleagues opposed his foreign policy, he resigned (and later got an earldom). He thus started a new process. A resignation was less drastic than an impeachment, a beheading or a skulking flight into exile. Ministerial turnover was being normalised.

By contrast, the characteristically long stable ministries were intercut with shorter periods of rapid turnover and 'interesting times'. For example, in the notable period of transition when the political challenge from the American colonies was intensifying, there were as many as five short premierships in the eight years between 1762 and 1770.[21] It took skill to juggle all the different issues and interest groups, and, in troubled times, the task became ever harder.

Particularly important was the special 'glue' of patronage. The historian Lewis Namier led the way in highlighting its importance, as Georgian politicians jockeyed for remunerative positions, for themselves, their families, and their allies.[22] Patronage systems, also known as political clientelism, can be justifiably criticised. Yet they can bind networks successfully, provided that rewards are spread widely (small monopolistic cliques are always disliked), and also provided that client-loyalties are not overridden by momentous policy issues. It was not true that all Georgian politicians were purely motivated by a quest for office, as assumed by some 'Namierites' who applied Namier's insights too uncritically.[23] But well-managed patronage could foster stability.

When crises did escalate, they tended, in this period, to be triggered either by foreign policy or taxation (or both). Public opinion was often bellicose in support of overseas wars, when fearing commercial rivalry from competitor nations. Yet it was equally keen on peace, if wars became too long and costly. And many then grumbled if the ensuing peace treaty seemed too generous to the defeated rival powers. One case in point was the ending of the Seven Years' War. The Peace of Paris (1763) confirmed notable gains for Britain in Canada, but restored some captured territories to France and Spain. Loud complaints then helped to accelerate the political eclipse of the peace-maker, the Earl of Bute.[24]

Notwithstanding those diverse pressures, Britain's ministers habitually faced the wider world with confidence. True, there were some galling defeats. In 1756 Britain lost the Mediterranean island of Minorca (today Menorca) after a naval battle with the French. Public opinion was outraged; and the losing commander, Admiral Byng, was court-martialled and shot.[25] Even more ignominious was the 1777 British surrender at Saratoga (New York) to the rebel Americans.[26]

Yet bullish Britons instead stressed their naval strength, their burgeoning trade and colonial assets, and their big victories worldwide. Those included Blenheim (1704) in Bavaria; Oudenarde (1708) in Flanders; Plassey or Palashi (1757) in West Bengal;[27] Quebec (1759) in Canada; Aboukir Bay (1798) off the Egyptian coast; Trafalgar (1805) off Spain's south coast; and, best known of all, Waterloo (1815) in Flanders.[28] The contribution of foreign allies to these successes was usually ignored in British legend. Behind the scenes, however, the king's ministers paid careful attention to diplomacy, just as the nascent civil service (discussed below, pp. 173–5) worked hard to organise the military and naval logistics.

Throughout everything, too, prudent politicians kept a careful check upon public opinion close to home. In the case of Scotland post-1707, consolidating the Union by consent was an absolute imperative, especially given the only slow withering of support for the Jacobites. At times, tough policies were enforced. After Culloden in 1746, civilians were banned from wearing the Scottish tartan. However, two generations later, in 1782, the kilt was re-legalised, being retained for ceremonial use, both officially and unofficially, as Scotland's national dress.[29]

Giving the Scots access to patronage became thereafter a conscious policy under the aegis of Henry Dundas in the later eighteenth century. A Midlothian lawyer, he became the Younger Pitt's right-hand man, taking office as secretary of state for war, and gaining the title of Viscount Melville. He presided over a period when many Lowland Scots in particular were sharing in Britain's colonial and economic expansion. But Dundas had critics, who dubbed him 'the uncrowned king of Scotland' or 'Harry the Ninth'.[30] In 1806 the opposition Whigs tried to impeach him for maladministration of Admiralty funds (the last case of impeachment in Britain). He was acquitted, but the associated political scandal ended his active career. Dundas did, however, gain one posthumous honour. In 1821 the lofty Melville Monument (modelled on Trajan's Column in Rome) was erected in St Andrew's Square, Edinburgh, following a special naval subscription. It was controversial then as it has become contro-versial again today – epitomising the difficulty of depicting complex historical lives in 'simple' public imagery.

Ireland, with its different constitutional arrangements, posed a separate set of challenges. Day-to-day management was left to successive lords-lieutenant, who were answerable to Westminster. But a role for Ireland's consultative assembly was confirmed when it was moved in 1729 into a new purpose-built building, with a striking octagonal debating chamber at its heart. (Today, after many vicissi-tudes, the old Parliament House serves as headquarters of the Bank of Ireland.) Furthermore, considerable flexibility was shown in 1782–83. The liberal lawyer Henry Grattan, buoyed by a special convention of Irish Volunteers (armed militias), persuaded the Irish Parliament in 1782 to vote for its full legislative independence.[31] And in 1783 politicians in Westminster agreed. They did not want to see an Irish equivalent of an American breakaway.

However, the liberal interlude which followed this partial step towards devolution was relatively short-lived. 'Grattan's Parliament' lifted various legal penalties upon Irish Catholics. Yet it did not gain the powers to supervise the lords-lieutenant or to hold them to account. And it could not withstand an abrupt shift in British policy, when wartime tensions heightened. In 1800–1, the Dublin and Westminster Parliaments agreed to merge. A reluctant Grattan acquiesced. However, the Irish Catholics remained excluded – at the insistence of George III, and contrary to Pitt's plan. A major grievance was thus left unresolved. The arts of patronage were enough to persuade MPs on all sides in 1801 to accept the Union. But, without structural reforms, they could not build long-lasting consent.[32]

Amidst all these multifarious concerns, the king's ministers also remained alert to domestic politics across England and Wales. Letters and messages constantly criss-crossed, sending information and advice from centre to peripheries and vice versa. Rival deputations from local, commercial, industrial and professional interest groups routinely lobbied central government. And Westminster politicians and local power-brokers worked together in an effort to maintain social order and, from time to time, to promote local 'improvements'.

Prime ministers had so much diverse business to coordinate that the role was not one for the idle or negligent. They also needed canny allies. Robert Walpole in the early eighteenth century deputed political patronage to the indefatigable Duke of Newcastle.[33] Meanwhile, ecclesiastical matters were entrusted to the Low Church Bishop Gibson of London, who also kept an unofficial eye upon the House of Lords.[34] And Walpole prudently shared court and military patronage with George II and his knowledgeable queen, Caroline of Ansbach. Likewise, the Younger Pitt relied upon the tireless Dundas and the efficient Charles Jenkinson, father of another prime minister, Lord Liverpool.[35]

To an extent, these men drew some additional power of command from their high social status. Quite a few had titles. Yet elevated rank did not itself guarantee success. The five Georgian prime ministers, who, as dukes, held the highest non-royal title in the land, all had very short periods at the top.[36] And the best known, Wellington, won his chief renown, and his title, in battle. Instead, working politicians were in demand. One exemplary case was that of a relative outsider, George Canning. He was the son of a failed Anglo-Irish businessman-cum-lawyer and a 'shady' mother who had worked on the stage. Nonetheless, relatives paid for Canning to get a good education. And his brains, oratorical flair and polemical skills brought him advancement as a liberal-conservative protégé of the Younger Pitt. Canning faced down social sneers from politicians on all sides to reach the top in 1827.[37] Alas for him, he died after no more than 119 days in power – logging the shortest premiership in British history. Nonetheless, Canning was an aide who rose because he understood the workings of the job – a portent of the steady professionalisation of politics.

Canning's ministerial efforts in supporting British trade had earlier won him plaudits from commercial interests, although his impetuous duel in 1809 with his colleague Viscount Castlereagh caused some shock. The two men were not only personal but also political rivals. As foreign secretary, Castlereagh played a key role in 1815 in founding a new framework for international diplomacy.[38] In a visionary plan, known as the 'Concert of Europe', the great powers of Britain, Austria, Russia, Prussia and (later) France agreed to convene trouble-shooting congresses in the event of potential conflict.[39] Some meetings were held, one significant one being convened in London in 1830. However, the system eventually collapsed, finding it hard to weld diverse national interests into international concord.

British politicians found themselves at odds over this momentous policy innovation. Patronage was not enough to smooth over disputes on issues of principle. Many of Castlereagh's closest colleagues feared and distrusted his diplomatic involvement with Europe. In 1820 he ruled out any further British military intervention overseas. But his critics were not appeased. As noted above (p. 107), anguished by personal and political worries, Castlereagh committed suicide in 1822. Canning, who succeeded him as foreign secretary, then tilted away from continental Europe towards a greater stress upon global and commercial concerns. The differences between their actual policies were not as deep as used to be thought. Nonetheless, their differing emphases heralded long-running tensions between a predominantly continental European, a potentially global or a defiantly insular focus for British foreign policy.[40] (These debates have become even more central to British politics after 1947 and the 'end of empire', whilst simultaneously raising questions about the survival of the historic Acts of Union.)

Parliaments and Parties

Georgian ministers paid great attention to their Parliaments. The prime minister generally sat in the Commons; and worked closely with the Speakers, who conducted the formal business. Not only were Parliaments summoned regularly, after the first Triennial Act in 1694, but settled conventions were becoming agreed to usher parliamentary bills through the system.[41] It was further accepted, after a row in 1702, that all money bills should be first introduced in the Commons, and that the Lords could not 'tack' financial clauses onto other matters. That practice was ruled as 'unparliamentary' and unconstitutional (and it remains a House of Commons standing order). To settle the rules of constitutional procedure and to safeguard the Commons' privileges, successive Speakers followed the lead of the 'Great Speaker', the long-serving Arthur Onslow.[42]

Above all, Parliament was the supreme forum for debate and, if possible, for the resolution of conflict. MPs when legislating were expected to consider the 'general good'.[43] It was a high ideal. In reality, many MPs had obligations to borough patrons; and in the nineteenth century some MPs were paid agents for colonial lobbies.[44] Yet the ideal was reiterated sufficiently to give it some political purchase. The House of Commons was not 'a congress of ambassadors from different and hostile interests', but 'a deliberative assembly of one nation, with one interest, that of the whole', as Edmund Burke specified in 1774.[45]

Sessions were not held throughout the year, and backbenchers often failed to attend with any assiduity. The Georgian Palace of Westminster, which then housed the law courts as well as the Houses of Parliament, was an ancient, ramshackle building.[46] It had coffee-shops and book-stalls within its purlieu. Yet its accessibility meant that, when big issues were at stake, MPs could hasten into the debating chambers, while citizens jostled in the passages to hear the latest gossip and news. (On one occasion in February 1783 a barking dog intruded into the Commons chamber, disrupting a serious debate about American affairs.)[47]

Keynote speeches were often very lengthy. Points were repeated and re-embroidered, for listeners who had no technological access to replay. Good oratory attracted attention – and votes. Afterwards, bravura contributions also were reconstructed in print and circulated to wider audiences.[48] It counted for something to hear or read renowned speakers like the Elder and Younger Pitts, Charles James Fox, the sonorous Edmund Burke or the playwright and Whig MP, Richard Brinsley 'Sherry' Sheridan, fizzing with wit.

Parliamentary legislation included both privately sponsored acts dealing with individual concerns and general acts pertaining to public affairs. Issues covered ran from family settlements and estate management to agrarian enclosures, bridge-building, establishing turnpike roads, civic improvements, trading policy, navigation laws and Georgian poor law policy. Some matters were introduced as bills but then failed or were withdrawn.[49] Others progressed steadily into law. Thus between 1689 and 1832 the Westminster Parliament passed almost 14,000 acts – a major increase, compared with very low seventeenth-century totals. Legislation was seen as essential to promote and entrench policies. Hence MPs were regularly lobbied by outside interests, and, in turn, they too lobbied ministers to expedite or to kill a bill.[50]

During the entire period from 1710 to 1838, there was a legal requirement that MPs upon election should own a specified amount of freehold land. The aim was a conservative one; but, from the start, candidates found ways to finesse the law. Some purchased the minimum land-holding, while rich patrons aided their bright but impecunious protégés to do the same. Then, after the election, the token estates were quickly resold. Hence, far from being a Parliament entirely of landowners, MPs had multifarious economic interests. Out of a total of 5,034 men elected between 1734 and 1832, over 50 per cent – a high proportion – had commercial, manufacturing or professional interests.[51] Indeed, among all the variegated occupational groups, it was the common lawyers, thronging the nearby law courts, who attended the Commons most regularly.

At times, these MPs were known to bond with like-minded allies to form political parties. These groups were often denounced as 'factious'. One 1747 sermon itemised *The Bad Consequences of Dissention and of Party-Rage*, while another tract of 1784 urged that Britain be saved from *The Calamities in which the Unhappy Divisions of Party have Driven it.*[52] Why don't people of goodwill unite to serve the national need? (It's a viewpoint often expressed.) Such regular complaints, however, indicated not the absence but the presence of organised groups. Yet one big caveat is essential. Georgian parties differed from later mass organisations, with their nationwide memberships, annual conferences, central offices and party whips. Political groupings in the long eighteenth century were fluid. Indeed, the old view, that there were always two rival parties, named Tories and Whigs, battling non-stop through time, was justly challenged by

Namier and his followers.[53] Throughout the long eighteenth century, backbench MPs in particular often maintained their independence and grumbled against 'parties'.

Nevertheless, looser groupings were active, with fluctuating strength and cohesion.[54] In Georgian London there were growing numbers of politically engaged society ladies – a new breed of confident femocrats (to borrow a useful Australian term). They hosted salons and social gatherings which functioned as unofficial party clubs.[55] Thus in the early nineteenth century the respective homes of the opposition Whig grandee Lady Holland, at Holland House in Kensington and the rival establishment figure of Lady Jersey at Osterley Park in west London were significant crucibles, where causes and careers were nurtured. Moreover, like-minded groups at Westminster actively cultivated links with supporters outside Parliament via constituency agents (often lawyers) and local ward organisers.[56] And MPs' wives and daughters often worked to foster the family's political interests too. For instance, after one county election, one elegant countess complained at the damage caused by throwing open her doors for campaign purposes. Not only were her floors ruined by yeoman farmers 'stamping about' in their hobnail boots, but her modish Chinese wallpaper was left stinking of punch and tobacco.[57]

Election contests prompted heightened efforts at wooing voters with rival party slogans, colours, songs, celebrity endorsements and supporters' clubs. The existence of known alignments did not stop politicians from making improbable alliances upon occasion, as happened when Lord North and the opposition Whig Charles James Fox formed a government together in 1783.[58] But their coalition of opposites immediately faltered amidst an outcry of shock and disbelief. In 1770 the ever-eloquent Edmund Burke had already offered a dramatic justification not just for making party alignments but for sticking with them: 'When bad men combine, the good must associate; else they will fall, one by one, an unpitied sacrifice in a contemptible struggle'.[59]

Once Parliament met regularly after 1694, then the fluctuating history of political parties got into its stride. From the start, those labelled as Whigs were supporters of the 1688–89 constitutional reforms and the Toleration Act, whilst Tories were those who stressed their allegiance to monarchical power and to the Anglican Church, worrying that the Toleration Act had gone too far. In 1714, however, the Tory ranks split over whether to support the Jacobites or Hanoverians. A prolonged period of moderate Whig hegemony followed. Walpole and his successors, the brothers Henry Pelham and Thomas Pelham-Holles, 1st Duke of Newcastle, sought a broad consensus – known as a 'broad-bottom' in Georgian parlance.[60] The term 'Whig', first coined in 1679 as a hostile caricature signifying a wild Scottish Presbyterian, assumed more moderate connotations.

Walpole tried to wrong-foot his opponents by dubbing them as either overt rebels or as sinister crypto-Jacobites. His chief critic, however, riposted by counter-attacking on different terrain. Viscount Bolingbroke denounced ministerial 'corruption' and defended liberty against Westminster 'tyranny'.[61] His ideas had traction not only at home but with critics of Britain in North America.[62] Indeed, attacks on 'corruption', with its connotations of moral, fiscal, cultural and biological decay, provide a powerful critique of patronage systems. Bolingbroke did not break the Whig hold on government. Yet he was purging the 'Tory' political label (a caricature dating from 1679, originally signifying a wild Irish Catholic backwoodsman) and trying to reposition conservatism as 'patriotic' opposition.

Then, after realignment in the 1760s, political control shifted away from the moderate Whigs. Instead, there was a prolonged era of conservative rule from 1770 to 1832 – with intermittent short interruptions. As always, the detailed political twists and turns were intricate and often hard to follow. Yet the broad outline was clear. By the later eighteenth century, the perceived 'threats' to British political stability (in the eyes of the nation's rulers) no longer came from the Jacobites but instead from rebellious colonists overseas and radical

reformers at home. That perception helped to sustain a run of traditionalist premiers, known as the 'King's Friends'. They ranged from
the unimaginative Lord North (prime minister 1770–82; 1783), to
the efficacious Younger Pitt (prime minister 1783–1801; 1804–6),
and the stately Lord Liverpool (prime minister 1812–27). They
supported monarchism and Anglicanism, whilst opposing constitutional reform and (worse still) radicalism. In the 1830s, their traditionalist stance morphed into an explicit conservatism. And their
supporters looked back to leaders like the Younger Pitt as heroes.[63]
These self-styled conservatives did not name themselves as 'Tories';
but the old label remained in use – as it still is, however unofficially,
today.[64]

Over time, too, opposition from the left of the political spectrum
was revived and renewed. That stance coalesced around calls for
checks upon an unfettered central government and support for
moderate reform. Opposition Whigs, wearing their blue-and-buff
colours, were led by the raffish but dogged Charles James Fox.[65] His
parliamentary duels with the Younger Pitt became legendary.[66] Fox
in fact faced a major setback in 1794. Edmund Burke and other close
allies shifted to support Pitt in the wartime emergency against
France.[67] But Fox persevered. He argued, against the prevailing
consensus, for a negotiated peace with France. And he ended his
career with a brief window of opportunity for reform, when, in the
'Ministry of All the Talents' of 1806–7, he legislated to end Britain's
role in the slave trade.

Thus the parliamentary system contained alternatives. Politicians
argued and negotiated – and at times switched their positions –
rather than fought in civil wars. Interest groups among the broad-
based property-owning oligarchy formed and reformed as different
issues surfaced. When the conservatives in 1832 became divided
between their own 'diehards' and relative liberals, they lost support –
and the opposition Whigs, led by Fox's heir, Earl Grey, were ready to
initiate constitutional change. Their moderate reformism morphed

in turn into nineteenth-century liberalism.[68] However, the old label of 'Whig' has quietly evaporated, even if patrician reformers may still be teasingly termed 'Whiggish'.

Expectations of adversarial politics between two or more parties were confirmed when the Palace of Westminster was rebuilt, after its accidental burning in 1834. No one favoured a circular auditorium, emulating revolutionary France. Instead, the traditional oblong room, lined by two sets of opposing benches, was reconstructed. Almost a century after the notion of one 'prime minister' had emerged in the 1720s, Georgian party politics by the 1810s had generated the countervailing concept of one 'leader of the opposition'. Yet the unofficial post was unsalaried – as were all MPs before 1911. Parliamentary advocacy, while much esteemed, was viewed as a civic duty to speak on behalf of the people, not as a salaried 'job'.

Civil Servants and Tax Collectors

Administrative underpinning for good governance meanwhile depended upon the expanding civil service.[69] That term was first used in 1785. As ministers were the real powers behind monarchs, so senior civil servants were becoming discreet powers behind prime ministers.[70] Under the aegis of the Treasury, itself descended from the old Exchequer, new specialist departments were formed. By 1800 the Home Office and Foreign Office (expanded from the Crown Secretariat and separated in 1782) were both well established, as were the Post Office (refounded 1660), the Ordnance Board (reorganised 1683), the exemplary Excise Board (1683), the Board of Trade (founded 1696, reorganised 1786), the Admiralty (1709), the War Office (founded 1722), the India Board (established 1784) and the Exchequer Loan Commissioners, later the Public Works Loan Board (1793).[71]

Collectively, these bodies were evolving an ethos of disinterested service to the nation. True, the convention was sometimes broken in practice. But the evolving ethos, derived from a Protestant concept of service, a classical (neo-republican) concept of civic duty and a national bullishness of communal resolve, was crucial in building respect for government and a tolerable willingness, among taxpayers, to fund it.[72]

Collecting taxes efficiently was a sine qua non. Much government funding came from loans raised in the international financial markets. Britain managed that well in this period, because its credit rating, backed by Parliament, was excellent. Moreover, taxation levels in peacetime were low. The land tax remained undervalued after a political fuss from landowners in 1697, when an upwards revaluation was proposed. And in 1733 a similar attempt by Walpole to expand the excise was halted by another furore.[73] By the end of the century, the Younger Pitt was urgently seeking ways of tapping the country's real wealth. In the 1780s he experimented with taxes on windows, gloves, servants and hair powder. Yet wealthy families reacted by blocking windows, shedding gloves, reassigning servants and wearing their hair *au naturel*.

Only in 1799, in the wartime emergency, did Britain see a new income tax introduced. It was deeply unpopular, because it bit deep. The Commons insisted that the tax be rescinded in peacetime. It was thus ended in 1816, even though by then income tax accounted for over half of all government revenue.[74] Its opponents hoped that it was gone for good. (It hadn't.) But it was politically obvious that collecting taxes successfully depended upon taxpayer consent.

Getting that agreement, not only in principle but in practice too, lay behind the eighteenth-century debates on 'corruption'. Public opinion was hostile to politicians and officials who feathered their nests. There was also resentment if appointments to state offices seemed to be made purely to 'buy' support for the government. Hence in 1780 – at a time when Lord North's wartime government was doing badly – the opposition Whigs won a dramatic parliamentary vote on a well-crafted resolution by the lawyer John Dunning. It stated simply that: 'the influence of the crown [i.e. the government] has increased, is increasing, and ought to be diminished'.[75] An ensuing commission in 1786 recommended scrapping many redundant posts.[76] And as the policy was slowly implemented, the number of MPs holding sinecures or pensions fell from *c.* two hundred in 1780 to eighty-nine by 1822, and sixty by 1833. The effect reduced ministerial patronage in the Commons, heightening the role of party loyalty as a rival political 'glue'. (Parties and patronage are not polar opposites, because parties often wield their own patronage. But they represent different principles of group organisation.)

Campaigners continued to canvass further reforms.[77] One vocal critic stirred readers by publishing *The Black Book: Or, Corruption Unmasked!* (1820–23).[78] Patronage, which helped ministers to reward supporters, could not guarantee efficiency. Thus civil service reform remained a simmering issue until the 1850s, when the policy of appointment by merit was introduced.

Dramatically, too, the House of Commons was searching for a suitable way of holding ministers to account. The traditional procedure of impeachment was revived in 1725, when Walpole's lord chancellor Thomas Parker, 1st Earl of Macclesfield was found guilty of taking bribes and fined. After that, Georgian judges were ultra-careful.[79] Yet impeachment was a clumsy device. It required proof of 'high crimes'. And the jurors were fellow politicians.[80] As noted above (p. 164), the impeachment of Dundas in 1806 failed. So did the case against Warren Hastings, Britain's first governor-general in Bengal.[81] Nonetheless, the opening speech by Edmund Burke in 1788 became a classic. He indicted Hastings, thrillingly, in the name of the law, the House of Commons, the British people, the Indian people and 'human nature itself'. Here was stated the clear principle of ministerial accountability, with the implication that good government owes a duty to all humanity. The proposition was epic (and remains fiendishly hard both to invigilate and to enforce).

ᘓ Time-Shift: Then and Now ᘗ

One means of encountering eighteenth-century British constitutionalism is to read – or better still read aloud – these extracts
from Edmund Burke's bravura opening speech, which took
place over four days (15, 16, 18 and 19 February 1788), as he
moved the impeachment of Warren Hastings, Britain's first
governor-general of Bengal, India.

Day 2, 16 February

My Lords, you have now heard the principles on which
Mr. Hastings governs the part of Asia subjected to the
British empire [meaning 'rule', since Britain did not claim a
formal empire in India until 1876] . . . Here he has declared his
opinion that he is a despotic prince; that he is to use arbitrary
power; and, of course, all his acts are covered with that shield
. . . *He* have arbitrary power!—my Lords, the East India
Company have not arbitrary power to give him; the king has
no arbitrary power to give him; your lordships have not; nor
the Commons; nor the whole legislature. We have no arbitrary
power to give, because arbitrary power is a thing which neither
any man can hold, nor any man can give . . .

It is blasphemy in religion; it is wickedness in politics,
to say that any man can have arbitrary power . . . We may bite
our chains, if we will; but we shall be made to know ourselves,
and be taught that man is born to be governed by *law;* and
he that will substitute *will* in the place of it, is an enemy to
GOD . . .

Day 4, 19 February

I impeach Warren Hastings, Esquire, of high crimes and
misdemeanours.

I impeach him in the name of the Commons of Great Britain in Parliament assembled, whose Parliamentary trust he has betrayed.

I impeach him in the name of all the Commons of Great Britain, whose national character he has dishonoured.

I impeach him in the name of the people of India, whose laws, rights and liberties he has subverted; whose properties he has destroyed; whose country he has laid waste and desolate.

I impeach him in the name and by virtue of those eternal laws of justice which he has violated.

I impeach him in the name of human nature itself, which he has cruelly outraged, injured and oppressed, in both sexes, in every age, rank, situation, and condition of life . . .[82]

Hastings pleaded not guilty. Hastings was acquitted, after many adjournments, in 1795. However, he later stated that listening to Burke's opening peroration he felt himself to be 'the most culpable man on earth'. Indeed, Burke's rolling oratory (here much abbreviated) became so famous that the text is often reprinted in collections of great speeches.

⟲ 10 ⟳

Participating in Public Life 'Out of Doors'

O pinion 'out of doors' was how the Georgians referred to the views of the wider public. Attitudes were often diverse and inchoate. Nonetheless, they sometimes had an impact. So Burke in opposition in 1775 noted to an ally that their cause would be 'absolutely crippled if it can obtain no kind of support out of doors'.[1] The cacophony of debate was not new in this period. In Elizabethan London, for example, the theatres had played a key role in circulating ideas. Yet Georgians saw public debates transformed through the combined impact of the end of the press licensing laws in 1695, the burgeoning of print culture and the spread of literacy.[2] News was everywhere in demand. A 1672 poem about the coffee houses had already noted, presciently, the avidity of public interest: 'There's nothing done in all the World,/ From Monarch to the Mouse;/ But every Day or Night 'tis hurl'd/ Into the Coffee-House.'[3]

'Free speech' was becoming a cultural talisman, albeit subject to the laws of libel. And there were creative ways to convey strong opinions. So a tract, entitled *The Art of Railing against Great Men* (1723), recommended that criticisms be made by analogy, such as comparing politicians to foxes or jackals: 'for what can be easier than to say the same dreadful Things of Beasts which are daily uttered in the Coffee-Houses and Clubs against our rational Governors?'[4]

Newspapers began to appear in some numbers.[5] Their contents included snippets of local, national and international news, often recycled from other sources, and advertisements which provided revenue. The first was the *Norwich Post* (1701), followed by London's *Daily Courant* (1702), the *Edinburgh Courant* (1705), and then scores more. One John Walter launched a new paper in London in 1785. It was first entitled the *Daily Universal Register*, before, in a stroke of inspiration, it was renamed *The Times*. Another famous name followed in 1821, when the *Manchester Guardian* was founded. Readerships were primarily local. Yet copies were widely circulated to travel hubs. So Bath's Circulating Library in 1784 stocked twenty-nine newspapers from twenty-four different urban centres, including the *Belfast Newsletter* and one from Dublin.[6]

Furthermore, the influence of the press was boosted, from the 1730s onwards, when sharp-eared journalists began to publish parliamentary reports. Those often contained errors, being based upon hasty shorthand. Yet there was clearly a market for this material. A test case in 1771 confirmed the press's right to report freely. Brass Crosby, the City of London's Lord Mayor (no less), was sent to the Tower by the Commons for treating a printer leniently, who had published the Commons' debates. This drastic punishment of an independent magistrate met with outcry. And the House of Commons backed down. ('Bold as Brass' Crosby is commemorated at his burial-place in Chelsfield, Kent, as a fighter for free speech.) Another confrontation followed in 1810, when the maverick William Cobbett was fined and imprisoned for publishing allegedly 'seditious' libel in his *Political Register*, which was the forerunner of Hansard.[7] He stoically continued to write from gaol. (A statue to Cobbett has recently been unveiled at his birthplace in Farnham, Surrey.)

Wrangling between journalists and politicians long continued. The press's right to publish, however, was becoming undisputed. Journalists saw themselves as the unofficial 'fourth estate' (a term coined in 1787), matching the high claims if not the formal powers of King, Lords and Commons. And some politicians, like George Canning, concurred. In 1822 he spoke of 'the mighty power of Public Opinion, embodied in a Free Press, which pervades, and checks, and perhaps, in the last resort, nearly governs the whole'.[8] It was a great compliment. Yet press power had limitations. Newspapers were discarded, as well as perused. People learned from many sources, including families, friends, neighbours, coffee houses, shops, taverns, clubs, churches, teachers, workplaces – and from books. In other words, newspapers were not controlling powers but, rather, sounding-boards in the great echo-chamber of public debate.

Contested Elections in the Open Constituencies

Given that opinion was often divided, one way to test the strength of rival views was to hold an election. The growing constitutionalism of British culture was seen in the adoption of formal voting by numerous civic bodies, such as gentlemen's clubs, banks, charities and some Nonconformist chapels, where the congregation balloted to choose a preacher.[9] In public affairs, the prime example occurred in the large, open constituencies, where MPs submitted to regular election by their constituents. This feature of Georgian politics is too often overlooked. Critics of the unreformed constitution before the Great Reform Act of 1832 focused their fire upon the patronage or 'pocket' seats, known as the 'rotten boroughs'. The anomaly of places like vanishing Dunwich (on the Suffolk coast) with its thirty-two voters, who from 1298 to 1832 returned two MPs, while fast-growing new urban centres like Manchester and Birmingham returned none, was increasingly hard to defend.

Yet, alongside the many rotten boroughs, there were a number of large 'open' constituencies, which were not controlled by one patron.

Their franchises were characteristically non-standardised. In some cities, the right to vote was vested in local rate-payers; in others, in the freemen; in the City of London, in the members of the Livery Companies (guilds).[10] Everywhere women were excluded by custom, rather than by explicit law, leaving them to lobby and campaign, usually behind the scenes.[11] Yet in big constituencies, like Bristol, London, Newcastle, Norwich and Westminster, the franchise extended 'down' the scale to include middling shopkeepers, traders, industrialists and professionals, as well as journeymen, porters and servants. Elections were thus socially inclusive events. As they cast their votes, rich and comparatively poor electors rubbed shoulders. And when elections in these constituencies were contested (not all were), their votes were taken to indicate public opinion.

Collectively, this electoral experience inaugurated a state of 'proto-democracy'.[12] Immediately after the 1694 Triennial Act, which made three years the upper limit for each Parliament's lifetime, there was an unprecedented frequency of elections. Local rivalries between Tories and Whigs intensified.[13] Individual alignments were often fluid, as noted in the previous chapter; but voters were able to identify polar positions. Key features of electoral partisanship soon sprang into exuberant existence. There were rival policies, slogans, placards, songs, party colours, celebrity endorsements, canvassing, partisan toasting and local ward organisers. In time, too, traders sold partisan tokens, plates, jugs, snuff-boxes and campaign mementos, to consolidate rival loyalties. The classic techniques of democratic politics were being invented.

So intensive was the fervour that in 1716 the Whigs at Westminster opted for a quieter life by promoting the Septennial Act. It extended the maximum life of each Parliament to seven years. That move tried to impose a brake on the proto-democratic ferment. (It was not until 1911 that the maximum term was cut to five years.) Yet, while elections become less frequent, partisan fervour during contests remained high. These events provided a chance to express choice and to resolve conflict by peaceful means. Once votes were counted, the verdict was accepted, although candidates called for a scrutiny if seriously dissatisfied.[14]

Throughout the Georgian era, moreover, the format was one of open voting. Over a period of several days, the length of the poll being determined locally, each elector approached the polling booth to declare his name, his address, his franchisal qualification and his vote. Doubting onlookers were entitled to challenge – and they sometimes did. Thus at a City of Westminster by-election in 1749, there were objections to one Peter Harris, a chandler of Wardour Street: 'It is the common repute of the neighbourhood that he is a Dutchman'.[15] In this case, however, Harris managed to refute the charge and his vote stood.

This episode showed how elections were monitored not just by presiding officials but by neighbourhood crowds, who often attended in some numbers. That public element of voting made it the purest form of electoral choice, according to the later verdict of the philosopher John Stuart Mill.[16] Not only did electors stand up, literally, to be counted but, afterwards, the poll books were published, listing all votes. Hence each elector's choice remained on the record for everyone to read – and for party canvassers to use at the next election.

Needless to say, there were some potential electors who did not use their votes; and some who did so in a state of confusion. At times, too, proceedings were disrupted by riots or affrays. In Westminster in 1741, an irate crowd 'threw dirt, stones, sticks, dead cats and dogs, so that the candidates, high bailiff, clerks and inspectors were obliged to retire into the church'. After a protest, the election was ruled to be invalid. Yet that drastic outcome was unique among all eighteenth-century contests. More common were pressures from partisan crowds, scuffles and loud chanting. On one disastrous occasion in 1784 a constable, summoned to keep order, was bludgeoned by an unidentified assailant and later died of his wounds. Generally, however, the big parliamentary contests were conducted with sufficient (if rowdy) order. Meanwhile, there were regular elections too for a multitude of municipal and ward posts, including some notable struggles over the London mayoralty.[17] These civic contests, whose results were printed in the local press, were much calmer affairs.[18]

At times, fears were expressed that voters were subject to 'treating', when party organisers made drinks available in local alehouses. A warning came from an anonymous American colonist in 1770, who proclaimed: 'That Great Britain will One Day Fall and that Glorious Constitution, which is the Envy of the World, Crumble into Ruin by the Influence of Corruption in Elections, No Body seems to Doubt'.[19] This diatribe paid a backhanded compliment to Britain's constitutionalist reputation. Yet its warning was exaggerated, at least in the case of the big open constituencies, with their thousands of voters. Those places were beyond the control of just one local power broker. Moreover, research into those open constituencies where individual electoral histories can be traced has shown that voters regularly displayed considerable discipline, sticking with their party from election to election, rather than changing tack for the price of a drink.[20]

Voting to select between rival candidates inculcated the concept of rational choice, even if seasoned by slogans, jibes and invective. The open nature of the process also fostered community participation, including from non-voters who came to witness, often generating a carnival atmosphere. There were chants, cheers and jeers as candidates spoke on the hustings. The tally of votes was posted at the end of each day, spurring extra effort from ward organisers. It was a form of basic political education. And, once the result was known, successful candidates were chaired through the streets. Aloft in a chair at King's Lynn, the new MP Horace Walpole nervously felt 'like the figure of a pope at a bonfire'.[21]

Candidates invariably addressed their electors with deep respect, saluting them as 'free' and 'independent'. After all, parliamentary elections marked a special moment of social inversion, when high-status politicians wooed electors from the middling and lower ranks.[22] As a result, electoral tracts were written in accessible styles, with catchy slogans. The entire electoral process, while not leading to the choice of a new government (a matter for negotiation between kings and ministers), allowed voters to put pressure on their MPs. Moreover, electors were keen to maintain their independence. In 1741, Robert Walpole manoeuvred to oust one of his vociferous political critics from the Denbighshire county seat. But disallowing many votes cast for a local landowner caused outrage. The rejected candidate regained the seat, on appeal to Parliament, and the sheriff, who had abetted Walpole, was imprisoned for electoral fraud.

One political thinker who meditated upon the relationship between MPs and their electors was Edmund Burke, who was, as ever, in the thick of things. Speaking to his Bristol electors in 1774 he explained that, as their MP, he would be their representative, not their mandated delegate. He would thus follow his own judgment. Yet Burke pledged simultaneously that an MP must work hard for his constituents: 'it is his duty to sacrifice his repose, his pleasures, his satisfactions, to theirs'.[23] (A high ideal.) In fact, Burke quit the seat in 1780, after disagreements with leading Bristol merchants over commercial issues. His departure for the quiet of a pocket borough indicated that 'open' electoral politics required a degree of accommodation all round. Nonetheless, a constitutionalist system was being forged by the Georgians, with participating voters and witnessing crowds.

From the 1740s onwards, the number of elections which were contested began to increase, and accelerated again from the 1780s. Thousands of voters understood the procedures and carried them out calmly. That point was stressed in 1832 by a later Whig reformer, Lord Macaulay. He reassured traditionalists, who were worried at the prospect of franchisal reform, that lower-class London electorates undertook their electoral responsibilities seriously. 'Experience, I say, therefore, is on our side.'[24] In the event, it took pressures both inside and outside Parliament to gain victory for the reform-minded Whigs. But, once passed, there was no backtracking from the principles of the Great Reform Act.[25] Across England and Wales, 143 borough seats were abolished. Birmingham, Leeds, Manchester and nineteen other large urban centres gained two MPs apiece and twenty-one smaller towns got one MP. And a newly uniform franchise was instituted for all urban constituencies, embracing all adult males with property worth at least £10 per annum. Similar legislation was passed for both Ireland and Scotland, where the size of the electorates was massively enlarged.

There was, however, one problem with the new 1832 franchise. It instituted a middle-class electorate on standard criteria. However, its impact was problematic in the big open constituencies. The new property qualification would have disenfranchised numerous working-class voters. Parliament, however, respected their prior constitutional rights. All established voters were free to continue voting in the constituencies where they were enfranchised. Thus in some places working-class electors continued to vote alongside the new middle-class electorate post-1832. That compromise did not mean that full democracy was one day inevitable. (History can spring surprises.) It did mean, however, that Parliament was not prepared to disenfranchise experienced voters. Hence some working-class men voted, long before the later extensions of the franchise in 1867 and 1884. Proto-democracy Georgian-style thus provided an accepted mechanism for opinion 'out of doors' to convey messages to those in power.

Street Politics and Riots

Direct action remained another option for aggrieved citizens. It generally took the form of impromptu public demonstrations, which often, but not invariably, escalated into angry riots, often with damage to property and (sometimes) loss of life.[26] In the very long term the incidence of such confrontations is falling, whilst participation in organised campaigning rises, with the spread of literacy and democracy. However, there was (and is) no sharp dividing line between orderly and disorderly protests. Historically, many rioters came from the disenfranchised masses, but enfranchised electors, if sufficiently angry or energised, do at times take to the streets in protests which may become rumbustious and out of control. (Indeed, plenty of evidence confirms that unruly gatherings have by no means disappeared in the era of mass democracies.)

The riotous Georgian masses did not emerge out of the blue. Rather, they were reacting to matters of serious concern, especially when other forms of redress seemed unavailable to them. Characteristic triggers to riots included: a steep rise in food prices, an unresolved wage dispute, a sudden rise in unemployment, unpopular taxation (anti-excise; anti-turnpikes), hostility to conscription (anti-pressganging), anger at costly entertainments (theatre riots), political antagonisms (election riots) and religious rivalries (including anti-Dissenter, anti-Methodist and anti-Catholic protests). However, as noted above (pp. 26–7), for over two centuries after 1689 there were no major riots directed against immigrant groups.[27]

A common procedure for disaffected crowds was to gather at known meeting-places, such as a market cross or common land, where drums and kettles were banged to arouse support. Symbolic items were ritually paraded, signifying popular grievances (a weaver's loom draped in black; a loaf of bread on a pole). Crowds also pressurised magistrates by shouting, hooting or 'groaning' at them.[28] Such actions initiated a rough-and-ready form of popular bargaining with the powers that be. As a result, the magistrates were sometimes able to provide at least limited redress, if they sympathised with the rioters' complaints. And central government was at times open to pressure, when extensive popular riots coincided with political lobbying within the system. So for example, that conjunction convinced Walpole in 1733 to drop his plans to extend the unpopular excise tax.[29]

Communal features of such riotous protests were particularly marked if women were present. They were often visible in market riots, not only in Britain but also in eighteenth-century France,

Germany and North America.[30] At times, too, protesting men wore dresses and shawls to escape detection. The Rebecca Riots in south Wales between 1839 and 1843, which opposed new tollgates as an oppressive tax on travel, were famed for their activist men, dressed as women. They blackened their faces, but wore white gowns, symbolically representing purity and female nurturing.[31] Those real-life women who did participate in riots were often denounced by critics as 'Viragos' or 'Amazons', just as all rioters were dismissed as insensate or insurrectionary 'mobs'.

Market protests were the most frequent of all Georgian popular tumults, and occurred in all three kingdoms. They were usually triggered by sudden spikes in grain prices, indicating local shortages – and, in some years in eighteenth-century Ireland, near-famine. The year 1766 saw the greatest number of all market riots, although they did not occur everywhere. Other poor harvests leading to unrest occurred in 1709, 1740, 1756/7, 1773, 1782–83, 1795 and 1800–1.[32] It was not uncommon for determined crowds to begin by seizing stocks of grain and selling them cheaply at a 'just price', although disorder then tended to escalate. Magistrates typically responded by trying to curb disorder, whilst procuring additional supplies, if available. In the peak crisis in 1766, the government instituted a temporary embargo on all grain exports.[33] Later, too, in the difficult 1790s, the Younger Pitt's ministry imported foreign grain specifically to feed London, where angry crowds posed a political danger.

Evidently, the authorities and rioters had contending views about how markets should operate. But equally clearly, the crowds were not purely 'mindless'. Instead, the historian E.P. Thompson argued that they favoured a community-based 'moral economy', as opposed to an unfettered commercial economy. His terminology has aroused contention.[34] It implies that the masses had a greater unity of beliefs than was probably the case. It also could be taken to imply that those opposing the crowds, for whatever reasons, were somehow 'immoral'. Nonetheless, Thompson showed successfully that the Georgian rioters had serious motives, which need to be understood historically, not just dismissed.

Some protests developed a festive atmosphere. At Nottingham's Goose Fair Riot in 1766, giant cheeses were rolled along the street, one knocking out the mayor, who was trying to reassert control.[35] Other protests, by contrast, were more aggressive but highly targeted. So in July 1719, unemployed journeymen weavers in Norwich slashed with knives at the imported calico (printed linen) dresses worn by well-to-do-ladies. Respectable society was shocked. Magistrates saw such actions as subversive *and* immoral. Yet the weavers were defending their textile industry against competitive imports, which were taking custom from them. And their militancy in this case helped to pressurise Walpole's government, which yielded to lobbying from the master weavers and introduced anti-calico legislation in 1721.[36]

Other protests, however, became much more brutal. In Edinburgh in April 1736, an indignant crowd stoned the City Guard, following the hanging of a popular smuggler. Their captain John Porteous ordered his men to fire, which they did, killing six protestors. He was later convicted of murder. But in September 1736 another crowd, fearing a reprieve, stormed the Tolbooth Prison, extracted Porteous, and lynched him.[37] The captain's fate entered legend, as recounted in Scott's *Heart of Midlothian* (1818).[38] The Porteous Riot was unusual in targeting one specific individual. (The ringleaders, incidentally, were never caught, despite offers of a reward.) Another riot, triggered in Newcastle upon Tyne in June 1740, attacked a different target. After a local plan to reduce high grain prices collapsed, irate Newcastle keelmen (the doughty boatmen who serviced the city's river port) and nearby mineworkers marched in protest. Shots were fired at the crowds. They retaliated by pelting the aldermen with stones and sacking Newcastle's Guildhall, burning the city's records.[39]

In both these cases, the official tactics of control affected the behaviour of the crowds, who resented anything seen as excess force.

Magistrates thus needed a judicious combination of firmness and negotiating skills. Legally, their responses were governed by the 1714 Riot Act, which remained on the statue book until 1967. It decreed that a disorderly group was not legally riotous until one hour after the magistrate had literally 'read the Riot Act' aloud to the crowd (the relevant text was brief). Sometimes protestors then simply dispersed. But, if they did not, the authorities were entitled to use a measure of force, calling upon any available troops.[40] The law was deliberately cautious, reflecting long-held fears of military interventionism – a lesson learned at the time of Cromwell. Protestors also understood the process. Thus in Montrose in 1812 the magistrate was interrupted while reading the Riot Act. One Elizabeth Beattie shouted: '*Will no person take that paper out of his hand?*' before attempting to do so herself.[41]

Although the system of curbing riots was cumbersome, it gave the magistrates an element of discretion. Upon occasions, indeed, they connived at early stages of popular protests, if they shared the crowd's distaste for the chosen targets. Some Anglican magistrates seem to have winked at anti-Methodist affrays in the 1750s. And the same attitude was seen in Birmingham in 1790, when rioters supporting the cause of 'Church-and-King' targeted the property of leading Dissenters.[42] The house and laboratory of the Unitarian Joseph Priestley were razed. He left the place for good, his optimism severely dented. Another Birmingham Dissenter, the businessman William Hutton, was equally horrified at the venom displayed against him, as his house, shop and warehouse were all wrecked.[43] On this occasion, the magistrates were willing (literally) to play with fire, to obtain a local political advantage. On the other hand, they did not want continued unrest; and in 1792 they halted further harassment of Hutton.

Generally, indeed, the nation's power-brokers were suspicious of too much street politics. And that attitude became even more marked after the incendiary Gordon Riots in London in June 1780.[44] The anti-Catholic agitator Lord George Gordon led huge demonstrations to petition against a bill to relax penalties on Catholics. Many Presbyterian Scots participated, full of anti-Popish zeal. (In 1779, Scottish Catholics in Edinburgh had already been attacked.) In 1780, one London constable, William Payne of Bell Yard, was so stirred by his militant Protestant zeal that he joined the protest.[45] For three days, the authorities dithered. Without opposition, the crowds became militant. Prisons were attacked, prisoners freed and Newgate Prison burned. Wealthy homes, including that of the Lord Chief Justice, were sacked. And the Bank of England was attacked – but not the Houses of Parliament. Eventually, troops were deployed. They killed several hundred and wounded as many. Many rioters were arrested and, in a show of rough justice, a few executed. Gordon was tried for treason but acquitted. London's mayor meanwhile was fined for failing to keep order, as in 1736 Edinburgh's Lord Provost was penalised for not halting the Porteous Riots.

The potential vulnerability of civic order was apparent. William Blake, who may have joined the crowds before the burning Newgate, poetically foretold such a terminal combustion: when 'the five gates were consumed, and their bolts and hinges melted;/ And the fierce flames burnt round the heavens and round the abodes of men'.[46] On the other hand, the Gordon rioters had unsure aims and no clear victory. Respectable reformers and Dissenters, who initially supported the anti-Catholic petition, recoiled as violence escalated. So there was no later glorification of either Gordon or the rioters in popular memory.

Hence the liberating of Newgate Prison in 1780 did not rank politically or psychologically with the fall of Paris's Bastille in 1789. By way of example, Charles Dickens's later novelising of the Gordon Riots in *Barnaby Rudge* (1841) was lacklustre in comparison with his intense account of the French Revolution: in *A Tale of Two Cities* (1859) he initially sympathised with the oppressed masses but then recoiled from revolutionary violence.[47] After 1780, indeed, there was

190

a heightened fear, especially among property-owners, that crowd protests might get dangerously out of hand. Furthermore, after Birmingham's 'Church-and-King' confrontations in 1790, leading reformers were aware they too might upon occasion become targets of popular hostility. Violence as a political weapon was double-edged.

Sporadic riotous protests continued, in an unplanned way (as they still do), arising out of strong popular feelings, albeit tempered by the forces of order. At times, militant protests made highly topical interventions. So the Bristol riots of 1831, challenging aristocratic opponents of constitutional reform, added a sense of urgency to the issue.[48] However, over three days the protests escalated. Rioters besieged the mayor's residence, attacked property and looted. In the chaos and military counter-charge, lives were lost. Later, the mayor was tried for negligence but acquitted. Four rioters were hung, despite a big petition for clemency. And the lieutenant-colonel in charge was court-martialled for undue leniency, shooting himself before his trial was ended. These outcomes were too messy and complex for the formation of a straightforwardly heroic legend.

Unsurprisingly, those seeking reforms began to consider other alternatives. After Peterloo, when an unarmed and peaceful assembly in 1819 was treated as though it was a riot (see below, p. 195), Shelley penned a poetic appeal to the masses: 'Stand ye calm and resolute,/ Like a forest close and mute,/ With folded arms and looks which are/ Weapons of unvanquished war'.[49] However, his ringing call for symbolic non-violence, which swayed later advocates of civil disobedience, had no great contemporary impact. Instead, many Georgian reformers were already seeking to convey public opinion via the power of organisation.

Reform Associations

Reform associations, seeking civic or constitutional improvements, formed part of the web of countless clubs and societies which were so characteristic of Georgian society. They depended upon ad hoc initiatives by individuals and small groups. Yet reform associations were increasingly being structured into national networks, with local branches in contact with a central team, together campaigning for the long term.

William Wilberforce was a campaigner buoyed by faith in the civic power of collective action. Apart from his role in anti-slavery movements, he also founded a new voluntary Society for the Suppression of Vice (1787; refounded 1802),[50] co-founded the Church Missionary Society (1799), and in 1824 the Society for the Prevention of Cruelty to Animals (the latter two still thriving). He saw that he had much more clout with organised backing than he had as a lone MP. Yet, to gain success, a cause had to reflect as well as to boost the tide of public opinion.[51] Notable Georgian associations promoted their own 'good causes': ranging from moral reform (first launched in 1699 by the Society for the Reformation of Manners), to missionary activity overseas, to social welfare at home, and on to a variety of trade union organisations among skilled workers. Such groups were both community-based and individualised, seeking active personal commitment to support, to lobby, to spread the word and, where possible, to provide funding.

Particularly significant from the late 1760s onwards were societies seeking systematic constitutional changes, including 'full and equal representation' of the adult male population. The first were organised by reform-minded individuals from respectable middle- and upper-class backgrounds. It was true that bodies like the Society for the Supporters of the Bill of Rights (1769–75), the Yorkshire Association (1780–84), the Society for Constitutional Information (1780–94) and the Whig Society of Friends of the People (1792–94) all failed in the short-term.[52] Yet they foretold the power of organised extra-parliamentary campaigning, as they held demonstrations, organised branches and developed alternative programmes. Some also used mass petitions. Those devices had been used before: in the warring

1640s, and by critics of Lord North's blundering policies in America.[53] Petitions in particular fused the authenticity of individual signatures (even if some were faked) into mass pressure from 'out of doors'.

Most notably of all, in the course of the ideologically charged 1790s, lower-class reformers also started their own organisations.[54] The pioneering body was the London Corresponding Society. It forged links with other radical associations across urban-industrial Britain – in places like Birmingham, Edinburgh, Glasgow, Manchester, Newcastle upon Tyne, Norwich, Perth and Sheffield.[55] The rank-and-file were 'honest men with leathern aprons', as one activist specified in 1794.[56] And leaders of the Sheffield Constitutional Society similarly stated themselves to be 'plain mechanics ... who are not gentlemen'.[57]

Embracing universal principles, they sought to transcend localism. Their radical call for adult male democracy had many roots, including the manifest experience of active voters in the big open constituencies. Some LCS leaders, like the Scottish-born London shoemaker Thomas Hardy, were also motivated by radical Nonconformity, stressing the equality of all believers. Others were inspired by England's seventeenth-century opponents of tyrannical kings. John Thelwall, the LCS's most powerful orator, named two sons as John Hampden Thelwall and Algernon Sydney Thelwall respectively, invoking earlier heroes of constitutional protest.[58] Others were enthused by the new American constitution (although its initial franchise excluded slaves). Thomas Paine, after returning to Britain from the USA, codified the democratic case in *The Rights of Man* (1791).[59] Emboldened, the LCS copied an opposition tactic from the Yorkshire Association. That body had summoned a constitutional convention in Edinburgh (1780) as a national forum.[60] In 1792 and again in 1793, the LCS did likewise.

However, it was difficult to coordinate support across working-class Britain. Furthermore, within the movement there were rival advocates of peaceful campaigning (the majority), or of armed protest (rumours of their actions serving to alarm respectable opinion). Meanwhile, meetings of the LCS were penetrated by government spies and informants.[61] Radical agitation was (and is) highly likely to generate countervailing action from alarmed opponents who support the status quo. In 1792, a new Association for Preserving Liberty and Property *against* Republicans exaggerated the aims of the LCS. It was not a republican organisation. Yet the Association's stark name neatly identified its own conservative fears and helped it to rally considerable support.[62]

Legal measures were also invoked to curb organised lower-class activism. In 1793 five Scottish radicals were tried before a hostile judge and sentenced to transportation. (The 1844 monument to these 'Scottish Martyrs' remains silhouetted on Edinburgh's skyline at Old Calton Hill.) And then in 1794 key leaders of the Whiggish reform Society for Constitutional Information and the LCS were put on trial in London for the crime of high treason. Sensationally, they were acquitted.[63] But an alarmed William Pitt the Younger responded by toughening the treason laws in 1795 and banning large outdoor meetings. He also ordered the construction of inland army barracks in populous towns, so that troops were readily available to enforce order.[64] Eventually in 1799, when calling for national solidarity in the wartime emergency, Pitt obtained legislation to ban the LCS outright (by name).[65] For good measure, too, he also persuaded Parliament to debar all 'unlawful combinations and confederacies', hence technically halting in its tracks the nascent trade union movement as well.[66]

Thereafter, this pattern of patchy but determined radical campaigning, followed by government repression, proved to be a common one. It was hard to convince the never-enfranchised that having the vote would help them, and harder still to persuade or force Parliament to adopt a change of such magnitude. Most respectable property-owners in this era thought it absurd and socially dangerous to give the vote to the under-educated, poorly literate, property-less masses, who constituted the 'Great Unwashed' (a term coined later, in 1830).

Opposing viewpoints remained clearly apparent in the 1810s, when democratic campaigning again revived. In particular, radicals and conservatives differed utterly over the bloodshed in St Peter's Field, Manchester, in August 1819. A big unarmed demonstration in favour of franchisal reform was charged by the panicked Yeomanry Cavalry (the Home Guard), their sabres drawn. In the mêlée, known as the Peterloo Massacre, at least eighteen people were killed and hundreds injured.[67] Yet Lord Liverpool in Westminster feared only a return to instability. He renewed the legislative repression, along the lines of the clampdown under the Younger Pitt in 1797. Calls for an inquiry into policing tactics had no success. Peterloo thus left reformers with a sorrowing legacy of popular heroism – and deep resentment at an undeserved attack upon a peaceful rally.

While not all excluded from the franchise were keen to vote (and subsequently voting in democracies has not proved as popular as the Georgian radicals had hoped), calls for enfranchisement were not permanently silenced. Radical campaigning re-emerged strongly in the mid-1830s, when the Chartists produced their six-point reform charter.[68] They developed yet more inventive organisational stratagems, including small Chartist churches and experimental Chartist land settlements.[69] En route, there was one big confrontation. In 1839 the Newport Rising in Monmouth caused shock-waves, as it teetered between a mass demonstration and an armed uprising.[70] Optimistic plans for a middle- and working-class reform alliance, proposed by Joseph Sturge, a Birmingham Quaker businessman, came to nothing, chiefly because of middle-class fears of Newport-style disorder.[71] Chartism, after its last big rally in 1848, also faded.

Against these radicals were ranged not only most property-owners but also the police and the army. However, civil government was not routinely militarised. As protests unfolded, heavy-handed responses at the wrong time could inflame rather than deter the populace.

Instead, officialdom tried to keep order with a mix of legal controls, exhortation, partial concessions (not always possible), local policing, and at times covert spying upon 'agitators'. Armed troops were generally used as backup, if order collapsed.[72] They then resolved matters with military 'rough justice'. But when the use of force was disproportionate, as most notoriously at Peterloo, it generated long-term popular resentment, defiance and anti-militarism, as circulated in songs and ballads.[73]

Organised campaigning, despite obvious setbacks, was gaining ground. It was less chaotic than rioting and might win partial concessions, even if not total success.[74] Numerous Georgians, nominally outside the political system, were gaining first-hand experience in civic activism. And as they did so, they were also finding that, just as riots prompted counter-reactions, so radical associations might prompt opposition from conservative counter-organisations. The world of pressure groups in a mass society was pluralistic and competitive. And public opinion, complete with its own divisions between rival and often unequal lobby groups, was becoming a factor with which national politicians had to reckon.

Wilkes, Liberty and the Sovereign People?

If asked 'Where in eighteenth-century Britain does (terrestrial) power lie?' most educated Georgians would reply with the stock phrase 'Crown-in-Parliament'. However, it took a series of constitutional test cases to clarify the working of the system in practice. In the eye of the storm was John Wilkes, a wealthy, witty and rakish Clerkenwell distiller's son with a gift for publicity.[75] His political journalism infuriated Bute's government in the early 1760s. Using a general warrant, issued under royal prerogative powers, Wilkes's home was raided by court officials and his private papers seized. A public outcry followed. In the ensuing test case, general warrants were declared illegal (and so confirmed by Parliament in 1766). In

effect, individual rights were upheld against the might of the executive. (This decision was echoed in the fourth amendment to the new
American constitution, which in 1791 banned arbitrary search
warrants.)[76] Having won his case, the irrepressible Wilkes sued for
wrongful arrest – and won damages.

Georgian culture was deeply legalistic, as seen in the contemporary saying (1732): 'be you never so high, the Law is above you' (the
principle which Burke adduced so powerfully against Warren
Hastings).[77] So Parliament, as the legislative branch, was equally
expected not to act capriciously. Again it was Wilkes who forced
another key issue, this time about determining disputed election
results. Between 1768 and 1774, he stood five times for election as
MP for Middlesex. Each time he topped the poll. Yet on four occasions, Parliament disallowed the result. Wilkes had in 1764 been
found guilty of seditious libel (as later was William Cobbett) and was
technically disqualified. However, after his fifth success in Middlesex,
Parliament yielded. Comparable cases in Britain remain very few in
number.[78] Nonetheless, Wilkes's victory set an unchallenged prece-
dent, indicating that electors, if they stand firm, have the final voice.

Within Britain's constitutionalist system, the 'people' thus
remained the ultimate 'sleeping' or reserve power.[79] Not that main-
stream opinion expected the populace to participate directly.
Nonetheless, radicals used the principle to put the case for wider
democracy. In 1776 it was Wilkes who moved (unsuccessfully) the
first reform bill in Parliament. His chameleon career, transitioning
from giddy rake to gadfly-journalist to radical hero and later to
conservative Mayor of London, meant that his legacy was not
straightforward. Yet Wilkes's victories were key blows against arbitrary action, whether from the executive or the legislative branch of
government – and were achieved only with the aid of popular protest
'out of doors'. Of course, the masses did not rule, whether directly or
indirectly. But the 'good people of Great-Britain' (in the eighteenth
century's polite rhetoric) were far from entirely powerless either.[80]

⟳ Time-Shift: Then and Now ⟳

To experience the force and humours of a large crowd 'out of doors' – and to consider how such events are best policed – try mingling, either virtually or personally, at big communal social or sporting events with Georgian (or even older) roots.

1. The Georgian Festival at Stamford, Lincolnshire. Held in the autumn, the festival is an updated version of the town's former bull-running festival: see https://stamfordgeorgianfestival.co.uk. Or, attend any other large urban or rural fair or festival with historic roots.

2. The annual Royal Shrovetide football match at Ashbourne, Derbyshire. Also known as hugball, the match is played over two days on Shrove Tuesday and Ash Wednesday, in a tradition with medieval roots which was certainly 'live' in Georgian times: see https://www.visitpeakdistrict.com/inspiration/blog/read/2019/02/your-guide-to-the-famous-ashbourne-royal-shrovetide-football-b104. Or, attend any other well-attended ball-game with historic roots.

3. Any large-scale tournament held at the Royal and Ancient Golf Club of St Andrews, Fife (founded 1754; and with continuous records since 1766). See https://www.randa.org/heritage/the-royal-ancient/the-royal-ancient-golf-club. Or, attend any other large golfing event at a historic venue.

4. The Epsom Derby (first run 1780) in north-east Surrey, especially on People's Saturday in early June: see https://www.thejockeyclub.co.uk/Epsom. Or, attend any other historic race meeting known as a 'derby', after the original.

5. Cowes Yacht Week, Isle of Wight, Hampshire, inaugurated 1826, following the establishment of the Royal Yacht Club (later Squadron) at Cowes in 1815, and boosted by patronage from the Prince Regent, later George IV: see http://www.cowesweek.co.uk. Or, attend any other well-attended nautical regatta.

6. The International Marching Bands Festival, Limerick, Ireland. Held annually on or around St Patrick's Day (17 March), the festival celebrates and showcases a long Irish tradition of commemorative marching bands: see https://www.limerick.ie/st-patricks-festival/limerick-international-band-championship/about-limerick-international-band. Or, attend any other well-attended music festival or carnival with historic roots.

ᥴᕔ 11 ᥱᕓ

Seeking Social Solutions at Home

The potential for protest ensured that, for reasons of prudence as well as of communal solidarity, the powers that be had an interest in maintaining social order and preventing discontent from escalating to dangerous levels. Coordinating mass societies and achieving collective harmony was a continuing preoccupation of Georgian social thought.[1] One ideal type of successful communal order was the beehive: 'A Spacious Hive, well stock'd with Bees,/ That lived in Luxury and Ease', versified the Anglo-Dutch political economist Bernard de Mandeville in 1705.[2] Its connotations were harmonious, productive and familiar. On the other hand, the beehive model did not help to explain or to resolve conflicts within human societies en masse.

Mandeville himself was aware of the complexities. His *Grumbling Hive* was a satire. It asked what would happen if all bees really lived simply and honestly. In response, Mandeville argued that strict morality would actually be harmful. Successful commerce relied upon the sophisticated knavery of traders and a self-indulgent love of luxury on the part of consumers. Hence Mandeville's paradoxical verdict that 'publick benefits' sprang from 'private vices'. In a terse conclusion, he added that some checks would still protect the general good: 'So Vice is beneficial found,/ When it's by Justice lopped and bound'.[3] However, Mandeville's final remark had much less impact than his depiction of an amoral and competitive economy, which he was often taken as endorsing.[4]

In practice, the beehive long remained a symbol for social order and harmony. (It was invoked in early Freemasonry and by Britain's nineteenth-century co-operative movement.) And Georgian society had plenty of visionary advocates of community-based alternatives, like the radical egalitarian Thomas Spence. In 1793, his *Real Rights of Man* proposed the common ownership of land. For good measure, Spence also invented a simplified phonetic script, intended to erase class differentials in literacy.[5] His efforts constituted one of many examples of utopian and visionary projects in this era.[6]

Alongside such communitarian visions, however, an alternative emphasis was also coming to the fore, one based upon individual 'rights'. The concept was familiar, being derived from law. 'Rights' were innate entitlements, not gifts conferred by the 'grace' of powerful kings or lords. Potentially, too, that doctrine could have radical implications – if invoked by people traditionally viewed as 'outsiders', like women, workers and enslaved Africans.

Yet whose claims were justifiable? There was no final court of socio-political arbitration. The result was a competitive society, jostling to assert rival rights and interests. Furthermore, within the human beehive, the affluent often had contradictory attitudes: hoping for low-cost welfare, yet fearing the dangers of disorder should the impoverished become too unruly. These competing pressures combined to shape the Georgians' evolving social policies.

Coping with Disabilities

A heightened awareness of the personal identity of each individual was helping to inculcate a greater sensitivity towards people with disabilities. It was becoming less acceptable to jeer at deformity or to guffaw if (say) a blind person bumped unknowingly into a brick wall. In fact, an old-style comic literature of cruelty was still published and enjoyed.[7] Yet the attitudes which it conveyed were being pushed onto the defensive, especially in respectable circles.[8]

Improved technology began to offer practical assistance to people with disabilities. Those with hearing difficulties could use new ear trumpets, which worked (in the era before amplification) by funnelling sounds. Those with poor vision were aided by improved eyeglasses, with fine-ground lenses, while all could look further with stronger telescopes and peer more closely with refined microscopes. There were new surgical techniques too. One pioneer was George III's German oculist, Baron Michael de Wenzel, who improved treatments for cataracts. By 1804, medical know-how had advanced sufficiently for London's Moorfields Hospital to emerge as a specialist centre for eye disease.[9] Practical help was also available for the young. In some large cities (Edinburgh, Newcastle, Norwich), asylums for blind children provided special training. And in 1791 Britain's longest running School for the Blind (now the Royal School) was founded in Liverpool by a group of philanthropists including the renowned blind poet and anti-slavery campaigner Edward Rushton.[10]

Meanwhile, therapists for people with hearing and speech difficulties were experimenting with what became codified into British Sign Language. One famous 'Academy for the deaf and dumb' was founded in Edinburgh by the Scottish educationalist Thomas Braidwood. Its most famous pupil was the deaf astronomer John Goodricke, who identified variant starlight signals, became a Fellow of the Royal Society, and won its Copley Medal, before dying at the age of twenty-two.[11] Another notable speech therapist was the radical orator John Thelwall. In the early nineteenth century, he redirected his political energies into running a special school for remedial elocution in London: a practical form of giving voice to the silent.[12]

All this interventionism helped to discourage fatalism. Disability was no longer an inescapable 'doom'. The mix of technology, therapy, treatment and special schooling served to boost change, as did the achievements of individuals who overcame handicaps. Thus Dr Johnson – no giddy enthusiast for innovation – was moved to observe, after visiting Braidwood's Edinburgh academy in 1773, that 'It was pleasing to see one of the most desperate of human calamities capable of so much help'.[13]

Many eighteenth-century doctors were similarly hopeful that they could assist patients with mental disorders. Traditional remedies included purges to cast out 'evil spirits', which were thought to have seized control. But up-to-date Georgians no longer saw 'lunacy' as a sign of demonic possession. Instead, the condition was becoming understood as a grievous illness, for which due legal acknowledgement was needed. Highly important in that respect was a new law in 1774, which required all private asylums to be registered and inspected annually. Crucially, too, patients were to be confined only by order of a qualified doctor. Before that, sufferers were processed by ad hoc 'commissions of lunacy'. For instance the father-in-law of the mercurial poet Christopher Smart obtained his committal into an asylum for seven years, before Smart was released in 1763 into the care of his adult children.[14] Medical controls were not infallible, but they offered some safeguard against abuse. Equally, an evolving Georgian case law allowed individual sufferers to plead insanity as a legal defence to a criminal charge. So emerged a set of conventions, codified in 1843 as the M'Naghten rules, which remain cited in many criminal jurisdictions to this day.[15]

However, the diversity of mental disorders was medically perplexing.[16] Furthermore, 'madness' could strike anyone. Best known was the case of George III. (It was later argued that his malady was porphyria, which causes confusion and hallucinations. But other experts disagree – and retrospective diagnosis is not a precise science.) In the event, the king recovered from his first illness in 1788, making his 'mad-doctor' Francis Willis instantly famous. However, the king's incapacity recurred, at first intermittently, and then, after 1810, permanently. Blind, deaf and amnesiac, George III lived his last years in seclusion.[17] There was no happy ending, after all.

Questing 'mad-doctors' began to seek alternative treatments. In 1796, the Quaker William Tuke demonstrated a new system at his York Retreat. His enlightened programme involved individually tailored educational plans for every patient and the abandonment of physical shackles. However, the Retreat's formula was hard to replicate everywhere. It catered for only thirty fee-paying patients, and its labour-intensive 'moral treatment' was costly.[18]

The greatest challenges were experienced in the large public asylums, where many patients with different mental maladies were congregated together. Most notorious was the City of London's Bethlem Hospital, known as 'Bedlam'. The institution was grandly rebuilt in 1675–76. Yet its palatial Baroque exterior belied its spartan interior. It soon began admitting the public (at first freely; after 1770 for a fee) to view the inmates, the unruly ones in chains. Intense controversies followed.[19] Public asylums, usually under-funded and crammed with distressed and difficult patients, were hard to run well. A parliamentary committee in 1815–16 revealed continuing evidence of harsh treatment. In the case of London's Bedlam, its inmates were removed to a purpose-built replacement. The new premises in St George's Fields, Surrey (now the Imperial War Museum) were also constructed in grand style, signalling philanthropic pride. However, the reality remained bleak.

Fresh anxieties in 1828 led to the creation of one permanent national body, known as the Lunacy Commission (updating the earlier ad hoc commissions of lunacy). The new board had powers to license and supervise all privately run institutions. This regulatory framework signalled to all 'mad-doctors' that the wider society was watching. However, public asylums still faced chronic problems. Further regulation followed in 1845. A full-time Commission of Lunacy was appointed, complete with a salaried inspectorate.[20] Crucially, it had overview of all asylums, both public and private. However, systems of monitoring themselves require constant review; and both the costs and methods of treating mental illnesses always remain controversial.

Overall, the Georgians' newly systematised help for disabilities, and the introduction of institutional regulation, was in some ways an optimistic story – not least in its ambition. Yet many people with disabilites still had sad experiences; some had disastrous ones. Literary testimony from troubled individuals, like the poets William Cowper and Christopher Smart, bore witness to the deadly despair induced by mental disorders.[21] Reverting to the apian metaphor, the beehive was newly ready, not to jeer, but to help any troubled bees. The remaining great challenge was to find viable assistance which really worked.

Relieving Poverty

Georgian society was capable of great complacency; yet individuals were often quick to respond to appeals for aid. So when in 1786 a charitable committee for the 'Relief of the Black Poor' was founded in London, considerable funds were raised. However, a crucial problem ensued. The committee proposed to resettle its clients in Sierra Leone (west Africa), but few of the indigent African and West Indian people wanted to remove to a distant land and lifestyle, for which they were unprepared.[22] It was a reminder that relief schemes worked best when realistically aligned with the recipients' expectations.

Throughout this period, needy Britons could apply to an immense array of private charities.[23] Some organisations were highly specialised. One charity, founded in 1741, supported poor widows and children of clergymen in Norwich and Norfolk.[24] Another, active in 1776, helped 'distressed' clerical families in Nottinghamshire.[25] There were also mutual aid groups. That stratagem was used in 1738 to generate funds for 'Decayed Musicians', with support from George Frederick Handel, no less. (Later in 1780 this body morphed into the Society of Musicians of Great Britain, which still flourishes.)

Charitable targets were sometimes highly specific; but not always. The Georgians were great funders of medical institutions. Some of the new charitable hospitals just admitted patients from their own localities. Yet others, like those in Birmingham (1779) and Nottingham (1781), notably accepted cases 'from whatever County'. Their open-door policies then assisted these institutions to offer a good breadth of training to their medical students.[26]

Needy individuals and families were used to surviving from hand-to-mouth in an 'economy of makeshift'.[27] Their experiences made them far from passive. When claimants requested aid, even if in semi-literate prose, their messages were usually clear and determined.[28] Similarly, petitions from tenants to landlords urged their cases in unequivocal terms.[29] However, it was easier for the young and mobile to assess relief options than it was for the old and infirm.

One recurrent and thorny issue was the question of how assistance should be disbursed. Begging in the street was a local offence: in theory, all wandering beggars who were seen as 'unruly' were to be confined in local houses of correction, known as Bridewells; and in 1824 the vagrancy laws were further tightened (and remain today on the statute book). But enforcement was subject to local discretion.[30] Unofficially, there was a trade-off between the desire of the affluent not to be harried in the streets for money, and their parallel concern not to pay too much to fund parochial welfare. The outcome generated a set of conventions, via a mixture of local policing and relief schemes. It thus became unusual in Britain and Ireland for large crowds of beggars to jostle potential donors or to threaten physical violence. But an individualised appeal was culturally tolerated. One accepted style was to stand or sit in dignified rags (and with fake deformities, according to cynics), with an outstretched hand or hat. Another more cheerful approach was to sing or play an instrument.[31]

Numbers of street beggars in practice fluctuated in line with economic pressures and local relief options. Central London became the special place of last resort for displaced vagrants, including many from Ireland. In 1796, a London merchant named Matthew Martin decided to intervene. He opened a Mendicity Office in Piccadilly, which tried to help 'deserving' beggars while prosecuting repeat offenders. It was a remarkable effort, redolent of an optimistic faith in individual action. What's more, Martin organised a Society for the Suppression of Mendicity, which survived until 1959.[32] Nonetheless, the deep causes of structural poverty and associated population migrations were not remediable by individual responses of this sort, no matter how well intentioned.

Buttressing the efforts of local policing was the social expectation that at least some safety-net support was available for the most destitute, even if there were sometimes hitches. In England and Wales, legislation in 1601 had codified a nationwide relief system. In theory, those qualifying included not only the 'impotent poor' (the elderly, the sick) but also, in times of special need, the 'able-bodied poor' (the unemployed). Implementation was delegated to local parishes; and poor rates were levied to meet the costs. A variant system emerged in Scotland from the later sixteenth century. Relief was available chiefly for the 'impotent poor', although in emergencies the 'able-bodied' might get ad hoc aid. Funds were habitually collected by the Presbyterian Kirk. Payments were voluntary, albeit subject to un-official social scrutiny. The result bound the Kirk closely into the fabric of Scottish society, although over time some municipal parishes instituted their own poor rates too.[33]

Eighteenth-century Ireland, by contrast, displayed another variant. Poor relief was disbursed via the different churches, in a voluntary system. One effect was to heighten religious bonds. Yet not all areas were equally able to pay. So there were also non-partisan special appeals after unusual disasters, such as big fires in Enniskillen in Fermanagh in 1705 and in Lisburn in Antrim in 1707. At the same time, numerous Irish charities ran hospitals and schools – not without controversies, when rival denominations accused one another of poaching custom.[34] The Dublin government intervened only when there was a risk of disorder. It discouraged begging by imprisoning 'sturdy' culprits in special Houses of Correction.[35] However, the scale of destitution, especially in harsh years (as in 1740–41), made strict implementation impossible. As noted above (p. 24), many poor Irishmen and women left for mainland Britain. If they fell foul of the authorities (not all did), they were liable to be repatriated. Thereupon, some savvy Irish travellers in London volunteered for a 'vagrant pass' to get a free, if utilitarian, no-ride back to Ireland.[36]

Recurrent pressures haunted all these relief systems. Potential rate-payers or charitable donors were often recalcitrant. In March 1763, the diarist Thomas Turner in East Hoathly, Sussex lamented the 'artifice and deceit, cunning and knavery', seen at the vestry meeting, as his affluent neighbours tried to avoid or reduce their assessments.[37] And the unpaid parochial officials in charge of relief payments were readily satirised as local tyrants. Relationships were liable to become fraught, as the parish officials known as 'Overseers of the Poor' regularly inspected people's paperwork.[38] The 'peasant-poet' John Clare in the early 1820s had no hesitation in scorning the parish bigwig, 'Who spouts of freedom as the thing he craves/ And treats the poor, o'er whom he rules, as slaves'.[39]

Continuing administrative changes also rendered these systems ever-more complex for claimants to negotiate. One perennially knotty question was the issue of who qualified for relief and where. In England and Wales, the original 1662 settlement law set strict criteria to establish parochial rights. But new legislation in 1697 inserted some flexibility. Migrants could settle with a certificate from their original parish, or gain new rights, via marriage, apprenticeship or payment of rates. A huge case-law developed around these questions.[40] Population mobility still continued, even while poor unmarried pregnant women were most liable to be removed, to prevent their children from gaining a birthright in a new place. Nonetheless, if migrants were sent back to their original parishes, the Overseers had no powers to keep them there.

Some regulations, furthermore, became too unpopular to implement. The 1697 legislation had decreed that recipients of relief should be 'badged'. Those wearing the letter P – for 'pauper' – were then forbidden to solicit further funds by begging; and the disobedient were to be publicly whipped. Yet this unpopular policy appeared to undermine any sense of trust and solidarity between claimants and rate-payers. Badging was thus widely evaded, well before the requirement was amended in 1782 and ended in 1810.[41]

Furthermore, new alternatives were evolving within the system. Workhouses were adopted where paupers could be lodged economically and set to work. Suitable tasks for pauper women included spinning yarn for the textile industry. (However, it was hard to find viable work for inmates with low skills and – often – poor health.) Workhouses, which emerged in the mid-seventeenth century, were boosted by enabling legislation in 1723 and again in 1782. As a result, contiguous parishes were enabled to group together in a single Poor Law Union. Many large cities had already led the way. Big urban workhouses were launched in Bristol (1696); Exeter (1697); Colchester, Hull and Tiverton (all in 1698); Dublin (1705); and Norwich (1712). These institutions fulfilled multiple roles.[42] Thus they contained workrooms, infirmaries for sick paupers, schools for poor orphans and, sometimes, lock-ups for the disorderly. These impersonal institutions were never very popular at best. Yet small acts of kindness did happen. In 1801 the Overseers at Terling (Essex) donated to an elderly inmate named Ann Cass the workhouse spinning-wheel, which she habitually used, so that Cass could bequeath it to her daughter as her personal property.[43]

Above all, the Old Poor Law (pre-1834) encompassed considerable local experimentation. In some industrial towns, for instance, young paupers were apprenticed to local employers, who welcomed their cheap labour whilst, in theory at least, teaching the youngsters new skills.[44] In Scotland, meanwhile, paupers were upon occasion lodged with wealthier families, as happened in Kilmartin in Argyl, Largs in Ayrshire and Greenock in Renfrewshire during Scotland's acute food shortages in the 1690s.[45] Elsewhere, elderly paupers were given doles (small payments) to live with their offspring, who were expected to help. And the small town of Tenterden in Kent tried another variant. The Overseers there gave extra funds to elderly paupers in their sixties and seventies, so that they could nurse house-bound older paupers in their eighties and nineties.[46] (That example offers a pertinent reminder that indigent old people were the most common group requiring parochial relief, before the Old Age Pension was introduced across the United Kingdom in 1909.)

Particularly controversial from 1795 onwards was the introduction in some southern rural counties of a new policy of wage-supplements. Known as the Speenhamland system (after Speenhamland in Berkshire), it saw landowners paying subsidies to their farm labourers, using a sliding scale based on the price of bread. It was a pragmatic response to sky-high food prices, designed to keep the rural workforce on the land. This policy variant, however, was absolute anathema to free-trade economists. They argued that wage subsidies warped the free market and pushed the poor into what was later termed 'welfare dependency'.[47] Moreover, high-cost relief in the arable south accentu-ated the differences with more spartan payments in the pastoral north.[48] Opposition to Speenhamland became a key plank in mounting criticisms of the Old Poor Law.

Eventually, the political momentum became such that the Whigs under Earl Grey legislated in 1834 to introduce the New Poor Law. In theory, all aid was to become 'indoor relief', dispensed in work-houses across England, Wales and Ireland, with a national commis-sion to invigilate. Inside these pauper institutions, conditions were to be discouragingly spartan, and the sexes were to be separated (including married couples). Reform in Scotland followed in 1845,

1. What does it all mean? *Self-portrait* (*c.* 1780) by the Swiss-born Henry Fuseli shows the intent, brooding gaze of the painter, who moved in London's literary and artistic circles, depicted fantasias and phantasms, and declared, musingly, that 'life is rapid, art is slow'.

2. William Hogarth's satirical print entitled *Gin Lane* (1751) pulses with sufficient demonic energy to delight every pessimist and it became instantly famous. Death, disease, drunkenness, urban degeneration and manifest child neglect are revealed as dire outcomes of the 1740s craze for cheap gin.

3. William Hogarth's optimistic contrast to *Gin Lane* is entitled *Beer Street* (1751). It offers a positive view of town life, with plump citizens drinking traditional English beers. Songs, merriment and emblems of plenty are affectionately depicted but the print, lacking shock value, did not gain fame.

4 & 5. Dynastic change – upheld by law, battles and bloodshed – saw (above) the 1714 arrival of the Protestant King George I, Elector of Hanover, as painted by G.W. Lafontaine, and (below) the departure, after the failed 1745 Jacobite rebellion, of the Catholic claimant Bonnie Prince Charlie, as later (1995) commemorated in a gallant statue at Derby, where his march on London halted.

6 & 7. One incomer in a great age of population turnover was (above) Dido Elizabeth Belle (from family portrait *c*. 1780) – daughter of a Scottish naval officer and an enslaved African woman in the West Indies – who lived in London, where she married a Frenchman. Meanwhile, one emigrant (below) was the Quaker William Penn (painted *c*. 1690) – son of an English admiral and a Dutch mother – who founded the settlement of Pennsylvania in North America, on principles of social and religious toleration.

8 & 9. Political debates took place both inside and outside Parliament: (L) the skinny
Prime Minister William Pitt, representing tradition and support for the war against France,
is caricatured (1798) as literally scourging the corpulent Whig opposition leader and reformer,
Charles James Fox; (R) meanwhile Fox stands on the hustings, wearing the buff-and-blue
colours of the reform Whigs and spreading his arms wide in his appeal for votes from his City of
Westminster electorate in 1796.

10 & 11. How to supervise British officials overseas? (above) Warren Hastings, in power as Britain's first governor of Bengal, is shown (1784) richly dressed, holding his wife's hand affectionately, and accompanied by a demure Indian attendant. But in 1788 (below) Edmund Burke, the Irish-born politician and political thinker, gave a famous speech to denounce Hastings at his public trial for crimes of corruption and misgovernment.

12 & 13. Celebrating Britain's flowering of literary and scientific talents: (above) the Lichfield-born Dr Samuel Johnson – cultural pundit and renowned *Dictionary*-compiler – is shown (1775) in characteristic pose, peering closely at his book in hand; and (below) a medallion (1833) salutes Mary Somerville, eminent Scottish mathematician and astronomer, whose name is commemorated by Somerville College, University of Oxford.

14 & 15. Rethinking religion and irreligion: (above) the Bristol statue (1932) of John Wesley recalls his non-stop missionary travels on horseback, book in hand, as he inspired the Protestant breakaway Wesleyan Connection. By contrast (below) the Edinburgh statue (1997) of David Hume, the Scottish philosopher, historian and religious sceptic, imagines him as a classical philosopher. Today tourists 'touch' Hume's right big toe for good luck, despite his own firm criticism of all superstition.

16 & 17. Exercising free choice in love and sexual fulfilment: (L) Rowlandson's *Elopement* (1782) shows a dashing soldier helping his feisty lover to escape her family – as they head for Gretna Green, where Scotland's laws permitted speedy marriage. But (R) others preferred same-sex relationships, usually conducted discreetly to avoid legal penalties. In 1780, two upper-crust Irishwomen Eleanor Butler and Sarah Ponsonby began a life-long association as intimate friends, sharing a house in Llangollen (north Wales) and eventually becoming iconic figures, identified by their distinctive dress and social poise, as they outlived scandal and guarded their privacy.

18 & 19. Celebrities who came to fame from 'nowhere': (above) Margaret 'Peg' Woffington, daughter of a Dublin bricklayer, appears (1753) as a romantic figure, as she won legendary fame on stage, plus lovers and wealth, before dying in mid-life; (below) London-born Kitty Fisher, a glamorous courtesan 'famous for being famous', is celebrated in a playful portrait (1765) – the kitten fishing for goldfish invoking her name – though Fisher's own fame faded after dying young.

20–23. Social diversification: (above L) the commercial middle class has poise and elegance, as displayed (*c.* 1790) by a female confectioner in Glasgow selling candied sugar-plums; and (above R) the professional middle class has growing social power, as shown by Dr Edward Jenner (1802), coolly vaccinating his incredulous but compliant patients. Meanwhile (below L) skilled workers celebrate industrial might, flagged in the Liverpool Tinplate Workers Society banner (1821), with symbols of plenty and patriotism under an all-seeing eye; while (below R) rural residents provide plentiful workforce and army recruits, as depicted in an affectionate cartoon (1794) of a tattered but indomitable Irish lad on his travels.

24–27. New thinking to challenge old ways: (above L) Scotland's pioneering economist Adam Smith advocates free trade, though accepting some basic regulation (1776); (above R) rationalist Thomas Paine urges equal political rights for all men (1791); and (below L) feminist Mary Wollstonecraft calls for improved female education and women's social liberation (1792); and (below R) radical businessman Robert Owen promotes factory reform, socialism, the cooperative movement and free co-educational schools (1813), developing a communitarian tradition with diverse roots, including Thomas Spence's 1790s campaigns for communal land ownership.

28 & 29. Maritime confidence and controversy: (above) applause for the Royal Navy, and Britannia's claim to 'rule the waves', is engraved on a Liverpool plate (*c.* 1790); yet (below) growing controversy erupts over Britain's role in the trans-Atlantic trade, taking enslaved Africans to work in the West Indian sugar plantations, especially after the Zong Massacre (1781) when, in a nautical crisis, the crew of the *Zong* threw Africans deemed expendable 'cargo' overboard to their deaths.

30 & 31. What legal and moral limits should be set to commercial interests? Campaigners to abolish the slave trade and then the institution of slavery itself strive to alert public opinion and to pressure governments: (L) this detail from a polemical engraving, *Inspection and Sale of a Negro* (1854), reveals the European dealer 'just doing his job', while the captive African is manifestly deprived of consent; (R) the dignified Nigerian-born Londoner, Olaudah Equiano, lectures and writes about his experience as a child-slave, in the cause of abolition. In 1789, he enquires pointedly: 'But is not the slave trade entirely a war with the heart of man?'

32. What did it all mean? William Blake's compelling vision of Lot (1794),
looking back at the beauty and horror of things past, evokes the challenge
of assessing an era which combines successes and progress in many fields,
alongside wars, exploitation and world crimes. Historians constantly grapple
with such issues – as do concerned citizens in their daily lives today.

on similar lines. Many new poorhouses (as workhouses north of the border were termed) were built, invigilated by a new Board of Supervision in Edinburgh.[49]

Such drastic changes, however, failed strikingly. The new system forfeited acceptability with most of its working-class clientele, whose poorest and oldest members were corralled into these unpopular 'bastilles'.[50] And the system was manifestly harsh upon pauper children, penalised for no fault of their own.

Equally devastating was the inoperability of the New Poor Law's central requirement that all aid be given 'indoors'. Especially in urban-industrial regions, big economic downturns quickly caused mass unemployment. Even if some workers left to seek work elsewhere, the remaining numbers were far too great to be corralled into workhouses. So, despite the rhetoric, 'outdoor' relief continued, discreetly. Some municipal and parish authorities gave handouts; others funded employment schemes (building bridges, roads).[51] And Ireland's unfolding crisis left no room for doubt that theories had to yield to stark realities. In 1838 the Irish Poor Law was remodelled into an even more draconian version of the English system.[52] But in the Famine years it became absurd as well as heartless to try to force the dying poor en masse to toil at menial tasks within spartan workhouses. In 1847, the London government under the Whig Lord John Russell changed tack. The Irish Poor Law Extension Act accepted the case for outdoor relief. However, costs were still left to be met locally. Thereupon many Irish landowners, acting uncharitably but 'realistically', evicted their desperate tenants.[53] Reliance upon punitive indoor relief stood revealed as an inadequate dogma; but outdoor relief also needed fundamental rethinking to cope with a fundamental crisis in a collapsing economy.

Levels of poverty were determined not just by the claimants' alleged or real moral and personal failings (idleness; guile; 'learned dependency'), but also by the workers' abilities and age structure, and equally by the nature and location of job opportunities. Furthermore, welfare policies had (and have) a socio-political as well as economic dimension. In the long eighteenth century, there was sufficient local flexibility under the settlement laws to give the poor some sense of claim and belonging, however complicated in practice.[54] After 1834, an element of shared community had to be smuggled back by ad hoc initiatives.

Many alternative approaches were canvassed. An anonymous plea for *The Civil and Religious Rights of the Poor to Relief and Support* appeared in 1766.[55] Yet the individualistic basis of much economic thought in the Georgian era – from Mandeville to the 'free market' of Adam Smith – did not include access to relief as a 'right'. Such a view was too communitarian. Thomas Paine's call in *Agrarian Justice* (1797) for a regular payment to all citizens living past the age of fifty – a prelude to ideas of Universal Basic Income – got no support.[56] Reverting to the beehive metaphor, the leaders of the colony were prepared, at least in theory, to help really impoverished bees who could not fend for themselves; but they always strove to keep costs down, fearing to encourage unproductive 'drones'. Meanwhile, proposals for income redistribution were not seriously considered. No doubt the existing beehive hierarchy was taken as optimal by those at the 'top'; but viewed from below, the relief systems were often too spartan and non-standardised to promote true communal harmony.

Punishing Criminals

During this period, there was also an unofficial quest to find acceptable forms of punishment, with the same debates over costs, efficacy and communal sensitivities. In fact, Georgian society was experiencing a long-term fall in random violence. But there were many other offences, including widespread instances of pickpocketing and shoplifting.[57] Many instances remained off the record, collectively constituting the 'dark figure' of unreported crime.[58] Nonetheless, the legal system, with the aid of juries in criminal cases, produced a steady stream of verdicts, which required condign punishment. One option was to levy fines, which were theoretically due after some civil offences (like swearing in public). However, the poor were chronically unable to pay – and, if pursued by bailiffs, were reduced to seeking welfare or begging.

So traditional punishments favoured instead physical chastisements which were intended to hurt and humiliate. Yet such assaults were becoming culturally unacceptable. Branding was first to lapse (discontinued long before it was officially outlawed in 1829), followed by 'whipping at the cart's tail', which was rare by the 1770s. One late case occurred in March 1817. A woman, identified only as Grant, was whipped through the Inverness streets for chronic intoxication and unruliness. Yet the *Inverness Journal* found the scene 'repugnant'; and the feisty recipient ridiculed the process even when under the lash.[59] Public floggings for women were abolished in 1820, and ended de facto for men in the 1830s, although prison floggings remained legal until 1948. (The abolition of corporal punishment in British schools and private homes is taking longer still.)

Similarly slow to disappear was the punishment of placing malefactors in the pillory for public mockery and humiliation. It did happen: the author Daniel Defoe was pilloried for one hour on three successive days in July 1703, after writing a tract condemned as a 'seditious libel'. In the event, it rained and few attended.[60] (Later mythology suggested that he was pelted with flowers.) Certainly, public responses were notoriously erratic. Sometimes malefactors were fêted, at other times attacked. In London in 1732 one John Waller, an 'affidavit man', whose testimonies had sent people to the gallows, was beaten to death in the pillory by supporters of his victims. Needless to say, such mayhem was not what the magistrates intended. Accordingly, public pillorying became rare, long before it was declared illegal by act of Parliament in 1837.[61]

Hanging on the gallows was the most drastic of all penalties in the Georgian era – and its historic role remains notorious. Between

1688 and 1800 the number of offences punishable by death more than quadrupled from 50 to 220. An array of laws, dubbed the 'Bloody Code', imposed that penalty, usually for very specific offences (damaging Westminster Bridge; impersonating a Chelsea Pensioner; pilfering from a naval dockyard; stealing from a shipwreck; pick-pocketing goods worth a shilling or more).[62] Most of those hung were men. But a few women were included, to add to the deterrent effect.[63] After the drop, bodies were left dangling for at least an hour. And, sometimes, cadavers were sent for scientific dissection – a callous refinement which denied convicts dignity after death.

Initially, all hangings were conducted in public, after processions, prayers and the malefactors' last dying speeches, which were quickly published, often becoming bestsellers.[64] All the main gallows sites – like London's Tyburn, Edinburgh's Grassmarket, Dublin's St Stephen's Green – were viewed with superstitious dread; and local Gallows' Fields (such as that at Ilchester, Somerset's historic county town) long retained their melancholic connotations.

When, rarely, people survived a hanging, the punishment was usually commuted. In 1724, the 'half-hanged' Maggie Dickson, convicted for infanticide, became a minor Edinburgh celebrity when she revived in her coffin.[65] It was not uncommon for friends of the condemned to stand below the gallows and pull the hanging body to ensure a quick death. In another case in 1770, friends of a convicted soldier, Thomas Dunk, snatched and mangled his corpse to save it from dissection.[66] Over time, scenes that were variously macabre, chaotic and carnivalesque convinced officialdom that tighter controls were needed. Public hangings were relocated to venues immediately outside prison gates; and, later still, brought in-house. In London, they were held outside Newgate from 1783 (and inside from 1868).

Educated opinion was gradually becoming hostile to reliance upon hanging as the chief deterrent. Uneven enforcement, plus the same harsh penalty for both great and small crimes, seemed grossly unfair. The number of hangings, already small, fell as a proportion of the rising population. In per capita terms, the peak occurred in the 1780s. By then hangings were unknown in some entire regions.[67] The Georgians, who invented the Bloody Code, also began its dismantling. In 1823, the death penalty was made discretionary for offences other than murder and high treason; and in 1834, the by that time rare practice of hanging in chains, which required the hanged corpse to be exhibited in a cage as a public warning, was abolished. This shift was part of the long process whereby the death penalty has lost support internationally, though not yet universally.[68]

Meanwhile, transportation overseas, in use from 1717 onwards, remained a major alternative option for British law enforcers. Yet exiling convicts from friends, families and familiar lives as a penalty for minor crimes seemed equally disproportionate. Moreover, this policy too was arbitrary in its implementation. Judicial discretion produced major regional variations in trial outcomes. After their conviction, too many prisoners then died in the insanitary ships – known as the 'hulks'– where they were kept while awaiting transportation.[69] And once they had arrived overseas, people's subsequent experiences were also variegated. Hence this penalty also lacked rationality, proportionality and fairness.

That said, the policy of criminal transportation, initially to the North American colonies (before 1776) and then to Australia, continued for a considerable time.[70] Most transportees were adult males from south-east England; but some women were sent too. One was Hannah Rosse, a Londoner described as 'a sort of a *dumb* [*sic*]', who was speech-impeded or (possibly) shamming. In 1745 she was sentenced to transportation for a second offence of larceny (non-violent theft of goods worth over 12 pence).[71] Rosse's disability won her no leniency, indicating that she had no incentive to be faking it. In all, some 162,400 convicts were taken to Australia between 1788 and 1868. However, this policy was also being slowed, long before it was finally halted. In its last years, it was more of a threat than an actuality. By 1851 the transportees (a number of whom later returned to Britain) constituted only a tiny proportion of the 27 million inhabitants of Britain and Ireland.

Imprisonment therefore remained the chief fall-back penal option. It had the apparent merit of getting criminals 'off the streets'. But large and labour-intensive incarceration centres were costly and chronically difficult to run. Numbers in prison began to rise from the 1770s onwards. Inmates usually found conditions tough. One young radical, Thomas Lloyd, locked in London's Newgate Prison in the 1790s for 'seditious' libel, kept a scribbled diary. In it, he recorded his illnesses and depression, along with the overcrowding and assaults from fellow inmates, even though he was detained in the smartest wing, relatively speaking.[72]

Poor debtors, without the means to discharge their liabilities, constituted a large contingent of inmates without hope of release. Often, too, their desperate families lodged with them. That practice was banned in London's King's Bench Prison in 1781. A bell was rung at closing time, when non-prisoners were supposed to leave. However, a compromise ensued. The bell was rung, but the families, with no other home, remained.[73] Only in 1828 was imprisonment for many forms of civil debt eventually abolished.

Conspicuously, the old-style village and urban lock-ups were becoming overwhelmed by the penal needs of a mass society.[74] There were frequent revelations of dire conditions. In 1729, a parliamentary inquiry uncovered many abuses in London's Marshalsea debtors' prison.[75] And all gaols were chronic incubators of disease. In 1777 a sweeping critique came from the penal reformer John Howard, a wealthy Calvinist.[76] He highlighted many problems, including the scandal of acquitted prisoners who remained inside because they could not pay their gaol fees (a requirement which was ended in 1815).

Howard's intervention prompted the start of a national penal policy. A new Penitentiary Act followed in 1779.[77] Hence the later eighteenth century saw considerable prison building and rebuilding. Some institutions drew specifically upon Howard's stress on good sanitation and opportunities for prisoner rehabilitation. The gaol at Gloucester (built 1786–91) was one example; as was the Dana Prison at Shrewsbury (built 1793). But there were always tensions between the requirements of incarceration and those of rehabilitation. Keen debates accordingly ensued. One school of thought favoured reformative austerity. The Calvinist reformer John Howard was, unsurprisingly, a key supporter. He advocated a regime of hard labour, strict discipline, spare diet and religious instruction, to foster moral rehabilitation. (His zeal was acknowledged in 1866, when the charitable pressure group, the Howard League for Penal Reform, adopted his name, albeit without endorsing his preferred methodology.)

Austerity was also the keynote vision of the philosopher Jeremy Bentham. His splendidly named 'All-Seeing-Eye' or 'Panopticon' proposed to keep isolated prisoners under remote surveillance from a central viewing-point (anticipating the idea of closed-circuit television).[78] However, his model gaol was never actually built. And, when versions of 'silent' austerity regimes were later tried in the UK and USA, the running costs plus the malign impact on prisoners' mental health eventually caused such projects to be halted.[79] Prisons were (and remain) micro-societies of the wider whole, not just aggregated cells of atomised individuals.

Liberal alternatives were equally canvassed. The Quaker philanthropist Elizabeth Fry worked, as a prison visitor in the 1820s, to humanise conditions. She sought above all to augment the prisoners' sense of self-worth. Thus she encouraged Newgate's female inmates to make their own rules for living together in crowded cells.[80] The gulf between these rival approaches was great, although both close invigilation and liberal mentoring were labour-intensive and costly.

Such proposals did, however, begin the long (and still incomplete) quest to find better means of coping with people who are adjudged to have illegally breached society's norms.[81] Viewed from the perspective of a beehive, all behaviour deemed criminal was aberrant, 'unnatural' and destructive of harmony. Yet human societies do not proceed so instinctually. They need also to have confidence in definitions of criminality as well as in systems of detection and judgment. And, as Georgian opinion turned against the drastic options of removing delinquent bees from the hive, the long quest also began to find alternative means of both punishment and rehabilitation.

Conflicts and Community within the 'Human-Hive'

Humans are indeed, like bees, instinctively social. However, human-hives are highly variegated, lacking the generic order of a beehive. In Georgian Britain, individuals by no means all played pre-allotted roles. They experienced mobility, whether geographical, socio-economic or educational. While most appreciated concord, yet people also experienced and at times generated conflict. And they expressed criticisms. The mass institutions of Britain – such as prisons, workhouses and asylums – were subjects of intensive debate, since their performance was often sub-optimal. In 1729, for example, an insolvent debtor in London's Fleet Prison wrote a bitter *Speech Without Doors*, deploring the harsh regime imposed by the repressive '*Gaol-archy*'.[82] Yet taxpayers were not keen on spending money to improve these mass institutions – or to sustain improvements, if made. These were chronic problems, without easy answers.

Analytically, too, human societies did not simply constitute one harmonious collectivity. People had intermediate sectional interests, within the whole. That point was made electrifyingly in 1848 by Karl Marx and Friedrich Engels, drawing upon Engels's experiences in Manchester. For them, class struggle not only existed but was the supreme motor force of all history.[83] Moreover, they were justified in stressing the force of economic conflicts. Yet historians observe that divisions are also generated by religious, cultural, regional, national, inter-generational and other rivalries. Hence group identities are as complex as individual ones, further complicating the human-hive.

Social policies in such intricate circumstances evolved dynamically.[84] In the very long term, there was growing support for liberal
attitudes – not to pillory people for behavioural oddities or for crimes;
not to badge paupers; not to keep 'lunatics' or convicts in chains; not
to adopt hugely disproportionate penalties for criminal transgressions; and so forth. Yet policies at any given moment were tugged by
contradictory pressures, just as public opinion veered between anxiety
at social 'problems' and resistance to high expenditure upon institutional reform. The human-hive was constantly balancing diverse
forms of conflict against the role of concord, whether sustained by
belief or by social controls. Hence, as Scotland's pioneering sociolo-
gist Adam Ferguson explained in his *Essay on . . . Civil Society* (1767),
outcomes *'are indeed the result of human action, but not the execution of
any [one] human design'*.[85]

∽ Time-Shift: Then and Now ∾

Three contrasting Georgian institutions for mental health
care, social welfare and punishment are worth visiting either in
person or virtually. These places invite consideration of the
merits (or otherwise) of concentrating facilities into large institutions in comparison with dispersal within the community.

1. The Lawn (built 1818–20)
Formerly Lincoln Lunatic Asylum (later the Lawn Hospital),
in use until 1985, and now commercially owned, with some
publicly accessible rooms. This asylum was famed in the 1830s
for treating patients without using physical restraints, as
directed by the progressive doctors E.P. Charlesworth and
R.G. Hill. Sympathetic help was intended to counter the over-
whelming sense of jeopardy so often experienced by mental
health sufferers. That misery was acutely invoked by John
Clare (*c.* 1844), who in his poem 'I Am!' felt lost in 'the living

sea of waking dreams,/ Where there is neither sense of life or joys'.

2. Southwell Workhouse (built 1824)

Now preserved and run by the National Trust, this Nottinghamshire venue challenges visitors to assess the merits or otherwise of the system of parochial poor relief, which provided a social safety net, however faulty, but whose institutionalised regime represented, in the words of George Crabbe's poem 'The Village' (1783), 'the cold charities of man to man'.

3. Shepton Mallet Prison (rebuilt 1793)

The seventeenth-century penitentiary was reconstructed in 1793 and again in the 1820s. It is now a visitor centre, offering guided and self-guided tours. People are invited to consider the fates of prisoners locked within 'the Dungeon's noxious gloom', as John Thelwall had it in his 1795 poem 'The Cell' (penned in another prison – Newgate – as he calmly awaited trial for high treason).

❧ 12 ❧

Encountering the World and Its People

The deeds and misdeeds of the Georgians overseas also show how history emerges from the sum of big trends *and* many individual decisions. There were structural forces at work (notably technological power imbalances), but there were also complex actions and interactions between many different peoples. Britons were to an extent prepared for overseas adventures by their imaginative travel literature. Readers could share with the hero of Defoe's *Robinson Crusoe* (1719) the thrill of fear, wonder and delight when he finds in the sand, after years as a solitary castaway, the fresh footprint of another human.[1]

Not every story was as epic. But writers, such as the anonymous author of *The Comical Pilgrim: Or Travels of a Cynick Philosopher through the Most Wicked Parts of the World* (1722), tried hard.[2] Much literature focused upon continental Europe. A stream of high-ranking British voyagers undertook the Grand Tour to Italy; and, by the end of the century, the social range of men – and women – undertaking such trips was increasing.[3] In time, however, the adventurous came to look further afield. A new *India Guide* (1801) invited British tourists to go east; another promoted *Tours in Upper India and in Parts of the*

Himalaya Mountains (1833); and *The Overland Traveller* (1838) outlined the long trek from India to Europe.[4]

Direct awareness of other cultures was further provided by visitors from overseas. One exotic arrival proved to be a bold impostor. George Psalmanazar gained fame in 1704 as the self-styled first native of Formosa (today Taiwan) to visit Britain. He documented the country's language, climate and customs. But critics expressed suspicion. And they were right to do so: it transpired that Psalmanazar was in fact a Frenchman with a lively imagination, who later settled in London as a jobbing writer.[5] His initial success indicated the public appetite for travellers' tales.[6] Yet his unmasking showed that sceptics were equally alert to detect frauds. Many other 'exotic' visitors also arrived in the course of this period. Britons were sometimes impressed. At other times, however, 'strangers' who seemed too 'primitive' in their ways were greeted with a certain condescension: a Cherokee chief and his entourage, visiting England in 1762, attracted excited crowds but were also dismissed by some newspapers as 'Savages' and 'Monsters'.[7]

Discovering the diversity of global experience was a source of endless interest.[8] Atlases and the new encyclopaedias sold well.[9] There were many great collectors of historical, geographical and biological curiosities, including some notable women, like Margaret Bentinck, Duchess of Portland, one of Britain's richest women at the mid-century.[10] Many museum collections were dispersed after an owner's death. But some major institutions, such as the Ashmolean in Oxford (founded 1686) and the British Museum in London (opened 1753), were accumulating what became major global collections.[11]

Simultaneously, botanists and biologists were importing foreign flora and fauna – often with distressingly high mortality rates for the first exotic animals brought to strange climes.[12] And with this cornucopia of knowledge came new challenges: to understand the role of Britain in the wider world – and the relationships of its people to 'others'.

Gaining and Losing Territories Overseas

Sometimes Britain's overseas history in this era is summarised as 'the colonial project'. The phrase implies an acquisitive set of linked procedures that led to the growth of Britain's colonial settlements – and eventually to their recognition as a seaborne 'empire'. Over time, the country's status was transformed from a minnow among European powers in 1650 to an emergent world leader (alongside a few other competitors for that title) by 1815. Yet there was nothing like a coherent master-plan – let alone one sustained over 200 years of history.

One case history demonstrates the haphazard nature of exploration and territorial claims. In 1792, George Vancouver, formerly an officer on Captain Cook's second and third voyages of circumnavigation, sailed back to Hawaii. There, in 1784, with the chief's concurrence, the Union Jack was raised over the island. However, since no message went to London, no proprietorial claims followed. Hawaii did not become a British colony, though it did remain a key maritime supply point. (As already noted, its state flag includes the Union Jack in tribute to these historic contacts.)[13] Vancouver's action was bold but uncoordinated. When he returned to Britain he got no great praise for his feats of Pacific exploration and cartography. Instead, he was harried and attacked by Thomas Pitt, 2nd Baron Camelford, an embittered fellow officer, who was backed by his eminent cousin, Prime Minister Pitt. Vancouver died in 1798, aged forty and in eclipse.[14] (Today he is widely commemorated; and a great Canadian city bears his name.)

Explorers like Vancouver were followed more routinely by traders, farmers, town settlers, missionaries, indentured servants, and (later) transported convicts. Naval doctors also gave practical help, one notable example being Dr David McBride who established, through trial and error, that sailors needed good supplies of vitamin C to combat scurvy on long voyages.[15] The Atlantic became a ready navigational highway for travellers in all directions.[16] Meanwhile, more slowly, the Pacific was also being explored by Europeans, aided by local islanders.[17]

Given that there was no straightforward pathway from Britain's overseas contacts to empire, explanations have to allow for the power of contingency and happenstance. But the role of pure chance should not be overplayed either. The Victorian historian J.R. Seeley announced in 1883 that Britain gained its empire in a 'fit of absence of mind'.[18] This phrase was undeniably arresting. Yet Seeley underestimated not only the cultural confidence of explorers but also the extent of British state support via diplomacy, naval protection, support for colonial governments, and warfare. Freelance actions and political power combined to foster accumulating changes, with a mixture of losses alongside gains.[19]

'Empire' in the eighteenth century referred not only to formal governance but, more loosely, to 'sway' or 'influence'. It was in that casual sense that it was initially applied in Britain. There were growing references to the country's maritime 'empire'. But expansion was not seen as a British monopoly. Thus the Irish philosopher Bishop George Berkeley, who lived for a while in Rhode Island, saluted New World dynamism by musing that: 'Westward the course of empire takes its way/ ... Time's noblest offspring is the last'.[20] (His poem has always had admirers in the USA.) However, a century later, the usage had become much more bullish and more specific. So the Scottish merchant Patrick Colquhoun penned his *Treatise on the Wealth, Power and Resources of the British Empire, in Every Quarter of the World* (1814) to quantify Britain's global colonial reach, under the rubric of 'empire' (even though, as noted above, p. 31, there was never a 'British Emperor' and Victoria did not gain the title Empress of India until 1876).[21]

Moreover, the country's political heartland in the Georgian era gave no signs of imperial grandeur. The royal court (before 1837) was modestly housed in the old Tudor palace of St James, while the prime minister's home was tucked unassumingly into a side street off Whitehall. There was no state residence in Georgian London on a par with the USA's neoclassical White House, built in 1792–1800 (later extended) as a presidential home and office. Indeed, a casual observer, looking for an ideal imperial capital in the early nineteenth century, might have nominated the monumental centre of Washington, DC or the palatial-urban edifices begun in the 1780s by the princely governors known as the Nawabs in Lucknow, Uttar Pradesh. In Georgian Britain, the most exotic royal palace was constructed not in London but at Brighton. The Royal Pavilion (1815–22) was a superb Indo-Islamic-Gothic fantasy, with ultra-modern amenities such as gas-lighting and flush toilets.[22] Yet this edifice had no royal-ceremonial role. In 1850 it was sold to Brighton Corporation, which put it to use, congenially, as the town's Assembly Rooms.

Politicians in London were, however, vigilant to support one bedrock policy which helped eighteenth-century Britannia to 'rule the waves'. They all upheld the Navigation Acts, which survived from 1651 until 1849. These laws confined all Britain's colonial trade to British ships, including all trade between British colonies. This manifest protectionism eventually faced criticisms, including from free-trade purists. Nonetheless, the system aided Britain's shipping interests, whilst binding its overseas settlements into a common network, patrolled by the powerful Royal Navy. Only over time were the Navigation Acts resented by the North American seaboard colonists, as their own commercial capacities grew.[23]

Throughout the period, too, British politicians paid close attention to commercial and colonial affairs. They relied upon a new Commission for Trade and Foreign Plantations (founded 1696), which grew into a major department of state, known after 1786 as the Board of Trade. And ministers were constantly lobbied by rival trading groups. One potent body was the West India Committee (founded 1780), which spoke for the plantation owners and merchants trading to the Caribbean.[24] Thus, while politicians could be casual about events in far-flung locations, they kept a close eye on Britain's Atlantic interests.[25] In particular, Gibraltar, ceded to Britain by Spain in 1713, was firmly defended as a strategic garrison, despite two Spanish onslaughts. One siege in 1727 was only brief, but the later 'Great Siege' lasted between 1779 and 1783 when Spanish and French fleets together blockaded and shelled the port, although without success. (Much jubilation followed in Britain, with triumphant paintings, cartoons and poems. There was even a congratulatory song from the young Mozart, who declared himself on this issue to be an 'arch-Englishman'.)[26]

Britain's overseas expansion accordingly relied upon a mixture of power, ad hoc acquisition and competitive energy from the would-be colonisers (both individual and state-directed), as checked by the nature of resistance and opposition from within the colonised territories. Simply put, there was a dynamic tension between the ambitions of the newcomers and the responses of the indigenous people. Furthermore, the balance of these forces was affected by wider responses from rival European powers, like France, which might potentially help those resisting.[27] For that reason, the earliest British overseas settlements tended to be in sparsely inhabited territories, with relatively little organised opposition.

The first successful resistance to Britain came, paradoxically enough, from its own North American-seaboard colonies. Once the 1763 peace settlement confirmed France's loss of Canada, many colonial Americans, relieved of military threat from the north, became restive under British tutelage.[28] Contentious issues of taxation and representation came to the fore. To one indignant British loyalist in 1778, the American rebels were nothing but 'Schism-blown Maggots'.[29] They were accused of ingratitude to their protector, the noble British lion. Yet the rebels won. The 'escape' of the new USA was forged in warfare, aided by the French, and confirmed by a new peace settlement in 1783. Had Britain's actions been more conciliatory – as some British opposition politicians urged – the original crisis might have been defused or postponed. Yet ultimately the consent of the colonial settlers was needed; and, if revoked, was liable to be further inflamed by attempted military suppression.

After American independence, however, the divorced parties became allies. Their peoples had long-standing links of religion, language and family. They shared a culture of constitutionalism, legalism, individualism, a stress upon rights and suspicion of an over-mighty state. And in practical terms, their economies were mutually and profitably interdependent. Traders and investors were not deterred by the political breach. Nonetheless, there was a process of adjustment. When the USA cast eager eyes upon Canada, Britain resisted strongly. During the war of 1812–14, its forces not only defeated the new republic, but in August 1814 set fire to Washington's most august buildings: the White House, the Capitol and the Library of Congress.[30] This exploit was not intended to undo American independence. Yet it showed that Britain was ready to defend its continuing interests in the region. Hence the emergent Anglo-American 'special' relationship was built upon turn-by-turn defeats and mutual respect.

Clearly, Britain's overseas expansion was not one of unalloyed triumph. The American Declaration of Independence had a long-term impact. It provided a template for a conscious anti-imperialism, which spread in nineteenth-century South America, and, later, worldwide. In the Georgian era, however, not all colonial settlers wished to stand alone. The plantation owners in the sugar islands remained reliant upon Britain for supplies, markets, naval protection and (for most of the period) political sanction for its slave economy.[31] The Caribbean saw frequent low-level skirmishes between the French, Spanish and British fleets, allowing naval officers (including the young Nelson) to hone their fighting skills. And there was one big confrontation in the form of Battle of the Saintes off Dominica in 1782, when Britain's victory halted the planned joint Franco-Spanish assault upon Jamaica. Little wonder then that the plantation owners were tenaciously loyal.

Canada, too, had a different set of reasons for sticking with the British, despite an initial plea in 1776 from Benjamin Franklin, who urged the French Canadians to join with the American rebels. There were many tensions between the Anglophone and Francophone communities, ever since James Wolfe's victory at Quebec in 1759 yoked them together. Yet British policy in that regard was decidedly pragmatic. The Quebec Act of 1774 allowed French Canadian Catholics to practise their religion freely and to participate in civic life, giving them rights not accorded to British Catholics before 1829.[32] The rival communities thereupon settled into a competitive co-existence, while a distant Britain held the ring. Indeed, Canada attracted many pro-British loyalists who left the new USA after 1776.[33] Thereafter a pragmatic ecumenicalism prevailed. The later union of the contending Canadian provinces was promoted in 1840 (and, later still, federal self-government accepted in 1867).[34] Britain's colonial interests were thus not halted by losing the USA, but were recalibrated.

Engaging with India

Pragmatic policies also helped to promote Georgian Britain's prolonged engagement with India.[35] That historic society had its well-entrenched rulers, social conventions, regional economies, languages, castes and multiple faiths. Prudently, Britain throughout its growing involvement with the region continued to respect all Indian religions and gave no official sanction to the quest for conversions by freelance Christian missionaries.[36] The two-way engagement remained intricate throughout.

Links were first initiated by adventurous British traders, organised from 1757 onwards by England's East India Company.[37] It soon established its own military force under British officers.[38] From London, strategic support – and sometimes conflicting advice – came from the India Board (established 1784). This arm's-length system left it to the Company to promote British trading interests, either in alliance with India's princely rulers, or, at times, by fighting or scheming against them. One sign of the East India Company's ambition was its launching in 1767 of the cartographic *Survey of India* (which thrives to this day, now under the Republic of India).[39] Accurate mapping was undeniably a great resource. Nonetheless, such data did not automatically ensure enduring political control, as shown by the contrary case of the well-mapped American colonies.

British admiration for India's wealth and might was far from unequivocal. One particularly brutal incident generated great negative publicity. In June 1756 over 100 British and other prisoners died when crowded for three days into a small, sweltering dungeon in Kolkata's Fort William, under the authority of the Nawab of Bengal. The prison was dubbed the 'Black Hole of Calcutta', launching a term still commonly used for any infamous goal. British opinion was outraged; and jubilation followed in 1759, when the Nawab was ousted by Clive 'of India'. (The tenacious British cultural memory of the Black Hole indicates a common phenomenon, whereby people often recall wrongs perpetrated against them, whilst ignoring or underestimating wrongs committed in their name against others.)

Nervous commentators also worried that India's great opulence was corrupting.[40] When British officials and traders returned home with massive financial gains, they were greeted with deep suspicion. A tract in 1783 denounced all '*Real, Spurious, Reputed, or Mushroom Nabobs*' as corrupting upstarts, recycling the term 'nabob' (a Mughal official) with pointed hostility.[41] Even the man dubbed by his British admirers as Clive 'of India', who had secured an agreement which placed Bengal thenceforth under the East India Company's administrative control, was repeatedly challenged about the large personal fortune with which he returned to Britain.[42]

More dramatically still, the opposition Whigs attempted in 1788 to impeach the returning first Governor-General of Bengal, Warren Hastings. As noted above (pp. 175–7), the procedure of impeachment was cumbersome, and did not really enable Parliament to scrutinise the day-to-day workings of the executive. Nonetheless, the indictment was savage. Hastings was charged with systemic misrule, including presiding over the disastrous Bengal Famine of 1769–70, aggravated by the East India Company's harsh land taxes. The prosecution urged that he had failed the Indian people, as well as the British under whose indirect auspices he governed. The case, however, did not test whether the East India Company should be in India at all. And Hastings was, eventually, acquitted. Nonetheless, the Company was being pushed to redefine its role, not as predatory, but as tutelary.[43] There were thus distinct stages in its operations.

Alongside some suspicion, there was also considerable interest in India's ancient languages and culture, as seen, for example, in *A History of Hindostan* (1770), which explored the 'religion and philosophy of the Brahmins'.[44] A number of English officials studied with Indian teachers. In 1784, Sir William Jones, a British judge in Kolkata, joined with colleagues to found the Asiatic Society. It was dedicated to studying Bengal and its culture (and flourishes today with a magnificent library and museum). Sir William was an enthusiastic polygot, who learned classical Sanskrit, which he greatly admired. Furthermore, he was one of a few pioneering scholars to suggest that there was a lost language (now known as the proto-Indo-European tongue), which was the common linguistic parent of Sanskrit, Persian, Greek, Latin and the Germanic languages.[45] (He also added to this list – this time erroneously – Egyptian, Japanese and Chinese.) Jones's work greatly boosted the new field of comparative linguistics. And it showed that far from all Westerners typically took a dismissive or condescending attitude towards 'the Orient'.[46]

Meanwhile, the East India Company was extending its geographical remit. The rival incoming power of France was by the 1790s weakened by prolonged wars and political upheavals at home. Seeking a dramatic way to reverse that state of affairs, Napoleon audaciously sought a new overland route to get his troops to India via Egypt. Yet he was foiled in 1798. His fleet was destroyed by Nelson at the Battle of the Nile in Aboukir Bay. Things then changed rapidly. In May 1799 the East India Company Army, with its Indian allies, defeated and killed at Seringapatam (now Srirangapatna) the formidable warrior ruler of Mysore, Tipu Sultan. The area under the Company's control was now greatly widened. A triumphant British medal showed an aggressive lion routing the 'Tiger of Mysore' – a fine foe but a losing one. Only in the long passage of time did Tipu, a Muslim, become in India a (controversial) hero of resistance.[47]

An unintended result of this battle was the diffusion of new military technologies. Tipu was known for his formidable arsenal of iron-cased rockets, and, after his defeat, Britain's army engineers hastened to study and to replicate this weaponry, which they then used to great effect when they bombarded America's coastal forts in the war of 1812–14. Their use of Indian-derived rockets indicated the speed with which new and successful military technologies were (and are) often copied. One American observer of the British bombardment penned a patriotic poem of resistance. Entitled 'Defence of Fort M'Henry' (and later adopted under the title of 'The Star-Spangled Banner' as the US national anthem) its first verse observes 'the rocket's red glare, the bombs bursting in air': an eyewitness account of this startling Indian-derived weaponry.

From the British government's perspective, its role in India was increasingly represented as holding the ring between rival interest groups, usually in alliance with the Indian princes, with regional administration delegated to the East India Company's civil service.[48] Yet there were tensions over whether its role was to conserve or to reform.[49] James Mill, the great admirer of utilitarian philosophy, wrote an influential *History of British India* (1817). This tract offered a coolly rationalist critique of what Mill saw as Indian and specifically Hindu 'backwardness'. For good measure, he also blamed British corruption and incompetence. (Mill, who prided himself on *not* being distracted by knowing the local languages, later rose to head the India Office in London.)[50]

Some traditional customs proved too contentious to ignore. So in 1829 the Hindu tradition of sati or suttee (widow self-immolation) was banned in Bengal, its chief redoubt, and later across all India. That move followed campaigning not only by Christian missionaries but also by the Hindu spiritual moderniser and political reformer, Ram Mohan Roy.[51] (On a visit to south-west England in 1833, he died suddenly in Bristol, where there are today many memorials to him as well as an annual remembrance service.)[52]

Providing paternalist administration was Britain's way of justifying its role. In the years 1828 to 1840, the liberal, upright and often controversial Charles Trevelyan – who *was* proficient in East Asian languages – saw that aim as his mission. In post in India, he strove to professionalise recruitment to its civil service (a prelude to his later efforts to achieve the same in Britain). He additionally abolished tariffs on India's internal trade; promoted Western-style education in literature and science; and established English, rather than the traditional Farsi, as a main language of Indian administration.[53] By this time, the intermediary role of the East India Company seemed ever more anomalous; but it was not until 1858 that Britain decided to rule directly, alarmed by the disruptive Army Mutiny of 1857. (And after that, over a decade passed before the residual business of the Company was settled by Parliament and the organisation itself finally dissolved in 1874 – two years before Queen Victoria was declared Empress 'of India'.)

This intricate encounter between two historic world-regions, both with their multiple peoples and cultures, showed that British views of India – and Indian views of Britain – were not homogeneous. Nor was there a straightforward pathway from the first trading connections, leading either to informal 'empire' or on to formal 'Empire'. In the later eighteenth century both Britain and France were foraging within the relative power vacuum of India; and it was not initially clear that the French competition would disappear as rapidly as it did. Nonetheless, there were distinct stages that can be detected in retrospect. An early phase of Britain's predatory commercial and military adventurism (to 1799) was replaced by a more stable era of administrative rule. By the early nineteenth century, many Britons began to rationalise their intervention in India as constituting a force 'for good'. Christian missionaries saw it as a chance to preach the word; liberal reformers as a chance to eradicate 'backwardness'. Eventually, however, the formalities of direct political rule tended to increase British lordliness vis-à-vis India. Class differences and ethnic prejudices were heightened.[54] A counter-reaction of explicit anti-imperialism began, which increasingly gained ground, not only in Britain but, most importantly, in India.[55]

During these shifts, the balance of benefits and disbenefits – political, economic, social, cultural, interpersonal – of the bilateral encounter oscillated between different eras of history.[56] Commercial, administrative and educational links were sometimes mutually beneficial, sometimes harmful, sometimes mixed. Profits from India reaching Britain fluctuated over time, as did British infrastructural investment in India. Urban traders often did well, while the rural economy stagnated. It is thus hard to model all the effects, whether direct or indirect. The British were not simply universal 'baddies' (or universal 'goodies', as some Britons may have hoped). Moreover, some influential sectors of Indian opinion came to support British rule, although decreasingly over time once the informal 'empire' turned into a more rigid and stratified Empire. Adam Ferguson's dictum is again relevant: outcomes emerge from the sum of many human actions, not from one plan. The two-way encounter between Indians and Britons was a complicated but mutual history, calling for understanding as well as careful assessments of its benefits and disbenefits.

Enslavement and Anti-Slavery

In practice, Georgian Britons first began to debate their actions overseas not via the question of territorial expansion but through the rights and wrongs of enslavement. Opinions during this period were divided – but slowly shifting. And, over time, British government policy was decisively changed, to oppose both the slave trade and slavery as an institution. It is therefore wrong to chide all Georgians retrospectively as 'racists' or condoners of enslavement (especially if it is erroneously implied that later centuries are without such blemishes). There were then passionate campaigners against slavery, from many backgrounds, who considered their cause to be the defining one of their era. The story however was not a straightforward one of liberal enlightenment and an end to oppression between peoples. The experiences of enslavement left complex and damaging legacies. In addition, this era saw an intricate new dimension added to the debates, in the form of would-be scientific theories of separate human 'races'.

Generally, British cultural attitudes in this period displayed great confidence, albeit shot through with competitive tensions vis-à-vis the French and, to a lesser extent, the Spaniards. And Britons settling overseas shared those attitudes. In North America, the cultural, technological and economic power imbalances between the newcomers and the indigenous peoples had destabilising effects upon the latter. But that reality was little appreciated by the incoming Britons. Moreover, the failure of rebellions such the Yamasee War in South Carolina (1715–16) not only marginalised the rebels but also divided the indigenous people, as some sided with the settlers against their tribal enemies.[57] A few missionaries did express concern. Yet, while an English commentator in 1740 denounced the Spaniards in South America for their cruelty to the 'poor Indians', most British colonial settlers were blithely unaware of the comparable motes in their own eyes.[58] (In the very long term, however, the settlers' poor treatment of the first Americans began to haunt later US culture and films, if with some ambivalence.)[59]

Problems and injustices at a distance were hard to grasp. Very much the same dynamic was apparent when the first British settlers arrived in Australia in the later eighteenth century. The abundant territory and sparse settlements of the indigenous Australians encouraged belief in the view that the land was vacant territory (*'terra nullius'*). There was no general 'colonial project' to erase the local population, although there were certainly cases of grim and dehumanising treatment.[60] Instead people in Britain were generally unaware of the hardships experienced even by many transported convicts, let alone those suffered by the indigenous Australians.

However, there was no such ignorance when it came to the international trade in enslaved Africans. No region or sector of British society was without some links to this commerce, whether directly or indirectly.[61] Merchants and shippers took manufactured goods to Africa, sold them to buy captives who were taken across the 'Middle Passage' to the West Indian plantations, and the traders returned with prized raw materials. The Beckfords were one example of a London merchant family who grew famously rich from the triangular trade and invested in estates in Jamaica to join the colonial plantocracy.[62] In all, it has been calculated that from the later sixteenth century until 1807, when Britain legally halted its role, some 3.1 million enslaved people were taken in British ships from Africa, of whom perhaps 2.7 million reached America. It was a colossal total – perhaps as much as one quarter of all such shipments. Only the Portuguese traders, who remained in the business after 1807, took more.[63]

Involuntary mass migration on this scale actually unbalanced those African societies which lost so many people.[64] But again, those realities were not widely apparent. On the other hand, it was hard to ignore shocking reports of African deaths in transit. One particularly notorious case occurred in 1781. The captain of the *Zong*, panicked by navigational difficulties, ordered that sick and 'surplus' captives be thrown overboard. Over 130 Africans drowned.[65] When the insurers refused to pay out over the lost 'cargo', the resulting court cases were seized upon by British abolitionists to publicise the inhumanity of the slave trade. The captain was never put on trial for murder. But his criminal actions and their aftermath helped to stir opposition to the entire trade. Moreover, a ruling on appeal in 1783 did at least refuse the shippers' claim to recover the insurance value of the lost lives. And a new law in 1788 sought to restrict the number of captives carried per ship.

Stubbornly defending their corner, slave-traders and Caribbean plantation owners relied upon the power of money, custom and law, while in the USA the southern plantation owners also appealed to the doctrine of states' rights. An unusual excuse was also attempted by 'Mad Jack' Fuller, the eccentric landowner with estates in Sussex and Jamaica. He blithely claimed that the unfree plantation workers enjoyed better living conditions than did the free British workforce.[66] But these advocates of enslaved labour struggled to frame a 'winning' narrative. Instead, they relied upon public apathy and a degree of ambivalence on the part of sugar-loving consumers. William Cowper caught that mood, ironically summarising their divided sensibilities: 'I pity them [the slaves] greatly. But I must be mum,/ For how could we do without sugar and rum?'[67]

To shake such complacency, the campaigners seeking to abolish the trade unleashed an intensifying barrage of moral outrage, humanitarian concern and statistical details, expressed in tracts, novels, plays, poems, sermons and speeches. Harrowing factual accounts were penned by Thomas Clarkson, who devoted his life to the campaign.[68] Articulate members of the African diaspora also bore witness. Olaudah Equiano, self-styled as Gustavus Vassa, toured Britain in the 1780s, lecturing on the case for abolition. And in a later generation, the Jamaica-born Robert Wedderburn penned *The Horrors of Slavery* (1824).[69] Christian campaigners, including radical groups like the Quakers, stressed the divinely instituted equality of humans: 'we are all one in the eyes of the Lord'. Many Nonconformists thus signed in 1783 the first petition against the trade.[70] And a secular strand of opinion maintained, equally firmly, that all sentient humans had individual rights, including to enjoy freely the fruits of their own labour. Economists, moreover, stressed that an independent workforce was more creative and productive than a coerced one, toiling in bondage.[71]

Collectively, all abolitionists agreed that enslavement contradicted the enlightened 'temper of the times'. While pro-slavers lobbied behind the scenes, they did not found pro-slavery associations. The abolitionists, by contrast, cultivated nationwide networks of local societies.[72] Many women, otherwise excluded from the front line of official politics, also became active in the movement, helping to organise the Anti-Saccharine Society's consumer boycott of sugar in 1792.[73] This tactic, which dented profits, was a warning to the slave-traders. But William Wilberforce, the evangelical MP for Hull who was the abolitionists' key spokesman – and the son and grandson of merchants – did not denounce commerce alone. Hence he urged forcefully in the Commons in 1789: 'We are all guilty – we ought all to plead guilty, and not to exculpate ourselves by throwing the blame on others.'[74]

Thus, while Britain's politicians were coping with multiple policies on many fronts, this single issue campaign steadily stoked the domestic pressures for change. And abolition did succeed – in two stages, a generation apart. In 1807 a coalition of Whigs and liberal Tories (allied in the brief-lived 'Ministry of All the Talents') legislated to abolish British participation in the slave trade. Because many shippers tried to evade detection or to sail under foreign flags, the Royal Navy was deployed to police the new policy. It took sixty years of naval patrols and diplomatic effort, working with the Americans, who in 1807 passed a federal law banning further importations of slaves into the USA, to halt the controversial shipments.[75] The power of vested interests was strong but not invincible.

Campaigners then transferred their efforts to abolish the real target: the institution of legalised slavery itself. This project took another generation. In 1831 a mass protest among the enslaved population in Jamaica, led by the charismatic Baptist preacher Samuel Sharpe, escalated into an uprising. It lasted a full ten days, before being crushed.[76] The plantocracy retaliated with severe reprisals. Yet such brutality boosted support for abolition, and in

1833 the new Whig government forthwith banned slavery in all British colonies. (Later legislation in 1843 clarified that the rule applied equally to India.) It became clear to all parties that abolition had legally 'won', even if implementation was a continuing struggle.

Twice the British state intervened to halt a trade and then a system of enslaved labour which were operated under its jurisdiction, but neither of which the state ran directly. In so doing, it advanced the case for international economic regulation. For all anti-slavery campaigners, Britain's eventual opposition to what is sometimes termed 'slave capitalism' was a principled policy, which took sustained political pressure to achieve.[77] At the same time, their victory was made easier by the accelerating global diversification of Britain's acquisitive economy, which diminished the earlier power of the West Indian sugar lobby. The plantation owners, who generally had not changed their minds, were bypassed in 1833, rather than educated into a different mindset or (more pro-actively) asked to make any kind of reparation.

Implementation of the changes following upon abolition was therefore problematic. As critics have noted, the abolitionists' attitudes towards those they were trying to help was often paternalistic and naive.[78] Compensation was paid only to the slaves' 'owners', who were losing specific property rights, and not to the enslaved people.[79] Many plantations shifted to a new regime of indentured labour, employing imported Indian and Chinese workers in semi-slavery for low pay.[80] Caribbean society was left to forge its own resilience, grappling with the aftermath of a system which had negated personal autonomy and especially undermined the authority of African males, removed from patrilineal societies.[81] (In Jamaica today Samuel Sharpe, who died on the gallows, is commemorated as a national hero.[82] But in both the USA and the Caribbean, a full process of truth and reconciliation awaits: the building up of the slave economy was a prolonged process; and shedding its legacy is proving similarly prolonged too.)

Inventing and Disputing Hierarchies of 'Race'

Overall, Georgian attitudes to strangers with different physiognomies covered a spectrum. Believers in a common humanity stressed the 'Brotherhood of Man' – a favoured motif in abolitionist tokens and medals. Yet social leaders in societies with marked power imbalances often looked down upon those at the 'foot' of society, especially if the 'others' looked and spoke differently. As a result, traders in captive Africans could view their cargoes as subhuman. Indian civil servants could rationalise their role by viewing Indians as 'backward' and 'uncivilised'. (Not all did.) Individuals also changed their minds. The ex-slave-trader John Newton renounced his former ways. He declared simply in his hymn 'Amazing Grace' (written 1772; published 1779) that he had come to his proper senses: 'I was blind, but now I see'. And he was not alone in initially accepting but then rejecting enslavement and all its works.

New formulations of social differences were, however, being added into the mix, from the later eighteenth century onwards, in the form of ostensibly scientific classifications of humankind. One approach, known as phrenology, had a brief success, with a dedicated Phrenological Society in Edinburgh (1820), and a best-selling textbook, George Combe's *Elements of Phrenology* (1824). It hoped to reveal criminal 'types' and individual personalities by measuring heads, jaws and cranial features. Yet phrenology, which had no scientific basis, proved to be an intellectual wrong turning. By the 1840s it was strongly debunked.[83]

Biologists sought instead more complex classifications. They were inspired by the Swedish botanist Carl Linnaeus, who in 1758 kindly named the human species as *Homo sapiens* (with *sapiens* meaning 'wise' or 'knowledgeable'). Some experts, like the English physician Charles White, held that there were many different breeds of humans, with 'whites' and 'negroes' constituting separate biological entities. This view was known as the theory of polygenism.[84] But, after much debate between scientists and theologians, it was accepted that humans collectively constitute one species (monogenism).

Within that generic category, however, were there any scientifically valid racial sub-classifications? On that point, no consensus emerged. Estimates ranged from two separate 'races' ('black' and 'white') to as many as sixty-three.[85] Linnaeus himself had proposed four geographically based indigenous groups: in America, in Europe and West Asia, in Asia, and in sub-Saharan Africa. Other biologists tried a range of definitional criteria: from skin colour to hair texture, average height, cranial formation, nose shape and testable intelligence. Phrenologists offered to help, by measuring head-sizes. Still the answers remained inconsistent.

Eventually, it transpired that the entire quest to find well-defined racial sub-groups within the species was another erroneous trackway – a pseudo-science, which is dying only slowly – like phrenology.[86] Geneticists show that millennia of migration have moved humans around the globe and frequent intermarriage has sufficiently merged genetic groupings within the species, so that all apparent genetic clusters actually contain immense diversity within them.[87]

Outward differences do not detract from underlying homogeneity. So humans, like dogs and horses, can interbreed with others of their species, while birds, which constitute many separate species, cannot. In 1766, the novelist Laurence Sterne already urged the universalist-humanist alternative. Indicating the rainbow spectrum of human skin colours, he asked pointedly: 'at which tint of these, is it that the ties of blood are to cease?' (Since 1950, the United Nations refers not to 'race' but to 'ethnic groups'.[88] And this terminology is now being updated as 'heritage', which may be mixed.) True, universalism then was easier to invoke abstractly than to put into everyday practice. Nonetheless, a growing number of Georgians responded affirmatively when the abolitionist Olaudah Equiano challenged them with the question: *'But is not the slave trade entirely a war with the heart of man?'*[89]

ᴄᴏ Time-Shift: Then and Now ᴄᴏ

Movement is a perennial part of global history as shown by five trees and shrubs which have become naturalised legacies of Georgian Britain's global explorations. These are reminders of the extent of global migration, not always welcomed, but regularly experienced by countless living organisms, from humans to microbes, on Planet Earth.

1. The cedar of Lebanon (*Cedrus libani*), introduced from the eastern Mediterranean *c.* 1700. One of the oldest living examples can be seen in the park of Adare Manor, Adare, Limerick.

2. The weeping willow (*Salix babylonica*), introduced from northern China in the early eighteenth century. One of the first in Britain grew in the Twickenham riverside garden of the poet Alexander Pope (1688–1744). A section of its trunk is kept in Pope's Grotto, Twickenham.

3. The common rhododendron (*Rhododendron ponticum*), introduced from the Middle East in 1763 and now classified as an invasive species. Visible in many parks, gardens and open countryside with suitably non-alkaline soils, such as the National Park at Snowdonia, the website of which gives advice on controlling its spread.

4. Wisteria (*Wisteria sinensis*), introduced from Canton in southern China. The oldest in Britain was planted as a cutting in 1816, began producing flowers within three years, and still flourishes at Fuller's Griffin Brewery, Chiswick.

5. Douglas fir (*Pseudotsuga menziesii*), an American evergreen conifer, named by two Scottish naturalist-explorers, David

Douglas and Archibald Menzies, and introduced to Britain in the early nineteenth century. Today the tallest Douglas fir in the UK reaches over 217 feet in height, and grows in Reelig Glen, Moniack, Inverness.

PART IV
The Georgians in Social Ferment

A marvelling crowd of men and women, young and old,
including a man of African heritage, view the social media
equivalent of their times, featuring variegated prints of
celebrities, fairy tales, satires and nudes.

ᥱᥩ 13 ᥩᥱ

Aristocrats, Plutocrats and
Cross-Class Gentlemen

Social interconnectedness for the Georgians was acknowledged by the concept of 'civil society'. In Britain, long before Adam Ferguson in 1767 analysed its core characteristics, the term was current at least by the 1690s.[1] The concept conveyed a secular sphere of human interaction, with shared values and peaceable intentions. Thus a tract of 1715, alarmed by heated political tensions, denounced all 'Fanatick' and 'Schismatick' fervour, showing *How Destructive it has been Both to Religion and Civil Society*.[2] Instead, a degree of mutual civility was required. Those at the 'top' were expected to display in public not a freezing hauteur but an affable bonhomie. Any who seemed too proud were open to satire, not admiration. Such unwritten rules welded society together – and guided social 'upstarts' on how to behave.[3] Thus, while British society at first glance still seemed highly traditional, headed by kings, dukes and earls, in reality it was in a prolonged state of flux at all social levels.[4]

At what was traditionally called the 'head' of society, the old landed aristocracy was merging with a new plutocracy, with some tensions in the process, to form a porous and broad-based 'upper class'. One slang usage from the 1790s referred, chaffingly, to its outward elevation as the 'upper crust'.[5] Another relevant term (first imported from France in 1823) named them as the 'elite'. Those terms were useful in shedding the idea that land was the sole source of social status and power. Instead, as will be seen, there were plural authority structures, with a diverse range of attributes and claims.

One sign of social flexibility was an extension of the honours system. Each British realm had a long-established chivalric body, with a socially and numerically restricted membership chosen by the monarch: England's Order of the Garter (founded 1348), Scotland's Order of the Thistle (re-founded 1687), and Ireland's Order of St Patrick (1783–1922).[6] Yet demand for social honours was fast outrunning the supply. Hence in 1725 the pragmatic premier Robert Walpole launched a new Order of the Bath. Initially, it had one Grand Master plus thirty-five (male) members. By 1815, however, its numbers had risen to around 500. So many of these were military and naval officers that later (in 1847) a specially designated civilian branch was added. The honour was personal, not heritable – the honours equivalent of a life peerage. Distributing these awards provided government ministers with useful patronage. And they gave scope to recognise meritocratic personal achievements, irrespective of an individual's social status. (The Order of the Bath was the forerunner of later civic awards, such as the Order of the British Empire, with its associated grades, instituted in 1917.)

Another feature of change at the 'top' was the marked long-term restriction in the number of hereditary titles. These were significant accolades, conveying high social prestige and a potential political role. Yet across all three kingdoms, those with noble titles numbered just 396 men in 1700, rising to 504 in 1800.[7] These totals were tiny – especially given Britain's fast-rising population. New peerages were awarded by the monarch, as advised by ministers, while all peerages both old and new were passed on by inheritance in the senior male line. (A few women did inherit specific titles in their own right.

However, an unchallenged custom debarred them from attending the House of Lords.)

Instead, flexibility was gained by the expansion of Irish titles. Those conferred prestige, but (before the Act of Union in 1801) no membership in the Upper House. Thus Lord Clive 'of India' gained an Irish title as 1st Baron Clive of Plassey in 1762, but remained eligible for the British House of Commons, where he sat as MP for Shrewsbury from 1761 to 1774. The relative paucity of titled people in Georgian Britain contrasted markedly with French society before 1789. There as many as 17,000 to 25,000 families were noble – including nobles by inheritance and nobles by office (*noblesse de robe*). Their jostling for power and incomes to match their outward status was one source of friction in pre-revolutionary France.[8] British society was also competitive, but titles were by no means the sole – or even chief – social prizes, as will be seen.

Landed Aristocrats

Outwardly grandest of all was the very small core of noble families, each headed by the holder of a leading non-royal title: a duke, an earl, a marquess, and so forth. They came from all three of the traditional realms, and they were usually proud of their status as social leaders. However, these titled men were not a separate caste, cut off from the wider society: in law, cadet members of noble families were legally commoners, unless they held another noble title in their own right. (A few families had multiple peerages, which were shared between family heads and eldest sons.) Otherwise, commoners with noble family ancestry were recognised only by 'courtesy titles'. Lord North, the prime minster who failed to retain the American colonies, was one such example. He was so named by courtesy, as the eldest son and heir of the 1st Earl of Guilford. As a result, Lord North hence sat for most of his political career in the House of Commons. Only in 1790, after his father's death, did he join the House of Lords as the 2nd Earl of Guilford.[9]

Beyond the ranks of the titled 'nobility', there was a broader swathe of high-status families, who were known loosely as the 'aristocracy'. This social category referred to those with substantial property in land (although they often had other assets as well), but not necessarily a noble title.[10] In literature, Jane Austen's proud *Mr* Darcy, the owner of Pemberley (modelled upon Chatsworth), was an aristocrat, in spite of his lack of title. Eighteenth-century Sussex also provided two real-life exemplars. One was Sir Harry Fetherstonhaugh, owner of Uppark House, high on the South Downs, whose house and grounds were elegantly remodelled in the eighteenth century. He was legally a commoner, as were all knights and baronets, but was an unquestioned Sussex bigwig. (His marriage in old age to a young dairymaid was noted above, p. 87.) The other was 'Mad Jack' Fuller, the squire of Brightling. He had immense wealth, gained partly from his family's Wealden iron manufactory, and partly from his Jamaican plantations (see above, p. 236). Yet he enjoyed his status as an independent and eccentric country squire. Indeed, he was reliably reported as having been offered and refused a peerage.[11] (Fuller's building projects included an observatory and his mausoleum within a 25-foot-high pyramid, erected in Brightling churchyard.)

Furthermore, buttressing these grandest families in the countryside were the many small landowners and country squires. In times of agricultural depression, their incomes were under pressure; and, in the very long run, small landed estates were disappearing. Nonetheless, for many years they provided a backbone of social stability. Jane Austen again penned an exemplar of a plain country gentleman, this time in *Emma* (1815). Mr Knightley, whose surname hints at his inner merits, has no title. His residence is the old-fashioned Donwell Abbey, which is described as 'rambling and irregular, with many comfortable and one or two handsome rooms'. It had not been remodelled in the latest style, but remains unmistakeably the residence of 'true gentility'.[12]

Signs of change overlapped within traditions of stability. That characteristic was evident in the contrasting fates of Britain's three hereditary (non-monarchical) offices of state. One post survived unaltered. The post of England's Earl Marshal, overseeing state ritual upon ceremonial occasions, was inherited by successive Dukes of Norfolk of the Howard family, as remains the case in the early twenty-first century. In Scotland, by contrast, the equivalent post disappeared entirely. Its hereditary holder in 1715 was the young George Keith, 10th Earl Marischal. However, he backed the losing Jacobites and, among other penalties, lost his post, which fell into abeyance.[13] When George IV visited Scotland in 1822, he met the head of the Clan Keith, who was dubbed Knight Marischal as a sign of reconciliation. Yet the old hereditary office was not revived.

By contrast, England's hereditary office of Lord Great Chamberlain, the ceremonial steward of the Palace of Westminster, saw an inventive variation. In 1779, the holder died without a son. His dukedom went, correctly, to the nearest male heir. But, remarkably, the House of Lords ruled in 1780 that the Duke of Ancaster's two daughters could jointly undertake the hereditary office. Since then, their descendants have provided the Lords Chamberlain, the job alternating (reign by reign) from one branch of the family to the other. When there are, through the continuing hazards of descent, female inheritors, they then appoint male deputies (usually husbands or sons).[14] The Georgians thus made a very limited nod towards gender equality. Perhaps a future woman Lord Chamberlain will further innovate by acting in her own right (that is, if the post remains a hereditary one).

Continuity in high places often turns out to conceal a mixture of persistence and innovation. That certainly applied to one exceptional privilege. Within Westminster Abbey, there is only one private vault, owned by the Percy family, Dukes of Northumberland. This special grant was made in the early eighteenth century. It went to a close confidante of Queen Anne named Elizabeth Percy, a noble heiress who was married to the 'proud' Charles Seymour, 6th Duke of Somerset. He had rebuilt Petworth House in palatial splendour; and he firmly declined to take his wife's surname.[15] However, in 1750 the family heiress in the next generation found a more accommodating husband. He was a politician on the rise, who gladly adopted the Percy surname and, later, gained the revived dukedom of Northumberland as well. Thus Westminster Abbey's only private vault still belongs to the apparently unchanging Percy dynasty. But the inheritance had actually moved to a different male line (in strict patrilineal terms), which had nonetheless discreetly renamed itself in response to the realities of female inheritance.

Grandeur at the very 'top' was boosted by appropriate ceremonial; but here again there were signs of adaptation. Upper-crust families would certainly expect to have retinues of liveried menservants. Unlike in earlier eras, however, great families in the Georgian era did not organise their staff into private armies. The one exception was the Duke of Atholl's infantry regiment, the Atholl Highlanders. This group had only a shadowy and undistinguished military manifestation between 1771 and 1783. Yet it was reconstituted in the 1840s as a purely private small ceremonial force, which won the favour of Queen Victoria. (This ad hoc regiment survives, intermittently, to this day, though its description as 'Europe's only private army' much exaggerates its size and role.)[16]

Reverence for male primogeniture, which governed the transmission of titles and land, was widespread among landowning society, although parents with entailed estates (restricted to male inheritors) and yet without male heirs (like the Bennets in *Pride and Prejudice*) might bewail the misfortunes of their non-inheriting daughters. In a few cases, families took steps to bypass primogeniture. Breaking an entail was legally possible, with the heir's consent, although it was both tricky and costly. (Fresh legislation eased the process after 1833.) Another legal procedure, again with the heir's consent, was resettlement, when annuities were attached to an entailed estate in favour of specific individuals, like widows, daughters and younger sons. But the core system continued unabated, despite sharp criticisms from radicals such as Thomas Paine and Mary Wollstonecraft, who described primogeniture as the eldest son 'trampling' on his siblings.

Rival fraternal rights were highlighted after the death of the 5th Earl of Berkeley in 1810. He and his long-term partner Mary Cole, a butcher's daughter, had twelve children, including seven sons. However, because their first union was deemed illegal, the Berkeley title went to the fifth son, who was the first to be born after their legally recognised (re)marriage. The family castle, meanwhile, was bequeathed by will to the eldest son.[17] Thereafter the officially legitimate 6th Earl declined to acknowledge his peerage or to attend the House of Lords. Yet two of his technically 'illegitimate' elder brothers stood for Parliament and sat as legislators in the Commons.

Disposal of personal property, outside the entail, gave the greatest scope for family heads to exercise discretion. Intense rivalries between siblings over such issues recur in Georgian novels and plays.[18] One fascinating literary example appears in Richardson's *Clarissa* (1748).[19] Disputes over the disposal of property stir the intrigue in this story of ill-fated love and lust between an aristocratic rake and an upwardly mobile daughter of the bourgeoisie. Richardson charts the protagonists' changing emotions with tender insight. No historical case history was quite so melodramatic. Yet one great public benefaction does stem from a family which used its wealth to amass not additional land but disposable property. During the eighteenth century, the first four Marquesses of Hertford invested in superb European artworks. The resultant collection, being outside the law of entail, passed through a sequence of private hands until it was eventually bequeathed to the nation. It is now on view as the Wallace Collection, exhibited at Hertford House in central London.[20]

Fluctuations in aristocratic family fortunes were legion. It took continuous effort to keep the grand show on the road. An incautious political or religious judgment at the wrong moment, a prolonged excess of expenditure over income, unsuccessful investments, a weak or nefarious estate steward, a string of daughters requiring expensive dowries, the lack of a male heir, or scandals causing social ostracism: these were some characteristic problems. However, the entail system put some ballast into the system, at least for the male heirs. For that reason, while the fortunes of individuals bobbed up and down, there was considerable (though not absolute) outward continuity at the top, in terms of the identity of the great houses and families in each region.[21]

Meanwhile, it is worth noting that, while there were very rich landowners without titles, there were also titled men without exceptional wealth. Take the politically grand Robert Jenkinson, 2nd Earl of Liverpool. He was the prime minister who in the 1820s was the epitome of staunch traditionalism. Yet he was no landed aristocrat. Instead, he was the son of a 'political' peer, Charles Jenkinson, who was ennobled as 1st Earl for serving as aide to George III.[22] Neither father nor son was mega-rich, neither acquired a large country estate, yet both seemed august, albeit working hard to attain their grandeur.

Aristocratic families who diversified their economic portfolios had the best chances of long-term success. Investments in financial markets, profits from overseas trade (including the slave trade), the exploitation of mineral resources, the emoluments of political office and marriages into wealthy commercial or professional families all contributed regularly to landed coffers. Some titled families flourished as owners of coal mines; and a proportion ran the collieries themselves – like the Earls of Dudley in the Black Country, with a long history of involvement in industrial and transport innovations.[23] Yet a spendthrift heir was always a dynastic hazard. Of the young George Villiers, for instance, it was reported in the 1760s that: 'His lordship is very ingenious in the art of wasting the most possible money in the least possible time'.[24]

Dips in family fortunes thus required urgent remedial action. The Cecils, ennobled under Elizabeth I, were a case in point. By the 1770s, the head of the family, the Catholic 6th Earl of Salisbury, was living as an impoverished recluse. The family home of Hatfield

House in Hertfordshire was left empty and dilapidated. His only companions were a set of 'old and rusty servants', his lower-class mistress (his 'old Dame') and their illegitimate children.[25] Recovery and a return to conventionality, however, began under the 7th Earl. He reverted to Anglicanism and won office at court, also gaining a marquisate. And the Cecil finances were substantially re-floated in 1821, when the 2nd Marquess married Frances Gascoyne. She was heiress to four different ancestral fortunes, gained in law, brewing, medicine and politics respectively. Her funds were used to restore the historic Hatfield House and estate. In tribute, the family surname was changed to Gascoyne-Cecil, as it remains to this day.[26] Hence the famous 3rd Marquess of Salisbury, thrice prime minister under Queen Victoria, who is often cited as proof of the long dominance of the landed aristocracy, was the heir to a hybrid estate, funded chiefly by business, professional and political fortunes.

Poised between town and countryside, those Georgian aristocrats who were able to ride the tides of history made an impressive show. They owned and renovated great country houses and surrounding estates. Many also had magnificent town houses as winter residences.[27] The eighteenth century saw a veritable rage for building, garden improvements and park landscaping.[28] Some leading stately homes were fully as majestic as royal palaces: Hopetoun House near Edinburgh, Castle Howard in Yorkshire, Chatsworth in Derbyshire, Holkham Hall in Norfolk, Vanbrugh's masterpiece Blenheim Palace in Oxfordshire, Stowe House in Buckinghamshire and Petworth House in Sussex (to name but a few). The spread of such residences, both large and small, in a shared Georgian-Palladian style gave an appearance of aristocratic confidence and unity across Great Britain. The effect was visible across the countryside in England and Wales, Scotland and Ireland.[29] And the impact was equally impressive within the great capital cities.[30]

Marriage strategies were important to advance family fortunes, although, as already indicated, sometimes individual heirs acted rashly rather than prudentially. Brides of good pedigree were welcome, but especially so were those with wealth. One study has investigated matrimonial decisions made by the titled peerage (nobility), at the absolute apex of society. Between 1600 and 1800, over one third (34.4 per cent) of the first marriages of 826 male English peers were unions with commoner brides. In other words, a significant number of wives marrying into the nobility were either daughters of merchants, bankers and professionals, or daughters of non-titled landowners.[31] Furthermore, those figures were calculated only by reference to the status of the brides' fathers. Had data on their mothers been available, the picture would be yet more complicated. Thus it is eminently possible that a good proportion of the 65.6 per cent of peers' brides with noble fathers may still have had 'commoner' mothers.

As a result, the British peerage was socially porous. It was a key characteristic which gave it a notable survivability, as well as ethnic breadth and pan-British range. One relevant exemplar was the family of John Stuart, 3rd Earl of Bute. Much pilloried in the 1760s for his perceived 'Scottishness', he lived most of his life in England, and he wed an English commoner, Mary Wortley-Montagu. Her father was a Yorkshire landowner-cum-diplomat, and her mother a well-esteemed English literary figure who first promoted smallpox inoculation. Among the Butes' eleven children, the eldest son inherited the Scottish peerage; four daughters wed English peers; one daughter wed a commoner; the youngest daughter stayed at home and wrote; while a younger son rose in the Church to become Archbishop of Armagh in Northern Ireland.[32]

Among this flexibility, any high-born individuals who stood too much upon their dignity were satirised rather than admired. In the later eighteenth century, Prince William Frederick, Duke of Gloucester, became known for his close attention to punctilio and obsessive following of ceremony. He was the great-grandson of George II, as well as the nephew and son-in-law of George III. Yet the duke remained very sensitive about his status, perhaps because his youth at court had been overshadowed by his mother's illegitimacy. At any rate, he insisted that courtiers must stand in his presence at all times. Such formality seemed excessive from one who was neither king nor heir to the throne. His unkind nickname was 'Silly Billy'.[33]

Indeed, any idea that 'blue blood' was on its own a valid claim to high status and haughty behaviour was coming under serious challenge in this period. Meritocratic ideas stressed that ability, not birth, provided the only true claim to respect, as discussed in Chapter 16. But one quotation here conveys the critical atmosphere, as Alexander Pope enquired rhetorically (1733): 'What can ennoble sots, or slaves, or cowards?/ Alas! not all the blood of all the HOWARDS'.[34] This allusion to England's premier ducal family no doubt stemmed from the poetic usefulness of a surname that rhymed with 'cowards'. Yet the couplet indicated that assured intellectuals like Pope, who stood tall in his own literary pulpit, spurned the idea that high birth alone guaranteed true inner nobility.

Monied Plutocrats

A parallel and increasingly overlapping elite of 'monied' families was also coming to the fore.[35] From the late seventeenth century onwards, references to the power of money became commonplace. A poem, published in York in 1696, stated that *Pecuniae Obediunt Omnia: Money Masters All Things*. And its subtitle explained: *The Power and Influence of Money over All Arts, Sciences, Trades, Professions, and Ways of Living in this Sublunary World*.[36] Another ballad lamented the sad fate of a youth who dissipated his wealth. The result was 'No Money, No Friend': 'So then was I despis'd by all,/ That me before did Master call'.[37] The power of lucre extended even into intimate daily life. Jonathan Swift was one observer of this trend. In the *Examiner* (1710), he exaggerated to make the point that '*Power*, which according to an old maxim was used to follow *Land*, is now gone over to

Money.[38] Certainly, too, John Gay's cynical Mr Peachum in *The Beggar's Opera* (1728) amused theatre audiences by remarking that: 'Money, wife, is the true Fuller's Earth [an absorbent clay] for reputations. There is not a spot or a stain but what it can take out.'[39]

In the early eighteenth century, successful bankers, financiers, brokers and overseas merchants were known as the 'monied interest', in contrast to the 'landed interest'. At first there was a strong rivalry between the two, with the Tories stressing 'land' and the Whigs favouring 'commerce'. However, the economic boundaries were always porous.[40] Over time, the conjunction rather than the opposition of land and business money became ever more apparent. In the early nineteenth century, Robert Southey defined Britain's social leaders as an 'aristocracy of wealth', explaining that the new 'commercial system' was generating a new 'manufacturing and mercantile aristocracy'.[41] By the 1830s the term 'plutocracy' was in use.[42] And Thomas Carlyle was blunt in detecting an 'Aristocracy of the Moneybag'.[43]

Traditionalists used to claim that being 'in trade' constituted an impediment to true gentility. (Snobbish sneers at commerce still resurface at times today.) But that attitude was already being rebutted in the later seventeenth century, as economic expansion took hold. In 1702 the Tory traditionalist Edward Chamberlayne updated the twentieth edition of his guide to *The Present State of England*, to agree for the first time that nobles and gentlemen were not degraded by having served an apprenticeship.[44] Yet a rival Whig handbook of 1691 was already vocal on the merits of wealth: 'Gentility with competent Means is an excellent Compound; but without it, 'tis but a wretched Condition, as the world goes now'.[45]

Hence whilst there was a lively Georgian literature of complaint about crass and intrusive commercial newcomers, such writings indicated unease at what was actually an accumulating process.[46] Complaints expressed concern but without halting change. The subliminal message to those making new fortunes was not to desist but to learn polite manners. Thus, while a few landed families tried to stay aloof from city money and court 'corruption', the long-term inter-mixing was pervasive.[47] In the course of the eighteenth century, most country landowners made investments in business and government bonds – and often also in overseas trade and the sugar plantations, tended by an enslaved workforce. Manifold connections between land and money were also generated by landed aristocrats sending their younger sons into banking, business, politics or the professions, including the army. Another link came from landowners marrying daughters of London merchants, as did Sir Robert Walpole (twice). Social links between 'old' land and 'new' money were everywhere widespread.

Successful plutocrats had no hesitation in aiming high. They sought titles and purchased country estates.[48] Among their number were some notable recruits from European Jewry, who made fortunes in commerce and banking as their families settled in Britain: Sampson Gideon in the early eighteenth century (see above, p. 28), the Rothschilds in the early nineteenth.[49] Yet not all 'monied' families wanted to go deep into the countryside. Some constructed their superfine residences just outside the big cities. Hopetoun House, 13 miles from Edinburgh, was one exemplar. It was built between 1699 and 1701 for the Hope family, whose fortunes were based upon law, political office and lead-mining. The property was later upgraded in 1721 by the rising Scottish architect William Adam, while his sons John and Robert Adam refurbished the sumptuous interior. Another case was the redevelopment of Osterley Park, 11 miles west of Charing Cross. The property, once home to the Greshams, the Tudor bankers, was later purchased by the Georgian banker Robert Child, who commissioned Robert Adam to build a new palatial mansion on its site. (Today it's an ornament of the National Trust, with the original Elizabethan stables nearby.)

However, one cadet branch of the Child family provided a cautionary tale. A string of successful marriages in the seventeenth century brought dowries into the family from commercial, legal and landed sources. In 1715, the super-wealthy Richard Child commissioned another Scottish architect, Colen Campbell, to build the first Palladian mansion in Britain, known as Wanstead House, located by Epping Forest, 8 miles north-east of Charing Cross. Completed in 1722, it was a princely seat, intended to rival the Baroque splendours of Blenheim. (It didn't.) Yet it was clearly fit for a viscount, as Child became in 1718 (he was later raised to an earldom in the Irish peerage). The house was gorgeously adorned with paintings, sculptures, furniture, plate and books.

In 1812, the heiress to this plutocratic fortune married a nephew of the Duke of Wellington. (The young couple hosted a big dinner to celebrate Waterloo.) But the bridegroom proved to be an inveterate gambler, and eventually, in 1825, he and his estranged wife agreed a settlement. To pay his debts and to save a modicum for their eldest son, their assets were auctioned. Wanstead House, having impressed everyone for just over 100 years, was razed to the ground, and the estate left as parkland, as it remains.[50] Grandeur could thus prove surprisingly impermanent.

Unsurprisingly, wealthy parents strove to prevent their daughters from marrying rakes and spendthrifts. And plutocrats at times had more specific requirements, such as gaining sons-in-law to continue the family business. In 1741 the wealthy ironmonger Sir Thomas Dunk refused to allow his daughter to marry George Montagu, 2nd Earl of Halifax, on the grounds that her destiny was to marry a man in commerce. But so much for fathers. Halifax purchased membership of a City Livery Company to gain his trading credentials. And the marriage went ahead, with the couple changing their surname to Montagu-Dunk.[51] This inventive suitor was the Halifax who later, as President of Britain's Board of Trade in the 1750s, fostered commerce in North America, and whose title was borrowed to name the city of Halifax in Nova Scotia.

Similar concerns underpinned another family dispute in 1782. The banker Robert Child wanted a son-in-law to take his name and run the bank. As noted above (p. 98), he was enraged when his only daughter Sarah Anne Child eloped with the 10th Earl of Westmorland. He disinherited both his daughter and her eldest son.[52] Yet this father was also thwarted. Eventually, for lack of other heirs, the house at Osterley Park and control of the bank passed to Child's eldest grand-daughter, the Countess of Jersey, who had married a peer. She remained the bank's chief shareholder until her death in 1867. Her husband, meanwhile, added her surname to his but spent his time happily in foxhunting and horse-breeding. It was the famously talkative countess who proved to be not only a noted political hostess in the conservative-plutocratic interest but also a discreet principal banker. Thus she cultivated, via her social connections, the high-class clientele for which Child's Bank is still known today.[53]

Plutocratic and aristocratic mergings were sufficiently common by the later eighteenth century for some arch-traditionalists to worry that the landed interest was being entirely ignored. So when in the 1790s, the Younger Pitt ennobled thirty new English peers to boost his support in the Lords, there were complaints that he had advanced 'monied' outsiders, Indian 'nabobs' and upstart 'mushroom men'.[54] However, in practice many of Pitt's recruits came from already landed or titled families, albeit often with commercial connections.[55] Signs of such yoking were seen in the custom of families tacking together surnames from both male and female lines. The case of the Gascoyne-Cecils has already been cited. Another was that of the 'Wiltshire heiress', Catherine Tylney-Long. When in 1812 she married the dissipated Richard Pole-Wellesley, he became Richard Pole-Tylney-Long-Wellesley, changing his name by royal licence.[56] It was a good gamble on his part, gaining him access to a fortune although not, as it transpired, to a happy marriage. Such surname diplomacy was an easy way to acknowledge diverse dynastic contributions.[57]

Two of the greatest Georgian fortunes came from landed and commercial mergers. William Thomas Beckford, born in 1760, was known as Britain's richest commoner, and lived more lavishly than many a duke. His wealth came from profits from enslaved labour on his Jamaican estates, from his Fonthill estate in Wiltshire and from his merchant father.[58] Beckford became a fabled art collector, sexual adventurer, architectural patron, phantasmagorical Gothic novelist, travel writer, MP and, finally, a serious recluse.[59] He commissioned the gigantic neo-Gothic Fonthill Abbey and, perhaps in a sign of hubris, its huge central tower fell down not once but thrice. After 1825 the property was left derelict. Here was consumption on a colossal scale, from a man with the temperament of an outsider, who saw polite society as composed of competitive 'wild beasts'. Yet the Beckfords were not shunned. He married (unhappily) an earl's daughter, and left his art collection to his younger daughter, the wife of a duke.

Beckford's titled counterpoint in the later eighteenth century was Britain's richest peer, George Granville Leveson-Gower, Viscount Trentham, later 1st Duke of Sutherland. He inherited profits from land, transport and mining interests in Midland England, and was described as a veritable 'Leviathan of wealth'.[60] And his wife contributed yet more lucre. Elizabeth Gordon not only owned vast estates in Sutherland but pushed to maximise their commercial yield, hastening the controversial Highland Clearances. Eventually, she was made Countess of Sutherland in her own right.[61] As a result, the couple were viewed locally with much ambivalence, notwithstanding their outward grandeur. (The duke's tall statue, known as the 'Mannie', erected in 1837 atop Ben Bhraggie in east Sutherland, raises debates today about how best to confront the history of past social conflicts.)

Together these merged economic interests were generating a plutocratic aristocracy, with a lifestyle to match. Landed and 'monied' families met as equals in town for the winter season, and at resorts, spas and country estates for summer recreation. The great Georgian art collectors – including the politician Robert Walpole, the sugar-heir William Beckford and the landowner George Wyndham, 3rd Earl of Egremont, who was Turner's patron at Petworth – all had multiple economic resources. The same applied to the top Georgian architectural sponsors, who included many creative and resourceful women.[62]

Moreover, this confident lifestyle was conveyed in the early nineteenth century to the new capitalist bosses who were making fortunes from engineering and industrial production.[63] Especially in single-industry towns with one large employer, such families were local kings. In south Wales, that role was filled by the Crawshays, who prospered as ironmasters in Merthyr Tydfil. Their works produced high-grade iron, tempered to make engines, machinery, railways and precision weapons. Pointedly, the Crawshay crest featured a mastiff, standing over a pyramid of cannon-balls.[64] And the family lived 'on the job' in Merthyr. In 1824 their newly commissioned home was built overlooking the works, in the form of the castellated Cyfarthfa Castle. (In the early twenty-first century, it houses both a school and museum.)[65]

Interestingly, one personal sign of this shared aristocratic-plutocratic lifestyle was identifiable via the Georgian merging of regional accents into a standard London-based 'upper-class English'. In the 1770s Sir Christopher Sykes of Sledmere, in the East Riding, sought a tutor for his sons 'who can correct their Yorkshire tones'. By contrast, a defiant descendant, Sir Tatton Sykes, refused to comply, startling polite society in the 1850s with his broad provincial vowels and his insistence on wearing his riding-boots indoors.[66] (He is also commemorated by an exuberant monument near Sledmere.) Yet the fact that his manners and accent caused surprise showed how much elite cultural assimilation had become the norm.

Far from being captivated and captured by land, the British upper crust was diversifying and shifting to a town-based lifestyle, with country estates to own or to visit during the summer season. And 'top' families did not depend upon land and noble titles to prosper. Plutocrats were fortified by their wealth, as they metaphorically rose from rags to riches. In practice, their social origins were varied. However, they still tended to view their wealth as a reward for 'merit'. (It was more difficult for later generations, who inherited plutocratic money, to make the same claim – thus indicating one of the problems within meritocracy over multiple generations.)[67] Yet for most Georgians, the social eminence of the ultra-wealthy bankers, merchants and industrialists seemed to confirm that 'Money Masters All Things', as the ballad claimed.

Cross-Class Gentlemen

Meanwhile, a significantly new cross-class ideal was successfully emerging in this era, which smoothed over the fine distinctions of life at the 'top'. To be known as a 'gentleman', with his wife graciously signalled as a 'lady', was a coveted accolade. This nomenclature was an unofficial (commoner) title, not awarded by the crown but at the bar of public opinion. There was no hard-and-fast rule. No rigid protocol. Instead, it was a matter of social judgment. As a concept, the ideal of the 'gentleman' conveyed not just coveted status but also attributes of probity, respectability, chivalric politeness and independence. It had moral as well as social meanings.

Strikingly, too, the unofficial designation did not lose its popularity with the aristocrats and plutocrats, even while its social elasticity spread. It kept its chivalric connotations. To take one celebrated exemplar, the portly Prince Regent, later King George IV, sought to associate himself with elegance and good style by pluming himself not as the 'first prince' but as the 'first gentleman in Europe'.[68]

During these years, the term was routinely attached to all untitled members of the country gentry: Jane Austen's Mr Knightley was indubitably a gentleman. Furthermore, from the later seventeenth century onwards, commentators referred to the generic concept of 'town gentry' as well as their rural counterparts.[69] Among those considered as 'gentlemen' were officeholders, members of the learned professions and all who made a respectable living without recourse to 'dirty' manual labour. Such key definitions dated back to Tudor times.[70] In this Georgian era, the usage was spreading fast.

To take one example, the common lawyers, a fast-expanding occupational group, were keen users of the courtesy title. It conferred status and helped them to overcome traditional suspicions that they were fleecing their hapless clients. Hence many individuals listed in the Georgian town directories (see below, pp. 272–3) simply as *John Smith, gentleman* turn out, upon cross-checking, to have been attorneys.[71] In other words, the title was elastic, straddling the upper and middle classes. By the later eighteenth century the great majority styled as 'ladies and gentlemen' were in fact urban residents, not country landowners.

Ideally, the concept implied a moral audit to find individuals of personal worth. The Whig journalist Richard Steele in 1713 had provided a classic pen-portrait of the refined dignity and courteous civility to all, which were the key qualities of a Christian gentleman.[72] That chivalric meaning was well understood, even if individuals fell short. Austen drew upon such expectations for a key encounter in *Pride and Prejudice* (1813). Elizabeth Bennet briskly rejects a lofty marriage proposal from the proud Fitzwilliam Darcy, telling him that she might have felt more compunction in refusing: 'had you behaved in a more gentleman-like manner'. As Austen precisely specifies, the rejected suitor is initially at a loss for words, caught between anger and surprise. Later, however, Darcy confesses: 'Your reproof, so well applied, I shall never forget'.[73]

Blurring Social Boundaries

Interpersonal encounters in everyday life were variegated, being often casual and fleeting. There was rarely time to undertake a careful moral audit of everyone encountered in a busy life. Hence for most purposes, the social accolade of being considered a 'gentleman' turned on self-presentation, particularly in smart clothing, manners, style and, to an extent, learning. Dr Johnson's *Dictionary* (1755) noted various shades of meaning. One was 'a term of complaisance', used to praise a respectable stranger as a 'fine gentleman'. Yet the usage could also be ironic. A dictionary-compiler in 1721 had already expressed alarm at the number of 'upstart gentlemen'. And he added sternly that: 'you cannot make a Silken Purse out of a Sow's Ear'.[74]

Satirical jibes at the rising numbers of city gentlemen signalled the increasing middle-class 'capture' of a valued designation. Fine upstanding townsmen did not see themselves as despised tradesmen, pettifogging lawyers, quack doctors, and so forth. Instead, they were confident in their gentlemanly claims, morally ranking themselves with princes. Furthermore, the gentleman's wife was termed a 'lady' (as in the salutation 'ladies and gentlemen'). This nomenclature was gratifying to the affluent bourgeois wife. She sounded, to the casual ear, as absolutely fine as any titled Lady, spelt with a capital L.

Finally, there was also a lurking radicalism within the concept. The concept of 'nature's gentleman' was also emerging, formed totally by inner personal qualities without any reference to external rank or smartness of dress. 'There is many a nobleman, according to the genuine idea of nobility, at the loom, at the plough, and in the shop,' wrote one schoolmaster-cleric in 1778.[75] Not many peers of the realm – let alone many shopkeepers and attorneys – were eager to hear such ideas. Yet old stereotypes were being challenged in this era of social ferment, even if the cultural challenge was often ahead of general public opinion – and was certainly well ahead of any systematic proposals to redistribute income in favour of the rank-and-file workforce.

⁓ Time-Shift: Then and Now ⁓

With these themes in mind, it's a good moment to reread Jane Austen's *Pride and Prejudice* (1813), not just for its narrative verve but also for its precise and witty social observation of manners and morals in Georgian Britain. It can also be compared with the TV adaptation (cited above, p. 113).

Notable themes include: the law of entail and its harsh message for dowerless daughters; a satire of undue pride; satire of undue servility; a satire of inadequate parenting (too fussy, or too negligent); a satire of intrusive relatives; a mild satire of jumping to conclusions too quickly; sympathy for a 'superfluous' not-so-young woman (Charlotte Lucas), who is socially deemed in need of a husband; the dangers in the charm of a sexual adventurer; social rather than religious concern when an unmarried couple run away together; marriage as a conventionally acceptable means of glossing over sin; the importance of 'true' gentlemanly behaviour; equality between gentlemen, even if from different ranks and background; respect for a sensible city businessman (Mr Gardiner); the art of learning to love; and the capacity of some – but not all – characters to gain wisdom.

14

Middlocrats

One major sign of social change in the Georgian era was the formative emergence of the middle class.[1] Their leading lights enjoyed being known as 'ladies and gentlemen', as already noted. One common eighteenth-century descriptive term for them was the 'town gentry'; another was the 'Persons of Consequence', as listed in the new town directories (see below, pp. 272–3), which were multiplying from the 1760s onwards.[2] Yet here they are termed 'middlocrats', an invented term to convey the authority of those in the so-called 'middle' between the ostensible rulers and the outwardly ruled, in both town and country.

Specifically, during this period, the language of 'class' was gliding slowly into currency. The new terminology, which later acquired its own rigidities, began as a loose form of social description, contrasting with earlier references to precise 'ranks' and 'degrees'.[3] It was an epic shift, slowly followed across western Europe by the nineteenth century: in French from *états* to *classes*; in German from *Stände* or *Schichten* to *Klassen*. These 'classes' were, however, never closely defined. And there was no consensus about their numbers. By the

1830s a broad threefold model of upper, middle and working classes was commonplace, but, as will be seen, far from universally accepted.

Written references to the 'middle class' began to appear in the 1740s. The term updated an older language of 'middling ranks' or 'middling sorts'. And it obviated circumlocutions, such as Defoe's usage when introducing Robinson Crusoe as a man from the 'middle state, or what might be called the *upper station of low life*'.[4] The existence of these middlocrats immediately contradicted any idea that British society faced a binary divide between extremes of great wealth and great poverty. Furthermore, in a pluralist social model, the centre could seem to embody the Aristotelian ideal of harmony, the 'Golden Mean'. Hence Daniel Defoe, himself the son of a middling tradesman, stated bluntly, again in *Robinson Crusoe* (1719), that the middle station of life was 'the best state in the world, the most suited to human happiness, not exposed to the miseries and hardships . . . of the mechanic part of mankind, and not embarrassed with the pride, luxury, ambition and envy of the upper part of mankind'.[5]

Over time, this chorus of praise strengthened. Those in the middle fostered public liberty, remarked David Hume in 1742, since they were neither so poor as to be submissive to authority nor so greedy as to be corrupted into supporting tyrants.[6] Others made similar claims. The 'middle class' boosted 'all the arts, wisdom, and virtues of society', and were true preservers of freedom (1766).[7] They symbolised social equipoise: 'neither too humble nor too great' (1784).[8] They were 'the most virtuous, the most enlightened, the most independent part of the community' (1790).[9] Their lifestyle was 'undoubtedly the happiest' (1792).[10] They constituted 'the middling, comfortable, modest and moderate, sober and satisfied, industrious and intelligent classes' (1800).[11] Joseph Priestley, himself the well-educated son of a skilled Yorkshire cloth finisher, further argued that, since men of moderate fortunes were 'better educated, and have consequently more enlarged minds and are . . . more truly independent than those born to great opulence', so the middle class should provide Britain's real rulers.[12]

Such comments indicated no shortage of public declarations of confidence and social visibility. Middlocrats were to be found throughout the three traditional realms, particularly in the towns; and they recruited families from diverse ethnic heritages. Theirs was a competitive world; and, as will be shown, fortunes fell as well as rose. Nonetheless, the middle-class way of life was gaining kudos and becoming ever more socially desirable. (In the USA today the designation is sufficiently valued that it is commonly stretched to include all workers, white-collar as well as blue-collar, excluding only the very poorest.)[13]

Social Rising and Falling

Social labels in Georgian Britain were never precise. 'The different Stations of Life so run into and mix with each other,' complained the Dean of Gloucester in the 1770s, 'that it is hard to say where one ends and the other begins.'[14] At the 'top' of the middle order, these Georgian middlocrats shaded into the lesser landowners and minor noblemen (all claiming the label of 'gentlemen'); and at the 'foot', there was a blurred line between the small master craftsmen and artisans and their skilled journeymen. One anonymous polemicist in 1753 confirmed the overlap by listing the middling sort as 'the *Gentry* [non-large land-owners], the *liberal Professions*, [and] the whole *mercantile Interest*', plus the *Yeomanry* of small farmers, while noting that the yeomen were in a 'waning Condition' – as later historians have confirmed.[15]

Middlocrats were certainly at home in the towns. Yet, as a commentator noted in 1753, there was a small rural middle class too, comprising yeoman farmers, estate stewards, country shopkeepers, a few lawyers, some affluent craftsmen and many clergymen. Those rural 'middlings' were much less numerous and assertive than were their urban counterparts, but they shared middle-class ideas and fashions. And they mediated socially between the great landowners and their labourers. So it is misleading to define the English middle class as purely an urban 'bourgeoisie'. There were many ties between town and country middlocrats: professional – such as when clergymen moved between parishes – and familial, such as when farmers' sons and daughters migrated into towns.

All estimates of middle-class numbers remain imprecise. But, if the hybrid elite of aristocrats and plutocrats constituted perhaps 1–2 per cent of the total population in approximate terms, then the middling sort or middle class was expanding from perhaps 5 per cent in 1700 to some 10–15 per cent by the early nineteenth century. Regional variations are easier to identify, since those reflected local economic conditions. Single-industry towns with one or two great factory employers and many industrial 'hands', like Bury in Lancashire, tended to have fewer middlocrats, whilst in places like Birmingham or Wolverhampton there were many middling master craftsmen in the metalware trades.

In the countryside, too, there were similar variations. Relatively larger numbers of small yeoman farmers and independent freeholders survived in unenclosed pastoral economies, as in Westmoreland and Cumberland, while the comparable middle ranks were being thinned in enclosing agrarian counties, such as Leicestershire and Northamptonshire.[16] These differences meant that inter-class relationships were also liable to vary. There was no automatic rule. Hence neither class antagonism nor class cooperation applied universally.

For the individuals concerned, life in the 'middle' was restless, competitive, acquisitive, often uncertain. There were many families who either rose or fell; and some who rose and fell more than once. Social uncertainties prompted poetic sympathy in 1765, from a youthful English republican named Michael Wodhull. He defined those in the social middle as 'motley Beings':

Who, dragged by Fortune into Middle Life,
That vortex of malevolence and strife,

Envying the Great and scoffing at the Mean,
Now swol'n with pride, now wasted with chagrin.
Like Mahomet's unsettled ashes dwell,
Midway suspended between Heaven and Hell.[17]

This dark pen-portrait offered an antidote to rhapsodies about middle-class happiness. (It was also interesting for Wodhull's assumption that his readers would understand Christian teachings about the posthumous fate of the Islamic prophet.) However, this ingenious poet was not writing from personal experience. Wodhull, who inherited landed estates in Northamptonshire, was a wealthy man, who became a renowned Georgian bibliophile. (Surviving books from his collection are dispersed between many British university libraries.)

Given the uncertainties of middle-class lifestyles, prudent families took a close interest in insurance and savings.[18] They typically invested in local improvement schemes, such as canal construction. And the more adventurous joined in pooled building projects, known as tontines, which offered to pay a life-time annuity, augmented as fellow contributors died, with the last survivor scooping the pool.[19] (In that context, it paid to be a young and healthy investor.) Meanwhile, a management challenge for all providers of goods and services was to collect the multitude of debts owed to them – an everyday problem in an economy that relied upon credit.[20] Anglican clergy proverbially struggled to levy tithes from recalcitrant or impoverished parishioners. The same applied to pew rents, which were legalised in 1818 to provide funds for building new churches. But the payments remained contentious and were often evaded.[21]

Bankruptcy courts were always busy.[22] One spectacular case in 1835 was the financial collapse of Thomas Daniell, with estates in both Trelissick in Cornwall and Michaelchurch in Hereford. His wealth was based upon a paternal legacy from tin- and copper-mining, and a maternal legacy from entrepreneurial landownership.

Yet Daniell became bankrupt through a mix of extravagance and a slump in demand for copper. To evade his creditors he moved to Boulogne, leaving many of them out of pocket. It took almost fifteen years for Daniell's assets to be sold. And even then his creditors were repaid at no more than 7 shillings per pound (just over one-third of the value). Their plight indicated the vulnerability of tradesmen to factors well outside their control.

Another drastic cause of middle-class family decline was a serious illness or sudden death of a male breadwinner. There were many genteel but hard-pressed widows and daughters in Georgian Britain, left with middle-class expectations but no independent income to sustain them. In Austen's *Emma* (1815), the widowed Mrs Bates and her daughter came into that category. 'She [Miss Bates] is poor; she has shrunk from the comforts she was born to; and if she live to old age, must probably sink more,' as Mr Knightley explains, rebuking the wealthy and heedless Emma Woodhouse for snubbing the ever-chattering spinster, whose determined good cheer masks her social plight.[23]

Large numbers of real-life middle-class widows and spinsters eked out small incomes at places like the resort city of Bath, with its array of cheap lodgings.[24] In fact, women constituted a majority of all urban populations in this era. But Bath was truly exceptional. In 1801 61 per cent of that city's population of 34,000 were women, many living alone.[25] Letting out rooms was one option for genteelly poor ladies. Another option was to work as a governess, although workloads could be heavy – and, in a glutted market, earnings often low.[26]

Those seeking to rise could consult advice manuals. One successful prototype was John Trusler's account of *The Way to Become Rich and Respectable: Addressed to Men of Small Fortune* (1755). He advised hard work – and no dissipation.[27] Trusler himself dabbled in many enterprises before prospering as a bookseller and social pundit. Families who did succeed were usually confident in their own merits. Accordingly, leading middlocrats – such as successful lawyers or merchants – moved on easy terms with aristocrats and plutocrats.

Indeed a good proportion of rising industrial families came from middling backgrounds.[28] Many middlocrats, however, were happy with their social eminence in their own bailiwick and were not desperate to climb higher.[29]

By contrast, those newly on the rise seemed to be most touchy about their status. Such characters recur in Georgian fiction, usually as butts of satire. Austen's *Emma* (1815) depicts a suitable target. The vicar's new wife Mrs Elton parades her 'high' family connections and her smattering of culture, affectedly calling her husband her '*caro sposo*'.[30] She seeks to lead the parish, whilst failing to note that her officiousness and self-promotion are not universally loved. Austen's depiction is unwaveringly satirical. Mrs Elton is ever-infuriating and, unlike Miss Bates, has no excuses. Social rising was best done with sensitivity.

The Commercial-Industrial Middle Class

Much of the impetus for the numerical expansion, social visibility and growing wealth of the middle class collectively came from deep-seated economic factors: the spread of urbanisation, commercialisation and eventual industrialisation. Living in affluent style within bustling towns encouraged a certain confidence. And, by this period, all middle-class adults were numerate and literate. They thus provided readers for earnest tracts like Thomas Gisborne's *Enquiry into the Duties of Men in the Higher and Middle Classes of Society in Great Britain* . . . (1794), which rehearsed their duties of social leadership.

Leading male middlocrats were listed individually in the growing genre of town directories. These utilitarian publications brimmed with confidence. So J. Bisset's *Poetic Survey round Birmingham* . . . *Accompanied by a Magnificent Directory* (1800) offered a verse 'ramble of the Gods' through town, plus its listing of leading inhabitants.[31] The *Staffordshire General and Commercial Directory* for 1818 mean-while lauded the great 'population, opulence, and knowledge' of the

Pottery towns.[32] These growing urban-industrial centres were sometimes disparaged. Austen's Mrs Elton predictably declares that: 'One has not great hopes from Birmingham. I always say there is something direful in the sound.'[33] Yet it is her triviality of judgment that is being satirised. Urban leaders saw things quite differently. So, to take one example, William Hutton, the Birmingham businessman, was an unapologetic enthusiast for his adopted home-town. 'When the word Birmingham occurs,' he wrote in 1781 without irony, 'a superb picture instantly expands in the mind, which is best explained by the other words grand, populous, extensive, active, commercial, and *humane*.'[34]

Characteristic male middlocrats, as revealed by the town directories, included a range of merchants, dealers, financiers, tradesmen, shopkeepers, manufacturers, office-holders and professionals, including the clergy. Their middling business culture was male dominated, and all posts in urban government were held by men from this social sector. In some places, a few honorary positions were filled by titled grandees with local economic interests. The *Hampshire Directory* of 1784 listed among Winchester's five aldermen – but not in first place – 'His Grace James 3rd Duke of Chandos'.[35]

But male dominance was far from absolute. Numerous businesses were run by women on their own account. Not only widows who inherited from a departed spouse, but also spinsters and wives circumvented the theoretical legal constraints. If they needed to go to law, they avoided the traditionalist common law courts and applied instead to Chancery, which, as the court of equity, was known as 'the woman's friend'.[36] Town directories in both England and Scotland in the 1770s and 1780s listed the names and occupations of hundreds of known female entrepreneurs. Most were engaged in shopkeeping or service industries, working locally. But some headed national business networks: in 1774 the London emporium for Stoughton's Elixir, a popular patent medicine (probably laudanum based), was run by a female-headed firm, Jane Kitteridge and Company, supplying retail outlets in fifty provincial towns.[37]

'Unexpected' female occupations (in the view of traditionalists) were widely found. In Southampton in 1784 there was a woman blacksmith, while Birmingham in 1780 had a woman thumb-latch-maker, a woman tinplate-worker and a woman clock-dial-maker. In Bristol in 1775, there was a female trader in ship's ballast, a female saddle-maker and a female sexton. Meanwhile, Dublin in 1784 had a woman funeral undertaker, and women wire-workers, brass-makers and cutlers. Edinburgh in 1773 had a female auctioneer; Liverpool in 1774 a female pilot; Newcastle in 1778 a female hackney-horse keeper; London in 1774 a female coal merchant; and Norwich in 1783 a female butcher.[38]

Most of these women had organisational roles and did not dirty their hands in the workrooms; and some were widows who had inherited from their husbands. Yet female economic participation was extensive and variegated. Women worked even in manufacturing businesses seen as characteristically 'male'. The first *Sheffield Directory* (1787) listed ten female steel-cutlers and nine female scissors-makers. Of these, two were spinsters: Mary Redfearn (trademark: *PARIS*) and Ann Drabble (trademark: *a small diamond*). Their roles were not instantly revolutionary – but they marked a process of quiet change.[39]

Even the world of high finance was open to determined women. In the later seventeenth century, Hester Pinney, the poorly educated youngest daughter of a Presbyterian minister from Dorset, moved to London as a lace-vendor in the family business. There she diversified into banking, moneylending and investments. And she later inherited landed estates from a married aristocrat's younger son, with whom she had a long-running liaison.[40] It was a remarkable trajectory, although, without connections and financial backing, Pinney did not try to institutionalise her success by founding her own bank. (In 2009 she came top in a British survey of historically impressive female entrepreneurship.)

Gender prejudices were still to be found. The sight of well-dressed women running their own shops caused some unease. It was sometimes unkindly implied that milliners, selling bonnets, ribbons and 'trimmings', were genteelly disguised prostitutes. John Cleland's *Fanny Hill* (1748) described a bawdy-house in Covent Garden which was fronted by a milliner's parlour, where 'sat three young women, very demurely employ'd on millinery work, which was the cover of a traffic in more precious commodities'.[41] But real-life tradeswomen, like Mary and Ann Hogarth, sisters of the celebrated painter, continued unabashed – in their case running a London frock-shop. Over time, the millinery business became so closely linked with women that a 'man milliner' came to indicate a man engaged in trifles. Trading trends were nothing if not topical: a 1798 comic opera entitled *The Man-Milliner* did its best to milk the humour accordingly.[42]

Shopkeeping remained throughout the quintessential middle-class occupation. New Georgian shops, with their jutting bow windows and enticing displays, were classic features of every urban high street.[43] (As they have remained, with architectural updatings – until the escalating challenge posed by today's online buying.) Smart Georgian salesrooms were furnished as pleasant parlours, where customers lingered to chat and view goods. Vendors also tried to stimulate demand by paying for newspaper advertisements and distributing trade cards. In this era, many in the clothing trades both made and sold their staple goods. Up-market tailors, shoemakers and hatters often had workrooms behind or above the store. There they sold both bespoke and 'off the peg' goods, enabling them to respond flexibly to changing demands. As a result, the occupational demarcation between 'makers' and 'sellers' was blurred. And consumers gave their own input when commissioning goods, thus helping to set and to respond to changing fashions, which emerged dynamically in the urban crucible.[44]

Traders who were not affluent enough to maintain their own shop premises became perambulating street vendors. They took their business to the customers (as do door-step sellers in the twenty-first century). Their street cries, itemising their wares, formed a staple feature of the soundscape of Georgian towns. In addition, there were weekly and seasonal markets for open-air trading. Rag fairs were famed places to buy cheap clothing (and, according to rumour, stolen goods).[45] And there were big regional gatherings at fixed points in the calendar. These traditional fairs, however, were in this era becoming better known for their unbuttoned social festivities rather than for their trading centrality.[46] Regular supply had moved to urban locations, encouraged by and in turn encouraging the great variety of urban retail outlets.

Year-round wholesale dealings were by this period being organised by national networks of dealers. These men – and a few women, like the already cited Jane Kitteridge – distributed and transported mass-produced wares from manufacturers and importers to retail outlets across the country. Their warehouses lined the major roads out of London and the leading provincial centres (as in the early twenty-first century the large packing houses for online dealers can be seen alongside Britain's motorways). Then as now, successful wholesale dealers became figures of some wealth and standing, able to hold their own in the 'best' circles. When in *Pride and Prejudice* the aristocratic Mr Darcy's pride is humbled, one of the many lessons he learns is to appreciate Elizabeth Bennet's admirable Uncle Gardiner, a man of wealth, standing and sound sense. And he was a London wholesale dealer, undeniably living 'by trade and within view of his own warehouses', as Austen carefully specified.[47]

Between them, these urban dealers and retailers acted as material gatekeepers to the expanding world of consumerism. Characteristic problems included the collection of debts from over-extended customers, and the need to check light-fingered shoplifters.[48] Yet there were characteristic pleasures too. Successful shopkeepers acted as intermediaries between shoppers of many different backgrounds, acting as informal hosts: the exchange of goods was equally associated with the exchange of news and gossip.

Advocating the collective interests of the commercial middle class from the mid-century onwards were the new Chambers of Commerce.[49] Early examples included the North Staffordshire

Potters (1767), the Liverpool Merchants (1774) and similar associations in Glasgow (1783), Leeds (1786), Hull and Belfast. Some were short-lived, torn by commercial rivalries. Nevertheless, 'common utility, mutual wants, and the necessity of mutual services', as the Liverpool merchants noted, encouraged them to persevere.[50] In the same spirit, Britain's first General Chamber of Manufacturers was founded in 1785, promoted by the Midlands ironmaster Samuel Garbett. This national body, with delegates from provincial committees and a rotating chair, in fact survived for only two years. It found it difficult to overcome regional rivalries and mutual recriminations.[51] Yet it marked the start of a long-term trend. The middlocrats, who were polite and duly ceremonious when dealing with their 'betters', equally firmly expected respect and attention to their own interests as a *quid pro quo*.

The Professional Middle Class

Commercial-industrial leaders shared overlapping concerns and working styles with leading figures among the professions. Indeed, all families of relative wealth and status had an interest in supporting social order, respect for property and opportunities for advancement. Nevertheless, there was also a notable element of bifurcation, even competition, among the middlocrats. Economic growth and the knowledge explosion were between them greatly multiplying the number and range of available specialist services (a marked long-term trend which is still continuing) and strengthening a separate professional ethos. If the commercial middle class was, by and large, money-motivated, socially conservative (with a small 'c') and outwardly deferential to the aristocratic-plutocratic elite, the professional experts tended, again by and large, to be relatively absorbed in their specialist roles, seeking validation from their professional subculture, and socially more liberal (with a small 'l'), especially among the 'caring' medical and educational professions.

Specialist know-how was the basis of professional claims to social and cultural authority.[52] High birth and great wealth were coincidental. And professional expertise was especially esteemed if it was used for the communal good.[53] So these occupations, at their best, represented an ideal above and beyond 'mere' money-grubbing. Practitioners were regularly invited into people's homes; and asked to give intimate counsel on personal matters, on a basis of trust. Their professional 'calling' was thus a source of cultural pride. 'My father was an eminent Button-maker, in Birmingham, but I had a soul above buttons,' declared a stage-hero in 1795: 'I panted for a liberal profession.'[54]

At the start of the eighteenth century, the most plentiful among the expert groups were still the clergy, distinctive in their clerical neck-bands and long black robes. By the mid-century, however, they had been joined by a remarkable expansion of the legal profession, bewigged and black-coated; and their rise was followed by another notable surge in the later eighteenth century, this time of the medical profession, also soberly dressed.[55] Some of these professionals had formal salaries. Many, however, relied on fees – supplemented by collateral charges, such as tithes collected by the Anglican clergy. Convention specified that professional fees be paid discreetly. Financial concerns were not supposed to obtrude into the relationship. Sometimes, however, such expectations were disappointed, and professionals also had to scramble to collect their dues.[56]

Throughout this period, meanwhile, the most respectable and well-trained experts were competing with a plethora of 'irregulars' or freelances, who profited from the huge market for services, in an initially unregulated economy. Thus many low-cost legal advisers, known as 'hedge attorneys', emerged to aid poor clients, who needed legal advice or help in writing letters. In the case of Georgian medicine, too, many early doctors were 'quacks', selling patent medicines in the market-place with well-honed, quick-fire rhetoric.[57] (The style had parallels with the ever-popular 'patter song' in comic opera.)

The number of 'irregulars' remains unknown: not only because totals were characteristically fluctuating but, more fundamentally, because there was also no hard-and-fast dividing line between reputable practitioners and 'quacks'.

Client disillusionment was a chronic risk, since the efficacy of many 'invisible' professional services was hard to gauge.[58] Georgian critics did not hold back. Satirising the professions was an old tradition, which gained fresh impetus in this era (and still continues). Plump and worldly clergymen were pilloried for greed in extracting tithes and financial benefits from the poor, as well as for their hypocrisy if they lived immoral lives. Medical 'quacks' were no better. They spouted hocus-pocus, whilst taking money from sick and desperate people in return for inadequate or positively dangerous treatments. High-flown professional claims were contrasted with too often prosaic realities.

Lawyers, meanwhile, were doubly satirised.[59] Either they were slow, dozy and incompetent, hiding their negligence behind legal jargon and obscurantism (ancestors of Messrs Slow and Bideawhile in the satirical magazine *Private Eye*), or were sharp-eyed leeches, battening upon unwary clients (*Private Eye*'s Messrs Sue, Grabbit and Runne). The barristers, as the senior rank within the legal profession, tended to get away more lightly, though they were still teased for their orotund delivery and legal obscurantism.[60]

Yet it was the 'pettifogging attornies [*sic*]', who faced the brunt of the satire. As their profession expanded, they were dealing with an ever growing range of sensitive matters, including estate management, moneylending, legal advice and conducting business for the illiterate. On stage in 1797, one legal practitioner, unsubtly named Mr Wolf, defended his profession with much irony: 'Let them say what they will respecting Pettyfogging and Chicanery Quibbling and Quirking: let them hold us up as public nuisances; still the profession of the law is a glorious one, it gives a man such opportunities to be a villain'.[61] The barrage of criticism became so great that attorneys in early nineteenth-century England began instead to use the parallel occupational label of 'solicitors'; and in 1873 that shift in nomenclature was confirmed in the Judicature Act.[62] Satire was an informal but hard-hitting way of holding the professions to account – and, in that case, the lawyers took heed. (However, in the different cultural context of the USA, the old Georgian terminology continues unchanged.)

Collectively, all these professional authority figures were readily visible. In countless urban high streets, the elegant Georgian residences of leading professional families were among the smartest to be seen. Most widely dispersed, geographically, were clergymen, since, in theory at least, every parish had its own minister. Yet they were also to be found in diocesan centres, capital cities and the smart resorts, where they sought sinners to save and wealthy patrons to lobby for their patronage (or so their critics jibed). Other professions also had their geographical clusters. Lawyers flocked to the law courts in Dublin, Edinburgh, London, and to the provincial assizes. And medical men frequented the successful spas, notably the city of Bath, as well as the big cities with teaching hospitals, led by the medical meccas of Edinburgh and London.

While the leading professionals did well, and some exceptionally well, there was also a long 'tail' of aspirants, struggling on the margins. Musicians and artists often fell into that category. Their skills were ones which were cultivated by amateurs, potentially undercutting the market for professionals. Educationalists were similarly over-supplied and often under-paid, particularly in the case of the many women who sought employment in this field. Indeed, while demand for education was expanding fast, the spread of literacy was simultaneously generating a glut of potential teachers. Women in particular clustered in a range of unglamorous service occupations, such as nursing, midwifery and teaching. In this era, there was no system to regulate the entry qualifications and training for such roles. Hence these 'semi-professions', as they are sometimes termed, had low prestige and variegated skills. Professional self-organisation, which began in occupations with highly technical know-how, was much less easy to achieve or to justify in less specialist sectors.[63]

Georgian assumptions about gender also played a role. The claims of a lawyer, a doctor, a clergyman, to enter a household and to provide confidential advice were associated with masculine authority and autonomy. All the 'learned ladies', who became female pundits in this era (discussed below, pp. 325–6) were, in organisational terms, free-lances, without any group identity. Among the professional men, however, the case for proper training and compulsory qualifications became increasingly apparent. Medical reformers in particular deplored the cheap 'quacks', who won custom whilst tarnishing the doctors' reputation for competence. Yet a number of free-trade enthu-siasts opposed the concept of regulation. Instead, they stressed the clients' right – and competence – to make their own decisions. Thus Adam Smith, the guru of free trade, noted sharply in 1774: 'That doctors are sometimes fools ... is not, in the present times, one of those profound secrets which is known only to the learned'.[64]

However, on the question of professional regulation, opinion was slowly moving against the free-traders. Reformers argued that the public needed impartial standards, to differentiate between rogues and experts. Sick and suffering patients could not easily assess the qualifications of those offering help. And, as the range of specialist expertise grew, even well-informed amateurs struggled to keep up with the latest medical know-how. Furthermore, clients tended by rogues might face serious injury as well as waste their money. Such malign outcomes damaged all doctors, by eroding public trust.

Hence the emergent Georgian quest for professional regulation contrasted with commercial policy moves to free trade. A potential ideological rivalry was apparent within middle-class society. A conservative commercial-industrial ethos which increasingly favoured free-trade was opposed by a liberal professional ethos, which favoured some regulation and social interventionism. Yet the division was far from absolute. It's worth noting that the commercial-industrial world also needed a common legal and tax framework. And at times, specific commercial-industrial interests favoured protective tariffs for their special purposes, and engaged in collective organisation to promote their special interests. Principles were sometimes overridden by immediate sectional interests. Nonetheless, the polarity between the two approaches of commercial free-trade versus professional regulation still persists, prompting debate to this day.

Self-organisation was the means by which the Georgian professions advanced a collective ethos. The clergy were sustained by their separate churches (there has never been one clerical professional body), doctors by association with the new teaching hospitals and barristers by their affiliations with the London Inns of Court.[65] In addition, the medical profession was further organised into a hierarchy of rival institutions. The elite physicians, who specialised in diagnosis, looked to the Colleges of Physicians in London (1518), Dublin (1667) and Edinburgh (1681).[66] The hands-on surgeons in England belonged to the Surgeons Company, which separated from the Barber-Surgeons in 1745 and gained a royal charter as an independent college in 1800.[67] In Edinburgh, the surgeons gained a charter in 1695.[68] In Dublin they formed a new organisation in 1780, chartered in 1784. Meanwhile, in England the workhorses of the medical profession, the apothecary-surgeons (forerunners of the later general practitioners) joined the Apothecaries Society of London.[69] Many local medical societies also thrived, such as those in Colchester (1774) and Plymouth (1794), where doctors met informally to discuss matters of mutual interest.

Medical regulation was then given a decisive boost in 1815. In the characteristic British way, moves to standardise qualifications happened in a piecemeal fashion. The Apothecaries Act of 1815 enshrined an absolute requirement for proper training, qualifications and registration for all rank-and-file medical practitioners in England and Wales. And Parliament conveyed, by law, full regulatory powers to the Apothecaries Society, which became the national licensing body.[70] Other systems followed in Scotland and Ireland. And later in 1858 the General Medical Council was founded, with representatives from all key medical bodies, to coordinate all British medical registration.

So was launched a devolved system of arm's-length professional self-regulation, undertaken with the authority of the state but not actually implemented by it. This compromise became prevalent within the English and American jurisdictions, contrasting with the alternative continental European system of state regulation.[71] For solicitors in England and Wales, their regulatory body began as the London Law Institution in 1823 (refounded 1825), which was then chartered by Parliament in 1831 as the Law Society. In effect, the professions were asked to act not as sectional cartels but as custodians of the public interest. It was both a compliment and challenge. But a medical reformer like Thomas Wakley, founding editor of *The Lancet* (1823), was keen that enlightenment would prevail: 'We hope that the age of *Mental Delusion* has passed, and that mystery and concealment will no longer be encouraged.'[72]

Parallel initiatives were seen, furthermore, in entirely new professions. Again, the process was ad hoc, with self-organisation preceding (often by some time) statutory registration. In 1774 a group of gentlemen architects met together to promote the improvement of their business. After many twists and turns within the competitive profession, a new Institute of British Architects was founded in 1837 – with statutory registration following almost a century later in 1931.[73]

The master builders who really caught the public imagination, however, were the civil engineers. They quickly set about fostering collective solidarity. In 1771, John Smeaton, celebrated for building the Eddystone Lighthouse (completed 1759), founded a new society.[74] This informal body, however, had no regulatory powers. So in 1818, a rival group established a new Institution of Civil Engineers, which then gained a royal charter in 1828.[75] Leading practitioners – like Smeaton, Metcalf, Telford, Trevithick, the Stephensons and the

Brunels – were becoming star figures in the public eye. They were seen as the technological equivalents of heroic generals, fighting successfully to 'tame' nature. As the Institution's optimistic motto, adopted in 1843, stated, 'By art, we master what would master us'.

Together, these professional experts were forming an identifiable and increasingly confident strand within middle-class society. They socialised together and their children often married partners from similar backgrounds. Indeed, over time, there emerged a range of illustrious (untitled) dynasties of legal, medical, clerical and engineering families.[76] Some, like the Darwins, welded both professional and industrial heritages.[77] These middle-class professionals also knew that much demand for their services came from a fellow middle-class clientele. 'The time for building palaces, castles, and cathedrals is gone by, or nearly so,' argued an architectural journalist in 1835.[78] He was not completely accurate; but his general point was clear. The old-style aristocratic patrons, with one or two big commissions, were morphing into everyday clients, often from affluent middle-class backgrounds, with everyday requirements ranging from the substantial to the mundane.

Standing Tall

Sustained by their authority (but not supremacy), these Georgian middle-class families were a fulcrum group within British politics and society.[79] They provided business, administrative and cultural leadership in the expanding towns, and saw themselves as socially 'standing tall'. Sometimes, as in the 1790s, most middlocrats aligned with the aristocratic-plutocratic elite when fearing that property rights might come under serious attack from lower class radicalism. At other times, however, middle-class reformers, especially from the liberal professions, were ready to challenge the powers that be if they seemed either too corrupt or too incompetent (or both).

Local conflicts often revealed a marked assertiveness and lack of deference towards aristocratic bigwigs. One example occurred in the tiny pocket borough of Monmouth. A long-running dispute in 1818–26 pitted leading traders, craftsmen and journalists against the borough's traditional patron, Henry Somerset, 6th Duke of Beaufort. He was publicly denounced as a 'Tyrant', who represented the 'huffing braggart puff'd Nobility'.[80] And his ducal 'corruption' was contrasted with the townsmen's 'independence', 'virtue' and 'freedom'. The rival factions went to law. Although the duke, with his capacious pockets, won his case, his critics' robust language and cultural confidence were striking. They had no hesitation in proclaiming that they held the moral high ground in opposing the local grandee.

Perceptibly and imperceptibly, the middlocrats were creating a legacy. From the early nineteenth century onwards, well-to-do masculine attire was increasingly adopting a non-flamboyant sleek style and dark colours for daily use. In the process, the old-style full wigs, ornate shoe-buckles and elaborate dress-swords were being transmuted into ceremonial wear for special occasions. The switch in style was made especially fashionable by the dandy Beau Brummell in the early nineteenth century. His elegance was costly but under-stated – making him a style guru (as recounted below, p. 316).[81] But where did the style originate? It was preferred by businesslike urban middlocrats; and especially endorsed by Protestant Nonconformists and by the plain-living Quakers both in Britain and North America.[82] Moreover, its arrival was more than just a fashion 'blip'. Discreet, dark, powerful but 'sensible' male attire was taking the social lead – setting the long-term style also for respectable 'toffs' and 'plebs' – and resisting attempts at rendering majority male garb in Britain more flamboyant ever since.

∾ Time-Shift: Then and Now ∾

Here are some significant Georgian middle-class residences to view physically or virtually (or find a local equivalent from many fine conservation projects). A visit to Dennis Severs'

House in particular draws attention to daily features which are hard to reconstruct – like past sounds, smells and tastes.

1. Dennis Severs' House, Spitalfields (1724)

A Georgian terraced house, originally owned by a Huguenot weaving family, and meticulously and lovingly curated by the artist Dennis Severs (1948–99), who used Georgian art and artefacts, plus smells, sounds and candlelight, to offer the experience of total immersion in eighteenth-century life. Now conserved by Spitalfields Historic Buildings Trust and offering themed tours; pre-booking required.

2. Tobacco Merchant's House, Glasgow (1775)

Built for himself by the Glasgow architect John Craig (a timber merchant's son), and later sold to a leading tobacco importer; the architectural style is restrained but redolent of professional-mercantile confidence. It is now the HQ of the Scottish Civic Trust.

3. Georgian House and Garden, Limerick (1835–38)

2 Pery Square is one of a terrace of six houses, constructed by a tontine (see above, p. 270) at the height of Limerick's pre-Famine growth, and restored by the Limerick Civic Trust, which also recreated its town garden with box hedges, pathways and flowerbeds to the original design.

ᖇ 15 ᖇ

The Advent of the Workers

As the tectonic plates were shifting in the upper and middle echelons of society, so too were changes afoot 'below', among the masses. The 'labouring poor' or 'lower orders' were turning into 'workers', with all the implications that terminology entailed.[1] Far from being passive beings at the foot of the social ladder, the Georgian masses were sharing in the general social ferment – and making their own history.[2] Britain's economic transformation had the effect of increasing the number of skilled workers, the range of their skills, and a new cultural awareness of their positive role. Traditionally those at the foot of society were described as either 'the poor' or the 'lower orders'. But there was long an informal search for a more complimentary way of referencing them in public.

Privately, those on high might talk harshly or disparagingly about the masses. (Although not all did.) Thus, when he first arrived in London in 1762, the young James Boswell, writing in his private diary, deplored the rumbustious directness of the 'English vulgar'.[3] And in 1764 an earl's mother referred dismissively to the liveried footmen, who were lobbying collectively to defend their financial perquisites, as 'those *beings*'.[4]

Yet when people of different backgrounds actually met face to face, a degree of civility was required, as already noted. A common salutation to strangers – 'even to the poor' – was 'Honest Man', noted a French visitor in 1719.[5] As reported, that phrase sounds rather stagey. Nonetheless, it signified the intention of verbal affability between fellow Britons. Indeed, it was as well to be polite, especially on first meeting, since it was often far from clear who outranked whom. A stage-lawyer named Quibble complained in 1701: 'Nay, the World is grown very impudent; and those strange creatures [the lower orders] imitate us [the middling sort] in every Thing. One can't have a Lac'd Hat, a ruffl'd Shirt, a pair of Clock Stockings, or red top't Shoes, but every City Prentice must follow us'.[6] Such sartorial copying was boosted by the buoyant market in second-hand clothing, recycling the dress of richer Britons onto the backs of poorer ones.[7]

When people from different backgrounds began to converse, however, most Georgian Britons could detect obvious divergences between 'refined' and 'low' speech, as well as the multitude of regional accents. Class and other differences did not suddenly disappear. For that reason, the radical autodidact Thomas Spence, who came from an impoverished but self-improving Tyneside family, tried in 1775 to popularise a phonetic alphabet. He hoped that its use would help speakers to improve their diction. 'Why should People be laughed at all their lives for betraying their vulgar education, when the Evil is so easily remedied?' he demanded in 1814, reasonably enough.[8] Nonetheless, despite the persistence of class and other differences in speech, the spread of standard English, aided by the output of the printing press, meant that most Britons could converse together without intermediaries. (The major exceptions to this state of affairs were found in rural Wales and rural Ireland, where Welsh and Gaelic continued to flourish.)

Language thus partly divided and partly united the British people in the Georgian era. And, while grammatical structures stood firm, linguistic usages were constantly open to adaptation. Many new terms were borrowed from overseas. Low-life 'cant' and regional dialects were topics of public interest; and various colloquialisms or 'vulgar idioms' were absorbed into respectable speech.[9] Indeed, some slang Georgian usages have come to stay, such as calling a hypocrite a 'humbug' or a tiresome person a 'bore'.[10] In this context, it was not surprising that the terminology of social description was itself in flux.

'Lower Orders' Morphing into 'Workers'

Concepts of social class were (and remain) fuzzy. As a result, individual positioning was not always easy to define, especially at the social margins. Commentators in Georgian Britain often disagreed in their usages. One wag in 1755 claimed that recent trends had abolished all social divisions: 'We are a Nation of Gentry. We have no such thing as Common People among us; between Vanity and Gin the whole Species is utterly destroyed'.[11] The verdict was intended as sardonic humour, but it nodded to the extent of social climbing ('Vanity') as well as the lethal drinks craze of the 1730s and 1740s ('Gin').

Most common, especially in times of crisis, were binary classifications. Some were witty. Thus in the later 1720s a French visitor declared that: 'In England ... in the daytime the lower classes get intoxicated with liquor [gin] and beer, the higher classes in the evening with Portuguese wines and punch [rum].'[12] Other twofold divisions were easily memorable. Variants included: high–low, great–mean, rich–poor, genteel–vulgar, haves–have-nots, the few–the many, them–us. *One Half of the World Knows Not How the Other Half Lives*, as an already cited pamphlet declaimed in 1752 (see above, p. 83).[13]

Radical activists were frequently drawn to binaries too. Thus Thomas Paine asserted bluntly in 1791 that 'There are two distinct classes of men in the nation, those who pay taxes – and those who receive and live upon the taxes'.[14] Another dichotomy was proposed in 1795 during a debate in the Commons. An opposition Whig MP praised the commercial interest, comprising the middle class and the masses, as 'useful', and defined the landowners as economically 'useless'.[15] (Unsurprisingly, the MPs present disagreed.) And this deliberately provocative usage did not gain currency.

It is worth noting too that one influential historian, E.P. Thompson, endorsed a twofold division in Georgian society before the 1790s.[16] For him, the great divide was between 'patricians' and 'plebeians' or, colloquially, 'plebs' – a term still being at times evoked today, usually dismissively. These concepts were certainly known in the eighteenth century. In 1719, two weekly papers, entitled respectively *The Plebeian* and *The Patrician*, offered rival views of the Whigs' controversial peerage bill.[17] Yet neither term was much used thereafter. When a new dichotomous permutation was deployed in 1835, it introduced a light-hearted comedy, entitled *Patrician and Parvenu*.[18] And in reality the eighteenth-century growth of a perceptible middle class, as already explained, meant that all these binary divisions, whether jovial or serious, were rhetorical tropes rather than realistic social descriptors.

The big challenge, when classifying the huge mass of the population – perhaps as many as 95 per cent of the population in 1700, or 85–90 per cent by the early nineteenth century – was whether to define them all as one big group, or to acknowledge gradations of skills and earnings. One classic definitional problem was (and still is) posed on the margin of the middle and lower classes. The 'artisan' in Georgian usage might refer to an independent master craftsman or to his skilled journeymen, who were economic dependants or employees.[19] Hence classifying individuals with this social label depends upon additional information about their work status, although over time the appellation was tending to become more 'lowly'.

Further challenges were associated with the split between skilled and unskilled workers. Again the boundaries were far from clear-cut. The ever-observant Daniel Defoe had already in 1705 noted that economic change was lifting some workers above others. ' 'Tis plain,' he wrote, that 'the Dearness of Wages forms our People into more

Classes than other Nations can show.' In 1709, he identified four groups among the lower orders. At the top of the heap, there were the 'working Trades', 'who labour hard but feel no want'. These were the equivalent of skilled workers. Then came the lower country people, 'who fare indifferently' – a separate rural category. They were followed by 'the Poor that fare hard', who matched those later defined as the 'unskilled' or, in Marx's hostile term, the 'Lumpenproletariat'. And at the bottom of the heap, Defoe detected 'the Miserable that really pinch and suffer want'; they would include outright beggars and vagrants, who risked falling through the poor-relief safety net.[20]

However, while recollecting the complexities within, it is still helpful to consider the lower-class population as a whole, not least because they all shared a lack of capital, relative poverty and insecure lifestyles. Moreover, people on low incomes were likely to face fluctuating fortunes during their precarious life-cycles.

Recognition of the positive economic input of the masses was slowly becoming a matter of comment. Disappearing were the old references, such as those made by Gregory King in the 1690s, to the poor as 'decreasing' the wealth of the country, allegedly by costing more in poor relief than they earned in wages.[21] Instead in 1751 a contributor in the *Monthly Review* wrote of 'a *class* of all others the most necessary and useful . . . yet the most neglected and despised; we mean *the labouring part of the people*'.[22] Attitudes of social disdain were equally rejected by the reformer Jonas Hanway, who stressed *The Importance of the Rising Generation of the Labouring Part of our Fellow Subjects* (1767). Another laudatory phrase was recorded in 1763, when a petition to Parliament from Norwich Corporation, seeking help for the city's textile industry, invoked the rank-and-file worsted weavers as the 'industrious class'.[23] Yet another variant was the 'laborious class' (1781), again stressing the positive case.

Such terms were verbal precursors of a resonant new description, the 'working class', which first appeared in print, almost in passing, in 1789.[24] 'Work' was a pithy, memorable term. Its implications were active, constructive. It echoed biblical notions of honest toil: 'the labourer is worthy of his hire'.[25] Again, Defoe was a pioneer, writing in 1725 of the 'working manufacturing People of England'.[26] It took some time, however, for 'working' to supersede 'industrious' or 'laborious'. Usages for a while overlapped. In 1790, a Birmingham workman addressed a pamphlet confidently to *My Fellow Labourers and Fellow Townsmen, the Honest, Well Meaning and Industrious Mechanics and Manufacturers*.[27] A radical ballad in 1795 also placed the incoming collective noun 'class' in close juxtaposition with the new adjective 'work', when it saluted: *'You lower class of Human Race, you working part I mean'*.[28] This song was entitled, sardonically, *Wholesome Advice to the Swinish Multitude*, poking fun at Edmund Burke's alarmed comparison of the revolting masses to swine (1790).[29]

Within a generation from the first scattered usages, the new terminology was becoming commonplace. The toil of the masses might be repetitive, sometimes 'dirty' and often backbreaking; but it was economically productive. Commentators by the 1810s routinely spoke approvingly of their efforts. People adopted or adapted the terminology as made sense to them. Some conservative thinkers preferred the plural usage of 'working classes', emphasising diversity among the workers. Equally, however, it was not unknown for working-class leaders in the Chartist movement also to self-refer to the 'working classes'.

Centrally, the key change was the positive reference to 'work'. It referred to the mass sector of society without capital, whose chief economic asset was their labour. There were remarkably few visual depictions of British society en masse; but one drawing, made by George Cruikshank in 1840, revived the image of *The Beehive*.[30] Each cell of the hive is shown as housing a distinct occupational group. (Unsurprisingly, the royal family is at the top.) Near the base of the hive are twenty cells with images of (male) 'worker bees': tailors, boot-makers, hatters, weavers, carpenters, bricklayers, smiths, masons, an upholsterer, engineers, a hackney-cab man, an ostler, a pavior (pavement-layer), a shoeblack, a boatman, a coal-heaver, a sweep, a costermonger (street seller of fruit and vegetables), a dustman and a (horse-drawn) omnibus conductor. It was a fascinating list, with highly skilled workers placed side by side with casual labourers. Their work experiences were very diverse. Engineers and sweeps had, outwardly at least, little in common. Yet, equally, these occupational groups underpinned Britain's economy: they were 'workers'.

Working-Class Lifestyles and Consciousness

Spreading literacy in the Georgian era expanded the number of articulate people from the 'lower orders' who gave personal testimony of their lifestyles. Before that, the poet Thomas Gray had mourned – in his *Elegy* (1751), the eighteenth century's most quoted poem – that individuals from poor backgrounds had very few chances to develop their talents: 'Full many a flower is born to blush unseen,/ And waste its sweetness on the desert air'.[31] In this era, by contrast, there was a new publishing phenomenon, as lower-class authors from a diverse array of backgrounds began to flower.[32] They provided direct accounts, whether embroidered or not, of non-elite experiences. A few wrote autobiographies.[33] Georgian poets from 'low-life' included Stephen Duck, the Wiltshire 'thresher poet'; Ann Yearsley, the Bristol 'milkwoman'; the little-known James Woodhouse, 'a journeyman shoemaker'; the world-renowned balladeer Robert Burns, son of an Ayrshire tenant farmer; and John Clare, a Northamptonshire farm labourer's son.[34] It was true that some found fame to be evanescent. Yet they were a portent of changing times.

Historians value such testimonies but they have perforce to go beyond individual experiences to consider working-class life in the round. There are great difficulties in finding reliable data which are, moreover, comparable over time. Hence there has been a prolonged debate about working-class living standards.[35] Did their conditions broadly improve over time (a thesis known as amelioration) or worsen (immiseration)? In parallel, historians also debate whether and when there was anything as distinctive as a working-class 'consciousness', and, if so, what form it took. One unmistakeable intellectual call to arms came from E.P. Thompson. For him, the 1790s constituted a watershed in the advent not only of a class-based society but also of a working-class consciousness, forged by the workers themselves.[36]

Common features which tended to unite those at the 'foot' of society included: their relative poverty; and (for many, though not all) their absolute poverty; their de facto exclusion from 'polite' society; their relatively greater unhealthiness; their crowded housing, which they rented rather than owned; their lack of capital; and their reputational association with 'dirty' manual labour. (In practice, some working-class occupations were clean and quiet, such as hand-loom weaving – though the repetitive work, protracted for long hours, could be sickeningly tedious.) The poorest, unskilled workers were particularly accustomed to living with chronic insecurity, in a precarious 'economy of makeshift'.[37] The volatility of their incomes sustained the flourishing Georgian service industry of pawnbroking.[38] But even the most diligent and skilled workers were liable to face sudden unemployment in an economic downturn, prompting a massive local surge in applications for charity and poor relief.

Positive bonding factors meanwhile had a mitigating impact, heightened in times of national success: pride in being 'freeborn'; confidence in constituting 'the people'; a willingness to demonstrate their views publicly; their capacity to self-organise; and their sense of superiority over foreigners, especially over the French. In the 1820s, the campaigning tailor Francis Place collected evidence to show that the masses were becoming more self-disciplined in manners and less dissolute in morals.[39] There was some wishful thinking in his account. In fact, Place also criticised workers who fought, drank and beat their wives. (His own father he thought 'cruel' and 'savage'.) Yet he also opposed those conservative thinkers who saw the masses as feckless and dissolute. Instead, many Georgian workers had good reasons – whether secular or religious – to value hard work, sobriety, self-discipline, saving for the proverbial 'rainy day', self-improvement and mutual organisation.[40]

By contrast, there were other factors which tended to fragment the working class, although not necessarily permanently. For a start, there were significant regional variations in the nature and performance of the economy.[41] Furthermore, there were other entrenched divisions between the highly skilled, moderately skilled, and unskilled; diverse work patterns between different industries and service occupations; difficulties facing workers on the margins of legality, like prostitutes; and the multitudinous personal variants based upon stages in life-cycle, health, family size, education, and so forth – let alone, in Ireland especially but not exclusively, religious rivalries. Ethnically, the masses were also the most diverse of all social sectors. Many immigrant groups were concentrated among the less well-to-do, as already noted. Their contributions, at times controversial, added variety and vitality and at times led to further tensions and disagreements.

Men and women who were young, healthy, resourceful, literate and without many dependants fared best. Conversely, the old, ill, socially isolated and illiterate faced problems; and partnerless women with dependant children were especially likely to suffer the worst slings and arrows of adversity.[42] At the 'foot' of society (viewed conventionally), there were the vagrants and street beggars.[43] There were also criminal networks and gangs, although reporters tended to exaggerate the scale of organised criminality among the lower orders.[44] (And, of course, there were unknown numbers of undetected affluent criminals, engaged in fraud or financial malfeasance.)

Trends over time must necessarily be painted in broad brush, allowing for many individual variations. In terms of capital-ownership, the relative gap between the very rich and the middle class on the one hand, and the masses on the other, was widening, thus increasing relative poverty.[45] At the same time, the distribution of wealth between the extremes was also shifting. Instead of a tiny elite ruling over an utterly indigent mass, there was a perceptible thickening of the intermediary band of the tolerably well-to-do, namely the middle class.

Furthermore, there was also an emergent industrial elite of the most highly skilled workers (perhaps 10 per cent of the workforce). These were later termed the 'aristocracy of labour'.[46] Classic Georgian exemplars were the Sheffield knife- and fork-grinders, whose annual earnings in the 1760s matched those of a poor middle-class curate.[47] However, the comparison should not be pushed too far. The grinders' long hours of highly focused toil – bringing with it the risk of pneumoconiosis from inhaled metal dust – meant that their lifestyles were far from luxurious or easeful. Nor did they have opportunities to translate their high earnings, when young and fit, into capital assets. They thus led the workforce, rather than joined the capital-rich.

For all workers, skilled or unskilled, one crucial variable in determining living standards was the price of basic foodstuffs. As noted above (pp. 187–8), one of the most common forms of popular disturbance in this era was the food riot, indicating the sensitivity of food supply. Hence when shortages became severe and prolonged, popular living standards were seriously challenged. Throughout much of the eighteenth century, grain prices in fact remained low, despite short-term fluctuations, providing relatively cheap food and cheap grain-based drinks. That favourable state of affairs applied particularly in the 1720s and 1730s – hymned as 'pudding-time' in popular song.[48]

Prices then began to move upwards in the 1770s and 1780s, before rising sharply from 1793 to 1820, during the wartime years and their immediate aftermath. That changed situation put severe pressure on lower-class living standards across the board.[49] Thereafter the Corn Laws continued to protect British farmers, by placing restraints on foreign grain imports. The system kept prices higher than they might have been, as the policy intended. Only after the Corn Laws were repealed in 1846 did Britain again experience another long plateau of relatively cheap food until 1914.[50]

Workers, however, were not all equally vulnerable when prices rose steeply. One option, for those in employment, was to work longer hours. Since many journeymen were paid by the piece of work, rather than by the hour, that tactic might sustain their living standards, even if at the cost of lost leisure. Such a response has been detected in England in the 1790s.[51] However, workers had that choice only if demand for their labour was booming, which was not equally the case in all industries. Another option was to send more family members out to work, including children. But again the feasibility of such stratagems depended upon the state of the local labour market.

There were also significant gender differentials. Women's earnings, especially among the unskilled, were tending to fall, in the early nineteenth century, offsetting a different trend for earnings among the male workforce, who were generally gaining a greater range of skills. One particularly poorly paid group of workers were those (usually women) working in the 'sweated' dress-making trades. They toiled around the clock at exacting, and repetitive tasks, in a market saturated with cheap labour.[52] The author Mary Lamb was one who worked as a seamstress in her youth, while struggling to cope with economic uncertainties, family ill-health and acute mental turmoil. Later in 1815 she recalled dryly the work's stultifying effects, with no time to read or think: 'Needlework and intellectual improvement are naturally in a state of warfare'.[53]

Given that there was, over the very long term, a moderate rise in average earnings, a rise in the proportion of the workforce in skilled occupations and an increase in the range of cheap consumer goods, such as cottons, available for mass consumption, the ultimate trend in living standards between (say) 1700 and (say) 1850 was one of amelioration.[54] Yet that process was punctuated by a long generation of immiseration from the 1790s to c. 1820, prompted by high food prices, as well as by protracted problems facing workers in declining industries. The Norfolk and Norwich hand-loom worsted weavers, once among the industrial elite, faced a complete occupational down-grading as they were undercut by the mechanised workforce in the new 'Worstedopolis' of Bradford.[55] Many youngsters in Norfolk left the industry and, indeed, the region.[56] Big, broad trends thus impacted differently upon rival groups – and big, broad trends were not constant, but were capable of being disrupted for considerable spans of time.

With so many diverse experiences, it was not likely that all those at the 'foot' of society would have a uniform set of attitudes or socio-political consciousness throughout successive generations.[57] Attitudes from 'below' towards the rich and powerful included cases of contin-uing deference and positive loyalty to 'King and Country'.[58] But at the same time there were also surges of anger and bitterness at perceived hardships and injustices. And there were calmer responses of self-reliance, in the form of self-help via benefit clubs. Or complex medleys of all those attitudes, varying according to circumstances. Nonetheless, E.P. Thompson was substantially right on the big general trend, even if working-class attitudes were not all radical – and instead remained variegated. The 1790s was the fulcrum decade when class politics arrived.

Radicals launched coherent calls to end the exploitation of Britain's workers across the board. The shift was encouraged by Georgian society's newly positive evaluation of their role, as noted above (pp. 291–2). And it was sharpened by the crisis of the 1790s, when high prices and unemployment (in many though not in all industries) balefully coincided, causing popular outrage. So an anon-ymous radical tract in 1795 stated that a key question from every poor man was: *'Who reaps the produce of his labour?'*[59] Building upon such ideas, radicals and then socialist thinkers called for a change to the economic basis of society.[60] Old ways were not sacrosanct. Instead, all should co-own the means of production – and all share its rewards.

Among later historians, leftists of a sentimental bent (not all are so) like to think that the sturdy plebs were groaning under a repressive state and that only adverse circumstances prevented them from rising up in justified indignation. Conversely, sentimental conservatives (not all are so) prefer to argue that the repression was only mild and incidental – and that the sturdy populace stood loyally with the government, especially when faced with threat of invasion by a foreign foe. Yet there were elements of truth in both scenarios – neither being completely right.

Britain's economic transformation was eroding belief in a hierarchic society, constructed of fixed 'ranks' and 'stations'. Instead, in the broadest of senses, there was a long-term 'Thompsonian' shift from lower-class deference towards much greater communal assertion from below, although never with complete unanimity. 'Class', after all, is not a static 'thing'. Workers' attitudes were forged dynamically, influenced by a combination of factors, including their circumstances, their grievances, their beliefs, their options and their interest in radical programmes proposed by activists, whilst equally being tempered by the nature of local and national government power, policies and policing. As a result, working-class unanimity (despite radical efforts) was rare. At the same time, however, total worker passivity (despite conservative hopes) was non-existent.

Workers' Self-Organisation

Welding community action into a coherent movement was a constant challenge. Regional and sectoral economic diversity meant that it was not uncommon for some areas or industries to experience booms, whilst others slumped. Warfare had a particularly differential impact, promoting activity in the dockyard towns and among the Midlands weapon manufacturers, whilst harming export industries that depended upon access to overseas markets, disrupted by the fighting. Moreover, these difficulties were known. Why did the masses not rebel and dispossess the rich? James Boswell was once discussing that question with Dr Johnson, who replied simply that 'the more numerous men are, the more difficult it is for them to agree in any thing, and so they are governed'.[61]

Communal self-help offered one positive means of combating the uncertainties of working-class lives. By banding into benefit or friendly societies, participants pooled their savings in a common fund, from which they could get aid in case of illness or unemployment. Such organisations did not include the poorest of the poor, who had no funds to contribute. But many small craftsmen, journeymen, and a few labourers, did participate – including some working women, as in the case of the York Female Benefit Society (founded c. 1788).[62] True, if the 'run' on their finances was greater than their collective savings, these bodies sometimes failed. There was also a perennial risk of fraudulent claims. By the 1840s, however, Friendly Societies were flourishing everywhere. They did not end the need for parochial poor relief. But they signalled a collective effort at mutual aid. 'Though of humble invention', wrote Thomas Paine, the Friendly Societies 'merit to be ranked among the best of modern institutions'.[63]

An associated move towards mutual support came in the forming of local trade unions, or 'combinations', as they were termed. Each society was organised around a specific trade, with the initiatives usually coming from skilled male workers, who knew that their labour was in demand.[64] These combinations then negotiated with local employers on pay. They often supported their claims with parades and marches, which served to foster their unity – and to assert their public visibility.[65] So in Bristol in 1754, an unmistakeably English crowd assembled to chant: '*No Lowering Wages of Labouring Men to 4d. a Day and Garlick*'.[66] If negotiations failed, the unions had the option of withdrawing their labour en masse. That drastic industrial action was called a 'strike' for the first time in 1766.[67] A counter-move from some employers was to employ new recruits instead. Such strike-breakers, who were often equally desperate for work, were described contemptuously by the regular workforce as 'scabs' (1777), and later as 'blacklegs' (1844). Against that danger, the strikers conversely tried to boost their collective solidarity – and to seek public support.

A dramatic case occurred in 1752. The skilled journeymen wool-combers in Norwich withdrew their labour entirely and camped together on Moushold Heath, a high bluff outside the city. As many as 300 men were reportedly assembled at that vantage-point, from which they sent messages to the local press, alerting the public to their cause. It was a visible stand-off. Their work was too technical to be under-taken quickly by substitutes, and, before long, the master combers agreed to stick to the established rates. Thereupon the journeymen returned to work, so it was reported, 'to the great joy of the city'.[68]

Other early trade unions were founded by similarly distinctive work-groups with recondite skills. Examples included the Devonshire serge weavers, the Midlands framework knitters, variously the Newcastle, Yorkshire and Lanarkshire colliers, and the Sheffield metalware workers.[69] Yet it was considerably more difficult to coor-dinate scattered and diversified workforces, especially in the service sector. (The problems faced by the liveried menservants in London in the 1770s have already been noted – see above, p. 86.)

Nonetheless, one metropolitan industrial group did prove suffi-ciently unruly – and close to the political hub of Westminster – that their grievances over rates of pay met with a special solution. Parliament in 1773 placated the Spitalfields silk-weavers by passing a protective law to regulate local piece rates, by agreement between the silk-masters and their journeymen weavers.[70] In the long run, this protective approach did not save the industry from being undercut by cheaper competitors outside London. Nonetheless, it gave the weavers a not negligible breathing-space of fifty years.

Official responses to early trade unions were varied. Some employers accepted them. Yet many were becoming hostile, as the doctrine of free trade began to spread in the light of Adam Smith's *Wealth of Nations* (1776). Fears were expressed that the workers' collective actions to raise wages or piece rates – or to prevent cuts – were harmful to the efficient working of the free market. Smith was no enthusiast for trade unions. Yet he did appreciate the logic of collective action, noting that big employers in concentrated industries often did likewise and that 'being fewer in numbers, they can combine much more easily'.[71] Over time, however, supporters of free trade grew more vocal, whilst forgetting Smith's perception that masters as well as workers combined.

Gradually, a long, rumbling struggle began between trade unionism and the central state, as successive governments veered between acceptance, regulation and attempts at suppression. The high-water mark of hostility actually came in 1799, when Prime Minister William Pitt the Younger was generally worried about the extent of lower-class radicalism in the mid-1790s (as noted above, p. 194) and specifically rattled by big naval 'mutinies' over pay and working conditions in 1797.[72] At his instigation, therefore, Parliament passed in 1799 and 1800 two acts to prevent 'unlawful combinations', known as the Combination Acts, which survived until 1824.

One unforeseen result, however, was that aggrieved workers resorted instead to unofficial organisations and secret activities. In the years 1811–17, that outcome was seen in the textile areas of Nottinghamshire and South Yorkshire. Under cover of darkness, militant workers attacked the mechanised stocking-frames, which were seen as taking jobs from the hand-powered frame-work knitters. Leading the machine-breakers, mythically, was one Ned Ludd.[73] He was a counter-cultural outlaw figure, sometimes depicted semi-disguised as a woman and wearing a French revolutionary bonnet. So, by association, the protestors became known as 'Luddites' – a resonant but uncomplimentary term. The lack of known leaders among the machine-breakers made it initially difficult for the authorities to clamp down, and added to the atmosphere of suspicion and fear. Eventually, however, Luddism was suppressed. Some ringleaders were executed, and frame-wrecking eventually ceased.

Luddism indicated that collective action by Georgian workers was not always designed to force up wages in growing industries, but also operated defensively. The machine-breakers testified to the outrage often felt when traditional jobs disappear as a result of changes which are defined as technological 'progress'. Writing in their support, the journalist William Cobbett argued that, if the Luddites' work was disappearing, then they owed little to 'a society whose compact is dissolved'.[74] Respectable opinion was unconvinced. In novels such as Charlotte Brontë's *Shirley* (1849), the machine-breakers are depicted as backward-looking, ignorant and one-dimensional beings. (Today, however, when concern over the impact of technological change is very far from disappearing, there is a new interest in various styles of neo-Luddism.)[75]

Trade unionism stubbornly failed to disappear. Its leaders were caricatured as dangerous rabble-rousers.[76] But their rank-and-file had grievances to express. In April 1820 there were massive strikes across Glasgow, Paisley and the central Lowlands. Politicians locally and nationally were sincerely alarmed, fearing that the crisis would launch a veritable 'Scottish Insurrection'.[77] Government ministers thereupon began to rethink the legal framework. Trade unions, aided by the veteran radical Francis Place, argued forcefully that their role should be normalised rather than proscribed. It was easier to nego-tiate with known leaders of known organisations than with unknown masses. In 1824, the Combination Acts were repealed, although lesser legal constraints followed in 1825.[78]

Most industrial disputes thereafter were matters to be resolved between employers and the unions. There was often a concealed contest as to which 'side' could gain public support and sympathy. However, if the aggrieved workforce overplayed its hand, then government repression was summoned, in the form of military support for the employers. That sequence was seen in the bitter wage dispute in industrial south Wales, known as the Merthyr Rising of 1831, which saw the first hoisting in Britain of the rebel red flag. For a brief time, the town was held by protestors, who included miners and industrial workers, while the magistrates and ironmasters were under siege within the Castle Hotel. Yet public support soon ebbed away and the army regained control, followed by rough justice for leading protestors.[79] It was no pathway to instant glory, either for rebels or employers. Hence as individual disputes continued to recur, so too did efforts at normalising industrial negotiations and labour relations.

From the trade unionists' point of view, there were some hopeful plans for transcending local divisions and forming a general union.[80] Yet divisions between different industrial sectors were hard to overcome, because working conditions and wage rates were so far from uniform. The new Grand National Consolidated Trades Union (GNCTU), founded in 1834 by the radical manufacturer Robert Owen, did not last.[81]

Nevertheless, the labour movement in this period was testing its role. The first trade unions were heavily dominated by skilled workers, who had some leverage with employers. However, there was one portent of change among the unskilled, which gave the movement its martyrology. In 1834, six agricultural labourers from Tolpuddle in Dorset were transported to Australia, following their conviction under antiquated laws against collective oaths.[82] The local magistrates had grossly over-reacted. Public opinion sided with the would-be trade unionists, whose actions were pacific and aspirations legal. A huge petition and protest march in 1836 led to their pardon by the Whig government. Today, the iconic Tolpuddle Martyrs are celebrated in an annual festival, organised by the Trades Union Congress – whose affiliated structure gives it longevity where plans for a consolidated union had failed.[83]

Organised labour has faced retreats and advances. It has witnessed both aggressive militancy and meeker martyrology. In the very long term, it faces the highly complex challenges of helping all forms of labour, including the ultra-casualised. Meanwhile, it urges fraternity with fellow workers as an antidote to uncertainty.

Multitudes but not Faceless Masses

People travelled up and down the Georgian social scale. A few from working-class backgrounds rose to fame, as discussed in the next chapter. An unknown but not negligible number 'sank' from prior respectability into poverty. Even the richest and grandest families sometimes had 'black sheep' who, for whatever reason, slipped into debts and obscurity, ending among the undifferentiated masses. Upon occasion, children from these downwardly mobile cadet branches were taken into their distant cousins' grand houses as servants or companions.

Accordingly, the masses were, in one sense, a multitudinous residual group of all Britons who did not have titles, land, capital, substantial commercial and industrial businesses or special professional expertise. Most petty criminals came from this background, as did most victims of petty crime. And the urban poor, especially in the large towns, were permeated by 'rogues and cheats', according to one police reformer in 1776, who urged strangers and locals in particular to watch out for the 'many atrocious artifices, tricks, seductions, stratagems, impositions, and deceptions which are daily committed'.[84]

But the masses did not generally see themselves either as faceless individuals or as 'bad hands'. They were well aware of the diversities of skills, interests, work experiences, incomes, ethnicities, religions, political views, regional affiliations, gender roles, lifestyles and moral values among the crowds. Poverty and wretchedness were constant risks. Yet, as already noted, they viewed themselves – and were viewed – as 'the people'. They were the sum of many individuals, with individual rights and claims. These 'lower orders' did not physically abase themselves before their 'betters', as is borne out by the many complaints at the 'uppishness' of servants, workers and urban crowds.

Collectively, their history was the sum of all these processes, propelling the masses into the national framework. Their presence was felt not only economically but also, diversely, by riots, demonstrations, political campaigns, votes, trade unionism, strikes, strike-breaking, and by Luddite machine-wrecking. A class does not need to be united to have impact (though the greater the unity, the greater the impact). In Georgian Britain, the 'workers' were becoming seen, heard and, by some, appreciated.

Thus George Cruikshank's *Comic Alphabet* (1836) imagined, under the letter E for Equality, a new world of social levelling, where a nobleman wearing his Garter star parades, arm-in-arm with a grimy dustman – both puffing tobacco smoke in a mutual cloud of satisfaction.[85] Needless to say, the scene was not drawn from life, although some male cross-class mingling did occur, for instance at race-courses and at boxing matches. Nonetheless, the image declared to its viewers that, as fellow humans, the dustman was as good as the duke, and indeed vice versa.

৵ Time-Shift: Then and Now ৵

Three icons to view in person or virtually constitute historic testaments to working-class experiences, including hazardous labour, insecurity and solidarity. It's also worth looking out for other public memorials to historic labour, such as the Leicester statue (1990) of a seamstress, celebrating women's work in the hosiery industry, or the Aberdeen fishing memorial (2018), showing a fisherman and woman with their catch. Such testaments of remembrance are comparatively rare, but are reaching towards the 'democratising' of the role of the public monument.

1. Hazard: kneeling coal-miner 'testing for gas' with a safety lamp (2005)
A bronze statue by Antony Dufort erected at the summit of Silverhill (a former spoils heap, now landscaped), near Teversal, Sutton in Ashfield, in tribute to all Nottinghamshire miners and the physical dangers faced by all workers underground.

2. Insecurity: pawnshop in the Black Country Living Museum, Dudley, West Midlands

The shop has been recreated within two workers' cottages dating from the 1840s and shows typical items pawned by poor people, with goods advertised for sale unless redeemed by original owners. Pawnshops, which are often said in times of general prosperity to have become socially obsolete, come into their own again in hard times.

3. Solidarity: Liverpool Tinplate Workers' Society banner (1821)

The world's oldest surviving trade union banner, containing emblems of commerce, justice and patriotism, and a large, long-lashed eye, signifying a watchful Divine Providence, can be seen at the People's History Museum in Manchester. The various insignia of such communal organisations publicly declared that the organised workers faced the world proudly in a justified cause.

∽ 16 ∾

The Allure of Celebrities and Meritocrats

Most of the famous Georgians, as known to history, were not traditional aristocrats or even new plutocrats. They were individual rising stars. Their advancement did not automatically shake the deeper structures of class and inequality. Some were shooting stars, who rose rapidly and fell as fast.

Nonetheless, the careers of exceptional individuals promoted a realisation that social positions were not set in stone. Power structures in Georgian Britain were already intricate. Celebrities, glittering in the public eye, added a further level of complexity, as did the array of Georgian meritocrats, including unknown influencers behind the scenes, as well as publicly known heroes.

Personal fame and merit certainly did not confer the same power as that wielded by leading politicians or businessmen. Yet those from modest backgrounds who won renown did gain an indefinable influence. And their success encouraged others to seek the same intangible prize. 'If it is advantageous to be born noble, 'tis far more so to ennoble oneself,' the anonymously authored *Treatise on Merit* asserted firmly in 1748.[1] This liberal tract invited ambitious people from 'below' to aim high. Women were equally held to be capable of self-advancement. In 1752, the antiquary George Ballard published a survey of over sixty notable female contributors to science and the arts. He sought both to praise the pioneers and to encourage others.[2]

Celebrities are here defined as all those from modest backgrounds who became, however briefly, 'famous for being famous'. A significant number were women who were bypassing conventional gender roles. Most Georgian celebrities had talents. Yet some advanced far with nothing but the power of ambition and good publicity. Supportive patrons also helped. These celebrities formed an amorphous, rivalrous group, rather than a homogeneous elite or an organised lobby. Their key distinction was gaining fame.

Meritocrats, by contrast, were not necessarily widely fêted or even much known in the wider society. Instead, they were individuals from modest backgrounds who advanced through their talents. They were usually well respected in their own fields and wielded a strong, if specialised, influence. Just as not all Georgian celebrities had outstanding personal merits, so not all meritocrats either sought or achieved fame. The two social categories, which considerably overlapped, were thus not the same, and are here discussed separately.

Celebrity Culture

The Georgians marvelled at an eclectic array of celebrities. They included: scientists, inventors, engineers, professional men, artists, novelists, poets, dramatists, musicians, dancers, singers, actors, sportsmen, society beauties, economists, philosophers, historians, freethinkers, evangelists, philanthropists, reformers, entrepreneurs, financiers, merchants, lawyers, doctors, architects, landscape gardeners, explorers, naval buccaneers, generals, ingenious rogues, and some politicians. There were also visits from international celebrities, the most famed being the Venetian-born dandy and adventurer Giacomo Casanova, who stayed in London in 1763–64 before leaving, ill with venereal disease.

Evidently, fame no longer depended upon land, title, a place at court or even great wealth. Instead, a stellar career in a special field could serve to define future expectations. In the early nineteenth century Joseph Grimaldi, from a London theatrical family of Italian descent, created the British model of a white-faced clown, known for sharp mimicry and sly catchphrases. (An annual 'Clowns' Service' is held in his memory at Holy Trinity Church, Hackney.)[3]

This emergent celebrity culture was boosted by the burgeoning mass media of print and graphic art. It was also abetted by the oral culture of news, views and gossip, circulated in conversation and songs.[4] The advent of a celebrity culture in Britain is sometimes dated to the so-called 'Romantic' literary movement of the early nineteenth century.[5] Yet the phenomenon long predated that. There were undoubted theatrical stars in the Restoration era. And during the eighteenth century, the cult of celebrity crossed from the stage to include poets, dramatists, actors, authors, wits, musicians, artists – and thence into ever-wider fields. The social cachet of the rich and powerful was not ended. Yet even in aristocratic-plutocratic circles, it took personality and dash, as well as wealth and high status, to become a fashionable icon in the Georgian *beau monde*.[6] Outward position and official title were not enough for 'fame'.

Definitions of 'celebrity' were never matters of precise calibration. Stars who were famed, say in sporting circles, might not be well known in other networks, such as, say those of physicists, and vice versa. Nonetheless, those who achieved stardom were usually not only successful in their own fields, but had some other special attraction or personal glamour. Foreign celebrities, like the Saxon-born Handel (son of a barber-surgeon) and the princely Ghanaian William Ansa Sessarakoo (son of an African slave dealer), had the extra allure of 'difference', even if in the case of the French-born George Psalmanazar, his self-claimed Formosan identity turned out to be faked (see above, p. 222). Celebrities, who lived in the public eye, thus risked jealous scrutiny alongside the benefits of adulation.

Incidentally, monarchs and peers of the realm knew something of that double experience of fame yoked with criticism. Their role was to represent publicly the social and political hierarchy and to accept homage (and sometimes brickbats) gracefully. Yet these dignitaries were doing the expected. The fame was attached to their position as much as to themselves personally – with a few aristocratic exceptions such as the Duchess of Devonshire, whose matrimonial exploits gave her a personal glamour.[7]

Self-made celebrities, by contrast, were doing the unexpected, lofted on the wings of opportunity and publicity. In addition, those who came from 'nowhere' often benefited from timely patronage. Ann Yearsley, the 'Bristol Milk Woman and Poetess' who became a literary sensation in 1785, was certainly helped by her fellow Bristolian, the educationalist Hannah More. More organised subscribers for Yearsley's works, thus guaranteeing advance sales (though the two women later quarrelled over the profits).[8] However, Yearsley's novelty value faded fast. She never replicated her initial fame; when she was applauded posthumously, it was with mild condescension in an 1836 group biography of the 'uneducated poets' by the Poet Laureate Robert Southey.[9]

Another poet from 'low life' had already experienced a similar fate. Stephen Duck was a largely self-taught Wiltshire farm labourer. His first book brought him fame as 'the Thresher Poet' in 1730. Yet his next works were coolly received, and he became a butt of satire. Adding to the pressures, Duck's apparent disdain for working women was well rebuked in a poem on *Woman's Labour* (1739) by Mary Collier, a Sussex washerwoman.[10] After early success and royal patronage, Duck then switched careers, becoming an Anglican clergyman. Later, severely depressed, he drowned himself. (Today an unabashedly cheerful Duck Feast is held annually in Charlton St Peter, the Wiltshire village of his birth, following a custom launched by an aristocratic patron in 1734. The event is claimed to be the longest consecutively running popular festival of this sort in the UK.)

Rising celebrities included many well-educated offspring of lesser professional families, including lawyers and clergymen. The Devonshire-born artist Joshua Reynolds provides one example. His clerical-schoolmaster father apprenticed his talented son to a London portrait painter. Brimming with energy, Reynolds rose to become founder and first president of the Royal Academy of Arts in 1768, gaining a knighthood en route. He simultaneously strove to raise the professional status of artists more generally. His magnetism was such that he was eulogised after his death in 1792 by his friend Edmund Burke as 'one of the most memorable men of his Time'.[11] (Each year Reynolds' statue, in the courtyard of London's Burlington House, is garlanded with flowers to herald the Royal Academy's summer exhibition – a series launched in 1769.)

A relatively small but distinctive number of celebrities, like Duck and Yearsley, came from truly humble origins. One who coped well with the psychological challenges of both class and geographical mobility was the actor Peg Woffington. A Dublin bricklayer's daughter, she starred on stage in both London and Dublin. Specialising in comedy, she won celebrity status, famous lovers and much wealth, which she invested well, before dying relatively young from a wasting illness, at the age of forty.[12]

Theatre continued to offer a great launching-pad for celebrity. Touring shows brought actors to public attention throughout the country.[13] Among the women, Eleanor 'Nell' Gwyn (sometimes Gwynne), from a poor London background, was a late seventeenth-century pioneer. She blended her theatrical stardom with her role as one of the royal mistresses of Charles II. (Via their illegitimate son, who was given a title, Gwyn's descendants today populate the British peerage.)[14]

Among the theatrical men, meanwhile, the outstanding figure was the captivating actor-impresario David Garrick, an army captain's son of Huguenot descent. He spent his youth in Lichfield before leaving to seek fame in London.[15] His death was keenly mourned by his old friend and fellow Lichfieldian, Dr Johnson, as eclipsing 'the gaiety of nations'. Many memorials and tributes followed. Also theatrically mesmerising was Sarah Siddons. Born into a theatrical family, she learned her craft on tour.[16] She also tended her image carefully, appearing with full dramatic effect as Lady Macbeth or 'The Tragic Muse' in Reynolds' famous 1784 portrait. (Best known of her subsequent memorials is the Sarah Siddons Award for distinguished acting, presented annually since 1952 in Chicago.)

A further public frisson ensued in 1779–81 when theatrical allure met establishment royal fame. The glamorous lovers of the day were the actor Mary 'Perdita' Robinson, a naval captain's daughter, and her swain, the Prince of Wales, later George IV. For a while, she was a style trendsetter, her clinging muslin draperies much copied. After their affair ended, however, Robinson turned to drama, poetry, fiction and polemic (as noted above, p. 104), urging the case for women's rights. Her trajectory was very different from that of Nell Gwyn.

A number of women from modest backgrounds won celebrity as courtesans, particularly if they had sexual glamour and social style. Although they were pilloried as the eighteenth-century equivalent of 'dumb blondes', it took skill and nerve to succeed in their risky lifestyles. Celebrated Georgian courtesans included mid-century fashion trendsetters like Fanny Murray, the daughter of a Bath musician whose lovers included the rakish 4th Earl of Sandwich.[17] Another was Nancy Parsons, a tailor's daughter who had a well-publicised affair with the Duke of Grafton, before going on to marry a viscount.[18] A third was Elizabeth Armistead, from obscure origins, who had numerous love affairs with titled patrons before a happy marriage with the Whig opposition leader Charles James Fox.[19]

But all were eclipsed in fame by Emma Hamilton, the daughter of a Cheshire blacksmith. Long before she wed Sir William Hamilton she was a minor sexual celebrity. Then, during the couple's unconventional *ménage à trois* with Nelson, she became a European-wide sensation. And she prospered as long as her devoted admiral was alive to sustain her social bravado.[20]

Remarkably, too, one Georgian courtesan demonstrated how to become famous purely for being famous. Kitty Fisher began her career as a milliner but, in a very short lifetime, revealed a huge talent for publicity. Her dresses, jewels and adventures were relayed in gossip, songs and mock biographies. And her image shone in portraits by leading artists. In her prime, Fisher was more famous than many a duchess, all without doing or saying anything momentous. She married the respectable owner of Hemsted Park in Kent, now the home of Benenden School.[21] Fisher, however, died at the age of twenty-five in 1767, and her legend soon faded. (Incidentally, her trajectory from celebrity to obscurity was the direct obverse of that of the visionary poet-artist William Blake. He was a Georgian non-celebrity, virtually unknown in his own era. Yet his slow-burn fame continues to rise, and his work is now internationally admired.)[22]

Not all Georgian women in the public eye, meanwhile, traded on their youth and beauty. One veteran Londoner became known both for longevity and eccentricity. She was Jane Lewson, informally dubbed 'Lady Lewson'. Allegedly born in 1700, she died in 1816, although her demise is better authenticated than her birth-date.[23] Widowed early and left well-to-do, she made her own rules. Strikingly, she always wore antiquated clothing, in the style of her youth. Early nineteenth-century prints showed Lewson as a figure 'out of time': seemingly an updated Shakespearean witch or a fairy queen in disguise. (Her image was a real-life precursor of Charles Dickens's time-defiant Miss Havisham (1861) and of many later fables of frozen femininity.)

Authors not only wrote about the famous but could also, in the right context, themselves become celebrities. The lexicographer Dr Johnson gained a magnetic reputation, as much on the strength of his authoritative writings as on his wit and bruising repartee.[24] Admirers like the young Boswell captured Johnson's punchy performances for posterity. (Much later, in an unexpected accolade, Samuel Beckett, the twentieth-century Irish master of tragicomedy, planned to write a play about Johnson.[25] It never appeared; but there was a resonance between the two wittily melancholic wordsmiths. *'You're on Earth. There's no cure for that'*; *'Life is a progress from want to want, not from enjoyment to enjoyment'*. Which dictum came from which of the two authors?)[26]

Outstanding Georgian literary stars included a dazzling string of poets and novelists: Addison, Steele, Defoe, Pope, Gay, Swift, Richardson, Fielding, Eliza Haywood, Cowper, Smollett, Charlotte Lennox, Sterne, Robert Ferguson and Fanny Burney in the eighteenth century, continuing on to Wordsworth, Coleridge, Southey, Maria Edgeworth, Mary Brunton, Burns, Jane Austen, Byron, Keats, Shelley, John Clare, Scott and Mary Shelley in the nineteenth – to name but the most famous. Here was a field amply open to women. The cautious were able to publish anonymously; while some who began anonymously, like Jane Austen, found success almost despite themselves.[27] Moreover, among these literary lions there was one famed aristocratic rebel: Lord Byron gained treble kudos for his title, his vivid poetry and the unconventionality of his politics and love life.[28] Indeed, the term 'Byronic' still sets the standard for stylish-raffish-sexy-androgynous fame.

Every specialist field generated its own heroes, some of whom gained wider renown. One noted personality was Jack Broughton, a pugilist of obscure social origins. Dramatically, he won all his bare-knuckle bouts. Known as the 'Champion Prize-Fighter of England', he later ran a boxing amphitheatre in London, which established the sport's basic rules. Upon his death in 1789, he was buried in Westminster Abbey, an unofficial accolade, agreed by the Dean and Chapter. Broughton thus joined the playwright Aphra Behn, the physicist Isaac Newton, the actor David Garrick and the literary lion Dr Johnson – a most eclectic list – who all gained this enduring tribute immediately after their deaths. (Many others have subsequently joined the Abbey's pantheon, their fame becoming accepted on a more leisurely timetable.)

Two male celebrities also helped to consolidate the social rules. In the mid-eighteenth century, Richard 'Beau' Nash was Bath's Master of Ceremonies. He acted as a social go-between, introducing people and facilitating the smooth running of balls and assemblies.[29] As a result, this man from a poor-to-middling Welsh family was known as Bath's 'uncrowned king'. When in 1752 the Pump Room was redecorated, a statue of Nash was pointedly placed between busts of Alexander Pope and Isaac Newton, celebrating his fame as an outstanding social compere between those two giants of poetry and science.

Later, another 'Beau' shone in the early nineteenth century. George Brummell, son of a minor politician, become *the* epitome of the Regency dandy, famed for both wit and sartorial elegance. He soared into exalted social circles. His cachet, however, fell steeply after a public show of displeasure from the Prince of Wales. By way of instant revenge, Brummell audibly asked his companion: 'Who's your fat friend?' It was a cool farewell to the social heights. Nonetheless, as noted above (p. 285), in his heyday Brummell signally boosted the fashion of well-cut plain dark clothing for men.[30] (And today, a statue of the 'Beau' stands aptly in London's Jermyn Street, the longtime home of gentlemanly tailoring.)

Living as a celebrity was a visible form of Georgian social mobility. It entailed a competitive lifestyle as stars jostled to stay in the spotlight which was often enjoyable, even if also stressful. Undoubtedly, the pursuit of fame was not an egalitarian project. Yet it did beckon to hopeful individuals to seek what in a later era would be termed their 'fifteen minutes of fame' – and some Georgians amply succeeded.[31] Their careers thus testified not only to the power of the press and portraitists to amplify their reputations but also to the multiple opportunities presented by Britain's social and economic diversification.

Praising Merit

Pathways to renown seemed highly individualised, with a component of good fortune and happy timing. Advancement through personal merit, by contrast, was seen by the Georgians as more solid, explicable and socially momentous. In fact, as already noted, there was a considerable overlap between celebrities and unofficial meritocrats. The people in that latter category, however, garnered respect rather than idolatry.

'Meritocracy' as an abstract noun was unknown in this era. (It was first coined as a term of criticism in 1958.)[32] Yet the Georgians used various synonyms for the admired qualities which brought relative outsiders to the fore. One vogue term was 'worth'. It conveyed a moral standing that was superior to a false pride in birth and title. Alexander Pope's critique of the blue blood of the Howards has already been cited (above, p. 255). He added a snappy sound-bite: 'Worth makes the man, and want of it, the fellow'.[33] That key word was later used in 1795 in a resonant phrase by Robert Burns. In a true and honest person, no matter how lowly, 'the Pith o' Sense an' Pride o' Worth' outranked all worldly titles.[34] In fact, the latter noun was sufficiently current for John Wesley in 1788 to complain at its overuse. In one sermon, he fulminated that 'worth' was 'one of the most silly, insignificant words that ever came into fashion'.[35] It was a significant admission, even if, for the evangelist Wesley, people should seek not just routine 'worthiness' but higher spiritual qualities.

Greater linguistic clarity was attached instead to the concept of personal 'merit'. It was a quality to be admired – and its lack deplored. Thus the anonymous author of the already cited *Treatise on Merit* (1748) declared that: 'Personal Merit is the only true Nobility – and the Lord, who inherits the Dignities without the Virtues of his Ancestors, is but a despicable Creature'.[36] Titles without fine character were hollow. Such commentaries were not egalitarian, since they accepted differences in status. Yet they were explicitly meritocratic, prizing personal merit from whatever social background.

An anonymous novel of 1784, which took the form of love letters between 'a lady of quality' and her suitor from an 'inferior station', had the same message. The 'lowly' lover hesitates to press his suit. However, the lady warmly encourages him, with a paean of praise for social mobility: 'My ancestors may have quitted the plough-share and the pruning hook a century before yours – and there is all the mighty difference between us. In *China*, where superior learning and virtue procure nobility, *you would have been a noble of the first class.* There is no rank to which superior merit and great talents may not aspire.'[37]

That statement was contextually not without irony. The author was William Combe, a hack writer who was downwardly socially mobile. His father was a rich ironmonger, whilst the son spent years in prison for unpaid debts. On the other hand, Combe's mother was a Quaker. She may have influenced her son's social liberalism, though she would not have approved of his chronic insolvency.

Either way, Combe's reference to China was striking. Fuelled by travellers' reports, scholars were fascinated by the meritocratic reputation of the Chinese mandarinate. This body provided the nation's civil service, as founded by the tenth-century Song Emperor Taizu. The mandarins were scholar-bureaucrats, chosen by competitive examination to provide rational rule, replacing the old militarised aristocracy. In fact, the western interpretation of China's system was very idealised. Yet the concept of rational authority struck an emphatic chord.[38]

Eventually, the term that emerged most clearly among Georgian commentators to denote meritorious qualities was 'talent'. Pure 'genius' was acknowledged to be extremely rare. Yet it did not strain credulity to assert that many talented individuals were making their mark in the world. Hence by the early nineteenth century, the synonymous phrase for what was later termed 'meritocracy' was the 'aristocracy of talent'. (One early user was the poet and wordsmith Samuel Taylor Coleridge in 1809.) The phrase simply updated traditional 'aristocracy', meaning the 'rule of the few', by adding the crucial ingredient of 'talent'. So in 1846 Benjamin Jowett, himself a meritocrat who rose from an impoverished London background to become Master of Balliol College, Oxford, observed that Britain's landowners were being blended with the new 'Plutocracy *and* the Aristocracy of Talent' – the latter emerging 'partly through the professions'.[39]

Praise for merit was not crystallised into a separate theory of society and government. It expressed a long-term hope as much as an immediate reality. But, a stress upon merit, not high birth, encouraged belief in a rational society with a rational government. This attitude was expressed most notably by authors, journalists, teachers, lawyers and others from the 'liberal professions'. They were in part flattering themselves, since the middle class was taken to be the repository of social intelligence. Yet the approach was potentially radical too, as the workers constituted a reservoir of talents awaiting greater fulfilment.

Interestingly, too, one defender of the nobility adopted the same concept. William Playfair, an ingenious Scottish political economist (and son of a Presbyterian minister), was aware that the tides were shifting. In 1809 his three-volume study of Britain's titled families accordingly promised to identify the *Origins and Progress of the Rank, Honours and Personal Merit of the Nobility of the United Kingdom.*[40] Yes, the nobility had merit too. Liberal inclusivity had no limits.

Emergent Meritocrats

Virtually all societies need some means to replenish pools of talent at the top. In the case of Britain, historic openings – mainly for men – were found in military affairs (especially in wartime), in the church, and in the lower rungs of government business. The really notable development, in the Georgian era, was the new breadth and diversity of roles open to emergent meritocrats from all backgrounds – and the declining role of patronage by the king and nobility.

Sociologically, most Georgian meritocrats came from the middling sort, though a significant minority came from further 'below'. They came from all three historic kingdoms; and, between them, they shared a range of ethnic heritages, since 'talent' opened doors that prejudice might otherwise keep shut. The eloquent Barbudan-British Henry Redhead Yorke overcame his obscure origins to become a radical spokesman in the 1790s, before switching sides to become a spokesman for conservatism.[41] Many meritocrats, like the celebrities with whom they overlapped, came from the lower ranks of the professions. Some were, socially speaking, 'rough diamonds'.[42] They faced teasing for their lower-class or regional accents and manners. But jibes and sneers marked the tensions of change, including anxiety from those 'above'.

One riveting confrontation occurred in Parliament in 1779. Edward Thurlow, son of a middling-status Norfolk clergyman, became Lord Chancellor and gained a modest title as 1st Baron Thurlow. He was certainly no radical. Nonetheless, whilst chairing the House of Lords, Thurlow was reproached for his 'lowly' origins and recent admission into the peerage.[43] The sneer came from the 3rd Duke of Grafton, a former prime minister and a man of indubitably high status (if not moral virtue).[44] It was, however, a blunder. In response, Thurlow issued a thunderous rebuke. He expressed amazement at the attack upon his high office. He dubbed the hapless duke the 'accident of an accident' (referring to his descent from an illegitimate son of Nell Gwyn and Charles II). And Thurlow ended proudly: 'as a MAN, I am at this moment as much respectable – I beg leave to add, I am at this time as much respected – as the proudest duke I now look down upon'.[45] Privately, Grafton decried the chancellor as 'coarse and dishonest'.[46] Publicly, however, there was no doubt who had won the contest.

Flexible attitudes allowed many aristocrats to engage the services of bright young protégés from humble backgrounds. Numerous political aides thus entered Parliament for seats in 'pocket' boroughs (see above, p. 180), especially if the patrons had no family candidates to promote. However, doughty meritocrats preferred to fly under their own colours. A confrontation in 1755 between Samuel Johnson and Lord Chesterfield became emblematic. When writing his *Dictionary*, over seven long years, Johnson sought financial sponsors. Lord Chesterfield initially obliged but did nothing more. Then, when the great work appeared, Chesterfield wrote to commend it, seemingly climbing onto the bandwagon. Angered, Johnson rejected his praise, asking acerbically: 'Is not a Patron, my Lord, one who looks with unconcern upon a man struggling for life in the water, and, when he has reached ground, encumbers him with help?'[47] His letter to Chesterfield, which became an open secret, was taken as an 'authorial declaration of independence'. Chesterfield, the master of suave politeness, was clever enough to praise the missive publicly, whatever his private thoughts. However, it was again clear which of the two had publicly won their confrontation.

Discreet behind-the-scenes patronage in fact never disappeared; but one major resource for emergent meritocrats was up-front and publicly apparent, in the form of cultural support from their peers. Psychologically, a few great outsiders were loners, none more so than Isaac Newton, the genius who recast the study of physics. Yet many abundantly talented meritocrats in the Georgian era were highly convivial and gregarious, attending clubs, societies and literary salons. In that way, they gained the boost of solidarity plus an element of piquant rivalry.[48] Indeed, the liveliest societies acted as informal mini-colleges, providing company and mental stimulus in ways that the Georgian universities, with their restricted entry, struggled to match.

Furthermore, friendships among rising meritocrats were antidotes to the risks of social hostility from 'above' or alienation from their social roots 'below'. In the early eighteenth century, one famed London literary association was the Kit-Cat Club. Its members included wits, authors and peers of the realm.[49] Another, founded in 1764 as a small dining group by Samuel Johnson, Joshua Reynolds and Edmund Burke, was known simply as 'The Club'.[50]

There were countless other male-only private societies across the country, and some open to women also. In addition, there were very many salons and drawing rooms, to be found across all three king-doms, where men and women habitually met together. Best known of these gatherings was the informal Blue-Stocking Society, hosted in Bath by Mrs Montagu (admired as one of the Muses mentioned above, p. 63). This was not the only group for learned ladies by that name, but it became the hegemonic example.[51] Another group of literary lumi-naries (both male and female) met regularly in the 1770s at the Streatham Park mansion of Hester Thrale, where she lived with her first husband, the wealthy Southwark brewer and MP, Henry Thrale.[52]

In the same decade, a noted role in stimulating Anglo-Irish cultural contacts was played by the well-connected Elizabeth Vesey. Politicians and literary lions flocked to her salons, held at different times in London, Dublin and in her country house outside Dublin. These clever and wealthy women, with serious intellectual interests, were gifted cultural impresarios. In another case in the 1780s, the Dublin salon of Elizabeth Rawdon, Countess of Moira, became a key centre for Irish antiquarian studies, in which she herself participated.[53]

Fields of advancement for all these Georgian meritocrats were legion. The nascent civil service recruited a number of clever young men from middling backgrounds, like Samuel Pepys, the son of a master tailor, who served in the late seventeenth-century Admiralty.[54] Law was another field where intelligence and technical competence allowed relative outsiders to flourish. One leading Georgian barrister, William Garrow, was the son of a middling Scottish clerical-school-teacher.[55] And the ultra-conservative lord chancellor in the early nineteenth century, John Scott, later ennobled as Lord Eldon, was the grandson of a coal fitter and the son of a Newcastle merchant.[56] High-born lawyers by no means disappeared, since the law was a favoured avocation for younger sons of landed aristocrats; but increasingly they competed with meritocratic newcomers.

Military and naval affairs constituted another great arena where rival social imperatives operated. Men of high status, with the habit of command, were traditionally favoured as leaders. Nonetheless, in wartime, technical abilities were at a premium. Horatio Nelson, as the sixth child of a modestly ranked Norfolk clergyman, would probably not have become a vice-admiral in peacetime. But in combat his strategic daring and his capacity for leadership brought him to the fore.[57] The Duke of Wellington was another whose military merits propelled him upwards.[58] From a relatively impoverished – though titled – Anglo-Irish family, he gained outstanding success in battles, a dukedom (the highest non-royal title) and, later, the top job in politics. Moreover, the careers of two such determined meritocrats in the army and navy were vital for Britain. After all, the country fought and eventually won against some of history's most famous military meritocrats: Napoleon and his twenty-six Marshals of France.

Able recruits, from no matter what background, were also needed in all arenas of work that required technical expertise, such as science and engineering. A number of Georgian women, mainly from middling families, contributed notably to mathematics and astronomy.[59] Engineering and technology, by contrast, were heavily male dominated. Famously, between 1775 and 1813 an outstanding group of industrialists, philosophers and scientists met monthly in Birmingham. Their Lunar Society, named for the full moon which lit their evening journeys, was a veritable meritocratic beacon.[60] Among those attending was James Watt, the Glaswegian instrument-maker of steam-engine fame.[61] (An evocative memorial to this Society, at Queslett in northwest Birmingham, takes the form of nine large carved sandstone monuments, known as *The Moonstones*, erected in 1999.)

And Britain produced two scientific giants, renowned not for the glamour of their lifestyles (far from it), but for their conceptual breakthroughs. In the later seventeenth century, Isaac Newton rose from a middling clerical family to a chair at Cambridge, a knighthood, and intellectual pre-eminence. En route he formulated the principles of gravitation and made key advances in mathematics and optics.[62] A century later, science also opened doors for the practical genius of Michael Faraday, born into an impoverished south London family in 1791.[63] He not only discovered the principles of electromagnetism – the spark of life, which combines electrical charge and magnetic field into many forms of energy – but in 1822 built the first electric motor. He also advised the government on mine safety; the operation of lighthouses; protection of shipping from corrosion; public health; and education. Faraday, who declined a knighthood, became the first Fullerian Professor of Chemistry at the Royal Institution (a chair endowed by 'Mad Jack' Fuller of Sussex, himself an amateur astronomer).

So notable was the rising status of science that a conservative commentator in 1825 observed with real consternation that: 'The Philosophers . . . are getting up what they are pleased to call a New Aristocracy – an Aristocracy of Science [which] . . . is to be the enemy and ruler of the old one'.[64] Needless to say, there was no such organised project. Still, the comment indicated the subject's rising status and nervous responses to the same. (Today the names of three British scientists are used internationally as standard technical terms, adopted long after their deaths.[65] Thus a *newton* (symbol: N) defines the force needed to accelerate 1 kilogram of mass at the rate of 1 metre per second, squared. A *farad* (symbol: F) constitutes the basic unit of electrical capacitance, meaning the ability to store an electric charge. And a *watt* (symbol: W) is the electrical unit for the rate at which energy is generated or consumed. These are great, and eminently practical, tributes to the pioneers.)

Within Britain's changing society, other specialist occupations were also providing occupations – and, as importantly, incomes – for many talented men and women. Tribes of artists produced an array of portraits, landscapes, seascapes, townscapes, farmscapes, animal like-nesses and sporting scenes for middle- and upper-class purchasers. Finding a specialist niche was one basis for a successful career. The self-taught Henry Raeburn, born near Edinburgh in 1756 and apprenticed to a goldsmith, became the paramount portrait painter of Scotland's professional and landowning classes.[66] George Stubbs, born in 1724, a Liverpool leather-dresser's son with little formal education, famously specialised in animal likenesses.[67] And Joseph Wright of Derby, born in 1734, a lawyer's son, spent his working life in the Midlands, celebrating the local world of technical experimen-tation.[68] (Today his Derby birthplace is distinguished by a spherical astrolabe on top of a marble pillar, erected in 1992 in deft tribute to his rapt paintings of scientific study.)

More patchy was the career of the Swiss-born artist Angelica Kauffmann. The daughter of a travelling mural painter, she too had a peripatetic life, which included some modest success in Britain in the 1770s. However, as often happened to pioneering women, she faced hostile innuendoes about her private affairs; her reputation was long eclipsed, before recent reassessments.[69] The meritocratic world remained deeply competitive; far from all succeeded.

The printing press, meanwhile, was opening up the equivalent of secular pulpits for opinion formers. New cultural arbiters emerged, to test the truth of the maxim – coined in 1839 – that 'the pen is mightier than the sword'.[70] Notable early eighteenth-century pundits were Joseph Addison (son of a clergyman) and Richard Steele (son of an attorney). And their mid-century counterparts included the thunderous Dr Johnson (son of a bookseller), Irelands' mellifluous Oliver Goldsmith (son of a curate) and the august Lord Chesterfield (an earl's son).

Later there were competing voices like those of Hannah More (daughter of a schoolteacher), Edmund Burke (son of an attorney), Adam Ferguson (son of a clergyman), Adam Smith (son of a Scottish advocate) and Jeremy Bentham (son of an attorney). And in a very different register, new views appeared from controversial young radicals like Wordsworth (son of an attorney), Coleridge (another son of a clergyman) and the even more controversial Mary Wollstonecraft (daughter of a failed small businessman-turned-farmer).[71] (The first public memorial to Wollstonecraft, unveiled in north London in 2020, has caused fresh outcry, with both applause and condemnation greeting Maggi Hambling's conceptual sculpture of a naked woman emerging from an indistinct and swirling mass of female forms.)

Over time, the number of pundits greatly multiplied. They formed loose-knit networks, centred especially in London and Edinburgh, and constituted an unofficial intelligentsia (although that term was itself not used in English before 1907). Instead, in 1818, Coleridge, who had self-transformed from youthful radical into unorthodox public sage, named his fellow thinkers as a secular 'clerisy', coining a new term.[72] Their era was 'an age of talkers', added the essayist William Hazlitt. Outstanding even among the greats, he nominated the eloquent Coleridge, who held audiences with the 'glittering eye' of an Ancient Mariner.[73] North of the border, in a very different style, Sir Walter Scott (another lawyer's son) used his fiction to weave the rival strands of history into a cultural 'Scottishness'. But he too, while luxuriating in the past, admired current boldness and ambition: 'He that climbs the tall tree has won right to the fruit'.[74] (In salutation to the man who became Laird of Abbotsford, the towering Scott Memorial was placed in 1846 between Edinburgh's Old and New Towns, adorned with figures of druids, former Stuart kings, eminent literary Scots and a statue of Scott with his dog – a truly stunning tribute to the power of the pen.)

Female pundits were also able to enjoy the role, provided that they could cope with frequent brickbats and disparagement. Harriet Martineau, daughter of a Norwich textile manufacturer, rose above her father's financial failure in 1825 – and her own increasing deafness – to make a solid living by her pen, expounding lucidly the principles of sociology and political economy. In her *Autobiography*, she exulted that: 'My business in life has been to think and learn, and to speak out with absolute freedom what I have thought and learned'. She also advocated universalism in educational rights: 'Everything possible should be done to improve the quality of the mind of every human being'.[75]

Above all, these advocates of meritocratic advancement stressed the power of reason. Thomas Carlyle, the man from Ecclefechan who became the 'Sage of Chelsea', advocated rule by the wise: 'Intellect *has* to govern in this world; and will do it', he declared.[76] 'The intelligent classes lead the government,' agreed John Stuart Mill (philosopher son of a philosopher father) in 1829, 'and the government leads the stupid classes.'[77] Well, no: nothing so simple. For the burgeoning intelligentsia, however, it was a hopeful prospect,

Openings for talented individuals came with an implicit reminder that their competitive world could lead to failure as well as success. Some in bohemian literary and artistic circles settled for a raffish freedom rather than great fortunes. Many, especially from impoverished backgrounds, found advancement precarious. 'Slow rises Worth, by poverty oppressed', as Dr Johnson reminded his readers.[78] Women were most likely to face difficulties and to feel thwarted. Their exclusion from the professions was an increasingly sore point, leading to later reform campaigns.

Nonetheless, Britain's pluralist society was generating pluralist sources of power and influence. In 1826, a new secular London University (now University College London) was founded by a group of liberal reformers, inspired by Jeremy Bentham.[79] Its first Warden was Leonard Horner, a Scottish geologist and radical educational innovator, who campaigned to improve working conditions in British factories.[80] The institution was itself a pledge of transition in a society grappling with fundamental changes. So the middle-class meritocrats were, in part, matching the overlapping elites of aristocrats, plutocrats plus celebrities, while also in part rivalling them, under the flag of brainpower.

Careers Open to Talent

Collectively, the new 'aristocracy of talent' had become a key part of Georgian society – and, as already noted, the most brilliant among them garnered a lasting fame that has eclipsed kings. To give one more example: Captain James Cook, the son of a poor Yorkshire farm labourer, is now globally memorialised. As a professional naval officer, he undertook three epic round-the-world voyages of exploration between 1768 and 1779, ended only by his death, in a confused struggle on a Hawaiian beach in 1779, about which complex debates still rage.[81] A controversial figure today, he nevertheless has many monuments, including institutions and places named after him. In addition, his ships' names were given to two American space shuttles, *Discovery* (launched 1984) and *Endeavour* (1992). And now there's a Cook Crater on the moon, no less.

Such experiences of social mobility were transformative, and not purely for the individuals concerned. They encouraged others to think big. Together, the successful celebrities and meritocrats constituted a liberal phalanx of change, even though some individually held conservative views. To take another example, the upwardly mobile prime minister George Canning was no supporter of radical politics. However, he was sociologically a relative outsider. Indeed, he was, paradoxically enough, taunted for his lowly origins by his aristocratic Whig opponent. The reformer Earl Grey reportedly sneered that Canning, as the son of an actress, was not a suitable candidate for high political office.[82] But so much for proud peers. Canning did reach the top; and he would no doubt have replied to the earl's barb that his success was already a tribute to the openness of British society.

Reformers in the following generations, however, wanted to open the doors to advancement more widely. They wanted to nurture hidden talents from all backgrounds. And it's a hard aim to oppose. Precisely what constitutes true social 'worth' – and how it can best be fostered – remain debated questions. But top-quality human abilities are always needed in urbanising, commercialising and industrialising societies like Georgian Britain. The trend was apparent, even if it required help on its way. As Robert Burns pointedly sang, when urging the case for respecting individual talent from whatever class background: 'Then let us pray that come it may/ As come it will for a' that'. For good measure, too, his lyrics end with a further appeal to the advent of universal human solidarity: 'It's coming yet, for a' that'.[83]

ᗡ Time-Shift: Then and Now ᗡ

Historically, the greatest social esteem went to those at the 'top' of the social ladder, usually on the strength of their birth, their titled status and (to an extent) their wealth. However, that expectation was being challenged in Georgian Britain by the success of individual celebrities and meritocrats.

One way of absorbing the liberal Georgian doctrine of the equal worth of all human beings is to sing, read or listen to the resonant declaration in the famous 1795 poem 'A Man's a Man for A' That' by Robert Burns (1759–96). The poem has a double message: it is a proud meritocratic manifesto in favour of individual sense and worth, but no fear is expressed that new meritocrats might form a new elite, and the poem ends by affirming universal brotherhood (although no doubt these days that sentiment would be expressed in gender-neutral terms).

After three verses stressing the worth of every individual of independent mind, the poem ends with these ringing words:

A prince can make a belted knight,
A marquis, duke, and a' that;
But an honest man's aboon [above] his might –
Guid faith, he mauna fa' [must not fault] that!

For a' that, and a' that,
Their dignities, and a' that,
The pith o' sense, and pride o' worth,
Are higher rank than a' that.

Then let us pray that come it may,
As come it will for a' that;
That sense and worth, o'er a' the earth,
May bear the gree [win the prize], and a' that.
For a' that and a' that,
It's coming yet for a' that,
That man to man the warld o'er
Shall brothers be for a' that.

The poem, sung to the tune of an old Scottish ballad, has been translated into many languages. It's often sung at annual Burns Night festivities on 25 January (Burns's birthday), as sponsored by the World Federation of Burns Clubs.

PART V
The Georgians Viewed Long

The Georgian age of experimentation attracted intense
public interest – as theoretical science was becoming ever
more challenging to understand, whilst applied science was
becoming visibly more transformative, both for good and ill.

❦ 17 ❦

Georgians in an Age of Experimentation

Just how, then, did the turbo-charged society of Georgian Britain and Ireland – at the hub of interlocking European, Indian, American, African and increasingly global networks – produce a major transformation in human history? This chapter explores the intersecting details. It's well to remember that the forces of historical continuity mean that not everything changed. It's also relevant to note that not all plans for innovation succeeded. Experimentation, which opened the floodgates, entailed 'trial and error' (a phrase first recorded in 1806).[1] Mistakes and the correction of mistakes were integral to the process. The challenge was to weld creativity with realism. And vice versa: to combine practicality with imaginative invention.

'Empiricism' became a Georgian cultural mantra. The concept was taken at once to signify the avoidance of dogmatic extremes and equally a willingness to apply ad hoc measures. Politically, it encouraged the arts of compromise. Philosophically, it fostered the need for rational debate. John Locke, the paramount Whig thinker and educationalist, had paved the way, arguing that knowledge comes not from innate pre-formed ideas but from experience, as interpreted by human reason.[2] Rational enquiry and debates were seen as central to all forms of learning. Hence the British contributions to the European-American intellectual ferment known as the Enlightenment were typically undogmatic and experimental.[3]

Scientists especially stressed the need for rational testing. (No waiting for miracles or thunderbolts from on high.) In 1661 the physicist Robert Boyle explained that: 'I look upon experimental truths as matters of ... great concernment to mankind'.[4] And his work bore practical fruits. Boyle's law, stating that a gas's pressure and volume are (at a constant temperature) inversely proportional, helped Britain's engineers to build new atmospheric pumps. Some theologians worried that new scientific speculations might clash with religious certainties. Boyle responded by funding annual lectures (which still continue) to explore that theme. But most Georgian experimenters were sure that human reason was divinely bestowed, to be used in full. Thus the devout, if unorthodox, Isaac Newton declared his confidence not in hypotheses but in 'Reason and Experiments'.[5] And the plain-living Michael Faraday, from the radical Protestant sect of Sandemanians, had a robust mantra: 'But still try, for who knows what is possible?'[6]

A cultural innovator like the visionary William Blake was unimpressed by the stress upon rationalism. 'I turn my eyes to the Schools & Universities of Europe,' he wrote in *Jerusalem* (1804): 'And there behold the loom of Locke, whose Woof rages dire/ Washed by the Water-Wheels of Newton'.[7] It was a graphic, if elliptical, critique. Yet Blake's own maxim was very Newtonian. 'The True Method of Knowledge is Experiment,' he agreed, as he welded a creative mix of radical religion, cabbalistic theories and a naturalistic lifestyle.[8] At the same time, the rationalist cleric-cum-social demographer Thomas Malthus – unlike William Blake in every other way – upheld the need to test and retest in order to confirm. 'It is an acknowledged truth in philosophy that a just theory will always be proved by experiment,' he stated firmly in 1798.[9]

Intriguingly, too, there was an echo of Malthus in the opening salvo of Jane Austen's *Pride and Prejudice* (1813). The novel starts with the resounding assertion, 'It is a truth universally acknowledged . . .', and then tests the proposition that a wealthy young bachelor must seek a wife.[10] In her tale of amatory trial and error, solid evidence proves to be more reliable than *First Impressions* (the novel's original title). Judgment is easily warped by self-interest. Elsewhere, Austen noted: 'How quick come the reasons for approving what we like!'[11] And the subjectivity of human brainpower was much debated by philosophers like David Hume and the Yorkshire physician-psychologist David Hartley. However, an antidote to error was offered by shared questioning and debate – and, for scientists, by repeated experimentation.

Entrenching Science through Highways and Erroneous Byways

The 'scientification' (my invented phrase) of British society indicated not solely the growth of systematic knowledge about the physical universe, but also the growing cultural acceptance of scientific authority, even while the subject was fast becoming too technical for most laypeople to understand. Many Georgian experts in 'natural philosophy' – known as 'scientists' once the term was first coined in 1834[12] – tried to explain their research. Books, lectures and demonstrations appeared in profusion. Audiences at eighteenth-century plays were being made familiar with 'eccentric' scientists.[13] And readers who had followed Gulliver's journey to the flying island of Laputa in 1726 had already been introduced to Swift's tribe of unworldly inventors. In real life, however, it was the successful technical applications of many new scientific ideas which managed to foster cultural conviction, though not close understanding.

Operating within an international galaxy of researchers across mainland Europe and North America, the scientists of Georgian

Britain had no lack of contacts with whom to share ideas and debates.[14] And between them they had no lack of confidence. Their pioneering work ranged widely. Impressive developments ranged from Robert Boyle's formulations of the properties of gases, to Isaac Newton's discovery of the laws of gravitation and motion, to the astronomer Edmond Halley's 1705 prediction that what became known as 'Halley's Comet' would return into view from Earth in 1786 (as it did). Then there were astronomical breakthroughs from the German-born siblings William and Caroline Herschel, whose specially built giant telescope enabled him to calculate the periodicity of sun-spots and her to classify star zones.[15]

Meanwhile, Henry Cavendish in the 1760s identified hydrogen and formulated the law of electrical attraction and repulsion. And Joseph Priestley in the 1770s discovered oxygen (as did, in parallel, Antoine Lavoisier in France) and pushed the boundaries in his experiments with electricity. In Scotland, Daniel Rutherford, the Edinburgh-born chemist-cum-botanist, isolated nitrogen in 1772. Moreover, a whole new field of electrochemistry was then synthesised in the 1790s by Humphry Davy, who first used electricity to identify minerals and gases.[16] His work was then dramatically advanced by Michael Faraday, who not only defined electromagnetism but also identified the practicalities of electrical-motor technology, thereby becoming the 'father of [later] electronics'.[17]

Together, these contributions used to be dubbed the 'scientific revolution'. However, that usage, with its parallels to political upheavals, suggests a finite, one-off event. Instead, expanding scientific knowledge and its multifarious technological applications have proved to constitute a very long-term and unfolding process, which is still continuing. Hence 'scientification': the spread and entrenchment of scientific know-how, both theoretical and practical.

En route, however, there were failed inventions and erroneous theories. William Herschel believed (incorrectly) that the Earth's moon and other planets in the solar system were populated, as some far-distant stars may perhaps be.[18] Mistaken theories did not necessarily halt research. They were often used as prompts to experiment, being then adjusted and revised before being (if need be) dropped entirely. To take one example, in the early Georgian era the physical process of combustion was thought to release into the air a fiery element: phlogiston (from the Greek for 'burned'). First propounded in Germany in 1667, the theory won many adherents. Hence when Rutherford identified nitrogen, he called it 'phlogisticated air' (burnt air). Critics, however, correctly observed that some metals became heavier after burning, not lighter as they would have been had they released phlogiston into the air. Believers tried hard to save the theory. Yet, before long, it was quietly dropped from the scientists' intellectual repertoire.[19]

Biological studies also travelled along some erroneous trackways. As noted above (p. 239), one would-be science, known as phrenology, had tried to classify human character traits and capacities by measuring cranial features. However, researchers did not produce results that could be tested and verified by others. The approach was shelved, though elements of phrenological thought lingered. Rather the same has happened to the prolonged attempts at scientifically subdividing humans into separate 'races' (see above, pp. 239–40). No consensus ever emerged. Geneticists now study the intricate cross-hatching of genetic clusters *and* genetic mixing within the shared human genome.[20] Questing for truth entails a continuous sifting of speculations, theories, errors and half-errors.

Establishing Medical Immunology

Many special remedies were explored by the multitude of Georgian doctors and vendors of patent medicines. Some cures, like taking mercury for syphilis, proved to be almost as harmful as the original diseases. Yet, among the ferment of ideas and the abundance of quack medicines, the outstanding Georgian innovation was the advent of medical immunology.

From the mid-seventeenth century onwards, a revivified and very virulent strain of smallpox was circulating across Europe. It was feared both for its high morbidity, especially among the very young, and for the grossly disfiguring scars left on survivors. From 1716 onwards, a new preventive technique, known as inoculation (technically 'variolation'), was promoted in England by Lady Mary Wortley Montagu, who had seen its efficacy in Constantinople (Istanbul). Not all were convinced. But doctors began to refine the treatment; and huge numbers were inoculated, helping to mute the ferocity of the disease.[21] Then in 1796 Edward Jenner introduced vaccination. It offered a better preventive technique via controlled exposure to cowpox, a less serious disease, which triggered a suitable immunity. Public opinion was still divided but, on witnessing the treatment's success, became increasingly favourable. And Jenner gained an enduring worldwide fame.[22]

Systematic medical immunology (needed today as much as ever) had arrived. It relied upon a mix of scientific study and public trust in medical authority, plus an experimental response to new diseases and well-honed organisation at grass-roots level. Such was the confidence generated that one Dr Maty predicted in 1767 that smallpox could eventually be eradicated worldwide. (It took over 200 years and massive global organisation. But it was achieved in 1980: an impressive world first in the human struggle to cope with contagion.)[23]

Applying New Technologies

Experiments leading to practical outcomes were mightily boosting the kudos of science. Newton invented a high-quality telescope in 1668, and (of long-term import) proposed that early prototypes of electrostatic generators could be improved by using a glass globe.[24] The adventurous Edmond Halley also devised a prototype of a magnetic compass, as well as in 1690 a diving bell with up to four hours' immersion capacity (inadvertently damaging his middle ear during a live trial).[25] They worked closely with other experimenters – Newton encouraging the career of his assistant Francis Hauksbee – indicating the absence of any barriers between 'pure' and 'applied' science.

Meanwhile, unnamed technicians across Britain's urban-industrial regions were refining designs of clocks, watches, telescopes, eyeglasses, microscopes and other precision instruments. These included both popular consumer goods and utilitarian machines. Constant technical upgrades both allowed for and encouraged a non-stop variegation of styles and products. Certain regions, as around Glasgow and Paisley, became hubs of industrial innovation. The metalware trades of Birmingham and the Black Country were also famed in that regard. Thus in 1757 the economist Josiah Tucker noted approvingly, if sweepingly, that 'almost every Master & Manufacturer hath a new Invention of his own, and is daily improving upon those of others'.[26] And many industrial towns and regions in Georgian Britain shared a hopeful culture of experimentation, as conveyed in the justly famed industrial art of Joseph Wright of Derby.

Above all, techno-optimism was especially boosted by the miner's safety lamp. When invented by Humphry Davy in 1815, it held out the promise that scientific know-how plus smart technology could 'fix' serious workplace hazards. In fact, it took years, including trials of rival lamps and campaigns for government regulation, before conditions underground were improved across the board. Nonetheless, Davy's lamp beamed a positive message.[27]

Mining Ever-Deeper Mines

New forms of power did not obviate the need for human muscle-power, especially in tough businesses like mining. On the contrary, the industrialising economy required huge natural resources. Coal, already saluted as the 'black gold' of the Georgian economy, provided abundant cheap fuel for domestic consumers and industrial producers alike. Improvements in surveying, rock-blasting and in hydraulic pumping opened new deep seams and coalfields.

However, as pits were sunk ever deeper, so the risks multiplied. In 1737, a disaster in Whitehaven, triggered by 'firedamp' (methane), killed twenty-two men and three horses. The colliers, initially unwilling to return to work, eventually had to succumb through economic necessity. Another large-scale disaster occurred in 1835 at the Wallsend Colliery by Hadrian's Wall. It killed 101 miners, ranging in ages from 8 to 75 – the great majority being young boys.[28] Legislation in 1842 banned all underground employment of women and children, but the male workforce still continued to face chronic hazards – even with the aid of safety lamps – in an industry then growing towards its all-time peak in the early twentieth century.[29]

Cornish tin- and copper-mining experienced even more dramatic rates of growth. Steam-powered pumps allowed miners to perform their hazardous labours in ever-deeper mines. In its mid-nineteenth-century heyday, Cornwall produced two-thirds of the global supply of copper. Ore was shipped in bulk across the Bristol Channel to Swansea, which, in parallel, flourished as at first a local, then European, and then between the 1770s and 1840s a global smelting centre.[30] Yet new overseas competition ensured that eventually Cornish miners were emigrating to rival mining areas in Australia, South Africa and America. Nonetheless, the hectic Georgian expansion is much saluted: in heritage sites; and in spirited historical novels like the *Poldark* series (1945–2002; twice adapted for television).[31]

Moreover, the Cornish experience of massive regional boom – linked in parallel with the boom in Swansea copper smelting – followed by undercutting from emergent rivals is proving to be a frequent theme in world economic development, as businesses characteristically migrate in search of lower costs.

Inventing Steam Power and Mechanising Industrial Production

Contemporaries were quick to note the impact of technological changes. The politician George Canning in 1822 voiced a new consensus when he identified steam as 'a new and mighty power ... which walks the water, like a giant rejoicing in his course; – stemming alike the tempest and the tide'.[32] Moreover, this mighty force did not come unheralded, out of the blue.

In 1712 the engineers Thomas Savary and Thomas Newcomen had invented a prototype steam pump. It was huge and cumbersome, being worked by atmospheric pressure; but it served to pump water from deep mines. (Its use spread throughout British and European mining regions; a working model operates today in Newcomen's home town of Dartmouth.)[33] As a result, access to Britain's plentiful coal and mineral resources was improved, providing raw materials for innovations in metallurgy. One significant pioneer was Abraham Darby, whose cast-iron furnaces began to refine a high-grade metal that was malleable but not brittle – and still tough enough to sustain the world's first cast-iron bridge at Coalbrookdale (opened 1781), today a World Heritage Site.[34]

Then the Greenock-born James Watt, an initially unknown instrument-maker, built a working steam engine, updating Newcomen's giant pump. By 1775, Watt was in partnership with the Birmingham businessman Matthew Boulton. Between them, they began to make engines which became the workhorses of Britain's industrialising economy.[35] Boulton also toured regularly, visiting the factories and mills which had installed their machines. His fine-tuning in situ not only trained local foremen to operate the new technology but also provided feedback to improve future models. (Today a number of surviving engines testify to Watt's remarkable breakthrough.)

Britain's industrial transformation, building upon these technological breakthoughs, is widely known as the 'industrial revolution'. And the changes were truly momentous.[36] But, again, the advent of the factory and mechanised production were key long-term trends, not a singular event. Much groundwork preceded James Watt's pioneering steam engine in 1776. In the wider economy, a notable subdivision of labour was already manifest, streamlining craft production in response to growing demand. That point was specifically stressed by Adam Smith at the start of *The Wealth of Nations*, citing the apparently humdrum example of pin-making.[37]

Employers thereupon began to experiment with bringing the workforce together into large factory workplaces and mechanising production. In the 1770s, Richard Arkwright's water-powered cotton-spinning mill at Cromford, Derbyshire, heralded a new workforce regime. (It's now a heritage industrial site.)[38] Inventors continually strove to remove production bottlenecks. James Hargreaves's mechanised spinning jenny (1764), with its multiple spindles, was followed by improved versions, as water power was upgraded to steam power. Hand-spinning became a thing of the past. Already in 1733, John Kay, a farmer's son from Walmersley, near Bury in Lancashire, had invented a mechanically propelled flying shuttle. But it lacked speed and accuracy.

Responding to burgeoning demand – and to the technological possibilities – Edmund Cartwright then in 1789 introduced a stream-powered loom at his Doncaster factory. He himself faced technical teething problems, and, eventually, financial failure. Yet, after many refinements, steam power became routine for both cotton-spinning and weaving, maximising output whilst keeping costs low.[39] The tireless Cartwright also devised a wool-combing machine, a rope-making machine and an engine that ran on alcohol. None of those later schemes bore fruit. Yet his efforts showed how changes sprang from many bright ideas, not all of which succeeded.

Crucial, moreover, was the spread of the new steam-powered technology from economic sector to sector. Witnessing in 1788 the transfer of mechanised production from one textile industry to another, Arthur Young remarked simply: 'a revolution is making'.[40]

It's important to stress once more that factory work did not become universal, and that industries had different timetables of change. In Sheffield a key shift dated from 1823. Greaves's Sheaf Works led the way, with the first integrated steel cutlery factory, soon followed by others as the old craft workshops disappeared. Before long, huge furnaces, working around the clock, lit the night 'in all the horrible splendour of their everlasting blaze', as William Cobbett observed, mixing admiration and alarm in 1830.[41] The coal-fuelled, steam-powered economy was arriving in stages, complete with its unintended counterpart in the form of cumulative environmental damage.[42]

Constructing Canals

Effortful human input was also required for another great change, this time produced from the 1760s onwards by the building of spectacular new canals. The muscle power of the navvies, as those who dug the canals were known, was never seen as romantic. Yet the fruits of their labours were certainly seen as heroic. An onlooker in 1767 wrote excitedly that: there 'never was a more astonishing *Revolution* accomplished in the internal System of any Country, than has been [done] within the Compass of a few Years'.[43]

A cross-country water-borne network was created, able to transport essential cargoes of heavy goods and raw materials (like coal) at low cost. Birmingham, without a major river, became a great canal interchange. Crucially, James Brindley invented a watertight puddling clay to line the new watercourses securely.[44] Later, engineers like John Rennie the Elder rose to the challenges of traversing difficult terrain with a mix of tunnels, aqueducts, pumping stations and locks, such as Caen Hill's impressive flight of twenty-nine locks on the Kennet and Avon Canal (completed 1810; now lovingly restored for tourism).

Thomas Telford also supplied his engineering imagination and organising skills. His stunning eighteen-arch aqueduct at Pontcysyllte (completed 1805), carrying the Llangollen Canal across the Dee Valley, took ten years to install. (It is today a highly popular World Heritage Site.)[45] Telford's reputation was such that, when in 1817 Parliament created a public body to promote work projects for the unemployed, he was chosen as lead commissioner. Yet not all his plans were golden. His Caledonian Canal (opened 1822) triumphantly linked the Scottish east coast at Aberdeen to the west coast near Fort William, with the aid of twenty-nine locks, four aqueducts and ten bridges. However, the canal's shallow draught, which had been reduced to cut costs, proved inadequate for the next generation of canal shipping; and the scheme lost commercial viability.[46] (Telford was buried in Westminster Abbey, and later his name fittingly bestowed upon Telford New Town, Shropshire, where a shirt-sleeved statue is located in the town square.)

Canals inspired veritable investment 'manias', as in the wartime 1790s. However, their unchallenged heyday lasted for no more than half a century. Technological change did not end the role of water-borne bulk transport. Far from it: different generations of transit systems regularly overlap and complement one another. Yet from the 1820s, the next 'shock of the new' was to run overland on rails.

There was not just one 'transport revolution', just as there was not just one 'scientific revolution'. Instead, there was a series of systemic upgrades, complete with failures, overshoots and wasted efforts. The status of engineers, however, rose unchecked – partly because the public were readily able to see and to marvel at their deeds. As already noted, these men were becoming the techno-heroes of their age. Their reputations were soon to be further enhanced by Samuel Smiles's five-volume *Lives of the Engineers* (1861).[47]

Inaugurating Steam Railways

Early efforts at harnessing steam power for mechanised transport were unsuccessful. James Watt had tried, but even he failed. In the course of the eighteenth century, however, coal wagons were being pushed and pulled along new iron rails at numerous pitheads, suggesting a viable trackway. The compound breakthrough began in 1801, when Richard Trevithick, son of a Cornish tin-mining family, invented a steam locomotive. At first, his 'Puffing Devil' ran on roads; but in 1804 it was exhibited in London, circling on specially constructed rails. The turbulent Trevithick would die in poverty. Yet his machine was an exciting portent of things to come.

After further experiments, it was George Stephenson who won global renown. From a Northumbrian mining family, he had already invented his own miner's safety lamp. Then in 1825, he and his son Robert, another virtuoso engineer, launched the world's first steam-powered railway. It ran for 25 miles between Stockton and Darlington, on wrought-iron rails.[48] And it was no mere curiosity. Between 1825 and 1835, Parliament authorised fifty-four more lines, and thirty-nine more during the railway 'mania' of 1836–37. The majority adopted George Stephenson's chosen narrow gauge of 4 feet 8½ inches, which remains an international standard. Together, the Stephensons constructed railways across Britain (the actual building done by their muscular railway navvies).[49] And Robert Stephenson constructed yet more in Belgium, France, Norway and Egypt.[50] (Both men are extensively commemorated, and Stephenson's Rocket remains a talismanic exhibit at York's Railway Museum.)

Steam power became more versatile once engineers had access to high-quality tempered steel. So the creative Isambard Kingdom Brunel, son of another gifted engineer, built not only railways, tunnels, dockyards and suspension bridges but also a pioneering steamship. The *Great Western* (completed 1838) crossed the Atlantic from Bristol to New York in just over fifteen days, with ample coal stocks still on board – another portent.[51] (Brunel, who is one of Britain's best known engineers, is aptly commemorated by the well-regarded university which bears his name.)

With the railways came greater speed and reliability when moving manufactured goods, raw materials and postal services. Other modes of transport were not superseded but increasingly had to complement the new technology. And the public proved keen to ride as well. Closed carriages were introduced, facilitating travel for leisure and tourism, as well as for work. The effect was to boost yet further local, regional and urban specialisation, within a national system. One conspicuous sign was the UK's 1840 standardisation of time zones into one national 'Railway Time', based upon Greenwich.[52] And every speeding of communications generated pressures for more.

Dreaming of Aviation

Following the success of the railways, inventors also began to experiment with powered road-carriages. However, the realisation of such plans awaited the advent of lightweight construction materials, and new fuels. Powered flight had the same requirements. It was thus much easier to conceptualise than to realise, although Georgian balloonists in Britain and France were busy experimenting. The first manned flight in a hydrogen balloon was achieved in Edinburgh in August 1784, the first in England in September 1784, and the first in Ireland in 1785.[53] There were also disasters, which dampened the excitement. In Ireland in 1785, a crashed balloon in Tullamore (County Offaly) led to a fire which burned more than 130 houses. (Today the town's shield displays a phoenix rising from the ashes, and an annual Phoenix Festival celebrates the recovery from the world's first aviation disaster.)[54]

Furthermore, these experiments prompted interest in the science of flight. In 1809–10, George Cayley, a Yorkshire baronet and prolific inventor, published an original treatise *On Aerial Navigation*, which identified the basic principles. Cayley also devised a manned fixed-wing glider, which was flown successfully for a short trip near Scarborough in 1853.[55] (A gliding champion in 1973 repeated the feat on camera for a TV programme.) Not all the techno-dreams of one generation are successfully realised by successor generations. Yet some are – and continuing experimentation ensured that powered flight has bcome a reality, again bringing unintended environmental consequences in tow. (Cayley today is honoured by Hull University, appropriately enough on its Scarborough campus, and in London by a discreet plaque at Westminster University, which he co-founded in 1838 as Britain's first polytechnic.)

The Georgian Age of Experiments

Remarkably, too, Britain's experimenters did not confine themselves to exploring just one major new source of power. Options multiplied, particularly once the Italian physicist Alessandro Volta had demonstrated the use of batteries to store electricity in 1800. His contribution was a further reminder that ideas and information were being shared and tested between international networks of scientists.

Research optimism was being collectively boosted, giving experimenters hope even during the slow processes of repeated trial and error. As the enthusiastic Joseph Priestley remarked: 'In completing one discovery, we never fail to get imperfect knowledge of others'.[56] Yet it's worth repeating that inventions do not automatically come on cue. There have been many failures, even after intensive effort; and there is also the phenomenon known as the 'technological plateau', when innovations stall and technical changes focus on refining systems incrementally rather than breaking fresh boundaries.[57]

Nonetheless, in this case, steam's successor world of electronics was appearing in vigorous embryo. In 1822 Michael Faraday built the first electrical motor; in 1823 the first electrical bell was rung; and in 1831 Faraday invented the world's first electrical generator. Later developments continued, of course, after this period of history. Yet Faraday, an intently persevering man, was aware of nature's power and its potential harnessing by humans, remarking that: 'The beauty of electricity or any other force is not that the power is mysterious, and unexpected ... but that it is under *law* [for Faraday, that meant the God-given law of physics], and that the taught intellect can even govern it largely'.[58]

All these dramatic changes encouraged dramatic responses. Impetuous action against 'nature' could lead to harm and remorse, causing Coleridge's *Ancient Mariner* (1798) to leave his listener 'a sadder and a wiser man'. A famously brilliant reverie on the perils of experimentation followed, in Mary Shelley's novel *Frankenstein: Or, the Modern Prometheus* (1818). What if a daring scientist could build a body and animate it via electrical power? Yet the inventor is dicing with danger, as did legendary Prometheus who gave fire to humans. Hence Shelley's tale now signifies that all innovations can unleash harm as well as good.[59] (One current example is the Frankensteinian career of plastic.)

At the same time, new technologies can produce positive benefits. And they can save workers from dangerous and backbreaking tasks. In 1833, one German-American techno-optimist foretold *The Paradise within the Reach of All Men, Without Labour, by Powers of Nature and Machinery* – foreseeing an automated future economy, 'beyond the common conceptions'.[60] (Yet being 'at work' is not always a negative experience, either for individuals or for society at large. Much depends on the type of work and working conditions.)

Georgian Britain's epic transformation into an urban-industrialised economy drew upon multiple interlocking roots, both theoretical and practical. Robert Stephenson once stated that: 'the locomotive is not the invention of one man; but of a nation of mechanical engineers'.[61] It was a gracious compliment to his fellow professionals. Yet their work was but one feature among many interlocking efforts within an economy, society and political system with multiple complementary roles. The inventive culture of 'trial and error' was pervasive. And so many aspects of life, communications and daily toil were being transformed.

Thus the most apt of all the Georgian age-namings comes from Benjamin Franklin, the experimenter, diplomat and sage, who was born in Boston, Massachusetts and resided in London for long periods between 1757 and 1775.[62] In his autobiography, Franklin mused: 'This is an age of experiments, and I think [that] a set [in conjunction], accurately made and combined, would be of great use'.[63] He was right, in that advances in scientific theory did not remain abstractions but can be applied to an extraordinary range of practical functions.

Georgian experimentation has proved world-changing in its impact, requiring people both to rethink and revise when things go wrong – and to celebrate when things go well. 'Trial and error' is a formula not for repose, but for effort.

ᘡ Time-Shift: Then and Now ᘧ

Here the suggestion is to view in person or virtually three new sources of power developed successively in the Georgian age of experimentation; and to consider the impact upon contemporaries witnessing these inventions for the first time. (Many aspects of twenty-first century life would surprise a time-traveller from 1700 or from 1840, but surely nothing would equal the amazement of encountering the miniaturised power within a mobile phone.)

1. Newcomen Memorial Engine (*c.* 1725)
This mighty atmospheric pressure pump was moved from its Midlands workplace to Thomas Newcomen's home town of Dartmouth, Devonshire, and is operated at stated times.

2. James Watt's 'Old Bess' Steam Engine (1777)
This is one of a handful of surviving engines which became tireless workhorses of industrialisation, viewable at the Science Museum in London. The harnessing of mechanical power to production was as massive a transformation in human history as the first use of tools in primeval times.

3. The Oxford Electric Bell, or Clarendon Dry Pile (constructed 1825 by instrument-makers Watkin and Hill; purchased by physicist Robert Walker 1840)

The world's oldest continuously ringing electric bell was a portent of the next big post-steam source of power. Two brass bells, with between them a small metal clapper, stand in a glass jar under two original dry-pile batteries. (Their tiny metallic ring is recorded on various YouTube videos.)

⚛ 18 ⚛

Georgians in an Age of Urbanisation

The great attention paid to improving communications, as discussed in the previous chapter, was not just an optional extra.
Instead, it was fundamental to the development of Georgian
Britain's internal integration, as well as to its expanding long-distance
trade, its growing overseas settlements, its dynamic naval power, its
assertive military campaigns, its heightened political reputation, and,
not least, to the sustenance of its multiplying urban population.
Successful towns depended upon regular communications. They
needed good incoming supplies of food, raw materials, population
recruits, visitors and news, as well as reliable outgoing networks for
the distribution of goods, services and urban 'value-added' culture.

Georgian artists, who painted many portraits of urban leaders and
celebrities, also produced striking townscapes – and depictions of
people on the move. Songs, stories and sayings regularly hymned
urban vitality. Townspeople walked fast. They shared bustle, ambition, knowingness. Walking the city streets was said to constitute an
education in itself.[1] The days were busy, as crowds thronged markets
and docksides. And urban night-life was newly flourishing too, as

oil-lamps (from the 1690s) and gaslights (from the 1800s) lit the main streets.[2] True, these pro-town views contained elements of the stereotypical. True, too, there were many lurking dangers among the urban masses. Yet their collective activities made for lively times, where all were enjoined to keep their eyes open, their wits about them, and their fob watches under close supervision.

Conversely, there was no glorification of the rank-and-file residents of the countryside. Instead, they were caricatured as slow-witted 'bumpkins' and 'clodhoppers'. Exile to rusticity was like living in 'a kind of healthy grave' or sleeping with one's eyes open, as the famed Georgian wit and parson Sydney Smith declared (no doubt to knowing laughter from his urban companions).[3] By contrast, the physical countryside was warmly admired by visiting towns-people. They hastened to buy landscape paintings, and they travelled to beauty spots as tourists, in growing numbers. Thus the Georgian towns, embarking upon a period of prolonged urban growth in all three kingdoms, became magnets, not to the exclusion of the countryside, but with an urbane view of their own centrality.[4]

Sending and Receiving Long-Distance Messages

To keep news and information in good circulation, the national postal services (dating back to Tudor times) were much expanded in the Georgian era; regular mail coaches ran on main routes from 1764 onwards. Letter-writing was a widespread practice, although, since the cost (before 1840) was paid by the recipients, some may have fretted at paying for unwanted missives.[5] There were also special arrangements for key purposes. Merchants established lookout posts outside the big ports, where marker flags were hoisted to inform them when their ships were 'in the offing'. Such news was vital, especially for long-distance traders, who faced nerve-racking waits between dispatch and returns.

In addition, governments established special systems to get rapid news of overseas military and naval engagements. Once reports reached the great dockyard towns, relays of signals were flagged between designated outlook points – often still styled as Telegraph or Beacon Hills – all the way to the capital city. Moreover, for special purposes, longer communications were taken by relays of fast horses. In June 1815 that system informed the government not only of the British-Prussian victory at Waterloo but also of the dramatic fact that the defeated Emperor of France had surrendered specifically to the British. As the news was carried to London, crowds promptly began to move in the reverse direction, flocking to Plymouth Sound to catch a glimpse of Napoleon (sombre but dignified in defeat) on board the British flagship HMS *Bellerophon*.

Given the premium upon rapid transmission, it is thus no surprise to find that Georgian experimenters were exploring the possibilities of electrical telegraphy. In 1816 the young Francis Ronalds, a London businessman, installed a working model, sending messages along subterranean iron wires for 8 miles from his base in Hammersmith. Exultantly, he wrote: 'Let us have electrical conversation offices communicating with each other all over the kingdom'. His pioneering system was then rejected by a dully unimaginative Admiralty spokesman as 'wholly unnecessary'.[6] Yet, by the late 1830s, engineers at home and overseas were starting to plan commercial telecommunications. Demand for ever-faster communications, whether for governments, businesses or private individuals, is in-built into urban-industrial societies.

Speeding and Safeguarding Shipping

Port authorities throughout the Georgian era paid much attention to dredging rivers, deepening and improving harbours and, from the 1790s, building docks. Around Britain's indented coastline, new lighthouses were also set in place. They signalled a practical optimism. Inspiring engineering feats like the Eddystone Lighthouse (completed 1698; rebuilt in 1759 after a fire) near

Plymouth Sound, and the Bell Rock or Inchcape Lighthouse (constructed 1807–10) off the Angus coast in the North Sea, acquired lasting fame.[7]

Navigation was meanwhile assisted by improved telescopes, quadrants, maps and, as noted above (p. 32), marine chronometers for determining longitude. Shipbuilders were making larger ships, still using durable English oak, but after 1783 using hardened copper rather than iron bolts. That change followed Humphry Davy's crucial proof that iron was liable to corrosion by lengthy contact with seawater. Sailing times were simultaneously being reduced by stream-lined adjustments to design and sails. By the 1820s and 1830s, sleek full-sailed tea-clippers, devised for rapid shipments from China, were marvels of maritime speed.

Important, too, were improvements to sailors' health on long-haul trips, following better understandings of dietary requirements. However, seafaring remained hazardous. The greatest disaster of the Georgian era occurred in mid-September 1782, when a ferocious gale off Newfoundland capsized an entire convoy. Two British warships, three captured French prizes and six merchant ships were sunk, with the loss of some 3,500 lives.[8] Many sombre Georgian memorials confirm that seafaring entailed risk.[9]

Expanding and Regulating Global Trade

Britain's commercial reach spread decisively from north-western Europe to become an emphatically global system. Again, this highly significant change was at one time saluted as a 'commercial revolution'. But, once again, a term suggestive of a single upheaval is misleading. 'Commercialisation' conveys more effectively the long-term process, by which Britain gained a global trading network linked to its colonies and to overseas commercial partners.[10] The 'jolly jack tars' who plied the seas remained great cultural favourites, featuring in songs and prints. They were also, in this era, losing many of their freelance competitors, as British shipping was effectively protected from piracy on the high seas by the vigilance of the Royal Navy.[11]

One specialist commercial service, provided in eighteenth-century London, Glasgow, Dublin and Cork, was both symbol and facilitator of change. That business was marine insurance, which was pioneered from 1688 onwards. Dealers, meeting at Lloyd's Coffee House in London (today institutionalised as Lloyds of London) offered a hedge against the many hazards facing long-distance shipping. Rationalist calculus was thus pitted against risk, even if not always effectively.

Most significantly, too, trade posed a major moral challenge. As already noted, Britain's mercantile involvement in trafficking in enslaved Africans became increasingly contentious. Policy was eventually changed in two stages: in 1807 Parliament banned British merchants from participating in the trade; and in 1833 it abolished slavery throughout its colonies. Other nations joined the process at different times. The USA banned the importation of slaves in 1807; and numerous other countries rejected the trade shortly afterwards. In practice, however, it took time to enforce the ban and to halt smuggling. Nonetheless, a principle was established, accepted today by international systems of regulation, that free trade must be conducted within legal and moral limits.[12] (It remains a constant struggle to close old loopholes and to prevent the invention of new ones.)

Improving Roads

Local and long-distance transport improvements both fostered and responded to growing urban demand. No region was self-sufficient. Shipping, canals and later railways catered for the heaviest of bulk goods, yet much traffic crowded onto the roads. Hence in this period the (initially unwritten) convention was consolidated that Britain's traffic drives on the left, thus collectively regulating the flows and diminishing the disputes.

Travellers' motivations were not exclusively work-related. Many journeys were made for leisure purposes. The Georgian commercialisation of organised sports, entertainments and tourism depended upon crowds flocking into town for urban events and heading out of town for rural tournaments, hunts and horse-races.[13] Local day-jaunts were also popular. The affectionate humour of William Cowper's comic poem *John Gilpin* (1782) embroidered freely upon a real-life tale. A London linen draper boldly hires a chaise-and-pair for a family dinner in a tavern out of town. Alas, Gilpin's own part in the trip goes badly wrong. He is no great rider. His horse bolts, taking Gilpin far beyond his waiting family who travelled by coach; the horse, startled again, then bolts straight back to Islington, once more past Gilpin's patiently waiting family. But these mishaps of mobility prompted much rueful mirth.[14] (Today, a street sculpture outside the Bell Inn in Edmonton, London commemorates the festive venue where Gilpin should have dined with his wife but didn't.)

After 1663, control over many sections of Britain's major thoroughfares was vested in new turnpike trusts, with the power to raise tolls. Not all these bodies were equally efficient. And high tolls had at times to be adjusted downwards, in response to angry anti-turnpike riots.[15] But successful trusts actively employed innovative road engineers. One star was John Metcalf, dubbed Blind Jack of Knaresborough (commemorated there with an engaging statue). Between 1765 and 1792, he installed roads across northern England, constructed with strengthened foundations and convex surfaces for better drainage.[16] Another pioneer was John Loudon McAdam, after whom the process of installing a firm surface of crushed rocks bound with gravel was named: 'McAdamisation'. (Later, when tar was added, this compound became tarmac.)[17] And a third star in the constellation was Thomas Telford, who built so extensively that he was dubbed, punningly, the 'Colossus of Roads'.[18]

Over time, a national system of (variably) maintained main routes was emerging, under local control. By 1825, there were over 1,000 trusts, which between them controlled some 18,000 miles of roads, some of which remained toll-free.[19] In Scotland, the British state post-1745 had made particular efforts, for obvious political reasons, to build new roads and bridges, linking from Fort Augustus to Fort William.[20] Meanwhile, eighteenth-century Ireland had a good-quality road network. And in 1765 grand juries were given powers to raise local funds for improvements. There were thus plenty of free roads providing alternatives to the Irish turnpikes. They, as a result, were relatively lightly trafficked, although used by mail coaches and hire-carriages.

Improved road surfaces thereupon allowed coach-builders to upgrade the quality and variety of conveyances. Those ranged from the drovers' heavy wagons to sturdy stage-coaches, hackney carriages for hire, heavy barouches, light chaises or gigs, through to simple pony carts.[21] Wealthy invalids could use wheeled Bath chairs (invented for use in the city's spa in the mid-eighteenth century), which were drawn or pushed. And elegant ladies with access to a pony cart could take the air without having to rely upon male drivers. Men and women alike rode their horses for short journeys. And the poor walked both near and far. In sum, all classes in Georgian Britain had at least some access to some form of mobility.

Moving and Safeguarding Money

Another form of mobilisation was that required to move flows of capital, as well as to invest and to safeguard outcomes. To aid those processes, the Georgians invented a range of specialist financial services. These began in London, with offices for fire insurance (after 1681), marine insurance (after 1688), life assurance (after 1706) and a stock exchange (after 1698). Specialist stockbrokers – a new profession – traded on behalf of domestic and foreign investors. Speculative fluctuations were common, as they remain to this day. Indeed, the notorious South Sea Bubble of 1720 is still a byword for investor gullibility and market volatility.[22] Yet investors sought a degree of security. Hence the London Stock Exchange strove to foster an ethos of responsible dealing: 'My word is my bond'. In 1812 it consolidated a professional code for all brokers, setting at the very least an aspirational bar of good conduct.

Banking was another major service that was institutionalised in this era, replacing the earlier role of individual moneylenders. Central stability was provided by the Bank of England. It was created by government in 1694 as an autonomous self-regulating institution, though it remained close to Whitehall and managed the national debt.[23] It also acted as clearing house for many private commercial banks.[24] Some became 'big beasts' (Lloyds; Barclays; Hoare's). But others remained localised. One such was the Quantock Savings Bank (founded 1817), with branches in Somerset's small townships, such as Nether Stowey, near Taunton.

Each business issued its own banknotes, usually relying on a London bank as guarantor. But financial services remained hazardous. The Anglo-Scottish bank of Neale, James, Fordyce and Down (founded 1757) experienced a sudden failure in 1772, following poor speculations. A ripple effect ensued. Neale's main clearing house, the Amsterdam-based bank of Clifford and Sons failed in turn, triggering further closures across Europe.[25] Prudent dealers began in ever greater numbers to employ mathematically trained risk assessors, who were first termed 'actuaries' in 1762.

London's role as an international financial hub was initially challenged by its closest rival, Amsterdam. However, by the late eighteenth century, the Dutch economy was in relative eclipse.[26] International investors responded favourably to Britain's fiscal and political stability, which allowed its governments to raise loans cheaply. With inflows from overseas, capital was abundant in Georgian Britain, and interest rates generally low.[27] The grid of English, Irish and Scottish banks meanwhile provided a flexible system for safe and speedy capital transfers.

Incidentally, however, it's not particularly helpful to classify the Georgian economic world as simply 'capitalist', based upon unfettered private capital. (Too many variants are cited under that generic label to make it a single phenomenon.)[28] In practice, the Georgian economy was considerably 'mixed'.[29] Its major asset-holders included not only individual men and women, but also chartered and private companies, colonial estates, charities, banks and, not to be forgotten, the British state, which had huge naval and military infrastructural resources, invested in a range of civilian projects,[30] and, throughout this period, upheld firmly protectionist policies, including the navigation laws.

Commercialising Agriculture

Mobility in this period – with outflows of people from the countryside, inflows of funds into agrarian improvements and efficient communications to get products quickly to market – greatly enhanced the commercialisation of agriculture. And that commercial integration prompted ever-increasing regional specialisation.[31] Farming inertia again did not disappear. But landowners faced pressures to adapt. Handbooks like *The Rational Farmer and Practical Husbandman* (1743) set the tone.[32] Stock breeders strove to upgrade the quality of sheep, cattle, pigs, farm-horses and thoroughbred racers; and in this era much British livestock was exported to North America and Australia. Other farmers experimented with scientific crop rotation, using fertilisers and nitrogen-fixing plants, like clover. Overall, grain yields per acre rose. And the extent of land lying fallow declined.

What's more, in the 1730s, the Berkshire agriculturalist Jethro Tull (a memorable name) invented a horse-drawn wooden seed-drill and horse-hoe. Before long, his machines were updated into cast iron, and later still mechanised. The long quest to substitute machines for person-power on the farm had begun; and, with that, the systematic reorganisation of agricultural labour.

Large-scale 'agribusiness' was arriving, while small farms were becoming squeezed. In 1801, Parliament passed a General Enclosure Act (updated 1845), which facilitated changes in land use. There were fierce individual protests.[33] Poachers continued also to flout the stern Game Laws, which regulated the hunting of wild game.[34] And community opposition to enclosures of common land was often spirited.[35] Commercial streamlining was, however, like an inexorably rising tide, sweeping all before it.

Thus an underlying rural discontent tended to be masked from view by neat farms, fertile fields, tidy hedgerows, nibbling sheep, plump livestock, mettlesome horses, well-tended orchards and gracious mansions in rolling estates, landscaped by Capability Brown.[36] Many farm workers were 'released' from primary agricultural production and left for the towns. Such migration eased rural pressures, albeit without ending rural poverty.[37]

An 'agricultural revolution' is too simple a concept for the multiple changes in British farming that occurred between the sixteenth and nineteenth centuries. There was not just one process on a par with one revolutionary event; and there were always regional variations. Nonetheless, the long eighteenth century did see the culmination of fundamental changes in the countryside. The older forms of subsistence farming for own-household consumption, long waning, finally disappeared in mainland Britain and across much of Ireland, while only in the west coastal regions of Ireland before 1845 were potatoes still being produced both for local subsistence and for commodity trading. In other words, commercialised agriculture had fully arrived.

Urbanisation

Sustained urbanisation in Georgian Britain was the visible counterpart to agrarian transformation. And both processes were integrally linked to commercial and territorial expansion, industrial innovation, transport improvements and the mobility of capital. Towns were themselves partly contributing factors to, and partly effects of, the wider transformation.[38]

However, it is not necessary to invoke a single 'urban revolution'. Urbanisation was a lengthy and patchy process. By 1851, the three traditional kingdoms within Great Britain and Ireland were together the first substantial regional power in the world (as opposed to the first small locality) to have developed an inbuilt and sustainable urban majority. That shift made Britain a world-leader in a world trend, which remains (to date at least) irreversible.[39]

As the urban population grew both absolutely and relatively as a proportion of the whole, so the urban system was simultaneously being refashioned.[40] The bedrock remained the multitude of small market towns; but a range of leading urban centres – some old-established, some new – were launched upon significant growth. A key factor was gaining or developing a chief economic specialism. Maritime centres included not only Britain's great international ports and the dockyard towns, but also from the 1760s onwards, the emergent seaside towns. Industrial towns flourished, often on or near the coalfields, including textile centres; boot- and shoe-making towns; metalware centres; brewing towns; and the Potteries. And specialist services were located in the popular spas, the university towns (which remained relatively small in this era), and the three capital cities, which were sites of government, law, services, some industry and much conspicuous consumption. Further specialisation was visible within London's large metropolitan region. The industrial East End differed from the commercial-entertainment West End, whilst the financial-trading hub in the City was demarcated from Britain's political-administrative headquarters in Westminster.

Mass urban living and the integration of diversity were becoming normalised. Of course, there were variations between areas of great wealth and great poverty. Nonetheless, the Georgians were also aware of the need to grapple with the challenges of mass living. Local authorities experimented with reforms. And from the mid-century, a string of new Improvement Commissions were appointed by

Parliament, each authorised to upgrade its own municipal lighting, paving, draining, policing and water supplies.[41]

Landmark buildings and facilities were also constructed, whether by individual investors, group subscriptions or local authorities. Together they were updating the customary townscape. Visitors increasingly expected to see paved main streets, promenades, a thriving market, shops, a town clock, a town hall, an Assembly Room, perhaps a theatre and a library, old and new churches, decorous Nonconformist chapels, hospitals, schools, (unromantically) a gaol, sometimes a local museum and art gallery, parks and, not least, urban pleasure gardens, many named 'Little Vauxhall' after the convivial pioneer at Vauxhall (1732) on London's South Bank.[42]

Their collective urban functioning, meanwhile, relied upon integration of their interlocking specialisms. Take the case of the smoky Staffordshire Potteries. The Five Towns were never fashionable. Yet their expansion was rapid, once a local potter, John Astbury, began in the 1720s to make cream-ware by mixing local red clay with ground flintstone. The area's distinctive bottle kilns multiplied. Leading businesses, like Wedgwood's Etruria pottery, became internationally known.[43] Also successful was Josiah Spode, famed for his blue-glazed bone china. His inexpensive version of the Chinese blue willow-pattern plate became popular from the 1780s, in a classic case of successful import substitution. Workers in the Potteries relied upon supplies from elsewhere. In return, they furnished Georgian households across Britain with Staffordshire pots, jugs, tea-sets, dishes and ornaments, such as matching pairs of spaniels dubbed 'fireplace dogs' (now collectors' items).[44] Hence countless people, who never expected to visit the Potteries, daily enjoyed their wares.

Cultural, Social and Ethnic Mixing

Despite their undoubted differences of rank and wealth, the Georgians enjoyed many occasions when social mixing was incorporated as part of the entertainment. In much earlier times, there were strict Sumptuary Laws which required people to dress according to their social rank. Such legislation, often poorly obeyed at best, was last contemplated in 1656.[45] The Georgians were able to dress as they pleased, and as their pockets allowed. They enjoyed inspecting the resultant social parade, whether strolling along urban promenades or seaside piers, flocking to fairs, or watching sports and alfresco entertainments. Not having to worry about the niceties of personal status was a liberating experience. Indeed some ultra-cautious commentators in the mid-eighteenth century worried that the fashion for masked balls among the well-to-do was encouraging too much incognito sexual and social mingling.

Nonetheless, even if some revellers might on occasion take intimacy too far, good manners required people from all backgrounds to get on easily. 'Politeness' and 'civility' were much admired social arts.[46] Thinking of others was the golden rule. Authoritative advice came from the courtier-diplomat Lord Chesterfield. His memoranda to his illegitimate son were posthumously aired in the best-selling *Letters . . . on the Art of Becoming a Man of the World and a Gentleman* (1774). 'Of all things, banish the egotism out of your conversation,' he wrote.[47] Aristocrats should not show undue pride; and the poor and lowly should not grovel. Nor should plutocrats brag about wealth. Any talk of money, outside the counting-house, should be discreet.[48] Moreover, specialist know-how was also to be carried lightly. So Chesterfield admonished intellectuals: 'wear your learning like your watch, in a private pocket; and do not pull it out, and strike it, merely to show that you have one'.[49] (Still good advice.)

Was such civility merely a facade to deceive the world? Some Georgian moralists disliked Chesterfield's Machiavellian implication that it was better to seem virtuous than actually to be so. Were onlookers really so easily deceived? Critics found his advice worldly and hypocritical. Samuel Johnson, never one to pull his punches, asserted that Chesterfield taught: 'the morals of a whore and the manners of a dancing-master'.[50] Yet the criticisms did not halt public interest in the joint tasks of cultivating good manners and 'getting ahead'. The array of conduct manuals testified that social mixing was in full train. So it was strangely apt that the blue-blooded Lord Chesterfield took the lead in declaring that high birth mattered less than a courteous ease of manner, open to all.

Ordinary life did not always match up to social ideals. Potential tensions between people with rival heritages never disappeared. As noted above (p. 5), mutual jibes and suspicions between the English, the Welsh, the Scots and the Irish already had a long history. And the contribution of so-called scientific hierarchies of 'race' added further pressures. It cannot be said, therefore, that the townspeople of Georgian Britain were always havens of mutual tolerance and respect. Racial prejudices in particular were often subtle, taking the form of covert as well as overt biases. Testimonies of those who suffered through hostility to their origins or physical appearance indicated the gross harm that could ensue.[51] And it was not only foreigners with different looks, clothing and speech who attracted mistrust. British-born children of mixed-heritage couples could also face significant stigmas, especially in cases of illegitimacy.[52]

At the same time, too, there were countervailing elements of integration, including the social conventions of civility between fellow citizens. Partial acceptance allowed some immigrant groups to concentrate in specific localities within large towns, where they had their own social venues and churches, as already noted (pp. 26–30). And full acceptance was not unknown either. Anti-racism and integration have histories too. There were plenty of Britons who accepted human diversity-in-unity, not just in theory but also happily in practice.

It is very hard to measure such attitudes retrospectively. Yet one potential signal comes from the considerable extent of intermarriage between different heritage groups. Thus George Africanus, the Nottingham businessman, the writer Olaudah Equiano, and Francis

Barber, Dr Johnson's factotum, plus two radicals of mixed West Indian ancestry, the Jamaican-Scot Robert Wedderburn and the Barbudan-British Henry Redhead Yorke, all found English brides. Furthermore, they all lived successfully in Britain and had families, whose descendants have merged into the hybrid British stock.

Another case is that of Dido Belle, the illegitimate daughter of a West Indian enslaved mother and a Scottish father. She was raised in the household of her uncle, the liberal law lord William Murray, 1st Earl of Mansfield.[53] Dido Belle herself married a Frenchman of middling status, raising a family with him in England. These experiences are among the documented cases, but most just quietly happened.

Many Britons today have 'foreign' ancestors, of whom they are completely unaware. The Georgian towns were thus places of de facto social and ethnic diversity, part suspicious but eventually mingling.

The Advent of the Egalitarian Handshake

Particularly interesting as an imperceptible but widespread sign of change was the slow change in Georgian styles of interpersonal greetings.[54] Traditional conventions expected men to greet their social 'superiors' with a deep bow and removal of the hat. Women in such circumstances were equally required to hold out their skirts and to give a deep curtsey. In this period, however, these gestures were being attenuated. Men were increasingly likely to give a brief touch or pull at the hat (codified as the salute from soldiers), while women gave a brisk bob. It was another sign of how changing social usages were catching up with the Quakers, who, ever since their emergence as a religious group in the turbulent 1650s, consistently refused to bare their heads to social 'superiors'.

But there was more. A new style of egalitarian greeting, the handshake, was spreading. It began as a gesture, initially between men, signifying mutual esteem and parity. Early users were international diplomats, confirming a treaty; commercial traders, settling a deal; and combatants, including working-class boxers, at the start and end of an honour fight.[55] Both noblemen and commoners who joined the new Freemason Societies, which were spreading across Europe in this period, also confirmed their membership with special hand-grips – the position of their fingers indicating not their rank in the wider world but their office within the society.[56] Moreover, this egalitarian greeting began to spread increasingly widely. At least by the 1790s, upper- and middle-class men and women on terms of close friendship were regularly shaking hands; women also shook hands with other women, usually in a more formal context. (Jane Austen, ever alert to styles of social signalling, incorporated regular handshakes in her novels.)

People meeting newcomers in crowded towns often found it hard to gauge their mutual status. The handshake effectively cut through such uncertainties. True, a conservative onlooker in 1828 bewailed the new style as unhygienic – and liable to erode social distinctions.[57] But such criticisms were rare. Instead, the growing use of soap and improved standards of personal cleanliness helped to boost the new custom.[58] The inexorable spread of the handshake (today used worldwide, though not universally) was one decisive sign that social trends did not simply start with kings 'at the top' and then 'trickle down'. (The 2020 pandemic is changing things yet again, at least temporarily, showing how views about acceptable touch are communally adapted.)

Gathering people into permanent and viable urban settlements thus entailed massive investments not only of capital but also of human labour, ingenuity and adaptability. By 1843 Robert Vaughan, a Congregationalist minister and professor of history at the new University of London, was inspired to define Britain as exemplifying *The Age of Great Cities*.[59] That characteristic meant therefore that it was also an age of mass communications, busily seeking new, faster and better systems.

Social and psychological effort was also required to ensure that mass living ran smoothly. People needed daily confidence to move securely among large numbers of strangers in crowded city streets. Social conventions therefore evolved to cope. One example in Britain was the agreement (as noted above, p. 355) that road traffic should drive on the left. And other conventions stipulated that people should not routinely carry dangerous weapons and use them to intimidate, threaten or harass others. These unwritten codes (which like all codes could be broken) assisted social mixing, as discussed above. All urbanised societies have their own variants, the USA being an exception (for historical and current reasons) in still permitting hand-weapons in daily possession.

Movements of living beings, goods, services, money, armies, navies, ideas, inventions, pollution and microbes happen in human societies worldwide.[60] Slowly, governments and international conventions have emerged to provide the organisational frameworks needed to hold the ring. (How much or little regulation is required remains disputed.) Yet it is apparent that mass living needs protection against mass hazards, including infectious diseases. In Britain, the campaign to eradicate smallpox was started by private initiatives but followed through by the state, which in 1853 made vaccination compulsory. How to get mass societies and accountable, constitutionalist governments to work in peaceful coordination remains a continuing work in progress. It was a quest not resolved but dynamically explored by the Georgians.

✍ Time-Shift: Then and Now ✍

Many town halls erected in the Georgian era have been later rebuilt or substantially transformed as their urban communities have grown around them. However, some still survive, even if with later embellishments. They are generally not as well known as their later Victorian counterparts. Yet they are eloquent testaments to municipal pride and the need for civic meeting places. Examples to view, in person or virtually, include the following five, chosen from a range of urban centres large and small (and listed chronologically by date of first building).

1. Town Hall, Laugharne, Caermarthenshire, Wales

Built 1747 to replace an earlier town hall, a clock tower and lean-to gaol extension were added in 1774, and the tower was further adorned with a bellcote and weathercock in 1786. Although altered over time, it is an excellent exemplar of a Georgian small town civic centre, where Laugharne Corporation continues to meet.

2. Liverpool Town Hall

Built 1749–54 to a design by the eminent architect John Wood, a dome was added to the already majestic building following rebuilding after a fire in 1795. It remains Liverpool's political hub, with Council Chamber, Mayor's Parlour and civic rooms (administration is conducted elsewhere).

3. The Tholsel, Kilkenny

Constructed in 1761, with a distinctive octagonal clock tower, the building was originally built as a toll-house, and was put to later civic use as a court house and guildhall. Today it is the town's city hall. Its attractive open arcades at street level make it a popular meeting place.

4. Town Hall, Newark-on-Trent, Nottinghamshire

Constructed in 1774–76, this town hall is at once imposing, with a pillared frontage, yet familiar, tucked into the street-scape. The civic rooms include a Council Chamber, Mayor's Parlour and main Assembly Room, used for balls and concerts. The building remains the municipal HQ, as originally planned, and also houses an art gallery and museum.

5. The Old Town House, Aberdeen

Built in the mercantile centre of Old Aberdeen in 1788–89, its simple but impressive granite design features today as the logo of Scotland's Architectural Heritage Society. Lovingly renovated in 2005, the building now houses the University of Aberdeen's King's Museum.

ᦔ 19 ᦕ

Georgian Deeds and Misdeeds

Illumination from past times helps to frame present decisions, which then affect the future. That point was made by the American jurist Patrick Henry, when he spoke in 1775 of consulting the 'Lamp of History'.[1] It's an evocative phrase, which is often attributed (wrongly) to Britain's leading eighteenth-century historian, Edward Gibbon. He certainly valued historical studies, which he conveyed with urbanity and wit.[2] Moreover the Lamp of History works best when it excludes factual errors, whether major or minor. (Gibbon, who had no need to borrow fame from others, would no doubt have agreed.) Historians therefore urge that retrospective assessments of the past should be undertaken with calm and, as far as possible, without error. It's not always easy, since controversial questions are often hard to reconstruct accurately and to judge without undue emotion. Nonetheless, that is the historians' aim. Historical studies seek to understand and to explain. There's no point in simply asserting that the past should not have happened as it did.

At the same time, however, understanding does entail some measured judgment. Historians assess whether individuals acted rightly or wrongly (viewed morally or practically), in their given circumstances; and they are entitled to make similar assessments of societies as a whole, provided that they explain their criteria for judgment. Above all, some historical events cast exceptionally long shadows. Hence it is just that they be assessed not only at the time they happened but also in the light of longer experience. The rest of this chapter examines specific Georgian legacies, which gain extra resonance when viewed through the unfolding of time.

Criminals Becoming Lovable Rogues

In popular culture, the era remains famed for roguery and uninhibited sexual romping. These themes energise an entire genre of Regency romances. The recasting of past crimes into roguery is a form of safe cultural distancing, whereby transgressions become enjoyable once they are past. So pirates on the high seas, formerly the scourge of transatlantic and Mediterranean shipping, become romantic once piracy is no longer a common danger to mariners. Georgian outlaws like Calico Jack and Anne Bonny are the ancestors of the swashbuckling figures who appear in children's yarns and escapist films. Their seafaring skills are welded with a dash of villainy – all to be savoured at a suitably safe distance in time.

Similarly, smugglers acquired a degree of sinister glamour once the deliberate wrecking of coastal shipping was going into real-life decline. The apotheosis of the genre is Daphne du Maurier's *Jamaica Inn* (1936), set in 1820s Cornwall. Individuals make moral choices against a backdrop of night-time skulduggery along Britain's intricate coastline. And characters in the novels are challenged to decide whether various outwardly respectable citizens or customs officials are actually villains (as sometimes occurred in real life).

Highwaymen are another category of retrospectively attractive outsiders. Travellers across Surrey's Bagshot Heath on the A30 today do not want to be robbed at gunpoint. Yet it is piquant to discover that (in legend at least) Nell Gwyn, celebrity actor and mistress of Charles II, was once robbed by a charming highwayman there, or that in 1689 the executed corpse of a serial highway bandit, a local farmer named Will Davis, was exhibited in chains at the now ironically named Jolly Farmer Roundabout.[3]

Above all, Dick Turpin, who in real life was an Essex petty horse thief and killer, was reinvented as a popular highwayman on the Georgian stage, before he was further transformed in the novel *Rookwood* (1834). His attributed feats of equestrianism, astride his valiant Black Bess, resonated in Britain's horse-loving society.[4] Since then, highwaymen – and a few highwaywomen – appear as fixtures in historical romances, while heist movies (a related genre) flourish on film.

Sociologically, the advent of regular policing, orderly transport, and the relative decline of interpersonal violence signalled not the end of crime (far from it) but its removal as an everyday danger when in transit. Criminals at a distance can thus become lovable, especially if they remain charming – and few in number. If instead all citizens are behaving criminally all the time in a totally corrupt system, then literature as well as everyday life would turn bleakly monotonous. And romance, which thrives on difference, would fade before grim realities.

Cultivating Style and Nonchalance

Nonchalant self-possession was much esteemed in Georgian Britain's fighting culture. Songs like 'Heart of Oak' (1760) hymned the stalwart sailors in the navy's oak-built ships: 'We ne'er see our foes but we wish them to stay,/ They never see us but they wish us away'. Coolness under fire was especially praised. A classic remark was attributed to the 2nd Earl of Uxbridge when wounded at Waterloo: 'By God, Sir, I've lost my leg'. The laconic reply from the Duke of Wellington confirmed the matter: 'By God, Sir, so you have!' This exchange was embroidered around a genuine crisis. Uxbridge was shot and lost a limb in a battlefield operation, without anaesthetic.[5] Later military museums exhibited memorabilia from the drama, including the surgeon's saw. Such stoicism was especially cultivated among men in Britain's military and sporting circles.[6]

Another favoured image was that of the outwardly nonchalant dandy who was secretly a heroic warrior. Such an elusive hero first appeared in a stage play as *The Scarlet Pimpernel* (1903) by the Anglo-Hungarian Emma Orczy, before being expanded by her into a string of novels (1905–40). Sir Percy Blakeney was a foppish English land-owner, who secretly rescued innocent victims from the guillotine during France's Reign of Terror (1793).

The historical detail was shaky. Yet the tale was potent. It fed into a popular literary and filmic archetype: from Zorro to Superman, and latterly Superwoman.[7] A rich and apparently privileged indi-vidual turns out to have a secret conscience and selflessly helps others, without seeking thanks. Those with wealth and power are thus chal-lenged to reveal an updated sense of chivalry and *noblesse oblige*.

Holding on for Victory

Nations also gain their stories of collective survival from history. Heroic soldiers lead by example. At the Battle of Dettingen (1743), an English hussar named Thomas Brown rescued his regimental standard from the French. In so doing, he sustained severe facial wounds. Thereafter Brown, who became an innkeeper at Yarm-on-Tees (Durham), sported a metallic mask and replacement nose. Prints were circulated to show his undauntedly stoical appearance. With that sort of encouragement, British cultural memory cultivated a potent wartime myth, which stated that the country would do badly at the start of a prolonged conflict, but that, if everyone held on doggedly, victory would in the end follow.

Military resilience among British generals was equally admired. John Churchill, 1st Duke of Marlborough (victor at Blenheim in

1704, Ramillies in1706 and Oudenarde in 1708) was carefully studied by his descendant Winston Churchill, who, as Britain's wartime leader in 1940, drew inspiration from his fighting ancestor.[8] Wellington was another general praised for his tenacity in the long campaigns before victory at Waterloo (1815). Unsurprisingly, that battle has its own impressive afterlife, appearing in both French and British novels, songs, films, TV programmes and games.

For many Britons, however, the lure of sea-power remained paramount. One maverick hero of the Royal Navy was the Scottish-born Thomas Cochrane, nicknamed the 'Sea Wolf'. His dashing raids upon enemy shipping in the 1800s were reminiscent of Drake's surprise attack on Cadiz (1587).[9] One real-life naval officer, Frederick Marryat, first gave Cochrane fictional life as the approximate model for *Mr Midshipman Easy* (1836). He was then re-invented by C.S. Forrester as the well-named *Horatio Hornblower* (1937–67), with a Nelson-like aura. And later still, Patrick O'Brian updated him as the spry Jack Aubrey in another series, rich in historical detail, flagged as *Master and Commander* (1969–2004). These updates spawned books, films, radio and TV programmes. Some tributes!

Moreover, Cochrane in death retained an international reputation. He had been an active naval supporter of independence movements in Brazil, Greece and, especially, Chile, where there is a grand monument to him in Valparaíso.[10] For Britons, the country's naval power, which had been used to liberate as well as to oppress, constituted their prime shield against the dangers of foreign tyranny. So even landlubbers were readily able to enjoy tales of heroic adventures at sea, bearing in mind that Britannia's first (distinctly optimistic) hope overseas was to 'rule the waves'.[11]

Combining Constitutional Invention and Continuity

At specific times, Georgian Britain saw the advent of harsh laws and draconian clampdowns. Yet a constitutionalist system was evolving, with in-built checks and balances. The Hanoverian monarchy grew into its new ceremonial-cum-political role, having defeated the military challenge from the Jacobites. Royal ministers learned to pull the levers of power discreetly. The civil service began to build an ethos of disinterested state service. And Parliaments, sitting regularly for the first time from 1694, emerged as political sounding-boards and ultimate authorisers of laws and taxes. Furthermore, two big political initiatives saw the Act of Union, uniting England and Wales with Scotland (1707), which survives, and the Act of Union with Ireland (1801), uniting Great Britain with Ireland, which survives only in part. Those changes relied upon consent from the politically engaged citizens, which remains even more needful in democratic times.

Two paradoxically opposite political reputations were also becoming crystallised. One accused the system of 'corruption'. Critics deplored the power of wealthy patrons to nominate MPs in constituencies which had few or no voters. These places were known as 'rotten boroughs' (see also above, pp. 180, 185). Defenders of the system argued that it allowed patrons to promote bright young protégés who would not otherwise succeed. But these 'rotten' elections were beyond challenge. By way of satire, Thomas Love Peacock in 1817 imagined that an orangutan, satirically named Sir Oran Haut-Ton, had been nominated to represent as MP the 'ancient and honourable borough of Onevote'.[12] Adding insult to injury, many fast-growing urban areas, like Birmingham and Manchester, lacked direct representation before 1832, when the rotten boroughs were finally abolished.

Paradoxically, however, the counterpart to 'old corruption' was a lively electoral culture in the large, open constituencies, which were outside the control of wealthy patrons. Not every seat was regularly contested. But many were. As a result, many Georgian voters were fostering a proto-democratic constitutionalist culture, wherein decisions were made by voting rather than by fighting. Indeed, the first campaign for a democratic male franchise was launched in 1769. (A few radicals supported votes for women; but that cause was then far too provocative for practical politics.) Hence, notwithstanding the impression of torpor conveyed by the 'rotten boroughs', Georgian political life was vigorous at grass-roots level, with protests and riots as well as organised campaigns.

Experiencing Slow Cultural Change

Socio-economic changes were also recasting Georgian Britain – but slowly. Gradual shifts lacked the excitements (and, often, the later disappointments) of political revolutions. Yet incremental adaptations were (and are) hard to resist. Most crucial was the spread 'down' the social scale of both literacy and numeracy. By 1801, all upper- and middle-class men in England and Wales could read and write, as could many lower-class men. Female literacy levels were also rising, if more slowly. The momentum was cultural and aspirational, expanding well ahead of the functional minimum required to run the British economy; and the outcome saw a glorious flowering of literary life.

Other slow-burn changes included Georgian Britain's once-and-for-all shift from a chiefly rural to predominantly urban society – plus the consolidation of commercialised agriculture; the growth of a global overseas trade; the advent of specialist financial services and a fully monetised economy; the spread of scientific know-how; the application of science to micro-technologies of precision instruments (clocks, watches) and macro-technologies of power (steam engines); an ensuing transformation of industrial work; and a great upgrading of transport and communications (canals and the railway).

Simultaneously, a part competitive, part cooperative culture of consumer choice was emerging. Prosecutions for blasphemy became rare, and de facto toleration for both religious diversity and personal irreligion was emerging (if not without continuing antagonisms). Power at the 'top' was shared between land and new money. A newly substantial middle class was then bridging between extremes of wealth and poverty. Many Georgian celebrities (famous for 'being famous') came from their ranks. Growing numbers of skilled workers, with good incomes in boom years, also headed a newly identified working class. (But the distribution of incomes and assets between the ultra-rich and the masses in urban-industrial societies continues to fluctuate, according to the state of the economy and political decisions about redistribution or otherwise. Trends do not invariably run in one direction.)

Within families, liberal alternatives to the old patriarchal authority were emerging, even if often thwarted in practice. The ideal of companionate marriage was spreading; women were taking a greater public role; and the ideal of a treasured childhood, without exploitation or physical abuse, was emerging. More still: a sexualised public culture was encouraging the exploration of sexual diversity, despite repressive laws and their sporadic implementation.

Framing such changes was a decline in random violence; a high respect for equality before the law; (in Britain) a low level of weapon-carrying; a minority tradition of duelling, which disappeared by the 1820s; as well as liberal campaigns to assist disabilities, to provide a safety-net for poverty (always contentious), to rationalise the Georgian penal code, and to promote animal welfare. Ideals were never perfectly matched by realities. Different religious and social groups sometimes had markedly different perspectives. Yet some common patterns in trends and attitudes have slowly emerged in literate and law-based urban-industrial societies (such as growing opposition to capital punishment).[13] It is, however, worth cautioning once more that no changes are inevitably here to stay.

Confronting Wrongs

Looking back at past conflicts and injustices is also vital for the education and good historical health of later generations. Confronting what happened adds crucially to the stock of collective experience.

Where major issues – like empire – have caused past divisions, it is vital to review all sides of the question to understand fully how and why such developments occurred; how they were maintained over many years; how they were challenged; how they continue to impact upon the present; and how oppressions can be prevented in the future.[14] Furthermore, a set of internationally (but not universally) shared humanist conventions urges that human autonomy be respected, free from lawless killing and violence in peacetime, and treated, even in wartime, with some restraint. However (to repeat), when making assessments, a degree of historical humility is in order, since humans in the twenty-first century are also perpetrating injustices at which later generations will look back in horror.

Big conflicted issues in Georgian history that challenge later generations include two cases of desolating collective exodus – from the Scottish Highlands during the economic Clearances in the later eighteenth century, and the Irish diaspora both before and especially after the disastrous Great Famine (1845–49), which was badly handled by the authorities. Other big issues highlight the often (though not invariably) contentious relationships between Britons overseas and the indigenous populations variously encountered. The histories of North America, Africa, India and Australasia are directly relevant here. And throughout these years there was also the leading role of British merchants (before 1807) in trafficking in enslaved Africans, plus Britain's official condoning of slavery within its colonies (before 1833). It was the campaign against that noxious business which first galvanised British, American, French and African campaigners into organised humanitarianism.[15]

Studying these big contested issues – all with different origins and outcomes – is assisted by the pooling of research. It has taken much effort to establish the full scale of the international trade in enslaved Africans. Between the fifteenth and the nineteenth centuries, some 12.5 million captives were taken to the New World by traders from Britain, France, Spain, Portugal and (after 1776) America, once it was freed from Britain's restrictive Navigation Acts.[16] Enforced migration on such a colossal scale is unique in human history. Hence in 1998, UNESCO designated 23 August as an annual day of remembrance. It's not only a world statement about an epic wrong, but also an encouragement to confront present-day racism, and to stop clandestine people-trafficking and contemporary neo-slavery.[17]

Many further issues still call for more research and public debate. These days, there are many excellent museum displays, both indoors and outdoors. They show the materiality of past conflicts and disasters, while giving contextual explanations and providing space for debate. Specially commissioned monuments also provide scope for reflection and act as markers for collective regret. These can work well but need to find the right tone. (The Boston Irish Famine Memorial is one disputed example, having both critics and defenders.)[18]

Conversely, different issues are raised by public statues of past worthies whose deeds do not seem admirable to many people today. Such matters call for broad-based community debates and thoughtful local decisions. Some statues will work best in museums. Both their making and their changing reception are matters of historical record for people to study. And where debated statues remain in their original locations, it's essential to have a plaque or information board to explain the context and express alternative viewpoints.

People also create interactive forms of remembering for themselves. There are official and unofficial commemorative walks, to and from significant places. (And sometimes conflict over rival walks, where the issues are still contested, calling for mediation.) There are songs, films, stories, community projects and invented rituals. In some cases, there are constructive forms of reparation and transnational memorial programmes. Importantly, too, British efforts can be pooled with those in other countries. Shared past histories invite shared research projects.

While humanity has a bad track record in generating conflict, it also finds inventive ways of coping. People learn from one another, so that historic encounters are not invariably negative. Complex past processes can't always be simply divided into 'all right' and 'all wrong'. Yet where there were undoubted offences against what most people accept as universal moral values, then such iniquities need acknowledgement. Later generations saying that they are sorry for agonising disasters in earlier times might at first seem futile, since those apologising are not the past perpetrators, and the past victims are dead. Yet because past and present are intertwined, it remains essential to understand how macro-disasters happen, to acknowledge and alleviate their adverse impact, with constructive remedial actions, and, above all, not to repeat them. Truth does not always lead to reconciliation; but it offers a better chance than do either silence or falsehood.[19]

Balancing Rights

Political thought in eighteenth-century Britain, America and France increasingly focused upon individual 'rights'. Those constituted autonomous and inalienable claims, which were not dependent upon the gift of a king or feudal lord.[20] The concept was legalistic, individualistic, assertive. It stood in opposition to the absolute power of central government. In Britain, the concept of 'rights' was seen as compatible with a limited constitutional monarchy; but in America and France, the language of rights became outright republican. This new emphasis was encouraged by enthusiasts like the wealthy English bibliophile Thomas Hollis, who reprinted and circulated many republican tracts, sending copies to both individuals and libraries across Europe and North America.[21]

Legalistic ideas of inalienable individual 'rights' resonated strongly across Europe and North America, especially among literate and assertive urban-commercial communities. Governments should no longer act capriciously or arbitrarily. Instead, the system of rule should spring from and respect the prior 'rights' of the people. A significant test case occurred in 1772. Petitioners sued on behalf of James Somersett, an enslaved African imprisoned in a ship in a British port, who claimed the right to freedom under British laws on British soil. The case was won and he was freed.[22] Soon, the concept was adopted to make generic claims. Thus in Britain Thomas Paine's *Rights of Man* (1791) asserted democratic capacities to be universal among adult males: 'Whatever is my right as a man, is also the right of another; and it becomes my duty, to guarantee as well as to possess'.[23] The terminology was powerful. Calls followed for *The Rights of Woman* (1792), *The Rights of Infants* (1796), *The Rights of Slaves* (*c.* 1796) and, somewhat later, *The Rights of Animals* (1838) to be treated humanely.[24]

Over time, the concept has extended to embrace personal as well as civic claims. Positive 'rights' range from freedom of speech and religious belief to free choice in one's sexual identity; and (still debated) gender identity, as well as women's 'rights' to control their own reproduction. Claims are also expressed in terms of the 'right' not to be oppressed by ageism, racism, sexism or prejudice on grounds of social class; plus 'freedom from fear and want'. And there are contested claims, including the 'right' of individuals to carry weapons daily, and the 'rights' of the unborn child.

Expectations vary from culture to culture. There are claims and counter-claims and, at times, strong backlashes against claims. Nonetheless, the eighteenth century's revolutionary language now pervades democratic thinking and international law. In 1948, the United Nations agreed the *Universal Declaration of Human Rights*, now translated into over 500 languages.[25] It is widely praised, though, needless to say, not universally upheld.

Eighteenth-century thought also acknowledged that 'rights' needed a framework of law. While they were inalienable to each individual, they could not be exercised arbitrarily. Societies thus often have to adjudicate between rival 'rights'. Thus it gradually became accepted (again in theory, well ahead of practice) that freedom of speech was subject to the laws of libel and slander; free expression of sexual identity did not legitimise rape, violence or assaults on minors;

and free exercise of religious beliefs did not extend to persecuting rival faiths, even if sincerely seen as heretical. Moreover, some tracts in the 1790s linked 'rights' to 'duties' in an approach which is now attracting fresh attention.[26] (Today an international law of human rights is still evolving, posing the challenge of achieving an impartial jurisdiction and upholding verdicts.)

Intricate individual choices are revealed by the history of Sarah 'Saartjie'- Baartman, a Khoi woman from Cape Province, South Africa. As already noted (p. 102), in 1810 she was publicly exhibited in England and later in Paris as the 'Hottentot Venus'. A legal challenge was mounted by anti-slavery campaigners. But it failed, as there was no evidence that Baartman was being coerced by her manager.[27] She herself left no statement, but could be taken as asserting her right to make her living as she chose (even if her realistic options were limited). Baartman died young in Paris, and her remains were displayed for many years (until 1974) in Paris's Museum of Man, next to a plaster cast of her body. But eventually her compatriots objected that her dignity in death was being violated, just as she had been presented as a 'freak' object during her life. After lengthy wrangles, the Khoi lobbyists, with the aid of President Nelson Mandela, won their case. In 2002, Baartman's remains were reburied in South Africa, where she is honoured. Sensitive questions for public debate and decisions are thus raised, not just in a person's lifetime but via their bones.[28]

Launching Urban-Industrial Society, between Regulation and Deregulation

Viewed over time, the Georgian economy was evolving from urban-commercial strength in the later seventeenth century – like the flourishing Dutch economy in the same era – towards an unprecedented urban-industrial economy. By the early nineteenth century, Britain had no direct analogues. The Dutch economy was then in comparative decline, as noted above (p. 358). Potential industrial rivals in northern France and the north-eastern states of the USA were starting to mount challenges.[29] Industrially, however, early nineteenth-century Britain was paramount. Its railways, belching steam, represented a new giant power in terrestrial guise; its coal-fired steam-powered technology was available for adoption and adaptation by all; and its engineers were busy building railways across many parts of the globe.[30]

Socially, Britain's creativity stemmed from both competition and cooperation. And, while its distribution of capital assets was profoundly unequal, there was also, especially in the towns, a robust absence of deference; and much movement up and down the social scale. A few radicals proposed egalitarian communities, without conspicuous success. But there was a strong current of thought which valued individual 'merit' above formal titles. Being born to high status conferred some advantages, argued one anonymous tract in 1748; but genuine self-advancement was far more admirable.[31] Hence Georgian Britain had some characteristics of a meritocracy. There were large numbers of modestly born 'stars'. (However, the role of inherited wealth meant that Britain did not remotely constitute a 'pure' meritocracy in which all had an equal chance of success from birth – a very hard state of affairs to achieve.)[32]

Sometimes British economic creativity is attributed to a single theory, such as a culture of 'free trade', as propounded by the seminal Scottish economist Adam Smith. Various organisations today cite his name.[33] However, the nostrums they adopt – that the state and all intermediate organisations, like trade unions, are economically harmful, and that progress comes from atomised individuals, preferably unfettered by taxation – do not match with Georgian experience. Eighteenth-century British society was not only formed of a multitude of different associations – famously defined as the country's 'little platoons' by Edmund Burke.[34] Georgian state policies also continually balanced between regulation and deregulation, with regulation winning on a number of significant issues – including the long survival of the protectionist Navigation Acts (1651–1849).[35]

'Free trade', like 'free speech', also needed a framework of rules to ensure fair play. One Georgian example focused upon the public certification of professional qualifications. As already noted in an earlier chapter (p. 281), some economic 'free-traders', influenced by Adam Smith, argued that clients should decide for themselves whether to employ a specific practitioner – such as a doctor. Against that, advocates of regulation replied that private citizens could not meaningfully assess complex professional qualifications. Moreover, allowing untrained quack doctors to prey upon patients was harmful not only to individuals but also to society as a whole.[36]

Collective good health is a communal asset, reducing the need for remedial policies to tackle physical and mental illnesses. And on social policies, the regulators slowly won the day, while free-traders had their own successes in some (but not all) economic policies. Parliament thus eventually legislated to empower the professional associations to certify recognised practitioners. And other laws began gradually to limit child labour, to control working conditions in factories and mines, and to create a framework of public health regulations.[37]

Arguments raged over both the details and principles of state intervention, as they do today. There were tensions between short-term prospects of financial gain and the long-term collective interest. Smith himself was not as dogmatic on these points as are some of his ultra-liberal later supporters. In fact, he believed that ultimately all interests were mutually compatible, smoothed by natural human sympathy.[38] Hence, he argued that, left to itself, the economy would be self-righting, as if run by an 'invisible hand' (also known as the 'hidden hand').[39]

However, many other social commentators – and not just cynics – were aware of the perennial competition, sometimes escalating into conflict, between rival interest groups. As a result, many concluded, often reluctantly (since Britain had a long tradition of suspicion of central government), that the state must hold the ring – not to dictate one outcome but to balance rival interests. (Much depended, then as now, on the effective workings of a consultative political system, free from control by one sectional lobby.)

Marking Through-Time Meanings

When summarising these collective meanings, it's sometimes said that Georgian changes marked the onset of 'modernity', with the further implication that it ushered in the start of a single definable stage in history. However, historical periods are not nearly so clear-cut.[40] Today the twenty-first century is variously described by different experts as either a straightforward case of 'modernity'; or as a vintage expression of 'late modernity'; or, amusingly, as an unstable state of 'liquid modernity';[41] or, more rarely nowadays, as having been superseded by a later condition of 'post-modernity'. In other words, world history now seems to be suffering an identity crisis – at least in the minds of expert analysts. So it's more helpful to look not for discrete stages but at big trends and patterns.

Clearly, one implication of Britain's development in the long eighteenth century was that its deeds and misdeeds were being enacted on a global stage, shared by a multitude of part-cooperating and part-competing interests worldwide. As trade and communications were expanded, so no developing country was left in isolation. The often painful readjustment between regions, which was part of the industrialisation process within Britain, soon began to be echoed by continuing world-regional processes of readjustment on a global stage.[42]

Tentative steps towards various forms of international agreement were simultaneously being explored, to set level playing fields between nations. One example was the long quest to establish international copyright agreements, Britain having pioneered its own copyright law in 1710.[43] Some attempts at international reform were led by individuals and pressure groups, as in the anti-slavery campaigns. Others were initiated by governments. Britain was thus one of the leading European powers in 1815 to join the Concert of Europe.

The hope that inter-governmental negotiations could avert conflict between nations proved too optimistic. The system, controversial within Britain from the start, was by the 1870s struggling to contain great power rivalries, let alone to cope with the forces of competitive nationalisms. However, these initiatives were part of multiple pressures, coming from many countries. And, over time, international laws and conventions have been adopted in the quest to regulate many issues, including: the conduct of war; disarmament; trading rules and standards; the law of the sea; copyright and patents; labour law; human rights; anti-discrimination; criminal justice; medical cooperation and protocols; and environmental protection.

The long-term fate of these plans falls well outside the scope of this study.[44] Nonetheless, these possibilities were prefigured in the debates between Georgian optimists and pessimists. On the one hand, there were high hopes that the world was entering a new era of light and concord. And on the other hand, there were dark warnings of social and moral ruin – and, in the Malthusian tradition, of the dangers of demographic overload and adverse environmental pressures. Today's global climate emergency is, after all, a direct legacy of the Georgian coal-mining boom and the invention of the steam engine – only 250 years ago.[45] In the big history of the cosmos, that's a very short time span.

So arguing for regulations (and action) to end air pollution, to curb climate change, to clean the oceans, to remove space junk, to restore the human heritage of dark skies by focusing street lighting downwards, to tackle world poverty, oppression and diseases (old and new), to eliminate food waste, to ensure harmonious relationships between all peoples, to confront the legacies of past epic injustices, to eradicate neo-slavery and sexual exploitation, to prevent violence against the less powerful of all species, to end international tax evasion, to civilise social media, to revalidate the quest for truth, to enhance the spirit of adventure and innovation and to promote genuine democracy – well, such great projects, complete, of course, with counter-arguments and an empirical testing by trial and error, can all become part of Georgian through-time meanings now.

ᘐ Time-Shift: Then and Now ᘐ

It's important to understand how and why inhumane policies in the past were implemented, as a means of attempting to prevent their equivalents in both present and future. In that spirit, three invented viewpoints from a slave-dealer, a captive African and 'Posterity' are offered for consideration. They are inspired by a polemical nineteenth-century print of the slave trade in action (see Plate 30).

1. The dealer would be bluff. He would argue that the trade in captives was invented long before he arrived on the scene. He would add too that if he did not take the business, then French or Spanish traders would do so instead. If he was particularly argumentative and living in the eighteenth century, he could further point out that the trade was sanctioned by the British Parliament and by numerous divines of the Church of England. Or he might say simply: 'I'm just doing my job'.

2. The African meanwhile shows no sign of being cowed by captivity or resigned to his lot. He is in the power of the dealer, but his keen eyes suggest that he is not willingly so. As he is about to be taken into enforced labour overseas, he stands to lose everything familiar to him: family, friends, community, religion, language, environment, food, daily customs, every-thing. The engraving presents the scene factually but it is not difficult to read the image as an indictment of the trade.

3. The verdict of posterity has not been sympathetic to the slave-traders. It's astounding to realise that, over five centuries,

12.5 million Africans were sold into slavery and taken to the New World, where they and their descendants were kept as slave labour. Here was 'man's inhumanity to man' (to quote Robert Burns) on a terrifying scale.[46] Furthermore, even if it helped with the economic development of the Americas (and the efficacy of slave labour is disputed), the enforced migration of so many young adults undoubtedly hindered the growth of Africa. In historical terms, it constituted a world crime, perpetrated by the Georgians who were following in the footsteps of countless slave traders in earlier generations.

Yet this era also saw, for the first time, systematic and organised opposition to the trade. Eventually, substantive measures were taken to end the slave trade and slavery as an officially sanctioned system, even though neo-slavery unofficially continues out of the limelight. Big tasks remain for later generations. But they have a great chance to go beyond simple condemnation. Instead they can seek to understand fully how the injustices of enslaved labour were perpetrated and defended, how these particular forms of injustice were abolished, how retrospective apologies can be made to work constructively, how imaginative processes of truth and reconciliation can be instituted across the continents and, finally, how the full lessons from the past can be understood and applied in both present and future.

CALENDAR OF GEORGIAN
COMMEMORATIONS

Regular commemorations link past, present and future. They answer to human needs and are continually open to amendment, in a living tradition. It was a surprise, when researching this study, to discover just how many Georgian personalities are celebrated today, and how many Georgian events are either mourned or appreciated. So, by way of finale, this calendar lists an eclectic range of such celebration – a selection of twelve different Georgian-related annual commemorations (chosen from among many).

25 January	Burns Night, celebrated with pipes, poems and haggis, organised by Burns Societies around the globe in commemoration of the birth of the Scottish poet and lyricist Robert Burns (1759–96)
first Sunday in February	Clowns Service at Holy Trinity Church, Hackney, east London, held in honour of Britain's pioneering clown Joseph Grimaldi (1778–1837) and the profession of clowning

22 March	Scottish Fiddle Festival, held in the Perthshire town of Dunkeld and Birnam, the home of legendary fiddler Niel Gow (1727–1807)
1 June	Duck Feast, first inaugurated in the eighteenth century, held at the Wiltshire village of Charlton, near Pewsey, the birthplace of the 'Thresher Poet', Stephen Duck (1705–56)
around 20 June	Commemorative walk to Bodenstown Graveyard, County Kildare, Ireland, to pay homage at the burial place of the Irish republican, 1798 rebel leader and founder of the United Irishmen, Theobald Wolfe Tone (1763–98)
July or August	Annual Bosphorus Cross-Continental Swim across the Hellespont (Dardanelles), organised by the Turkish Olympic Committee, and held in commemoration of the 1810 swim by George Gordon, Lord Byron (1788–1824)
18 September	Commemoration, with church service and Johnson Society dinner, serving the favourite dishes of Britain's most famous lexicographer; held in Lichfield, the birthplace of Dr Samuel Johnson (1709–84)
around 27 September	Memorial service at Bristol's Arnos Vale Cemetery to celebrate India's religious, social and educational reformer; the venue being very far from his Bengal birthplace, but marking the sudden death in Bristol from meningitis of Raja Ram Mohan Roy (1772–1833)

18 October	UK Anti-Slavery Day (adopted 2010), a national day to raise awareness of the need to eradicate all forms of slavery, human trafficking and exploitation; school projects are organised to raise awareness of neo-slavery today, echoing Georgian efforts to open people's eyes to injustice, such as the work of the African-born and later Westminster-based abolitionist Olaudah Equiano (1745–97)
21 October	Trafalgar Day of remembrance and celebration of the British victory over the French at Trafalgar on 21 October 1805, held on board HMS *Victory*, Royal Navy Museum, Portsmouth, with the ceremonial flying of the famous flag message ('England Expects ...') from Vice-Admiral Horatio Nelson (1758–1805)
mid-November	Sarah Siddons Award for Distinguished Achievement, given, from 1952 onwards, to the best performer on the Chicago stage, after Joseph Mankiewicz conceived the event in his 1950 film *All About Eve* and Chicago theatrical patrons made his idea into a reality in tribute to the Welsh-born thespian Sarah Siddons (1755–1831)
late November	Jonathan Swift Festival, Dublin, held in the city where he was born and where he was from 1713 onwards Dean of St Patrick's Cathedral, in honour of the Anglo-Irish wit, satirist and author Jonathan Swift (1667–1745)

ENDNOTES

The place of publication is London unless otherwise indicated.

Chapter 1: Introducing the Georgians

1. S. Madden, *Memoirs of the Twentieth Century, Being Original Letters of State under George the Sixth . . .* (1733); Anon., *The Reign of George VI, 1900–25* (1763); for context, see A. Sandison and R. Dingley, *Histories of the Future: Studies in Fact, Fantasy and Science Fiction* (Basingstoke, 2000).
2. E. Vassall, *The Journal of Elizabeth Lady Holland*, ed. G.S.H.F. Strangways, 2 vols (1908), vol. 2, p. 54; and context in D. Skilton, 'Tourists at the Ruins of London: The Metropolis and the Struggle for Empire', *Cercles* 17 (2007), pp. 93–119.
3. T. Clayton, *Caricatures of the Peoples of the British Isles* (2007).
4. N. Groom, *The Union Jack: The Story of the British Flag* (2006).
5. *His Majesty's Most Gracious Speech . . . 18 November 1760* (1760), p. 3.
6. J. Bew, *The Glory of Being British: Civic Unionism in Nineteenth-Century Belfast* (Dublin, 2009).
7. Anon., *Popular Prejudice Concerning Partiality to the Interests of Hanover* (1743), p. 13; S. Conway, *Britain, Ireland and Continental Europe in the Eighteenth Century: Similarities, Connections, Identities* (Oxford, 2001).
8. As asserted by a speaker in the Irish Parliament: see J.C. [J. Caldwell], *Debates Relative to the Affairs of Ireland in the Years 1763 and 1764* (1766), vol. 1, p. 11.
9. S. Murphy, 'The Dublin Anti-Union Riot of 3 December 1759', in G. O'Brien (ed.), *Parliament, Politics and People* (Dublin, 1989), pp. 49–68.
10. Act of Union (Ireland) 1800 (40 Geo. III c. 38) in the Parliament of Ireland, followed by the similar Union with Ireland Act (39 and 40 Geo. III c. 67) in the Parliament of Great Britain.
11. P.A. Clark, *British Clubs and Societies, 1580–1800: The Origins of an Associational World* (Oxford, 2000), p. 300; C. Bailey, *Irish London: Middle-Class Migration in the Global Eighteenth Century* (Liverpool, 2013).

12. J. Oldmixon, *The British Empire in America . . .* (1708).
13. F. O'Gorman, *The Long Eighteenth Century: British Political and Social History, 1688–1832* (1997); W. Prest, *Albion Ascendant: English History, 1660–1815* (Oxford, 1998); D. Allan, *Scotland in the Eighteenth Century: Union and Enlightenment* (Harlow, 2002); T.S. Barnard, *Improving Ireland? Projectors, Prophets and Profiteers, 1641–1786* (Dublin, 2008); R.C. Allen, *The British Industrial Revolution in Global Perspective* (Cambridge, 2009).
14. I. Mortimer, *Centuries of Change: Which Century Saw the Most Change and Why It Matters to Us* (2014).
15. T. Moore, *Lalla Rookh: An Oriental Romance* (1817; 1842), p. 68.
16. F. Warner, *The Ecclesiastical History of England to the Eighteenth Century* (1756–57).
17. 'Andrew Merry' (pseud.), *The Last Dying Words of the Eighteenth Century . . .* (1800).
18. Anon., *The New Century in Verse* (1801).
19. A. Sibbit, *Thoughts on the Frequency of Divorces in Modern Times* (1800).
20. J. Adams, *The Flowers of Modern History . . .* (1788; and many later edns).
21. H. Walpole in W.S. Lewis and C.H. Bennett (eds), *Horace Walpole's Correspondence, Vol. 15: With Sir David Dalrymple* (New Haven, 1951), p. 128.
22. E.P. Thompson, *The Making of the English Working Class* (Harmondsworth, 1968 edn), p. 12.
23. D. Rapp, 'Inventing Yahoo!', *American Heritage*, 12 April 2006; online at https://web.archive.org/web/20100716081021/http://www.americanheritage.com/events/articles/web/20060412-yahoo-internet-search-engine-jerry-yang-david-filo-america-online-google-ipo-email.shtml (archived from the original; accessed 21 January 2021).
24. H. Fielding, *The History of Tom Jones* (1749), ed. A.R. Humphries, 2 vols (1962), vol. 1, pp. 208, 250–1.
25. J. Black, *The Continental Commitment: Britain, Hanover and Interventionism, 1714–93* (Abingdon, 2005); A. Thompson, *Britain, Hanover and the Protestant Interest, 1688–1756* (Woodbridge, 2006).
26. K. Schweizer and J. Black (eds), *Politics and the Press in Hanoverian Britain* (Lewiston, NY, 1989); P. McNally, *Parties, Patriots and Undertakers: Parliamentary Politics in Early Hanoverian Ireland* (Dublin, 1997).
27. Anon., *The Georgian Era: Memoirs of the Most Eminent Persons . . .* (1832); for context, see too B.W. Young, *The Victorian Eighteenth Century: An Intellectual History* (Oxford, 2007).
28. S. Riches, *St George: Hero, Martyr and Myth* (Stroud, 2000).
29. H.C.R. Edwards, *Georgian Furniture* (1958); A. Jennings, *Georgian Gardens* (Swindon, 2005); J. Summerson, *Georgian London* (1945) and J.S. Curl, *Georgian Architecture in the British Isles, 1714–1830* (Swindon, 2011).
30. D.B. Webster, *Canadian Georgian Furniture* (Toronto, 1981); M. Dupain, *Georgian Architecture in Australia* (Sydney, 1971).
31. S. Parissien, *The Georgian Group Book of the Georgian House* (1995), p. 11.
32. A.J. Youngson, *The Making of Classical Edinburgh, 1750–1840* (Edinburgh, 1966); R. Mudie, *The Modern Athens: . . . By a Modern Greek* (1825), pp. 293, 295, 298, 302
33. 'In the particular is contained the universal': R. Ellman, *James Joyce* (Oxford, 1982), p. 505; for context, see D. O'Gráda, *Georgian Dublin: The Forces that Shaped the City* (Cork, 2015).
34. P.N. Lindfield, *Georgian Gothic: Medievalist Architecture, Furniture and Interiors 1730–1840* (Woodbridge, 2016).
35. P.J. Corfield, 'British History: The Exploding Galaxy', *Journal for Eighteenth-Century Studies* 34 (2011), pp. 517–26.
36. See e.g. J. Black and D.M. MacRaild, *Studying History* (Basingstoke, 2007), pp. 1–23, 123–55.
37. E. Chambers (ed.), *Cyclopaedia: Or, an Universal Directory of Arts and Sciences*, 2 vols (1728), vol. 1, dedication.

38. Anon. [J. Brown], *An Estimate of the Manners and Principles of the Times*, 2 vols (1758), vol. 1, p. 15.
39. Idem, *An Explanatory Defence of the Estimate . . .* (1758), p. 5.

Chapter 2: Locating the Georgians at Home and Abroad

1. H. Walpole in W.S. Lewis and R.S. Brown (eds), *Horace Walpole's Correspondence, Vols Nine and Ten: Horace Walpole's Correspondence with George Montagu*, 2 vols (New Haven, 1941), vol. 1, p. 386.
2. C.M. Cipolla, *The Economic History of World Population* (Hassocks, 1978); R. Rotberg and T.K. Rabb, *Population and History: From the Traditional to the Modern World* (Cambridge, 1986).
3. G. White, *The Natural History and Antiquities of Selborne* (1789), ed. A. Secord (Oxford, 2013), p. 176.
4. M. Lefebure, *Samuel Taylor Coleridge: A Bondage of Opium* (1974).
5. W. Fox, *An Address to the People of Great Britain* (Sunderland, 1791), p. 4.
6. G.E. Barnett (ed.), *Two Tracts by Gregory King* (Baltimore, 1936), pp. 37–8.
7. J. Bolton, 'The World Upside Down: Plague as an Agent of Social and Economic Change', in W.M. Ormrod and P.G. Lindley (eds), *The Black Death in England* (Stamford, 1996), pp. 17–79, esp. pp. 26, 28; R. Nicholson, *Scotland: The Later Middle Ages* (Edinburgh, 1974), pp. 2, 148–9.
8. K.H. Connell, *The Population of Ireland, 1750–1845* (Oxford, 1950), p. 25.
9. Verses by J. Swift, sung to the tune of 'I'll Tell Thee, Dick', in W. Scott (ed.), *The Works of Jonathan Swift, DD*, 19 vols (Edinburgh, 1824), vol. 12, pp. 269–73.
10. G. Donaldson, *The Scots Overseas* (1966), pp. 57–80.
11. J. Livesey, *Civil Society and Empire: Ireland and Scotland in the Eighteenth-Century Atlantic World* (New Haven, 2009); T. Devine, *To the Ends of the Earth: Scotland's Global Diaspora, 1750–2010* (2011); B.S. Glass, *The Scottish Nation at Empire's End* (Basingstoke, 2014).
12. See https://en.wikipedia.org/wiki/Francis_Buchanan-Hamilton (accessed 25 March 2021).
13. B. Boelens et al. (eds), *The Eponym Dictionary of Reptiles* (Baltimore, 2011), p. 114.
14. S. Daultrey, D. Dickson and C. O'Gráda, 'Eighteenth-Century Irish Population: New Perspectives from Old Sources', *Journal of Economic History* 41 (1981), pp. 601–28.
15. J. Gamble, *Views of Society and Manners in the North of Ireland . . .* (1819), pp. 422–3. For further discussion of cultural context, see also I. McBride, *Eighteenth-Century Ireland: The Isle of Slaves* (Dublin, 2014); V. Morley, *The Popular Mind in Eighteenth-Century Ireland* (Cork, 2017).
16. W.E. Vaughan and A.J. Fitzpatrick (eds), *Irish Historical Statistics: Population, 1821–1971* (Dublin, 1978); P. Fitzgerald and B. Lambkin, *Migration in Irish History, 1607–2007* (Basingstoke, 2008).
17. P.J. Corfield, *The Impact of English Towns, 1700–1800* (Oxford, 1982), pp. 66-81; L. Schwarz, *London in the Age of Industrialisation: Entrepreneurs, Labour Force and Living Conditions. 1700–1850* (Cambridge, 1992); D. Hancock, *Citizens of the World: London Merchants and the Integration of the British Atlantic Community 1735–85* (Cambridge, 1995); D. Barnett, *London, Hub of the Industrial Revolution: A Revisionary History, 1775–1825* (1998); N. Zahedieh, *The Capital and the Colonies: London and the Atlantic Economy, 1660–1700* (Cambridge, 2010); J. White, *London in the Eighteenth Century: A Great and Monstrous Thing* (2012).
18. T.W. Freeman, 'Irish Towns in the Eighteenth and Nineteenth Centuries', in R.A. Butlin (ed.), *The Development of the Irish Town* (1977), pp. 101–38; J. Crowley (ed.), *Songs from the Beautiful City: The Cork Urban Ballads* (Cork, 2016).

19. S.J. Campbell, *The Great Irish Famine* (Strokestown, 1995); J. Mokyr, *Why Ireland Starved: A Quantitative and Analytical History of the Irish Economy, 1800–50* (Abingdon, 2002); M. Kelly and C. O'Gráda, 'Why Ireland Starved after Three Decades: The Great Famine in Cross-Section Reconsidered', *Irish Economic and Social History* 42 (2015), pp. 53–61; L. Kennedy, *Unhappy the Land: The Most Oppressed People Ever, the Irish?* (Sallins, 2016), pp. 81–124.

20. P. Gray, *Famine, Land and Politics: British Government and Irish Society, 1843–50* (Dublin, 1999); T.P. Coogan, *The Famine Plot: England's Role in Ireland's Greatest Tragedy* (Basingstoke, 2012), pp. 101–17.

21. D. Defoe, *The True-Born Englishman: A Satire* (1701; 1703), lines 25–6.

22. D. Quataert, 'Clothing Laws, State and Society in the Ottoman Empire, 1720–1829', *International Journal of Middle East Studies* 29 (1997), pp. 403–25.

23. R.D. Gwynn, *The Huguenots in Later Stuart Britain*, vol. 1, *Crisis, Renewal and the Ministers' Dilemma* (Eastbourne, 2015); V. Larminie (ed.), *Huguenot Networks, 1560–1780: The Interactions and Impact of a Protestant Minority in Europe* (New York, 2018).

24. *The Proceedings of the Old Bailey, 1674–1913*, April 1761, trial of Theodore Gardelle (t17610401-27); online at https://www.oldbaileyonline.org (accessed 21 January 2021).

25. D.S. Katz, *The Jews in the History of England, 1485–1840* (Oxford, 1994).

26. E. Samuel, 'Gideon, Sampson (1699–1762), financier', *Oxford Dictionary of National Biography* (2004); online at https://www.oxforddnb.com/view/10.1093/ref:odnb/9780198614128.001.0001/odnb-9780198614128-e-10645 (accessed 21 January 2021).

27. For further context, see S. Feiner, *The Origins of Jewish Secularisation in Eighteenth-Century Europe*, trans. C. Naor (Philadelphia, 2010); T.M. Endelman, *Leaving the Jewish Fold: Conversion and Radical Assimilation in Modern Jewish History* (Princeton, 2015).

28. See L.I. Newman, *Richard Cumberland: Critic and Friend of the Jews* (New York, 1919); and, for wider context, M. Ragussis, *Theatrical Nation: Jews and Other Outlandish Englishmen in Georgian Britain* (Philadelphia, 2010).

29. R. Visram, *Ayahs, Lascars and Princes: Indians in Britain, 1700–1947* (1986), pp. 11–20, 34–40, 70; M. Fisher, *Counterflows to Colonialism: Indian Travellers and Settlers in Britain, 1600–1857* (New Delhi, 2004).

30. S.D. Smith, *Slavery, Family and Gentry Capitalism in the British Atlantic: The World of the Lascelles, 1648–1834* (Cambridge, 2006), pp. 325–6.

31. R. King (ed.), *Ignatius Sancho: An African Man of Letters* (1997). A play, *Sancho: An Act of Remembrance* by P. Joseph (2015), re-imagines Sancho's life, illuminating themes of both integration and difference.

32. J. Walvin, *An African's Life: The Life and Times of Olaudah Equiano, 1745–1797* (1998); and context in B. Carey, M. Ellis and S. Salih, *Discourses of Slavery and Abolition: Britain and Its Colonies, 1760–1838* (Basingstoke, 2004).

33. R. Hanley, *Beyond Slavery and Abolition: Black British Writings, c. 1770–1830* (Cambridge, 2019).

34. A growing number of studies document their experiences: see P. Fryer, *Staying Power: The History of Black People in Britain* (1984); G. Gerzina, *Black London: Life before Emancipation* (New Brunswick, 1995); R. Costello, *Black Liverpool: The Early History of Britain's Oldest Black Community, 1730–1918* (Liverpool, 2001); K. Chater, *Untold Histories: Black People in England and Wales during the Period of the British Slave Trade, c. 1660–1807* (Manchester, 2009); C. Molineux, *Faces of Perfect Ebony: Encountering Atlantic Slavery in Imperial Britain* (Cambridge, MA, 2012); D. Olusoga, *Black and British: A Forgotten History* (2016).

35. W.A. Hart, 'Africans in Eighteenth-Century Ireland', *Irish Historical Studies* 33 (2002), pp. 19–32.

36. E.g. the Black Cultural Archives (founded 1981), now located in Windrush Square, Brixton, London SW2; the International Slavery Museum (Liverpool); and the Huguenot Museum (Rochester).
37. G. Williams, *The Expansion of Europe in the Eighteenth Century: Overseas Rivalry, Discovery and Exploitation* (1966), pp. 143, 171–2; W. Reinhard (ed.), *Empires and Encounters, 1350–1750* (Cambridge, MA, 2015).
38. C. Evans, *Slave Wales: The Welsh and Atlantic Slavery, 1660–1850* (Glamorgan, 2010).
39. N. Owen, *British Remains: Or, a Collection of Antiquities . . .* (1777), p. 119.
40. Anon. [A. Anderson], *An Historical and Chronological Deduction of the Origin of Commerce . . .*, 2 vols (1764), vol. 1, p. [v]. See context in K. Wilson, *The Sense of the People: Politics, Culture and Imperialism, 1715–85* (Cambridge, 1995); P. Lawson, D. Cannadine and K. Munro (eds), *A Taste for Empire and Glory: Studies in British Overseas Expansion, 1660–1800* (2020).
41. A. Phillips and J.C. Sharman, *Outsourcing Empire: How Company-States Made the Modern World* (Princeton, 2020); and further discussion, pp. 228–32.
42. J. Ogden, *The British Lion Rous'd . . .: A Poem in Nine Books* (Manchester, 1762), p. 11. For the sailors' viewpoint, see S. Taylor, *Sons of the Waves: The Common Seaman in the Heroic Age of Sail, 1740–1840* (New Haven, 2020); and recruitment problems in N. Rogers, *The Press Gang: Naval Impressment and its Opponents in Georgian Britain* (2007).
43. H. Hobden and M. Hobden, *John Harrison and the Problem of Longitude* (Lincoln, 1993); P. Glennie and N. Thrift, *Shaping the Day: A History of Timekeeping in England and Wales, 1300–1800* (Oxford, 2009), pp. 329–406.
44. S. Huler, *Defining the Wind: The Beaufort Scale and How a Nineteenth-Century Admiral Turned Science into Poetry* (New York, 2004).
45. T. Benjamin, *The Atlantic World: Europeans, Africans, Indians and Their Shared History, 1400–1900* (Cambridge, 2009).
46. Devine, *To the Ends of the Earth.*
47. W. Edmundson, *A History of the British Presence in Chile* (New York, 2009).
48. Anon. [J. Price], *The Saddle Put on the Right Horse: Or, an Enquiry into the Reason Why Certain Persons Have Been Denominated Nabobs . . .* (1783); T.W. Nechtman, *Nabobs: Empire and Identity in Eighteenth-Century Britain* (Cambridge, 2010).
49. P.J. Marshall, 'British Society in India under the East India Company', *Modern Asian Studies* 31 (1997), pp. 89–108; T.R. Travers, *Ideology and Empire in Eighteenth-Century India: The British in Bengal* (Cambridge, 2007); D. Gilmour, *The British in India: Three Centuries of Ambition and Experience* (2018).
50. B.P. Bach, *Calcutta's Edifice: The Buildings of a Great City* (New Delhi, 2006); T. Hunt, *Cities of Empire: The British Colonies and the Creation of the Urban World* (New York, 2014).
51. J. Peakman, *Licentious Worlds: Sex and Exploitation in Global Empires* (2019), pp. 168–74.
52. V. Anderson, *Race and Power in British India: Anglo-Indians, Class and Identity in the Nineteenth Century* (2015).
53. N. Barley, *The Golden Sword: Stamford Raffles and the East* (1999); C.M. Turnbull, *A History of Modern Singapore, 1819–2005* (Singapore, 2009).
54. J. Laughton and A. David, 'Flinders, Matthew (1774–1814), naval officer and hydrographer', *Oxford Dictionary of National Biography* (2011); online at https://www.oxforddnb.com/view/10.1093/ref:odnb/9780198614128.001.0001/odnb-9780198614128-e-9750 (accessed 22 January 2021).
55. K.V. Smith, *King Bungaree* (Kenthurst, 1992).
56. M.H. Ellis, *Lachlan Macquarie: His Life, Adventures and Times* (1952).
57. H. Reynolds, *The Other Side of the Frontier: Aboriginal Resistance to the European Invasion of Australia* (Sydney, 2006).
58. A. Ward, *An Unsettled History: Treaty Claims in New Zealand Today* (Wellington, New Zealand, 1999); M. Hickford and C. Jones (eds), *Indigenous Peoples and the State: International Perspectives on the Treaty of Waitangi* (2018).

59. E. Richards, *Britannia's Children: Emigration from England, Scotland, Wales and Ireland since 1600* (Abingdon, 2004), p. 255.

60. A. Shimbo, *Furniture-Makers and Consumers in England, 1754–1851: Design as Interaction* (Farnham, 2015).

61. J. Beresford (ed.), *The Diary of a Country Parson: The Reverend James Woodforde, Vol. 1, 1758–81* (Oxford, 1968), p. 201.

62. R. Platt, *Smuggling in the British Isles: A History* (Stroud, 2007).

63. P. Dillon, *The Much-Lamented Death of Madam Geneva: The Eighteenth-Century Gin Craze* (2002).

64. J. Grainger, *The Sugar-Cane: A Poem* (1764), book 3, l. 491.

65. B.W. Cowan, *The Social Life of Coffee: The Emergence of the British Coffee House* (New Haven, 2005).

66. J.T. Merritt, *The Trouble with Tea: The Politics of Consumption in the Eighteenth-Century Global Economy* (Baltimore, 2017).

67. T. Bickham, *Eating the Empire: Food and Society in Eighteenth-Century Britain* (2020).

68. N.A.M. Rodger, *The Insatiable Earl: A Life of John Montagu, 4th Earl of Sandwich* (1994).

Chapter 3: Georgian Voices of Gloom

1. H.F. French, *Vanishing Borders: Protecting the Planet in the Age of Globalization* (Abingdon, 2000); T. Langan, *Surviving the Age of Virtual Reality* (Columbia, 2000); J. Ellis, *Seeing Things: Television in the Age of Uncertainty* (1999); O. Guinness, *Time For Truth: . . . in a World of Lies, Hype and Spin* (Leicester, 2000).

2. B.A. Goldgar (ed.), *The Grub Street Journal, 1730–33* (Abingdon, 2002); P. Rogers, *Hacks and Dunces: Pope, Swift and Grub Street* (1980).

3. J.S. Mill, *The Spirit of the Age* (1831), with introductory essay by F.A. Von Hayek (Chicago, 1942), p. 1.

4. E.H. Coleridge (ed.), *Letters of Samuel Taylor Coleridge*, 2 vols (1895), vol. 1, p. 115.

5. Anon., *Another Estimate of the Manners and Principles of the Present Times* (1769), p. 96.

6. R. Ward and R.P. Heitzenrater (eds), *The Works of John Wesley*, 23 vols (Nashville, 1962), vol. 22, p. 67.

7. P.B. Shelley, *The Revolt of Islam* (1817), in T. Hutchinson (ed.), *The Complete Poetical Works of Percy Bysshe Shelley* (Oxford, 1934), pp. 33–4.

8. E. Wallace, *The Age of Lead: A Satire in Verse* (1840), p. 3.

9. A. Murphy, *The Upholsterer* (Glasgow, 1758), in idem, *The Works of Arthur Murphy, Esq.*, 7 vols (1786), vol. 2, p. 118.

10. C. Hibbert (ed.), *An American in Regency England: The Journal of a Tour in 1810–11* (1968), p. 119; with thanks to Gillian Williamson for this reference.

11. Anon. [E. Stephens], *A Plain Relation of the Late Action at Sea . . . With Reflections . . . upon the Present State of the Nation* (1690), p. 49.

12. Anon., *The Compleat Mendicant: Or, Unhappy Beggar . . .* (Harrow, 1699), preface, p. [ii].

13. Anon., *The Cheating Age Found Out . . . (c.* 1705).

14. Anon., *The Age of Mad-Folks* (1710).

15. H. Sacheverell, *The Answer of Henry Sacheverell, DD, to the Articles of Impeachment* (1710), p. 16.

16. G. Miège, *The Present State of Great-Britain and Ireland* (1716), p. 150.

17. Anon., *The Plebeian Prayer-Book* (1726), p. [1].

18. C. Pitt, 'On the Masquerades' in his *Poems and Translations* (1727), p. 69.

19. T. Castle, *Masquerade and Civilisation: The Carnivalesque in Eighteenth-Century English Culture and Fiction* (Palo Alto, 1986).

20. Anon., *Several Discourses and Characters, Address'd to the Ladies of the Age* (1689), p. 136.

21. Anon. [F. Bordoni], *Faustina . . .: A Satyr on the Luxury and Effeminacy of the Age* (1726), pp. 4–5.
22. Anon. [C. Churchill], *The Times: A Poem* (1764).
23. Anon. [E. Jones], *Luxury, Pride and Vanity: The Bane of the British Nation* (1736), p. 5.
24. Anon. [P. Delany], *Sixteen Discourses . . . against the Reigning Vanities of the Age* (1754), p. 316.
25. 'A. Fitz-Adam' (pseud.), *The World* 58 (1753), p. 351; O. Goldsmith, *She Stoops to Conquer: Or, The Mistakes of a Night* (1773), p. 36; H. More, *An Estimate of the Religion of the Fashionable World* (1793), p. 14; J. Trusler, *Modern Times: Or, the Adventures of Gabriel Outcast* (1785), p. v; Anon., *Argentum: Or, the Adventures of a Shilling* (1794), p. i.
26. Anon., *The Nabob: Or, Asiatic Plunderers – A Satyrical Poem . . .* (1773), p. 41.
27. O. Goldsmith, *The Deserted Village* (1770), lines 51–2.
28. T. Judt, *Ill Fares the Land: A Treatise on Our Present Discontents* (2010). See also the film *Ill Fares the Land* (dir. B. Bryden, 1983).
29. Anon. [Delany], *Sixteen Discourses*, p. 316.
30. 'Civis', 'The Prevalence and Bad Effects of Luxury', 5 September 1754, in *London Magazine and Monthly Chronicler, 1753* [actually 1754], vol. 22, pp. 457–8.
31. A. MacLaren, *The Days We Live In: . . . A Dramatic Piece, with Songs* (1805), p. 12.
32. J. Burgh, *Britain's Remembrancer: Or, the Danger Not Over* (Edinburgh, 1746).
33. Anon. [Brown], *Estimate of the Manners*, vol. 1, p. 15.
34. G. Walker, *A Sermon . . . to a Congregation of Protestant Dissenters at Nottingham* (1778), pp. 11–12.
35. J. Mitford (ed.), *The Correspondence between Horace Walpole, Earl of Orford, and the Rev. William Mason*, 2 vols (1851), vol. 2, p. 210.
36. Mirabeau [H.G. Riquetti, comte de Mirabeau], *Mirabeau's Letters during His Residence in England . . .*, 2 vols (1832), vol. 2, pp. 162, 140.
37. E. Burke, *Reflections on the Revolution in France* (1790), ed. C.C. O'Brien (Harmondsworth, 1979), p. 170.
38. P.J. Corfield and C. Evans, *Youth and Revolution in the 1790s: Letters of William Pattisson, Thomas Amyot and Henry Crabb Robinson* (Stroud, 1996), p. 47.
39. J. Bowles, *Reflections on the Political and Moral State of Society . . .* (1800), pp. 122, 128.
40. Idem, *Remarks on Modern Female Manners . . .* (1802), pp. 8, 12.
41. A.L. Barbauld, 'Eighteen Hundred and Eleven: A Poem' (1812), in L. Aikin (ed.), *The Works of Anna Laetitia Barbauld*, 2 vols (1825), vol. 1, pp. 235, 249.
42. R. Cruikshank, *Spirit of the Age Newspaper, for 1828* (Durham, 1829), p. xiv.
43. J. Wade, *The Black Book: Or, Corruption Unmasked! Being an Account of Persons, Places, and Sinecures*, 2 vols (2nd edn, 1828), suppl., p. 5.
44. R. Palmer, *The Sound of History: Songs and Social Comment* (Oxford, 1988), pp. 71–2.
45. Defoe, *True-Born Englishman*, p. 4.
46. J. Farooq, *Preaching in Eighteenth-Century London* (Woodbridge, 2013).
47. P.J. Corfield, *Power and the Professions in Britain, 1700–1850* (Oxford, 1995), p. 114.
48. J. Woodward, *Fair Warnings to a Careless World: Or, the Serious Practice of Religion Recommended . . .* (1707).
49. For details, see G. Holmes, 'The Sacheverell Riots: The Crowd and the Church in Early Eighteenth-Century London', *Past & Present* 72 (1976), pp. 55–85.
50. Anon. [J. Denne], *Some Observations upon the Present State of Religion in England* (1734), p. 2.
51. 'M.W.', *The Sacred Outcry upon a View of the Principal Errors and Vices of Christendom . . .* (1788), pp. vii, x.
52. T. Jervis, *Reflections on the State of Religion* (1801), p. 19.
53. S. Johnson, *A Dictionary of the English Language*, 2 vols (1766), vol. 1, *sub* 'Infidelity'; and 'Irreligion'.

54. W. Warburton, *Faith Working by Charity to Christian Edification* (1738), preface, p. [iv], with thanks to John Walsh for this reference.

55. Among them, see the following, many written by clergymen: J. Glanvill, *Seasonable Reflections . . ., in Order to the Conviction and Cure of the Scoffing and Infidelity of a Degenerate Age* (1676); J. Edwards, *Some Thoughts Concerning the Causes and Occasions of Atheism, Especially in the Present Age . . .* (1695); W. Tilly, *A Preservative against the Growing Infidelity and Apostasy of the Present Age* (1729); W. Crawford, *A Short Manual against the Infidelity of this Age* (Edinburgh, 1734); Anon. [H. Lindsay?], *An Essay . . . against the Infidelity of the Age* (Edinburgh, 1736); Anon., *An Essay . . . Serving to Illustrate . . . the Truth and Certainty of Christianity against the Prevailing Infidelity of the Age* (Edinburgh, 1752); 'Credens' [C. Fleming], *An Antidote for the Rising Age, against Scepticism and Infidelity . . .* (1765); 'Clericus', *The Excellency of the Sacred Writings . . .* (1780), p. iv; J. Bennett, *Divine Revelation Impartial and Universal: Or, an Humble Attempt to Defend Christianity . . . against the Infidelity and Scepticism of the Age* (1783); J. Jamieson, *An Alarm to Britain: . . . the Causes of the Rapid Progress of Infidelity . . .* (Perth, 1795); 'A Layman' [T. Williams], *The Age of Infidelity, in Answer to Thomas Paine's* Age of Reason (1795), p. 1.

56. R. Hall, *Modern Infidelity Considered . . .* (Cambridge, 1800); idem, *Anffyddiaeth diweddar yn cael ei ystyried yn ei effeithiau ar gymdeithas: mewn pregeth* (Caenarfon, 1840).

57. G. Ion, *A Sermon Preached at Bubwith* (York, 1780), pp. 16, 18, 20–3.

58. Anon., *A Sermon Preached in Hackney Church . . .* (1780), p. 16.

59. J. Bowdler, *Reform or Ruin: Take Your Choice!* (Dublin, 1798), p. 21.

60. R.B. Nickolls, *Considerations on the Present Times . . .* (Chesterfield, 1798).

61. E. Weber, *Apocalypses: Prophecies, Cults and Millennial Beliefs through the Ages* (Toronto, 1999).

62. R. Campbell, *The London Tradesman: Being a Compendious View of All the Trades . . .* (1747), p. 33.

63. G. Burder, *Evangelical Truth Defended* (Lancaster, 1788), pp. 14, 16.

64. Anon. [attrib. J. Swift], *A Letter to a Young Gentleman, Lately Enter'd into Holy Orders* (1721), p. 25.

65. J. Berridge, *Cheerful Piety: Or, Religion without Gloom . . .* (1794).

66. *Spectator* 165 (December 1731), repr. in *Gentleman's Magazine*, vol. 1 (December 1731), p. 514.

67. W. Jesse, *Parochialia: Or, Observations on the Discharge of Parochial Duties* (Kidderminster, 1785), p. 188.

68. Anon., *A Dissuasive from Entering into Holy Orders . . .* (1732), pp. 24, 41.

69. R.H. Popkin and A. Vanderjagt, *Scepticism and Irreligion in the Seventeenth and Eighteenth Centuries* (Leiden, 1993); J. Redwood, *Reason, Ridicule and Religion: The Age of Enlightenment in England, 1660–1750* (1976).

70. J. Ogilvie, *An Inquiry into the Causes of the Infidelity and Scepticism of the Times* (1783), pp. 436–8. See also 'T.W.' [T. Williams], *The Age of Credulity* (Philadelphia, 1796), p. 7.

71. Edwards, *Some Thoughts Concerning the Causes . . . of Atheism*, pp. 96, 123, 119 (repeated pagination).

72. J. Vanbrugh, *The Provok'd Wife* (1697), in idem, *Plays . . .*, 2 vols (1730), vol. 1, pp. 126 (act 1, sc. 1) and 191 (act 5, sc. 2).

73. W. Thom, *An Enquiry into the Causes of the Decline of Religion . . .* (Glasgow, 1761), p. 5.

74. J. Griffin, *The Decline of Religion: An Inquiry into the Causes of the Decline in Religion in Christian Churches . . .* (1819); T.B. Clarke, *The Church and State in Danger: Or, Cause and Effects of the Decline of Religion* (1821).

75. P.J. Corfield, '"An Age of Infidelity": Secularisation in Eighteenth-Century England', *Social History* 39 (2014), pp. 229–47.

76. D. Vaisey (ed.), *The Diary of Thomas Turner, 1754–65* (Oxford, 1984), p. 146.

77. R. Scruton, *The Uses of Pessimism and the Danger of False Hope* (2010).
78. A. Gramsci, *Letters from Prison*, ed. F. Rosengarten (New York, 2011): 19 December 1929. See also F. Antonini, 'Pessimism of the Intellect, Optimism of the Will: Gramsci's Political Thought in the Last Miscellaneous Notebooks', *Rethinking Marxism* 31 (2019), pp. 42–57.
79. N. Perrin, *Dr Bowdler's Legacy: A History of Expurgated Books in England and the USA* (1970).
80. T.R. Malthus, *An Essay on the Principle of Population ...* (1798), ed. A. Flew (Harmondsworth, 1970), p. 186.
81. R. Reeves, *John Stuart Mill: Victorian Firebrand* (2007), pp. 1–2, 51, 482.

Chapter 4: Georgian Voices of Optimism

1. G. Jacob, *The Country Gentleman's* Vade Mecum (1717), p. 117.
2. R. Bell (ed.), *Ancient Poems, Ballads and Songs* (1857), p. 243.
3. R. Havens, *The Influence of Milton upon English Poetry* (New York, 1961).
4. Corfield, *Power and the Professions*, pp. 42–69; C. Davies, *The Mirth of Nations* (New Brunswick, 2002), pp. 17–49; V. Gatrell, *City of Laughter: Sex and Satire in Eighteenth-Century London* (2006); M. Knights and A. Morton (eds), *The Power of Laughter and Satire in Early Modern Britain: Political and Religious Culture, 1500–1820* (Woodbridge, 2017).
5. R.W. Bevis, *The Laughing Tradition: Stage Comedy in Garrick's Day* (Athens, GA, 1980).
6. 'Ali Mohammed Hadgi' (pseud.), *A Brief and Merry History of Great Britain* (1710?), p. 26.
7. Anon., *The Caledonian Jester ...* (1806); Anon., *The Welsh Jester: Y digrifur Cymraeg: neu Feddyginiaeth i'r tristwch; sef, ychydig o ffraethineb oferwyr yr oes bresennol ...* (Caerfyrddin, 1820); Anon., *The Female Jester: Or, Wit for the Ladies. Compiled by a Woman* (c. 1780).
8. C.N. Cole (ed.), *The Works of Soame Jenyns, Esq.*, 4 vols (1790), vol. 2, p. 149.
9. L. Sterne, *The Life and Opinions of Tristram Shandy, Gentleman*, 9 vols (1759–67; 1967), p. 36.
10. D. Defoe, *A Tour through the Whole Island of Great Britain*, 3 vols (1724–27), ed. G.D.H. Cole and D.C. Browning, 2 vols (1962), vol. 1, p. 1.
11. J. Sekora, *Luxury: The Concept in Western Thought, Eden to Smollett* (Baltimore, 1977).
12. Defoe, *Tour*, vol. 1, p. 168; idem, *Weekly Review of the Affairs of France* 2 (1705), p. 9.
13. H. Fielding, *An Enquiry into the Causes of the Late Increase of Robbers* (1751), p. 6.
14. Anon., *The Prosperity of Britain Proved from the Degeneracy of its People* (1757), p. 32.
15. [Riquetti], *Mirabeau's Letters*, vol. 2, pp. 162, 140.
16. W. Combe, *A Word in Season to the Traders and Manufacturers ...* (Ipswich, 1793), p. 15.
17. S. Copley and A. Edgar (eds), *David Hume: Selected Essays* (Oxford, 1993), pp. 156, 160–1, 164–5.
18. J. Harris, *Navigantium atque Itinerantium Biblioteca: Or, A Complete Collection of Voyages and Travels*, 2 vols (1744–48), vol. 1, pp. [i–iv].
19. W. Hutton, *An History of Birmingham to the End of the Year 1780* (Birmingham, 1781), pp. 61–2.
20. A. Ferguson, *An Essay on the History of Civil Society* (Edinburgh, 1767; in Hardpress.net reprint of 8th edn, 2006), p. 197.
21. P. Carter, *Men and the Emergence of Polite Society: Britain, 1660–1800* (Harlow, 2000); L. Klein, 'Politeness and the Interpretation of the British Eighteenth Century', *Historical Journal* 45 (2002), pp. 869–98.
22. Anon., *An Enquiry into the Manners of the Present Age: By a Lady* (1778), p. 1.
23. A. Sibbit, *A Dissertation, Moral and Political: On the Influence of Luxury and Refinement on Nations ...* (1800), p. 80.

24. D. Defoe, *The Compleat English Tradesman*, 2 vols (1726–27), vol. 1, p. 55. But for the same phrase intended as condemnation, see Anon. [Jones], *Luxury, Pride and Vanity*, p. 4.

25. Burgh, *Britain's Remembrancer*, p. 42; and context in C.H. Hay, *James Burgh: Spokesman for Reform in Hanoverian England* (Washington, 1979).

26. 'J. Buncle' [T. Amory], *The Life of John Buncle, Esq: Containing Various Observations . . .*, 2 vols (1756–66), vol. 1, p. 460.

27. J. Hanway, *The Defects of Police, the Cause of Immorality . . .* (1775), p. 265.

28. Letter in *Gentleman's Magazine* 24 (August 1754), p. 347.

29. Anon., *A New Estimate of Manners and Principles, Part 3: Of Happiness* (Cambridge, 1761), p. 125.

30. See variously J.B. LeBlanc, *Letters on the English and French Nations*, 2 vols (Dublin, 1747), vol. 1, p. 127; Anon., *German Cruelty: A Fair Warning to the People of Great Britain* (1756), p. 1; Anon. [E.D. Davenport], *The Golden Age: Or, England in 1822–3, in a Poetical Epistle . . .* (1823); S.T. Coleridge, *On the Constitution of the Church and State, According to the Idea of Each* (1830), pp. 71–2.

31. J. Arbuthnot, *Law is a Bottomless Pit: Or, the History of John Bull* (*c.* 1712?), p. 72; Corfield, *Power and the Professions*, pp. 26–7, 47–52, 70–101.

32. Anon. [S. Johnson], *The Adventurer* 115 (11 December 1753), p. 266.

33. W. Green, *The Art of Living in London* (1768), p. 1.

34. Anon. [T. Beck], *The Age of Frivolity: A Poem* (1806), pp. 47, 50.

35. J. Tucker, *Instructions for Travellers* (1757), pp. 20–1.

36. Anon., *England Displayed: Being a New, Complete and Accurate Survey . . .* (1769), p. [iii].

37. B. Franklin, *The Autobiography and Other Writings*, ed. P. Shaw (Toronto, 1982), p. 151.

38. J. Stuart, *Critical Observations on the Buildings and Improvements . . .* (1771), p. 17.

39. J. Boswell, *Life of Johnson*, ed. R.W. Chapman (1976), p. 1211 (April 1783).

40. *Telegraph* (26 May 1795), cited in N. McKendrick, J.H. Plumb and J. Brewer, *The Birth of a Consumer Society: The Commercialisation of Eighteenth-Century England* (1983), p. 160.

41. *Public Advertiser* (13 April 1785).

42. W. Jackson, *The Four Ages: Together with Essays on Various Subjects* (1798), p. 79.

43. *Preston Chronicle* (28 February 1824), with thanks to Amanda Vickery for this reference.

44. Anon. [T. Beck], *Age of Frivolity*, pp. 47, 50.

45. R. Southey, *Letters from England* (1807), ed. J. Simmons (1951), pp. 362–3.

46. T. Carlyle, 'Signs of the Times', *Edinburgh Review* 98 (1829), pp. 441–2.

47. Burgh, *Britain's Remembrancer*, p. 18; C. MacLaurin, *An Account of Sir Isaac Newton's Discoveries . . .* (1748), p. 62; J. Millar, *Observations Concerning the Distinction of Rank in Society* (1771), p. 76; J. Ives, 'Preface', in H. Swinden, *The History and Antiquities of the Ancient Burgh of Great Yarmouth* (Norwich, 1772), p. [i]; J. Cartwright, *Give Us Our Rights! Or, a Letter to the Present Electors of Middlesex* (1782), pp. iii, 35; E. Gibbon, *The Autobiography of Edward Gibbon, as Originally Edited by Lord Sheffield* (1796), ed. J.B. Bury (1959), p. 19; J. Priestley, *The Theological and Miscellaneous Works . . .*, 25 vols (1817–32), vol. 25, p. 375; 'A Woman', *Monthly Magazine* 2 (1796), p. 469.

48. C. Vereker, *Eighteenth-Century Optimism: A Study of the Interrelations of Moral and Social Theory in English and French Thought between 1689 and 1789* (Liverpool, 1967); M. Scrivener, *The Cosmopolitan Ideal in the Age of Revolution and Reaction, 1776–1832* (Abingdon, 2007).

49. Anon. [J. Gordon], *A New Estimate of Manners and Principles, Being a Comparison between Ancient and Modern Times . . .* (Cambridge, 1760), pp. 49–50.

50. W. Combe, *The Diaboliad: A Poem* (1777), p. iii.

51. 'Constant Reader', *Gentleman's Magazine* 53 (November 1783), p. 938.

52. A. Thomson, *Essay on Novels: A Poetical Epistle . . .* (Edinburgh, 1793), p. iii.

53. 'A Cornish Tinner', *The Age of Light: Or, Truth Unveiled* (Bristol, 1818), p. 7.
54. T. Sprat, *The History of the Royal-Society of London . . .* (1667), pp. 1, 76.
55. MacLaurin, *Account*, p. 91.
56. J. Bentham, *Fragment on Government* (1776), p. i.
57. T. Paine, *The Rights of Man: Being an Answer to Mr Burke's Attack on the French Revolution* (1791), ed. H. Collins (Harmondsworth, 1969), p. 141.
58. Malthus, *Essay on the Principle of Population*, pp. 67–8.
59. R. Griffiths (ed.), *Monthly Review*, n.s. 27 (1798), p. 441.
60. M. Wollstonecraft, *Letters Written during a Short Residence in Sweden, Norway, and Denmark* (1796), pp. 59, 264; C. Tomalin, *The Life and Death of Mary Wollstonecraft* (1974); B. Taylor, *Mary Wollstonecraft and the Feminist Imagination* (Cambridge, 2003); N.E. Johnson and P. Keen (eds), *Mary Wollstonecraft in Context* (Cambridge, 2020); S. Tomaselli, *Wollstonecraft: Philosophy, Passion and Politics* (Princeton, 2020).
61. The Muses constituted the poet Anna Laetitia Barbauld (née Aikin), linguist Elizabeth Carter, novelist Charlotte Lennox (née Ramsay), dramatist Elizabeth Griffith, historian Catherine Macaulay (née Sawbridge), religious writer Hannah More, singer Elizabeth Sheridan (née Linley), painter Angelica Kauffmann and salon hostess Elizabeth Montagu (née Robinson).
62. R.B. Sheridan, *The Rivals: A Comedy* (1775), ed. E. Duthie (1979), p. 26 (act 1, sc. 2).
63. S. Tucker, *Protean Shape: A Study in Eighteenth-Century Vocabulary and Usage* (1967), pp. 149–55; R.J. Smith, *The Gothic Bequest: Medieval Institutions in British Thought, 1688–1863* (Cambridge, 1987).
64. J. Richardson, *Two Discourses, No. 2: A Discourse on the Dignity, Certainty, Pleasure and Advantage of the Science of a Connoisseur* (1719), p. 221.
65. Fielding, *Tom Jones*, vol. 1, p. 261.
66. S. Foote, *The Orators* (1762), in idem, *The Dramatic Works . . .*, 2 vols (1830), vol. 2, p. 146.
67. Tucker, *Instructions for Travellers*, p. 37.
68. *Monthly Review* 1 (December 1773–June 1774), p. 11, cited in Tucker, *Protean Shape*, p. 150.
69. F.A. Wendeborn, *A View of England towards the Close of the Eighteenth Century*, 2 vols (Dublin, 1791), vol. 1, p. 232.
70. Lindfield, *Georgian Gothic*.
71. T. Paine, *The Age of Reason: Being an Investigation of True and Fabulous Theology* (Paris, 1794).
72. See variously K. Thomas, *Religion and the Decline of Magic: Studies in Popular Beliefs in Sixteenth- and Seventeenth-Century England* (1971); M. Hunter, *The Decline of Magic: Britain in the Enlightenment* (New Haven, 2020).
73. J.B. Bury, *The Idea of Progress: An Inquiry into its Origin and Growth* (1920); D. Spadafora, *The Idea of Progress in Eighteenth-Century Britain* (New Haven, 1990); C. Lasch, *The True and Only Heaven: Progress and Its Critics* (New York, 1991); P. Slack, *The Invention of Improvement: Information and Material Progress in Seventeenth-Century England* (Oxford, 2015).
74. J. Bunyan, *The Pilgrim's Progress . . .* (1678).
75. Hogarth's six-print series *Harlot's Progress* (1732) and eight-print *Rake's Progress* (1735), in S. Shesgreen (ed.), *Engravings by Hogarth* (New York, 1973), plates 18–23, 28–35.
76. J. Macure, *A View of the City of Glasgow: Or, an Account of Its Origin, Rise and Progress* (Glasgow, 1736); Anon., *The Mathematician, Number 1: Containing a Dissertation on the Rise, Progress and Improvement of Geometry* (1745); C. Ingram, *The Rise and Progress of the Present Taste in Planting Parks . . . etc.* (1767).
77. Priestley, *Theological and Miscellaneous Works*, vol. 25, p. 375; idem, *An Essay on the First Principles of Government* (1768), pp. 5–7; idem, *Miscellaneous Observations Relating to Education* (Bath, 1778), pp. 3–4.

78. W. Wordsworth, *The Prelude* (in 1805 version), in J. Wordsworth, M.H. Abrams and S. Gill (eds), *The Prelude, 1799; 1805; 1850: Authoritative Texts* (New York, 1979), p. 396.

79. T. Paine, letter of 17 January 1790, in Sheffield City Library, Wentworth Wodehouse Muniments: repr. in *Durham University Journal* 43 (1951), pp. 50–4; Paine, *Rights of Man*, p. 168.

80. A. Goodwin, *The Friends of Liberty: The English Democratic Movement in the Age of the French Revolution* (1979), pp. 109–10.

81. A. MacLaren, *Old England for Ever! Or, a Fig for the Invasion* (Bristol, 1799), p. 30.

82. *Gentleman's Magazine* 75 (1805), part 1, preface, p. iii.

83. E. Cobbold, *Ode on the Victory of Waterloo* (Ipswich, 1815), p. 18.

84. M. Thale (ed.), *Selections from the Papers of the London Corresponding Society, 1792–99* (Cambridge, 1983), p. 134: resolution dated 14 April 1794.

85. Cited in Goodwin, *Friends of Liberty*, pp. 244–5 n. 162, 326, 329 n. 114.

86. J. Thelwall, *The Rights of Nature against the Usurpations of Establishments* . . . (1796), p. 21.

87. R. Owen, *A New View of Society* . . . (1816).

88. J.F.C. Harrison, *Robert Owen and the Owenites in Britain and America: The Quest for the New Moral World* (1969); R.G. Garnett, *Cooperation and the Owenite Socialist Communities in Britain, 1825–45* (Manchester, 1972); N. Thompson and C. Williams (eds), *Robert Owen and His Legacy* (Cardiff, 2011).

89. Anon. [William Fox], *An Address to the People of Great Britain* . . . (11th edn, 1791), p. [i].

90. O. Equiano, *The Interesting Narrative: And Other Writings*, ed. V. Carretta (1995), p. 233.

91. W. Roscoe, *Manifesto against African Slavery, Issued by the Liverpool Anti-Slavery Society* (1830); idem, *Wrongs of Africa: A Poem* . . . (1787), p. i.

Chapter 5: Sharing Family Lives between Private and Public Worlds

1. Arbuthnot, *Law is a Bottomless Pit*, p. 90.

2. H.P. Brougham, *Historical Sketches of Statesmen* . . ., 3 vols (1839), vol. 1, p. 52.

3. J. Brewer, *The Sinews of Power: War, Money and the English State, 1688–1783* (1989), pp. 82–3, 92–3.

4. G. Smith, *Robert Burns, the Exciseman* (Ayr, 2006).

5. P. Laslett, 'Size and Structure of the Household in England over Three Centuries', *Population History* 23 (1969), pp. 199–223; '2011 Census: Population and Household Estimates for the United Kingdom', Office for National Statistics (March 2011).

6. P. Laslett, 'Characteristics of the Western Family Considered over Time', in idem, *Family Life and Illicit Love in Earlier Generations* (Cambridge, 1977), pp. 12–49.

7. N. Tadmor, *Family and Friends in Eighteenth-Century England: Household, Kinship and Patronage* (Cambridge, 2001); K. Harvey, *The Little Republic: Masculinity and Domestic Authority in Eighteenth-Century Britain* (Oxford, 2012).

8. F.A. Pottle (ed.), *Boswell's London Journal, 1762–1763* (1951), p. 50.

9. W. Saint, *Memoirs of the Life, Character, Opinions, and Writings of . . . John Fransham* (Norwich, 1811).

10. E. Sitwell, *English Eccentrics: A Gallery of Weird and Wonderful Men and Women* (Harmondsworth, 1983), pp. 47–55.

11. *Gentleman's Magazine* 23 (March 1753), p. 123.

12. N. Groom (ed.), *Thomas Chatterton and Romantic Culture* (Basingstoke, 1999).

13. W. Wordsworth, 'Resolution and Independence' (written 1802; publ. 1805).

14. B. Hill, *Women Alone: Spinsters in England, 1660–1850* (New Haven, 2001).

15. J. Austen, *Persuasion* (1817–18; in Harmondsworth, 1980), pp. 165–7, 200.

16. J. Rowbotham and K. Stevenson (eds), *Criminal Conversations: Victorian Crimes, Social Panic and Moral Outrage* (Columbus, 2005).

17. L. Stone, *The Family, Sex and Marriage in England, 1500–1800* (1977); R. Trumbach, *The Rise of the Egalitarian Family: Aristocratic Kinship and Domestic Relations in Eighteenth-Century England* (New York, 1978); A. Giddens, *The Transformation of Intimacy: Sexuality, Love and Eroticism in Modern Societies* (Cambridge, 1992).
18. G.J. Barker-Benfield, *The Culture of Sensibility: Sex and Society in Eighteenth-Century Britain* (Chicago, 1996); S. Holloway, *The Game of Love in Georgian England: Courtship, Emotions, and Material Culture* (Oxford, 2019), pp. 166–74, esp. pp. 166–8.
19. Sheridan, *The Rivals*, pp. 100–1 (act 5, sc. 1).
20. E. Ehrman, *The Wedding Dress: Three Hundred Years of Bridal Fashions* (2014).
21. J.R. Gillis, *For Better, For Worse: British Marriages, 1600 to the Present* (Oxford, 1985); R.B. Outhwaite, *Clandestine Marriage in England, 1500–1850* (1995); R. Probert, *Marriage Law and Practice in the Long Eighteenth Century: A Reassessment* (Cambridge, 2009).
22. L. Leneman, *Promises, Promises: Marriage Litigation in Scotland, 1698–1830* (Edinburgh, 2003); K. Barclay, *Love, Intimacy and Power: Marriage and Patriarchy in Scotland, 1650–1850* (Manchester, 2011).
23. M.E. Bowes, *Confessions of the Countess of Strathmore . . .* (1793); D. Parker, *The Trampled Wife: The Scandalous Life of Mary Eleanor Bowes* (Stroud, 2006).
24. M. Finn, 'Men's Things: Masculine Consumption in the Consumer Revolution', *Social History*, 25 (2000), pp. 133–55; A. Vickery, *Behind Closed Doors: At Home in Georgian England* (2009), esp. pp. 83–128, 166–206, 291–307.
25. Shimbo, *Furniture-Makers and Consumers.*
26. Anon. [J. Collier], *An Essay on the Art of Ingeniously Tormenting . . .* (1753; 1804), p. 90.
27. 'Redhead v. Redhead' (1690): testimony of William Eason, labourer, cited in J. Akamatsu, 'Gender, Power and Sensibility: Marital Breakdown and Separation in the Court of Arches, 1660–1800' (PhD thesis, London University, 2009), p. 149.
28. M. Bird, *Mary Hardy and Her World, 1773–1809, Vol. 1: A Working Family* (Kingston upon Thames, 2020), p. 279.
29. E.A. Foyster, *Marital Violence: An English Family History, 1660–1857* (Cambridge, 2005); J.A. Sharpe, *A Fiery and Furious People: A History of Violence in England* (2016), pp. 187–9.
30. S. Staves, *Married Women's Separate Property in England, 1660–1833* (Cambridge, MA, 1990); A.L. Erickson, *Women and Property in Early Modern England* (1993).
31. L. Stone, *Broken Lives: Separation and Divorce in England, 1660–1857* (Oxford, 1993).
32. Akamatsu, 'Gender, Power and Sensibility', pp. 134–222.
33. F.A. Montgomery, *Women's Rights: Struggles and Feminism in Britain, c. 1770–1970* (Manchester, 2006); A. Chernook, *Men and the Making of Modern British Feminism* (Stanford, 2010).
34. A. Foreman, *Georgiana: Duchess of Devonshire* (1998). She features in a number of historical films, including *The Divine Lady* (dir. F. Lloyd, 1929), *Berkeley Square* (dir. F. Lloyd, 1933) and *The House in the Square* (dir. R.W. Baker, 1951), and constitutes the central role in *The Duchess* (dir. S. Dibb, 2008).
35. M. Morgann, *A Letter to My Lords the Bishops . . .* (1779).
36. E.P. Thompson, 'Rough Music', in idem, *Customs in Common* (1991), pp. 467–538.
37. T. Hardy, *The Mayor of Casterbridge* (1886).
38. S. Menafee, *Wives for Sale: An Ethnographic Study of British Popular Divorce* (Oxford, 1981); E.P. Thompson, 'The Sale of Wives', in idem, *Customs in Common*, pp. 404–68.
39. J. Lane, *Apprenticeship in England, 1660–1914* (1996).
40. B. Trinder, *The Market Town Lodging House in Victorian England* (Leicester, 2001); Vickery, *Behind Closed Doors*, pp. 34–8, 49–82.
41. G.S. Thomson, *The Russells in Bloomsbury, 1669–1771* (1940), pp. 226–7, 238.

42. J.J. Hecht, *The Domestic Servant Class in Eighteenth-Century England* (1956; 1980), pp. 209–12; B. Hill, *Servants: English Domestics in the Eighteenth Century* (Oxford, 1996), pp. 66–70; C. Steedman, *Labours Lost: Domestic Service and the Making of Modern England* (Cambridge, 2009).

43. J. MacDonald, *Memoirs of an Eighteenth-Century Footman: Travels, 1745–79*, ed. J. Beresford (1927), pp. 57, 59; Hill, *Servants*, pp. 52–3, 58–9, 104.

44. Ibid., pp. 25–6, 84–5.

45. Anon., *The Vices of the Cities of London and Westminster* (Dublin, 1751), p. 27.

46. R. Dodsley, *A Muse in Livery . . .* (1732); Hill, *Servants*, p. 245.

47. J. Townley, *High Life below Stairs: A Farce* (1759).

48. Hill, *Servants*, pp. 15, 19, 31–43.

49. J. Walvin, 'Black People in Britain: The Eighteenth Century', *History Today* 31 (1981).

50. M. Bundock, *The Fortunes of Francis Barber: The True Story of the Jamaican Slave who Became Samuel Johnson's Heir* (2015).

51. Mary Hardy's Register of Maidservants, ledger 4 (1793–97), in M. Bird (ed.), *The Diary of Mary Hardy, 1773–1809: Vol. 3, Farm, Maltings and Brewery* (Kingston upon Thames, 2013), p. 407.

52. L. Stone, *Road to Divorce: England, 1530–1987* (Oxford, 1992), pp. 220–30; J. Akamatsu, 'Revisiting Ecclesiastical Adultery Cases in Eighteenth-Century England', *Journal of Women's History* 28 (2016), pp. 13–37.

53. Hecht, *Domestic Servant Class*, pp. 207–8; M. Jourdain, 'Dumb-Waiters and What-Nots', *Country Life* 47 (1945), p. 286.

54. C. Smart, *Mrs Abigail and the Dumb-Waiter: Fable 15* (1755).

55. Boswell, *Life of Johnson*, ed. Chapman, pp. 316–17 (July 1763).

56. Hecht, *Domestic Servant Class*, pp. 158–68; Hill, *Servants*, pp. 76–92.

57. Vickery, *Behind Closed Doors*, pp. 25–48, 307.

58. B. Bryson, *At Home: A Short History of Private Life* (2010), pp. 153–4.

59. E. Smith, *Memoirs of a Highland Lady: Being the Autobiography of Elizabeth Grant of Rothiemurhus . . . 1789–1830* (Edinburgh, 1897), p. 151.

60. Hill, *Servants*, pp. 44–63.

61. S. Richardson, *Pamela: Or, Virtue Rewarded* (1740); Hill, *Servants*, pp. 208–24.

62. Ibid., p. 209.

63. A. Warner, 'Finding the Aristocracy, 1780–1880: A Case Study of Rural Sussex', *Southern History* 35 (2013), pp. 117–19.

64. J.A. Sharpe, *Crime in Early Modern England, 1550–1750* (1984), p. 110.

65. L.A. Pollock, *Forgotten Children: Parent-Child Relations from 1500 to 1900* (Cambridge, 1983); P. Ariès, *Centuries of Childhood*, trans. R. Baldick (Harmondsworth, 1973).

66. J. Locke, *Some Thoughts Concerning Education* (1693); W. Cadogan, *An Essay upon Nursing and the Management of Children . . .* (1750).

67. W. Wordsworth, 'Sonnet: My Heart Leaps Up' (written 1802), in T. Hutchinson (ed.), *The Poetical Works of William Wordsworth* (Oxford, 1920), p. 79.

68. J.H. Plumb, 'The New World of Children in Eighteenth-Century England', *Past & Present* 67 (1985), pp. 64–95.

69. M.O. Grenby, *Children's Literature* (Edinburgh, 2008); A. O'Malley, *The Making of the Modern Child: Children's Literature and Childhood in the Late Eighteenth Century* (2003).

70. T. Cosslett, *Talking Animals in British Children's Fiction, 1786–1914* (Aldershot, 2006), p. 37.

71. Corfield and Evans, *Youth and Revolution in the 1790s*, p. 19.

72. P. Laslett, K. Oosterveen and R.M. Smith (eds), *Bastardy and Its Comparative History . . .* (1980); R. Mitchison and L. Leneman, *Girls in Trouble: Sexuality and Social Control in Rural Scotland, 1660–1780* (Edinburgh, 1998); R. Mitchison and L. Leneman, *Sin in the City: Sexuality and Social Control in Urban Scotland, 1160–1780* (Edinburgh, 1998).

73. A. Blaikie, *Illegitimacy, Sex and Society: Northeast Scotland, 1750–1900* (Oxford, 1993); K.L. Gibson, 'Experiences of Illegitimacy in England, 1660–1834' (PhD thesis, University of Sheffield, 2018); A.J. Muir, *Deviant Maternity: Illegitimacy in Wales, c. 1680–1800* (2020).

74. Corfield, *Power and the Professions*, p. 236; R. Gore-Browne, *Chancellor Thurlow: The Life and Times of an Eighteenth-Century Lawyer* (1953).

75. J. Austen, *Emma: A Novel* (1816), ed. R. Blythe (Harmondsworth, 1969), p. 463.

76. T. Evans, *Unfortunate Objects: Lone Mothers in Eighteenth-Century London* (Basingstoke, 2005); S. Williams, *Unmarried Motherhood in the Metropolis, 1700–1850: Pregnancy, the Poor Law and Provision* (Basingstoke, 2018).

77. A. Levene, *Childcare, Health and Mortality at the London Foundling Hospital, 1741–1800: 'Left to the Mercy of the World'* (Manchester, 2007); D.S. Allin, *The Early Years of the Foundling Hospital, 1739/41 to 1773* (2010).

78. J. Styles, *Threads of Feeling: The London Foundling Hospital's Textile Tokens, 1740–70* (2010), pp. 63–9.

79. A.M. Kilday, *A History of Infanticide in Britain, c. 1600 to the Present* (Basingstoke, 2013).

80. J. Hanway, *A Sentimental History of Chimney Sweepers . . . Showing the Necessity of Putting Them under Regulations . . .* (1785).

81. Idem, *Essays on the Importance of the Rising Generation of the Laboring* [sic] *Part of Our Fellow-Subjects* (1767), p. 176.

82. H. Cunningham, *The Invention of Childhood* (2006); J. Humphries, *Childhood and Child Labour in the British Industrial Revolution* (Cambridge, 2010).

83. T.W. Laqueur, *Religion and Respectability: Sunday Schools and Working-Class Culture, 1780–1850* (New Haven, 1976); S. Orchard and H.Y. John (eds), *The Sunday School Movement: Studies in Growth and Decline of Sunday Schools* (Bletchley, 2007).

84. C.J. Holmes, *Ideology and State Intervention in Nineteenth-Century Britain: The Case of the Factory Acts, 1833–80* (Kingston, 2002); D. Greer and J.W. Nicolson, *The Factory Acts in Ireland, 1802–1914* (Dublin, 2003).

85. R.G. Cowherd and A.H. Cole, *The Humanitarians and the Ten-Hour Movement in England* (Boston, 1958).

86. J. Habermas, *The Structural Transformation of the Public Sphere: An Inquiry into a Category of Bourgeois Society*, trans. T. Burger (Cambridge, 1989), p. 40; M. McKeon, *The Secret History of Domesticity: Public, Private and the Division of Knowledge* (Baltimore, 2005).

87. J.A. Downie, 'The Myth of the Bourgeois Public Sphere', in C. Wall (ed.), *A Concise Companion to the Restoration and Eighteenth Century* (Oxford, 2004), pp. 58–79; A. Vickery, 'An Englishman's Home Is His Castle? Thresholds, Boundaries and Privacies in the Eighteenth-Century London House', *Past & Present* 199 (2008), pp. 147–73.

88. R.B. Shoemaker, *Gender in English Society, 1650–1850: The Emergence of Separate Spheres?* (1998).

89. C. Taylor, *The Design, Production and Reception of Eighteenth-Century Wallpaper in Britain* (2018).

90. C. Casey, *Making Magnificence: Architects, Stuccatori and the Eighteenth-Century Interior* (New Haven, 2017).

91. C. Ehrlich, *Social Emulation and Industrial Progress: The Victorian Piano* (Belfast, 1975).

Chapter 6: Exploring Sexualities

1. T. Hitchcock, *English Sexualities, 1700–1800* (Basingtoke, 1997); J. Peakman, *Lascivious Bodies: A Sexual History of the Eighteenth Century* (2004); W. Gibson and J. Begiato, *Sex and the Church in the Long Eighteenth Century* (2017).

2. R.B. Outhwaite, *The Rise and Fall of the English Ecclesiastical Courts, 1500–1860* (Cambridge, 2006); B. Till, *The Church Courts: The Revival of Procedure, 1660–1720* (York, 2006); Gibson and Begiato, *Sex and the Church*, pp. 85–107.
3. F. Dabhoiwala, *The Origins of Sex: The First Sexual Revolution* (2012).
4. G. Frankl, *The Failure of the Sexual Revolution* (2003); A. Marwick, *The Sixties: Cultural Revolution in Britain, France, Italy and the United States, c. 1958–c. 1974* (2012).
5. G.R. Searle, *Morality and the Market in Victorian Britain* (Oxford, 1998).
6. Holloway, *Game of Love*.
7. Pottle (ed.), *Boswell's London Journal*, pp. 255–6.
8. P. Laslett, *The World We Have Lost* (1966), p. 89; E.A. Wrigley and R.S. Schofield, *Population History of England, 1541–1871: A Reconstruction* (Cambridge, 1981); E.A. Wrigley, 'The Growth of Population in Eighteenth-Century England: A Conundrum Resolved', *Past & Present* 98 (1983), pp. 121–50.
9. Wrigley and Schofield, *Population History of England*, p. 260: table 7.28.
10. H.R. Stiles, *Bundling: Its Origins, Progress and Decline in America* (Albany, 1869); A.R. Ekirch, *At Day's Close: Night in Tmes Past* (New York, 2005), pp. 197–202.
11. H. Abelove, 'Some Speculations on the History of Sexual Intercourse during the Long Eighteenth Century in England', *Genders* 6 (1989), pp. 15–20; T. Hitchcock, 'Redefining Sex in Eighteenth-Century England', *History Workshop Journal* 41 (1996), pp. 72–90.
12. W. Hazlitt, *Liber Amoris: Or, the New Pygmalion* (1823).
13. Holloway, *Game of Love*, pp. 141–65, esp. p. 147.
14. M. D'Ezio, *Hester Lynch Thrale Piozzi: A Taste for Eccentricity* (Newcastle upon Tyne, 2010).
15. B. Brophy, *New Statesman* (15 November 1963).
16. S. Holloway, '"You Know I Am All on Fire": Writing the Adulterous Affair in England, c. 1740–1830', *Historical Research* 89 (2016), pp. 317–39.
17. R.M. Wardle (ed.), *Godwin and Mary: Letters of William Godwin and Mary Wollstonecraft* (Lincoln, NA, 1966), p. 46, with thanks to Louise Falcini for this reference.
18. R. Perry cited in Naomi Clifford, 'The Bristol Elopement: Clementina Clerke and Richard Vining Perry', *Recovering Stories of Women in History: Stories from the Long 18th Century* (blog); online at http://www.naomiclifford.com/the-bristol-elopement (accessed 15 February 2021).
19. Goldsmith, *She Stoops to Conquer*.
20. D. Constantine, *Fields of Fire: A Life of Sir William Hamilton* (2001).
21. P. Woodland, 'Dashwood, Francis, eleventh Baron Le Despencer (1708–1781), politician and rake', *Oxford Dictionary of National Biography* (2009); online at https://www.oxforddnb.com/view/10.1093/ref:odnb/9780198614128.001.0001/odnb-9780198614128-e-7179 (accessed 15 February 2021).
22. Peakman, *Lascivious Bodies*, pp. 103–28; J.M. Kelly, 'Riots, Revelries and Rumour: Libertinism and Masculine Association in Enlightenment London', *Journal of British Studies* 45 (2006), pp. 759–95.
23. A.H. Cash, *John Wilkes: The Scandalous Father of Civil Liberty* (New Haven, 2006).
24. R. Porter and G.S. Rousseau (eds), *Sexual Underworlds of the Enlightenment* (Manchester, 1992).
25. D. Stevenson, *The Beggar's Benison: Sex Clubs of Enlightenment Scotland and Their Rituals* (East Linton, 2001).
26. K. Harvey, *Reading Sex in the Eighteenth Century: Bodies and Gender in English Erotic Culture* (Cambridge, 2004).
27. L. Hunt (ed.), *The Invention of Pornography: Obscenity and the Origins of Modernity, 1500–1800* (New York, 1993); J. Peakman, *Mighty Lewd Books: The Development of Pornography in Eighteenth-Century England* (Basingstoke, 2003).
28. I. Gibson, *The English Vice: Beating, Sex and Shame in Victorian England and After* (1978).

29. Anon., *A Treatise on the Use of Flogging . . .*, trans. J.H. Meibom (1718).
30. L. Stone, 'Libertine Sexuality in Post-Restoration England: Group Sex and Flagellation among the Middling Sort in Norwich in 1707/8', *Journal of the History of Sexuality* 2 (1992), pp. 511–26.
31. B.J. Hurwood, *The Golden Age of Erotica* (Los Angeles, 1965), p. 69.
32. D.D. Gray, *Prosecuting Homicide in Eighteenth-Century Law and Practice: 'And Must They All Be Hanged?'* (Abingdon, 2020), pp. 156–87.
33. N. Aston, 'Worsley, Sir Richard, seventh baronet (1751–1805), antiquary and politician', *Oxford Dictionary of National Biography* (2009); online at https://www.oxforddnb.com/view/10.1093/ref:odnb/9780198614128.001.0001/odnb-9780198614128-e-29986 (accessed 15 February 2021).
34. T. Henderson, *Disorderly Women in Eighteenth-Century London: Prostitution and Control in the Metropolis, 1730–1830* (1999).
35. B. de Mandeville, *A Modest Defence of the Public Stews: Or, an Essay on Whoring* (1724; 1740).
36. L. Linker, *Dangerous Women, Libertine Epicures and the Rise of Sensibility, 1670–1730* (2016).
37. B. White, *Queen of the Courtesans: Fanny Murray* (Stroud, 2014).
38. F. Wilson, *The Courtesan's Revenge: The Life of Harriette Wilson, the Woman who Blackmailed the King* (2003).
39. A.F. Randall [Mary Robinson], *A Letter to the Women of England on the Injustice of Mental Subordination* (1799), p. 3; P. Byrne, *Perdita: The Literary, Theatrical and Scandalous Life of Mary Robinson* (New York, 2004).
40. A. Greenfield (ed.), *Interpreting Sexual Violence, 1660–1800* (2014); Foyster, *Marital Violence*.
41. R. Norton, 'Homosexual Terms in Eighteenth-Century Dictionaries', *Homosexuality in Eighteenth-Century England: A Sourcebook* (website, 2008; updated 2013); online at http://www.rictornorton.co.uk/eighteen/diction.htm (accessed 15 February 2021).
42. R. Trumbach, *Sex and the Gender Revolution, Vol. 1: Heterosexuality and the Third Gender in Enlightenment London* (Chicago, 1998); idem, 'Male Prostitution and the Emergence of the Modern Sexual System: Eighteenth-Century London', in A. Lewis and M. Ellis (eds), *Prostitution and Eighteenth-Century Culture: Sex, Commerce and Morality* (2014), pp. 185–202; Carter, *Men and the Emergence of Polite Society*; M. Cook (ed.), with H.G. Cocks, R. Mills and R. Trumbach, *A Gay History of Britain: Love and Sex between Men since the Middle Ages* (Oxford, 2007).
43. C. Upchurch, *Before Wilde: Sex between Men in Britain's Age of Reform* (Berkeley, 2009).
44. Gibson and Begiato, *Sex and the Church*, pp. 195ff; J. Weeks, *Sex, Politics and Society: The Regulation of Sexuality since 1800* (2017).
45. R. Norton, *Mother Clap's Molly House: The Gay Sub-Culture in England, 1700–1830* (1992); A. Clark, *Desire: A History of European Sexuality* (New York, 2008).
46. L. Moore, *Amphibious Thing: The Life of Lord Hervey* (2000); idem, 'Gay Love Letters of John, Lord Hervey to Stephen Fox', in R. Norton (ed.), *My Dear Boy: Gay Love Letters through the Centuries* (San Francisco, 1998), pp. 1727–31.
47. A. Pope, 'Epistle from Mr Pope to Dr Arbuthnot' (1735), in J. Butt (ed.), *Poems of Alexander Pope* (1975), p. 608.
48. Anon., *A Treatise, wherein are Strict Observations upon that Detestable and Most Shocking Sin of Sodomy, Blasphemy and Atheism* (1728); C. McFarlane, *The Sodomite in Fiction and Satire, 1660–1750* (New York, 1997).
49. Anon. [Churchill], *The Times* (1764), p. 19.
50. T. Cannon, *Ancient and Modern Pederasty Investigated . . .* (1749), in H. Gladfelder, 'In Search of Lost Texts: Thomas Cannon's *Ancient and Modern Pederasty Investigated and Exemplifi'd*', *Eighteenth-Century Life* 21 (2007), pp. 22–38; D.M. Robinson, *Closeted Writing and Lesbian and Gay Literature: Classical, Early Modern, Eighteenth-Century* (Aldershot, 2006).

51. J. Bentham, *Offences against One's Self* (1785), ed. L. Crompton, *Journal of Homosexuality* 3 (1978), pp. 389–405; Gibson and Begiato, *Sex and the Church*, pp. 201–3.

52. R. Norton, 'The First Public Debate about Homosexuality in England: The Case of Captain Jones, 1772', in idem, *The Gay Subculture in Georgian England* (19 December 2004; updated 10 May 2014); online at http://rictornorton.co.uk/eighteen/jones1.htm (accessed 25 March 2021).

53. A. Simpson, 'Blackmail as a Crime of Sexual Indiscretion in Eighteenth-Century England', in L.A. Knafla (ed.), *Crime, Gender and Sexuality in Criminal Prosecutions* (Westport, CN, 2002), p. 74; J. Bew, *Castlereagh: A Life* (Oxford, 2012).

54. N.M. Goldsmith, *The Worst of Crimes: Homosexuality and the Law in Eighteenth-Century London* (Aldershot, 1998); B. Lacey, *Terrible Queer Creatures: Homosexuality in Irish History* (Dublin, 2008).

55. E. Donoghue, *Passions between Women: English Lesbian Culture, 1668–1801* (1993); R. Jennings, *A Lesbian History of Britain: Love and Sex between Women since 1500* (Oxford, 2007); M. McAuliffe and S. Tiernan (eds), *Tribades, Tommies and Transgression* (Newcastle upon Tyne, 2009); J.C. Beynon and C. Gonda (eds), *Lesbian Dames: Sapphism in the Long Eighteenth Century* (Farnham, 2010).

56. S. Toulalan, 'Extraordinary Satisfactions: Lesbian Visibility in Seventeenth-Century Pornography in England', *Gender and History* 15 (2003), pp. 50–68.

57. W. King, *The Toast* (1732); J. Medd (ed.), *The Cambridge Companion to Lesbian Literature* (Cambridge, 2015).

58. R.M. Dekker and L.C. van de Pol, *The Tradition of Female Transvestism in Early Modern Europe* (Basingstoke, 1989); H. Bauer (ed.), *Women and Cross-Dressing, 1800–1939* (2006).

59. Anon. [H. Fielding], *The Female Husband: Or, the Surprising History of Mrs Mary, Alias Mr George Hamilton . . .* (1746).

60. R. Norton, 'Lesbian Marriages in Eighteenth-Century England', *Homosexuality in Eighteenth-Century England: A Sourcebook* (website, 2009; updated 2010); online at http://rictornorton.co.uk/eighteen/lesbmarr.htm (accessed 15 February 2021).

61. 'Dublin's First Recorded Transgender Person?', *Irish History Podcast* (2018); online at https://irishhistorypodcast.ie/dublins-first-recorded-transperson (accessed 15 February 2021).

62. McKeon, *Secret History of Domesticity*, p. 564. *The Favourite* (2018), dir. Yorgos Lanthimos, provided a black-comedy film interpretation of these amatory intrigues: see above, p. 112.

63. R. Norton (ed.), 'A Sapphick Epistle, 1778', *Homosexuality in Eighteenth-Century England: A Sourcebook* (website, 1999; updated 2003); online at http://rictornorton. co.uk/eighteen/sapphick.htm (accessed 15 February 2021).

64. M. Vicinus, *Intimate Friends: Women who Loved Women, 1778–1928* (Chicago, 2004), p. 45; A. Steidele, *Gentleman Jack: The Biography of Anne Lister . . .*, trans. K. Derbyshire (2018).

65. E. Mavor, *The Ladies of Llangollen: A Study in Romantic Friendship* (1971); L. Moore, '"Something More Tender Still than Friendship": Romantic Friendship in Early Nineteenth-Century England', *Feminist Studies* 18 (1992), pp. 499–520.

66. M. Vacherie, *An Account of the Famous Hermaphrodite: Or Parisian Boy-Girl . . .* (1750).

67. M. de Decker, *Madame le chevalier d'Éon* (Paris, 1987); G. Kates, *Monsieur d'Éon Is a Woman: A Tale of Political Intrigue and Sexual Masquerade* (Baltimore, 1995).

68. C. Mounsey (ed.), *Presenting Gender: Changing Sex in Early Modern Culture* (2001).

69. L. Syson, *Doctor of Love: Dr James Graham and His Celestial Bed* (Richmond, 2008).

70. Anon., *Onanism: Or, A Treatise on the Disorders Produced by Masturbation* (1766); T.W. Laqueur, *Solitary Sex: A Cultural History of Masturbation* (New York, 2003); Gibson and Begiato, *Sex and the Church*, pp. 34–9.

71. R.S. Morton, 'Dr William Wallace, 1791–1837, of Dublin', *Medical History* 10 (1966), pp. 38–43; K.P. Siena, *Venereal Disease, Hospitals and the Urban Poor: London's 'Foul Wards', 1600–1800* (Rochester, NY, 2004); N. Gallagher, *Itch, Clap, Pox: Venereal Disease in the Eighteenth-Century Imagination* (2018).
72. E. Chevallier, *The Condom: Three Thousand Years of Safer Sex*, trans. P. White (1995).
73. Pottle (ed.), *Boswell's London Journal*, p. 227.
74. J.M. Riddle, *Eve's Herbs: A History of Contraception and Abortion in the West* (Cambridge, MA, 1999); H. Cook, *The Long Sexual Revolution: Women, Sex and Contraception, 1800–1950* (Oxford, 2004).
75. L.F. Cody, *Birthing the Nation: Sex, Science and the Conception of Eighteenth-Century Britons* (Oxford, 2005).
76. A. Macfarlane, 'Illegitimacy and Illegitimates in English History', in Laslett, Osterveen and Smith (eds), *Bastardy*, pp. 76–8; L. Rose, *Massacre of the Innocents: Infanticide in Great Britain, 1800–1959* (1986).

Chapter 7: Gaining Literacy and Numeracy

1. D. Cressy, *Literacy and the Social Order: Reading and Writing in Tudor and Stuart England* (Cambridge, 1980), esp. pp. 186–9; D. Allan, *Commonplace Books and Reading in Georgian England* (Cambridge, 2010).
2. M. Goldie and G. Kemp (eds), *Censorship and the Press, 1580–1720, Vol. 4: 1696–1720* (Abingdon, 2009).
3. A. Fox and D. Woolf (eds), *The Spoken Word: Oral Culture in Britain, 1500–1850* (Manchester, 2002).
4. D. Johnson, *Music and Society in Lowland Scotland in the Eighteenth Century* (1972); R. Ganev, *Songs of Protest, Songs of Love: Popular Ballads in Eighteenth-Century Britain* (Manchester, 2009); M.W. Dowling, *Traditional Music and Irish Society: Historical Perspectives* (Burlington, VT, 2014).
5. L.A.M. Butterworth, *Robert Burns and the Eighteenth-Century Revival in Scottish Vernacular Poetry* (Aberdeen, 1969); D.S. Thomson (ed.), *Gaelic Poetry in the Eighteenth Century: A Bilingual Anthology* (Aberdeen, 1993); D. Fairer, *English Poetry of the Eighteenth Century, 1700–89* (Harlow, 2002); C. MacLachlan (ed.), *Before Burns: Eighteenth-Century Scottish Poetry* (Edinburgh, 2010); J. Henigan, *Literacy and Orality in Eighteenth-Century Irish Song* (2015).
6. I. Watt, *The Rise of the Novel* (1957); J.P. Hunter, *Before Novels: The Cultural Contexts of Eighteenth-Century English Fiction* (1990); R. Maioli, *Empiricism and the Early Theory of the Novel: Fielding to Austen* (2017); H.R. Steeves, *Before Jane Austen: The Shaping of the English Novel in the Eighteenth Century* (2020).
7. D. Cook and N. Seager (eds), *The Afterlives of Eighteenth-Century Fiction* (Cambridge, 2015).
8. J.C. Rather and W. Goldwater, *According to Hoyle, 1742–1850: A Bibliography . . .* (New York, 1983).
9. P. Downey, *Edward Bunting and the Ancient Irish Music . . .* (2017).
10. Pope, 'An Essay on Criticism' (1711), in Butt (ed.), *Poems of Alexander Pope*, p. 151.
11. L. Stone, 'Literacy and Education in England, 1640–1900', *Past & Present* 42 (1969), pp. 69–139; R.A. Houston, *Scottish Literacy and the Scottish Identity* (Cambridge, 1985).
12. M.O. Grenby, *The Child Reader, 1700–1840* (Cambridge, 2011), pp. 4–6, 70–85, 91–2, 284–9.
13. J.W. Hullim, 'Barbauld's Lessons: The Conversational Primer in Late Eighteenth-Century British Children's Literature', *Journal for Eighteenth-Century Studies* 43 (2020), pp. 101–20; D. Wakefield, *Anna Laetitia Barbauld* (2001).
14. Corfield, *Power and the Professions*, p. 78.
15. Sheridan, *The Rivals*, pp. 24, 26 (act 1, sc. 2).

16. A. Stott, *Hannah More: The First Victorian* (Oxford, 2004), pp. 103–25.
17. Stone, 'Literacy and Education', pp. 114–15.
18. P.M. Heath (ed.), *The Works of Mrs Trimmer, 1741–1810* (Saarbrücken, 2010).
19. Stone, 'Literacy and Education', pp. 93, 104–5.
20. Ibid., p. 119; R.S. Schofield, 'Dimensions of Illiteracy in England, 1750–1850', in H.J. Graff (ed.), *Literacy and Social Development in the West* (Cambridge, 1971), pp. 201–13.
21. Idem, *The Literacy Myth: Literacy and Social Structure in the Nineteenth-Century City* (New York, 1969).
22. Stone, 'Literacy and Education', pp. 121, 123, 126–7,135; contrasted with Houston, *Scottish Literacy*, pp. 70–83, 211, 257–8, 264.
23. Ibid., p. 80.
24. N.Ó. Ciosáin, *Print and Popular Culture in Ireland, 1750–1850* (Basingstoke, 1997), pp. 154ff.
25. W.K. Webb, 'Working Class Readers in Early Victorian London', *English Historical Review* 65 (1950), pp. 333–51; J. Rose, *The Intellectual Life of the British Working Classes* (New Haven, 2001).
26. S. Cowan, 'The Growth of Public Literacy in Eighteenth-Century England' (PhD thesis, Institute of Education, London University, 2012), pp. 169–77.
27. S. Whyman, *The Useful Knowledge of William Hutton: Culture and Industry in Eighteenth-Century Birmingham* (Oxford, 2018).
28. M.G. Jones, *The Charity School Movement: A Study of Eighteenth-Century Puritanism in Action* (Cambridge, 1938; 1964); W.B. Stephens, *Education in Britain, 1750–1914* (Basingstoke, 1998).
29. Laqueur, *Religion and Respectability*.
30. H. McLachlan, *English Education under the Test Acts: Being the History of the Nonconformist Academies, 1662–1820* (Manchester, 1931); J.W.A. Smith, *The Birth of Modern Education: The Contribution of the Dissenting Academies, 1660–1800* (1954); B.W. Kirk, *The Taunton Dissenting Academy* (Taunton, 2005).
31. F.M.L. Thompson, *Gentrification and the Enterprise Culture: Britain, 1780–1980* (Oxford, 2001), pp. 123–4, 126, 131.
32. S.M.S. Pearsall, *Atlantic Families: Lives and Letters in the Later Eighteenth Century* (Oxford, 2008); L. O'Neill, *The Opened Letter: Networking in the Early Modern British World* (Philadelphia, 2015).
33. S. Whyman, *The Pen and the People: English Letter-Writers, 1660–1800* (Oxford, 2009).
34. A. D'Ancourt, *The Lady's Preceptor: Or, A Letter to a Lady of Distinction upon Politeness* (1743), p. 59; L. Hannan, 'The Imperfect Letter-Writer: Escaping the Advice Manuals', in P.J. Corfield and L. Hannan (eds), *Hats Off, Gentlemen! Changing Arts of Communication in the Eighteenth Century/Arts de communiquer au XVIIIe siècle* (Paris, 2017), pp. 53–72; esp. pp. 57–9.
35. E.G. Ravenstein, 'On the Celtic Languages of the British Isles: A Statistical Survey', *Journal of the Statistical Society of London* 42 (1879), pp. 579–643; C.W.J. Withers, *Gaelic in Scotland, 1698–1981: The Geographical History of a Language* (Edinburgh, 1984).
36. Anon., *An Account of the Character and Manners of the French . . .*, 2 vols (1770), vol. 2, p. 113.
37. Tucker, *Protean Shape*; D. DeWispelare, *Multilingual Subjects: On Standard English, Its Speakers and Others in the Long Eighteenth Century* (Philadelphia, 2017).
38. *Tatler* (1709–11) 147 (March 1709): commonly attributed to Steele, though some editions also name Joseph Addison.
39. A. Williams, *The Social Life of Books: Reading Together in the Eighteenth-Century Home* (New Haven, 2017); M. Towsey and K.B. Roberts (eds), *Before the Public Library: Reading, Community and Identity in the Atlantic World, 1650–1850* (Leiden, 2017).
40. C. Lupton, *Reading and the Making of Time in the Eighteenth Century* (Baltimore, 2018).

41. S. Johnson, 'Apothegms, Sentiments, Opinions, Etc.', in J. Hawkins, *The Works of Samuel Johnson LLD* . . ., 11 vols (1787), vol. 11, p. 197.
42. L. Hannan, 'Women, Letter Writing and the Life of the Mind in England, *c.* 1650–1750' (PhD thesis, London University, 2009), pp. 177–9; A.J. La Vopa, *The Labour of the Mind: Intellect and Gender in Enlightenment Cultures* (Philadelphia, 2017).
43. U. Heyd, *Reading Newspapers: Press and Public in Eighteenth-Century Britain and America* (Oxford, 2012).
44. M. Purcell, 'The Private Library in Seventeenth- and Eighteenth-Century Surrey', *Journal of Library History* 19 (2003), pp. 119–27; idem, *The Country House Library* (2017).
45. J. Raven, *Lost Libraries: The Destruction of Great Book Collections since Antiquity* (Basingstoke, 2004); Towsey and Roberts (eds), *Before the Public Library*.
46. University histories provide details, while there is scope for a good comparative study of all these monumental Georgian libraries.
47. D. Allan, *A Nation of Readers: The Lending Library in Georgian England* (2008).
48. J. Crawford, 'The Community Library in Scottish History', IFLA [International Federation of Library Associations] Conference (2002); online at file:///C:/Users/PROFCO~1/AppData/Local/Temp/063-111e-1.pdf, p. 7 (accessed 8 March 2020).
49. A.M. Fazle Kabir, 'English Libraries in Eighteenth-Century Bengal', *Journal of Library History* 14 (1979), pp. 436–56.
50. T.F. Dibdin, *Bibliomania: Or, Book Madness* (1809).
51. R. Myers and M. Harris (eds), *Spreading the Word: The Distribution of Networks of Print, 1550–1850* (Detroit, 1990); J. Raven, *The Business of Books: Booksellers and the English Book Trade, 1450–1850* (New Haven, 2007); J.-P.A. Ghobrial, *The Whispers of Cities: Information Flows in Istanbul, London and Paris in the Age of William Trumbull* (Oxford, 2013).
52. J. Raven, *Publishing Business in Eighteenth-Century England* (Woodbridge, 2014).
53. O. Field, *The Kit-Cat Club: Friends who Imagined a Nation* (2008).
54. R. Garnett, 'Murray, John (1778–1843)', *Oxford Dictionary of National Biography* (1894); online at https://www.oxforddnb.com/view/10.1093/odnb/9780192683120.001.0001/odnb-9780192683120-e-19634 (accessed 15 February 2021); see also W. Zachs, P. Isaac, A. Fraser and W. Lister, 'Murray family (per. 1768–1967), publishers', *Oxford Dictionary of National Biography* (2016); online at https://www.oxforddnb.com/view/10.1093/ref:odnb/9780198614128.001.0001/odnb-9780198614128-e-64907 (accessed 15 February 2021).
55. C. Smylitopoulos, 'Expanding the View: The Cultural and Artistic Impact of Thomas Tegg's Graphic Satire', in Corfield and Hannan (eds), *Hats Off, Gentlemen!*, pp. 273–92.
56. P. Hopkins (ed.), *The Life of James Lackington, Bookseller, 1746–1815* (Morden, 2004).
57. F. Lambert, *Pedlar in Divinity: George Whitefield and the Transatlantic Revivals, 1737–70* (Princeton, 1994), p. 85.
58. C.L. Carlson, *The First Magazine: A History of the Gentleman's Magazine* (Providence, RI, 1938); G. Williamson, *British Masculinity in the Gentleman's Magazine, 1731 to 1815* (2015).
59. R. Watson, *The Literature of Scotland, Vol. 1: The Middle Ages to the Nineteenth Century* (Basingstoke, 2006), p. 253.
60. J. Mullan, *Anonymity: A Secret History of English Literature* (2007).
61. D. Looser, *The Making of Jane Austen* (Baltimore, 2017).
62. K. Thomas, 'Numeracy in Early Modern England', *Transactions of the Royal Historical Society* 37 (1987), pp. 103–32; P.C. Cohen, *A Calculating People: The Spread of Numeracy in Early America* (Chicago, 1982), esp. pp. 15–46.
63. R. Poole, '"Give Us our Eleven Days!" Calendar Reform in Eighteenth-Century England', *Past & Present* 149 (1995), pp. 95–139; idem, *Time's Alteration: Calendar Reform in Early Modern England* (1998), pp. 1–18, 159–78.

64. J. Saward, 'The Chaldon Labyrinths', *Labyrinthos: Labyrinth and Maze Resource Photo Library and Archive* (website, 2017); online at https://www.labyrinthos.net/The%20 Chaldon%20Labyrinths.pdf (accessed 15 February 2021).
65. B. Wardhaugh, *Poor Robin's Prophecies: A Curious Almanac and the Everyday Mathematics of Georgian Britain* (Oxford, 2012), pp. 63ff.
66. Scottish Record Office GD18/695, fol. 81; GD18/1017, as cited in Houston, *Scottish Literacy*, p. 195.
67. J. Ward, *Young Mathematician's Guide: Being a Plain and Easie Introduction to the Mathematicks* (1707); B. Wardhaugh, 'Consuming Mathematics: John Ward's *Young Mathematician's Guide* (1707) and Its Owners', *Journal for Eighteenth-Century Studies* 38 (2015), pp. 65–82.
68. E. Cocker, *Cocker's Arithmetic* (1677); idem, *Cocker's Arithmetic, Revised and Corrected by John Mair* (Edinburgh, 1751).
69. B. Wardhaugh, 'Learning Arithmetic in Georgian England', *Plus* (online magazine, 2013); online at https://plus.maths.org/content/learning-arithmetic-georgian-england (accessed 15 February 2021).
70. Clark, *British Clubs and Societies*.
71. Anon., *The Caledonian Conjuror, Mr Arbuckle . . .* (Nottingham, 1808).
72. N. Guicciardini, 'Hutton, Charles (1737–1823), mathematician lieutenant in the Royal Artillery', *Oxford Dictionary of National Biography* (2004); online at https://www.oxforddnb. com/view/10.1093/ref:odnb/9780198614128.001.0001/odnb-9780198614128-e-14300 (accessed 15 February 2021).
73. S. Costa, 'The Ladies Diary: Gender, Mathematics, and Civil Society in Early Eighteenth-Century England', *Osiris*, 2nd ser. 17 (2002), pp. 49–73.
74. M. Ogilvie, 'Bryan, Margaret (*fl.* 1795–1816), educator and writer on natural philosophy', *Oxford Dictionary of National Biography* (2004); online at https://www.oxforddnb. com/view/10.1093/ref:odnb/9780198614128.001.0001/odnb-9780198614128-e-3791 (accessed 15 February 2021).
75. K.A. Neeley, *Mary Somerville: Science, Illumination and the Female Mind* (Cambridge, 2001).
76. B.A. Toole, *Ada, the Enchantress of Numbers: Prophet of the Computer Age* (Mill Valley, rev. edn 1998), pp. 234–5; B. Woolley, *The Bride of Science: Romance, Reason and Byron's Daughter* (2015); C.D. Hollings, U. Martin and A.C. Rice, *Ada Lovelace: The Making of a Computer Scientist* (Oxford, 2017).
77. A.R. Hall, *Philosophers at War: The Quarrel between Newton and Gottfried Leibniz* (Cambridge, 1980); R.C. Brown, *Tangled Origins of the Leibnitzian Calculus: A Case Study of Mathematical Revolution* (2012).
78. H.J. Graff, *The Literacy Myth: Literacy and Social Structure in the Nineteenth-Century City* (New York, 1969); idem (ed.), *Literacy and Historical Development: A Reader* (Carbondale, IL, 2007); Houston, *Scottish Literacy*, pp. 218–20, 250–5.
79. S. Johnson, *The Rambler* 121 (14 May 1751).
80. T. Carlyle, *The Hero as Man of Letters* (1840).
81. T.L. Peacock, *Crotchet Castle* (1831), ed. D. Garnett (1948), p. 656.
82. G.N. Cantor, *Michael Faraday, Sandemanian and Scientist: A Study of Science and Religion in the Nineteenth Century* (Basingstoke, 1991).
83. 'P. Pry' [William Heath], *The March of Intellect* (1829).

Chapter 8: Redefining Religion and Irreligion

1. A.D. Gilbert, *The Making of Post-Christian Britain: A History of the Secularisation of Modern Society* (1980); C. Brown, *The Death of Christian Britain: Understanding Secularisation, 1800–2000* (2000); S. Bruce, *Secularisation: In Defence of an Unfashionable Theory* (Oxford, 2011); Corfield, '"An Age of Infidelity"'.

2. R. Stevens, *Protestant Pluralism: The Reception of the Toleration Act, 1689–1720* (Woodbridge, 2018); and for a variant view, more favourable to James II, see S. Sowerby, *Making Toleration: The Repealers and the Glorious Revolution* (Cambridge, MA, 2013).
3. D. Davie, *The Eighteenth-Century Hymn in England* (Cambridge, 1993); E.P. Hood, *Isaac Watts: His Life and Hymns* (Belfast, 2001).
4. Anon., *The Mother's Advice and Instruction to Her Children . . .* (c. 1739).
5. D. Norton, *The King James Bible: A Short History from Tyndale to Today* (Cambridge, 2010), pp. 162–73.
6. E.S. Cunha and L. Davies (eds), 'Writing Religion, 1660–1830', *Journal for Eighteenth-Century Studies* 41 (2018).
7. R. Warren, *The Daily Self-Examinant: Or, an Earnest Persuasive to the Duty of Daily Self-Examination . . .* (1720).
8. C. Hill, *'A Turbulent, Seditious and Factious People': John Bunyan and His Church, 1628–88* (Oxford, 1988); R.L. Greaves, *Glimpses of Glory: John Bunyan and English Dissent* (Stanford, 2002).
9. J. King, *William Cowper: A Biography* (Durham, NC, 1986).
10. D.B. Hindmarsh, *The Evangelical Conversion Narrative: Spiritual Autobiography in Early Modern England* (Oxford, 2005).
11. Farooq, *Preaching in Eighteenth-Century London*; J. van Eijnatten (ed.), *Preaching, Sermons and Cultural Change in the Long Eighteenth Century* (Leiden, 2009).
12. J. Swift, 'On Sleeping in Church' (1744), in idem, *The Works of the Rev. Jonathan Swift, DD . . .* (1801), p. 136.
13. J. Butler, *Fifteen Sermons Preached at the Rolls Chapel* (1726); A. Duncan-Jones, *Butler's Moral Philosophy* (Harmondsworth, 1952).
14. Anon. [C. Lloyd], *Particulars of the Life of a Dissenting Minister . . .* (1813; 1911), p. 175.
15. C. Parolin, *Radical Spaces: Venues of Popular Politics in London, 1790–c. 1845* (Acton, Australia, 2010).
16. C.M. Eckhardt, *Fanny Wright: Rebel in America* (Cambridge, MA, 1984); L. Schwartz, *Infidel Feminism: Secularism, Religion and Women's Emancipation, England, 1830–1914* (Manchester, 2013), pp. 45–6.
17. Corfield, *Power and the Professions*, pp. 28–36.
18. S. Slinn, *The Education of the Anglican Clergy, 1780–1939* (Martlesham, 2017); and for individuals, see the comprehensive Clergy of the Church of England Database (CCEd); online at http://www.theclergydatabase.org.uk (accessed 9 March 2021).
19. Corfield, *Power and the Professions*, pp. 52–6, 109–10, 131 n. 49.
20. G. Berkeley, *A Defence of Freethinking in Mathematics* (1735), p. 7.
21. R. Rouse and S.C. Neill, *A History of the Ecumenical Movement, 1517–1948* (Philadelphia, 1954).
22. P. Virgin, *The Church in an Age of Negligence: Ecclesiastical Structure and Problems of Church Reform, 1700–1840* (Cambridge, 1989); J. Walsh, S. Taylor and C. Haydon (eds), *The Church of England, c. 1689–1833: From Toleration to Tractarianism* (1993); N. Yates, *Eighteenth-Century Britain: Religion and Politics, 1713–1915* (Harlow, 2008).
23. K.R.M. Short, 'The English Indemnity Acts, 1726–1867', *Church History* 42 (1973), pp. 366–76.
24. J. Richardson, *Two Discourses* (1725; repr. Bristol, 1998), no. 2, p. 230.
25. Gibbon, *Autobiography*, p. 163.
26. Gibson and Begiato, *Sex and the Church*, pp. 109–34.
27. A. Burns, *The Diocesan Revival in the Church of England, c. 1800–70* (Oxford, 1999); J. Gregory, *Restoration, Reformation and Reform: The Archbishops of Canterbury and Their Diocese, 1660–1818* (Oxford, 2000).
28. T. Lathbury, *A History of the Non-Jurors* (1842).

29. W. Benbow, *The Crimes of the Clergy: Or, the Pillars of Priestcraft Shaken* (1823); Gibson and Begiato, *Sex and the Church*, pp. 228–30.
30. C. Hill, *The Economic Problems of the Church from Archbishop Whitgift to the Long Parliament* (Oxford, 1956); Corfield, *Power and the Professions*, pp. 109–10, 125–8.
31. R.P. Jones, *Nonconformist Church Architecture* (1914).
32. A.D. Gilbert, *Churches and Church-Goers: Patterns of Church Growth in the British Isles since 1700* (Oxford, 1977).
33. Corfield, *Power and the Professions*, pp. 117–18.
34. C. Hill, B. Reay and W.M. Lamont, *The World of the Muggletonians* (1983); W.M. Lamont, *Last Witnesses: The Muggletonian History, 1652–1979* (Aldershot, 2006).
35. J.H. Smith, *The Perfect Rule of the Christian Religion: A History of Sandemanianism in the Eighteenth Century* (Albany, 2008).
36. R. Lines, *A History of the Swedenborg Society, 1810–2010* (2012).
37. W. Blake, *The Garden of Love* (1794), verse 2; E.P. Thompson, *Witness against the Beast: William Blake and the Moral Law* (Cambridge, 1993).
38. J.M. Court, *Approaching the Apocalypse: A Short History of Christian Millenarianism* (2008).
39. F. Brown, *Joanna Southcott: The Woman Clothed with the Sun* (Cambridge, 2002).
40. C. Haydon, *Anti-Catholicism in Eighteenth-Century England: A Political and Social Study* (Manchester, 1994); G. Glickman, *The English Catholic Community, 1688–1745: Politics, Culture and Ideology* (Woodbridge, 2009).
41. Corfield, *Power and the Professions*, pp. 118–19, 122.
42. Catholic Qualification and Convert Rolls, 1701–1845 (Ireland); online at http://census. nationalarchives.ie/search/cq/home.jsp (accessed 15 February 2021).
43. T. Barnard, *The Abduction of a Limerick Heiress: Social and Political Relations in Mid-Eighteenth-Century Ireland* (Dublin, 1998).
44. J.D. Brewer with G.I. Higgins, *Anti-Catholicism in Northern Ireland, 1600–1998: The Mote and the Beam* (Basingstoke, 1998).
45. R.E. Burns, 'Parsons, Priests and the People: The Rise of Irish Anticlericalism, 1785–1789', *Church History* 31 (1962), pp. 151–63.
46. Corfield, *Power and the Professions*, pp. 119, 207, 226–7.
47. D. Keenan, *The Grail of Irish Emancipation, 1793–1829* (Philadelphia, 2002).
48. G.M. Ditchfield, *The Evangelical Revival* (1998); G. Atkins, *Converting Britannia: Evangelicals and British Public Life, 1770–1840* (Woodbridge, 2019).
49. 'W.H.' [W. Hole], *The Ornaments of Churches Considered* (1761); D. Aston, *Art and Religion in Eighteenth-Century Europe* (2009), pp. 68–72, 205–12, 252–4.
50. A.M. Lyles, *Methodism Mocked: The Satiric Reaction to Methodism in the Eighteenth Century* (1960); Gibson and Begiato, *Sex and the Church*, pp. 136–55.
51. E. Miller, *John Wesley: The Hero of the Second Reformation* (1906); R. Hattersley, *A Brand from the Burning: The Life of John Wesley* (2002).
52. E. Evans, *Daniel Rowland and the Great Evangelical Awakening in Wales* (1985); G. Tudur, *Howell Harris: From Conversion to Separation, 1735–50* (Cardiff, 2000); E. Evans, *Bread of Heaven: The Life and Work of William Williams Pantycelyn* (Bridgend, 2010); D.M. Valenze, *Prophetic Sons and Daughters: Female Preaching and Popular Religion in Industrial England* (Princeton, 1985).
53. D. Hempton, *Methodism: Empire of the Spirit* (New Haven, 2005).
54. F. Cook, *Selina, Countess of Huntingdon* (Edinburgh, 2001); G.W. Kirby, *The Elect Lady* (Reading, 2003).
55. J.S. Werner, *The Primitive Methodist Connexion: Its Background and Early History* (Madison, 1984); R.W. Ambler, *Ranters, Revivalists and Reformers: Primitive Methodism and Rural Society, South Lincolnshire, 1817–85* (Hull, 1989).
56. C.D. Field, 'Counting Religion in England and Wales: The Long Eighteenth Century, *c.* 1680–*c.* 1840', *Journal of Ecclesiastical History* 63 (2012), pp. 693–720; esp. p. 711.

57. R.G. Usher, *The Rise and Fall of the High Commission* (Oxford, 1913).

58. M. F. Graham, *The Blasphemies of Thomas Aikenhead: Boundaries of Belief on the Eve of the Enlightenment* (Edinburgh, 2013); and context in J. Marsh, *Word Crimes: Blasphemy, Culture and Literature in Nineteenth-Century England* (Chicago, 1998).

59. A.M. Matytsin, *The Specter of Skepticism in the Age of the Enlightenment* (Baltimore, 2016).

60. J. Locke, *A Second Vindication of the Reasonableness of Christianity* (1697), p. 36, in idem, *Vindications of the Reasonableness of Christianity*, ed. V. Nuovo (Oxford, 2012).

61. A. Campbell, *A Discourse Proving that the Apostles Were No Enthusiasts* (1730).

62. J. Wesley, *The Case of Reason Impartially Considered* (1781): sermon 71.

63. B.P. Copenhaver, *Magic in Western Culture: From Antiquity to the Enlightenment* (New York, 2015).

64. M. Gibson, 'Witchcraft in the Courts', in idem (ed.), *Witchcraft and Society in England and America, 1550–1750* (Ithaca, NY, 2003), pp. 1–9; J.C.D. Clark, *English Society, 1660–1832: Religion, Ideology and Political Practice during the Ancien Regime* (Cambridge, 1985), pp. 169–71.

65. P. Chambers, *The Cock Lane Ghost: Murder, Sex and Haunting in Dr Johnson's London* (Stroud, 2006); S. McCorristine, *Spectres of the Self: Thinking about Ghosts and Ghost-Seeing in England, 1750–1920* (Cambridge, 2010).

66. D.P. Walker, *The Decline of Hell: Seventeenth-Century Discussions of Eternal Torment* (1964); G. Rowell, *Hell and the Victorians: A Study of Nineteenth-Century Theological Controversies Concerning Eternal Punishment . . .* (Oxford, 1974).

67. Combe, *Diaboliad*, p. 1.

68. Redwood, *Reason, Ridicule and Religion*; S. Charles and P.J. Smith (eds), *Scepticism in the Eighteenth Century: Enlightenment, Lumières, Aufklärung* (2013).

69. R. Iliffe, *Priest of Nature: The Religious Worlds of Isaac Newton* (Oxford, 2017).

70. Voltaire, *Dictionnaire philosophique* (Geneva, 1764), in idem, *Oeuvres completes*, 92 vols (Paris, 1785), vol. 55, p. 96; T.C. Pfizenmaier, *The Trinitarian Theology of Dr Samuel Clarke, 1675–1729: Context, Sources and Theology* (Leiden, 1997).

71. P. Byrne, *Natural Religion and the Nature of Religion: The Legacy of Deism* (1989); J.R. Wigelsworth, *Deism in Enlightenment England: Theology, Politics and Newtonian Public Science* (Manchester, 2009).

72. J. Toland, *Christianity Not Mysterious: A Treatise Showing that There is Nothing in the Gospels Contrary to Reason, nor above It . . .* (1696), p. 6; R.R. Evans, *Pantheisticon: The Career of John Toland* (New York, 1991); J.A.I. Champion, '"Manuscripts of Mine Abroad": John Toland and the Circulation of Ideas, c. 1700–22', *Eighteenth-Century Ireland: Iris an dá chultúr* 14 (1999), pp. 9–36.

73. J. Agnesina, *The Philosophy of Anthony Collins: Free-Thought and Atheism* (Paris, 2018).

74. S. Lalor, *Matthew Tindall, Freethinker: An Eighteenth-Century Assault on Religion* (2006).

75. R.E. Schofield, *The Enlightened Joseph Priestley: A Study of his Life and Work from 1773 to 1804* (Philadelphia, 2004).

76. J. Taylor and E. Taylor, *History of the Octagon Chapel, Norwich* (1848).

77. M. Hunter and D. Wootton (eds), *Atheism from the Reformation to the Enlightenment* (Oxford, 1992).

78. W. Hammon, *Answer to Dr Priestley's Letters to a Philosophical Unbeliever* (1782).

79. T. Holden, *Spectres of False Divinity: David Hume's Moral Atheism* (Oxford, 2010); T.S. Yoder, *Hume on God: Irony, Deism and Genuine Theism* (2011); D.W. Purdie and P.S. Fosl (eds), *David Hume on God: Selected Works, Newly Adapted for the Modern Reader* (Edinburgh, 2019).

80. P.B. Shelley, *The Necessity of Atheism* (1811; 1813), pp. 4, 5; H. Williams, *Shelley at Oxford* (Oxford, 2012).

81. E. Royle, *Robert Owen and the Commencement of the Millennium: A Study of the Harmony Community* (Manchester, 1998); I. Donnachie, *Robert Owen: Social Visionary* (Edinburgh, 2005).

82. M.L. Bush, *The Friends and Following of Richard Carlile: A Study of Infidel Republicanism in Early Nineteenth-Century Britain* (2016).

83. Beresford (ed.), *Diary of a Country Parson*, vol. 1, p. 212 (October 1777); Corfield, *Power and the Professions*, pp. 112–13.

84. K.D.M. Snell and P.S. Ell, *Rival Jerusalems: The Geography of Victorian Religion* (Cambridge, 2000); A. Crockett, 'Variations in Churchgoing Rates in England in 1851: Supply-Side Deficiency or Demand-Led Decline?', *University of Oxford Discussion Papers in Economic and Social History* 36 (2000).

85. Voltaire, *Letters Concerning the English Nation* (English trans., 1733), p. 45.

Chapter 9: Negotiating Political Power 'Indoors'

1. S. Pincus, *1688: The First Modern Revolution* (New Jersey, 2009); R. Kay, *The Glorious Revolution and the Continuity of Law* (Washington, 2014),

2. B. Worden, *Roundhead Reputations: The English Civil War and the Passions of Posterity* (2001).

3. A. Pope, 'An Essay on Man' (1733–34), epistle 3, in Butt (ed.), *Poems of Alexander Pope*, p. 534.

4. W. Paley, *Principles of Moral and Political Philosophy* (1785), book 6, ch. 7.

5. Clark, *English Society*.

6. Anon., *A Guide to the Knowledge of the Rights and Privileges of Englishmen . . .* (1757; 1771); J. Cairns and G. MacLeod (eds), *The Dearest Birthright of the People of England: The Jury in the History of the Common Law* (Oxford, 2002).

7. D.J. Sturdy, 'The Royal Touch in England', in H. Duchhardt, R.A. Jackson and D.J. Sturdy (eds), *European Monarchy: Its Evolution and Practice from Roman Antiquity to Modern Times* (Stuttgart, 1992), pp. 171–84.

8. J. Oates, *Sweet William or the Butcher? The Duke of Cumberland and the '45* (Barnsley, 2008).

9. A.H. Byrne, *The Noble Duke of York: The Military Life of Frederick Duke of York and Albany* (1949); J. Black, *Britain as a Military Power, 1688–1815* (1999), p. 195.

10. B. Fothergill, *The Cardinal King* (1958; 2010); J. MacLeod, *Dynasty: The Stuarts, 1560–1807* (1999).

11. R. Hatton, *George I: Elector and King* (1978; 2001); J. Black, *George III: America's Last King* (New Haven, 2006); A.C. Thompson, *George II: King and Elector* (2011).

12. H. Smith, *Georgian Monarchy: Politics and Culture, 1714–60* (Cambridge, 2006).

13. J. Prebble, *The King's Jaunt: George IV in Scotland, August 1822* (1988).

14. F. Fraser, *Princesses: The Six Daughters of George III* (2004).

15. E.A. Smith, *Queen on Trial* (Stroud, 1993); M. Morris, *Sex, Money and Personal Character in Eighteenth-Century British Politics* (2014); S. Tillyard, *George IV: King in Waiting* (2018).

16. I. Kramnick *Republicanism and Bourgeois Radicalism: Political Ideology in Late Eighteenth-Century England and America* (Ithaca, NY, 1990); A. Taylor, *'Down with the Crown': British Anti-Monarchism and Debates about Royalty since 1790* (1999).

17. F.K. Prochaska, *Royal Bounty: The Making of a Welfare Monarchy* (1985).

18. K.W. Schweizer (ed.), *Lord Bute: Essays in Reinterpretation* (Leicester, 1988).

19. J.H. Plumb, *Sir Robert Walpole, Vol. 1: The Making of a Statesman* (1956); idem, *Sir Robert Walpole, Vol. 2: The King's Minister* (1960); H.T. Dickinson, *Walpole and the Whig Supremacy* (1973); B.W. Hill, *Sir Robert Walpole: 'Sole and Prime Minister'* (1989); W.A. Hay, *Lord Liverpool: A Political Life* (Woodbridge, 2018); P. Whiteley, *Lord North: The Prime Minister who Lost America* (2007).

20. A. Seldon, *10 Downing Street: The Illustrated History* (1999).
21. The Earl of Bute (prime minister 1762–63); George Grenville (prime minister 1763–65); the Marquess of Rockingham (prime minister 1765–66); William Pitt the Elder (prime minister 1766–68); the Duke of Grafton (prime minister 1768–70).
22. L.B. Namier, *The Structure of Politics at the Accession of George III*, 2 vols (1929), vol. 1, pp. 1–191; D. Hayton, *Conservative Revolutionary: The Lives of Lewis Namier* (2019).
23. H. Butterfield, *George III and the Historians* (1957), pp. 10–11, 200–15, 293, 297–9.
24. B. Simms, *Three Victories and a Defeat: The Rise and Fall of the First British Empire, 1714–83* (2007).
25. C. Ware, *Admiral Byng: His Rise and Execution* (Barnsley, 2009).
26. R. Furneaux, *Saratoga: The Decisive Battle* (1971).
27. R. Harvey, *Clive: The Life and Death of a British Emperor* (1998).
28. R.E. Foster, *Wellington and Waterloo: The Duke, the Battle and Posterity* (Stroud, 2014).
29. M. MacDonald, *The Clans of Scotland: The History and Landscape of the Scottish Clans* (1995).
30. M. Fry, *The Dundas Despotism* (Edinburgh, 1992).
31. J. Kelly, *Henry Grattan* (Dundalk, 1993); E.M. Johnston-Liik, *A History of the Irish Parliament, 1692–1800* (Belfast, 2002); J. Hoppit (ed.), *Parliaments, Nations and Identities in Britain and Ireland, 1660–1850* (Manchester, 2003).
32. P.M. Geoghegan, *The Irish Act of Union: A Study in High Politics, 1798–1801* (Dublin, 1999); M. Brown, P.M. Geoghegan and J. Kelly (eds), *The Irish Act of Union, 1800: Bicentennial Essays* (Dublin, 2003).
33. R.A. Kelch, *Newcastle, a Duke without Money: Thomas Pelham-Holles, 1693–1768* (1974).
34. N. Sykes, *Edmund Gibson, Bishop of London, 1669–1748* (1926).
35. J. Ehrman, *The Younger Pitt, Vol. 1: The Years of Acclaim* (1969); idem, *The Younger Pitt, Vol. 2: The Reluctant Transition* (1983); M. Duffy, *The Younger Pitt* (2000; 2016).
36. Ducal first lords of the Treasury were: the 1st duke of Newcastle (1754–56); the 4th duke of Devonshire (1756–57); the 3rd duke of Grafton (1768–70); the 3rd duke of Portland (1783; 1807–9); the 1st duke of Wellington (1828–30).
37. S.M. Lee, *George Canning and Liberal Toryism, 1801–27* (Woodbridge, 2008).
38. Bew, *Castlereagh*.
39. J. Lowe, *The Concert of Europe: International Relations, 1814–70* (1990); J.-A. de Sédouy, *Le concert européen: Aux origines de l'Europe, 1814–1914* (Paris, 2009).
40. W. Mulligan and B. Simms (eds), *The Primacy of Foreign Policy in British History, 1660–2000: How Strategic Concerns Shaped Modern Britain* (Basingstoke, 2000); J. Black (ed.), *The Tory World: Deep History and the Tory Theme in British Foreign Policy, 1679–2014* (Farnham, 2015).
41. J. Hoppit, 'Patterns of Parliamentary Legislation, 1660–1800', *Historical Journal* 39 (1996), pp. 109–31.
42. M. Clayton (ed.), *A Portrait of Influence: Life and Letters of Arthur Onslow, the Great Speaker* (Chichester, 2017).
43. P. Langford, *Public Life and the Propertied Englishman, 1689–1798* (Oxford, 1991), pp. 138–206; C. Jones (ed.), *A Short History of Parliament: England, Great Britain, the United Kingdom, Ireland and Scotland* (Woodbridge, 2009).
44. M. Taylor, 'Colonial Representation in Westminster, *c.* 1800–65', in Hoppit (ed.), *Parliaments, Nations and Identities*, pp. 206–19.
45. E. Burke, *Speech to the Electors of Bristol* (1774), in idem, *Select Works of Edmund Burke*, ed. F. Canavan, 4 vols (Indianapolis, 1999), vol. 3, p. 5ff.
46. R. Eagles, '"Got Together in a Riotous and Tumultuous Manner": Crowds and the Palace of Westminster, *c.* 1700–1800', *Journal of Eighteenth-Century Studies* 43 (2020), pp. 349–66.
47. Ibid., p. 360.

48. C. Reid, *Imprison'd Wranglers: The Rhetorical Culture of the House of Commons, 1760–1800* (Oxford, 2012).
49. J. Hoppit (ed.), *Failed Legislation, 1660–1800: Extracted from the Commons and Lords Journals* (1997).
50. S.E. Finer, *Anonymous Empire: A Study of the Lobby in Great Britain* (1966; 1969); J. Hoppit, 'Petitions, Economic Legislation and Interest Groups in Britain, 1660–1800', *Parliamentary History* 37 (2018), pp. 52–71.
51. G.P. Jupp, *Members of Parliament, 1734–1832* (New Haven, 1955; 1972), pp. 54–73; R. Sedgwick (ed.), *The House of Commons, 1715–54*, 2 vols (1970), vol. 1, pp. 3, 139–53.
52. Anon., *The Bad Consequences of Dissention and of Party-Rage* . . . (1747); Anon., *Fellow-Citizens: At This Alarming* . . . *Period, It Is Necessary for Every Man* . . . *to Lend his Aid* . . . (1784).
53. K.G. Feiling, *The Second Tory Party, 1714–1832* (1938).
54. F. O'Gorman, *The Emergence of the British Two-Party System, 1760–1832* (1982); B.W. Hill, *British Parliamentary Parties, 1742–1832: From the Fall of Walpole to the First Reform Act* (1985); M. Skjönsberg, *The Persistence of Party: Ideas of Harmonious Discord in Eighteenth-Century Britain* (Cambridge, 2021).
55. J.S. Lewis, *Sacred to Female Patriotism: Gender, Class and Politics in Late Georgian Britain* (2003); E. Chalus, *Elite Women in British Political Life, c. 1754–90* (Oxford, 2005).
56. E.A. Smith, 'The Election Agent in English Politics, 1734–1832', *English Historical Review* 84 (1969).
57. R. Fletcher, *The Parkers at Saltram, 1769–89: Everyday Life in an Eighteenth-Century House* (1970), p. 65; and for fashionable chinoiserie, see too D. Porter, *Chinese Taste in Eighteenth-Century England* (Cambridge, 2010).
58. J. Cannon, *The Fox–North Coalition: Crisis of the Constitution, 1782–4* (Cambridge, 1969).
59. E. Burke, *Thoughts on the Cause of the Present Discontents* (1770), p. 106.
60. J.B. Owen, *The Rise of the Pelhams* (1957); J.W. Wilkes, *A Whig in Power: The Political Career of Henry Pelham* (Evanston, IL, 1974).
61. H.T. Dickinson, *Bolingbroke* (1970); L.J. Colley, *In Defiance of Oligarchy: The Tory Party, 1714–60* (Cambridge, 1982).
62. J.G.A. Pocock, *The Machiavellian Moment: Florentine Political Thought and the Atlantic Republican Tradition* (Princeton, 1975); C. Gerrard, *The Patriot Opposition to Walpole: Politics, Poetry and National Myth, 1727–42* (Oxford, 1994).
63. J.J. Sack, *From Jacobite to Conservative: Reaction and Orthodoxy in Britain, c. 1760–1832* (Cambridge, 1993).
64. A. Seldon (ed.), *How Tory Governments Fall: The Tory Party in Power since 1783* (2016).
65. L.G. Mitchell, *Charles James Fox* (Oxford, 1992); P. Corfield, E.M. Green and C. Harvey, 'Westminster Man: Charles James Fox and His Electorate, 1780–1806', *Parliamentary History* 20 (2001), pp. 157–85; L.G. Mitchell, *The Whig World, 1760–1837* (2005).
66. N.G. Howe, *Statesmen in Caricature: The Great Rivalry of Fox and Pitt the Younger in the Age of the Political Cartoon* (2019).
67. F. O'Gorman, *The Whig Party and the French Revolution* (1967).
68. P. Mandler, *Aristocratic Government in the Age of Reform: Whigs and Liberals, 1830–52* (Oxford, 1990); K. Henry, *Liberalism and the Culture of Security: The Nineteenth-Century Rhetoric of Reform* (Tuscaloosa, 2011).
69. P. Harling, *The Waning of 'Old Corruption': The Politics of Economical Reform in Britain, 1779–1846* (Oxford, 1996); R. Lowe, *The Official History of the British Civil Service* (2011).
70. R. Knight, *Britain against Napoleon: The Organisation of Victory, 1793–1815* (2013).

71. J. Pellew, *The Home Office, 1848–1914: From Clerks to Bureaucrats* (1982); C. Browne, *Getting the Message: The Story of the British Post Office* (Stroud, 1993); W.J. Ashworth, *Customs and Excise: Trade, Production and Consumption in England, 1640–1845* (Oxford, 2003); D, Coffman, *Excise Taxation and the Origins of Public Debt* (Basingstoke, 2013); M. Moir, *The Examiner's Office: The Emergence of an Administrative Elite in East India House, 1804–58* (1979).

72. E. Bridges, *Portrait of a Profession: The Civil Service Tradition* (Cambridge, 1950); S. Horton, 'The Public Service Ethos in the British Civil Service: An Historical-Institutional Analysis', *Public Policy and Administration* 21 (2006), pp. 32–48.

73. P. Langford, *The Excise Crisis: Society and Politics in the Age of Walpole* (Oxford, 1975).

74. A. Hope-Jones, *Income Tax in the Napoleonic Wars* (Cambridge, 1939); P.K. O'Brien, 'The Political Economy of British Taxation, 1660–1815', *Economic History Review*, 2nd ser. 41 (1988), pp. 1–32; D. Stasavage, *Public Debt and the Birth of the Democratic State: France and Great Britain, 1688–1789* (Cambridge, 2003), pp. 88–9, 93–5.

75. J. Cannon, *Parliamentary Reform, 1640–1832* (Cambridge, 1973), p. 78.

76. P. Harling, 'Parliament, the State and "Old Corruption": Conceptualising Reform, c. 1790–1832', in A. Burns and J. Innes (eds), *Rethinking the Age of Reform: Britain, 1780–1850* (Cambridge, 2003), pp. 98–113.

77. J. Innes, '"Reform" in English Public Life: The Fortunes of a Word', in Burns and Innes (eds), *Rethinking the Age of Reform*, pp. 71–97.

78. Wade, *The Black Book, or Corruption Unmasked! Being an Account of Persons, Places, and Sinecures*, 2 vols (1820–23; and later edns).

79. Corfield, *Power and the Professions*, p. 93.

80. R. Berger, *Impeachment: The Constitutional Problems* (Cambridge, MA, 1973); M.J. Gerhardt, *Impeachment* (New York, 2018).

81. E. Burke, *Speech of the Rt. Hon. Edmund Burke . . . in Opening the Impeachment, 15 February 1788* (1859); P.J. Marshal, *The Impeachment of Warren Hastings* (1965); M. Mukherjee, 'Justice, War and the Imperium: India and Britain in Edmund Burke's Prosecutorial Speeches in the Impeachment Trial of Warren Hastings', *Law and History Review* 23 (2005), pp. 589–630.

82. Burke, *Speech . . . Opening the Impeachament*, from idem, *The Works of the Rt. Hon. Edmund Burke*, 12 vols (1887), vol. 9, pp. 1452–3, 1455, 1458 (16 February1788); vol. 10, pp. 144–5 (19 February 1788); online at https://www.gutenberg.org/files/13968/13968-h/13968-h.htm and https://www.gutenberg.org/files/18192/18192-h/18192-h.htm (accessed 10 March 2020).

Chapter 10: Participating in Public Life 'Out of Doors'

1. Burke to Rockingham, 23 August 1775, in N.E. Koehn, *The Power of Commerce: Economy and Governance in the First British Empire* (1994), p. 186.

2. Heyd, *Reading Newspapers*; B. Dooley (ed.), *The Dissemination of News and the Emergence of Contemporaneity in Early Modern Europe* (Farnham, 2010).

3. See Anon., *The Coffee House: Or, News-Monger's Hall . . .* (1672); and context in M. Green, 'The Lost World of the London Coffeehouse', *Public Domain Review* (7 August 2013); online at https://publicdomainreview.org/essay/the-lost-world-of-the-london-coffeehouse (accessed 15 February 2021).

4. Anon., *The Art of Railing at Great Men . . .* (1723), p. 12.

5. G.A. Cranfield, *The Press and Society: From Caxton to Northcliffe* (2016).

6. T. Fawcett, *Voices of Eighteenth-Century Bath* (Bath, 1995), p. 119.

7. J. Grande, *William Cobbett, the Press and Rural England: Radicalism and the Fourth Estate, 1792–1835* (Basingstoke, 2014).

8. G.D.H. Cole, *William Cobbett* (1925; 2010); R. Therry (ed.), *The Speeches of the Right Honourable George Canning . . .*, 7 vols (1828), vol. 6, pp. 404–5.

9. D. Hirst, 'A Culture of Voting in Seventeenth-Century England', in S. Ferente, L. Kunčević and M. Pattenden (eds), *Cultures of Voting in Pre-Modern Europe* (2018), pp. 129–40.

10. E.M. Green, P.J. Corfield and C. Harvey, *Elections in Metropolitan London, 1700–1850*, 2 vols (Bristol, 2013), vol. 1, pp. 175–216.

11. See e.g. Z. Dyndor, 'Widows, Wives and Witnesses: Women and Their Involvement in the 1768 Northampton Borough Parliamentary Election', *Parliamentary History* 30 (2011), pp. 309–23.

12. P.J. Corfield, 'Summary: Proto-Democracy in Eighteenth-Century London', in Green, Corfield and Harvey, *Elections in Metropolitan London*, vol. 1, pp. 55–67. See also W.J. Bulman, *The Rise of Majority Rule in Early Modern Britain and its Empire* (Cambridge, 2021).

13. G.S. Holmes and W.A. Speck (eds), *The Divided Society: Party Conflict in England, 1694–1716* (1967).

14. E. Chalus, 'Gender, Place and Power: Controverted Elections in Late Georgian England', in J. Daybell and S. Norrhem (eds), *Gender and Political Culture in Early Modern Europe, 1400–1800* (2016), pp. 179–96.

15. Green, Corfield and Harvey, *Elections in Metropolitan London*, vol. 1, p. 220.

16. J.S. Mill, *Considerations on Representative Government* (1861), ed. C.V. Shields (New York, 1958), pp. 154–71; J.C. Mitchell, *The Organisation of Opinion: Open Voting in England, 1832–68* (Basingstoke, 2008).

17. N. Rogers, *Whigs and Cities: Popular Politics in the Age of Walpole and Pitt* (Oxford, 1989); E. Bland, '"We Care Not a Fig, who Is Lord Mayor of London, or Tory or Whig": Popular Political Culture in the City of London, *c.* 1725–46', *London Journal* 42 (2017), pp. 34–52.

18. Green, Corfield and Harvey, *Elections in Metropolitan London*, vol. 2, pp. 482–858.

19. Anon., *To the Public: That Great Britain Will One Day Fall . . .* (New York, 1770).

20. Corfield, Green and Harvey, 'Westminster Man', pp. 157–85.

21. H. Walpole in Lewis and Bown (eds), *Horace Walpole's Correspondence, Vols Nine and Ten*, sub-series 2, p. 254.

22. F. O'Gorman, *Voters, Patrons and Parties: The Unreformed Electoral System of Hanoverian England, 1734–1832* (Oxford, 1989).

23. Burke, *Speech to the Electors of Bristol*.

24. T.B. Macaulay, 'Speech on the Reform Bill' (20 September 1831), in idem, *The Miscellaneous Writings and Speeches of Lord Macaulay*, 4 vols (1889), vol. 4, pp. 46–7.

25. D. Wahrman, *Imagining the Middle Class: The Political Representation of Class in Britain, c. 1780–1840* (Cambridge, 1995); N.D. LoPatin, *Political Unions, Popular Politics and the Great Reform Act of 1832* (Basingstoke, 1999); E. Pearce, *Reform: The Fight for the 1832 Reform Act* (2010).

26. J. Stevenson, *Popular Disturbances in England, 1700–1870* (1979); P. Jupp and E. Magennis (eds), *Crowds in Ireland, c. 1720–1920* (2000); R.B. Shoemaker, *The London Mob: Violence and Disorder in Eighteenth-Century England* (2004); J. Bohstedt, *Provision: Food Riots, Moral Economy and Market Transition in England, c. 1550–1850* (2010).

27. N. Goose, 'The Dutch in Colchester in the Sixteenth and Seventeenth Centuries: Opposition and Integration', in R. Vigne and C. Littleton (eds), *From Strangers to Citizens: The Integration of Immigrant Communities in Britain, Ireland and Colonial America, 1550–1750* (2001), pp. 88ff.

28. E.P. Thompson, 'The Moral Economy of the English Crowd in the Eighteenth Century' (1971); idem, 'The Moral Economy Reviewed' (1991); both in idem, *Customs in Common*, pp. 185–258, 259–351.

29. Langford, *Excise Crisis*.

30. J. Bohstedt, 'Gender, Household and Community Politics: Women and English Riots, 1790–1810', *Past & Present* 120 (1988), pp. 88–122; B. Clark Smith, 'Food Rioters and

the American Revolution', *William and Mary Quarterly* 51 (1994), pp. 3–38, esp. pp. 3–5, 26–9.

31. R.E. Jones, *Petticoat Heroes: Rethinking the Rebecca Riots* (Cardiff, 2015).

32. R.B. Outhwaite, *Dearth, Public Policy and Social Disturbance in England, 1550–1800* (Basingstoke, 1991); J. Kelly, *Food Rioting in Ireland in the Eighteenth and Nineteenth Centuries: The 'Moral Economy' and the Irish Crowd* (Dublin, 2017).

33. T.S. Ashton, *Economic Fluctuations in England, 1700–1800* (Oxford, 1959), p. 22.

34. D.E. Williams, 'Morals, Markets and the English Crowd in 1766', *Past & Present* 104 (1984), pp. 56–73.

35. D.J. Chambers, 'Population Change in a Provincial Town: Nottingham, 1700–1800', in L.S. Pressnell (ed.), *Studies in the Industrial Revolution* (1960), p. 111.

36. M.C. Harris, 'The Moral Economy of the 1719/20 Anti-Calico Riots' (PhD thesis, University of Alberta, 2015).

37. R. McNeil, *The Porteous Riot* (1988).

38. W. Scott, *The Heart of Mid-Lothian* (1818); S. Lelly, *Scott-Land: The Man who Invented a Nation* (2010).

39. Thompson, 'Moral Economy Reviewed', pp. 310–11.

40. T. Hayter, *The Army and the Crowd in Mid-Georgian England* (1978).

41. K.J. Logue, *Popular Disturbances in Scotland, 1780–1815* (Edinburgh, 1979), p. 22.

42. R.B. Rose, 'The Priestley Riots of 1791', *Past & Present* 18 (1960), pp. 68–88.

43. Whyman, *Useful Knowledge of William Hutton*, pp. 133–54, esp. p. 141.

44. G. Rudé, 'The Gordon Riots: A Study of the Rioters and Their Victims', *Transactions of the Royal Historical Society*, 5th ser. 6 (1956), pp. 93–114; I. Hayward and J. Seed (eds), *The Gordon Riots: Politics, Culture and Insurrection in Late Eighteenth-Century Britain* (Cambridge, 2012).

45. J. Innes, 'The Protestant Carpenter: William Payne of Bell Yard (*c.* 1718–82) – The Life and Times of a London Informing Constable', in idem, *Inferior Politics: Social Problems and Social Policies in Eighteenth-Century Britain* (Oxford, 2009), pp. 279–341.

46. W. Blake, *America: A Prophecy* (1793), final lines.

47. J. Tambling, *Dickens, Violence and the Modern State: Dreams of the Scaffold* (1995).

48. J. Capie, *The Bristol Riots of 1831 and Social Reform in Britain* (Lampeter, 1991); S. Poole and N. Rogers, *Bristol from Below: Law, Authority and Protest in a Georgian City* (Martlesham, 2017).

49. P.B. Shelley, *The Masque of Anarchy* (1819), lines 319–22; A.P Young, *Shelley and Non-Violence* (The Hague, 1975).

50. M. Roberts, *Making English Morals: Voluntary Associations and Moral Reform in England, 1787–1886* (Cambridge, 2004), pp. 67–8, 73–7, 85–9, 134, 136, 170 n. 100.

51. P. Hollis (ed.), *Pressure from Without in Early Victorian England* (1974).

52. N.C. Davies, 'The Bill of Rights Society and the Origins of Radicalism in Britain' (MA dissertation, University of Wales, 1986); I.R. Christie, 'The Yorkshire Association, 1780–4: A Study in Political Organisation', *Historical Journal* 3 (1960), pp. 144–61; Goodwin, *Friends of Liberty*, pp. 63–117, 209–10, 215–17, 238–9, 252–4, 317–18, 329–30, 332–3, 389–90.

53. See variously N. Carlin, *Regicide or Revolution? What Petitioners Wanted, September 1648–February 1649* (2020); J.E. Bradley, *Popular Politics and the America Revolution in England: Petitions, the Crown and Public Opinion* (Macon, 1986); H. Miller, 'Petition! Petition!! Petition!! Petitioning and Political Organisation in Britain, *c.* 1800–50', in H. te Velde and M. Janse (eds), *Organising Democracy: Reflections on the Rise of Political Organisations in the Nineteenth Century* (2017), pp. 43–61.

54. A. Goodrich, *Debating England's Aristocracy in the 1790s: Pamphlets, Polemics and Political Ideas* (Woodbridge, 2001); M. Philp, *Reforming Ideas in Britain: Politics and Language in the Shadow of the French Revolution, 1789–1815* (Cambridge, 2014).

55. Goodwin, *Friends of Liberty*, p. 139.

56. Thompson, *Making of the English Working Class*, p. 142 n. 1.
57. Goodwin, *Friends of Liberty*, p. 327.
58. J. Thompson, *John Thelwall in the Wordsworth Circle: The Silenced Partner* (2012).
59. R. Lamb, *Thomas Paine and the Idea of Human Rights* (Cambridge, 2015).
60. Goodwin, *Friends of Liberty*, pp. 284–5, 295–304; L. Curelly and N. Smith (eds), *Radical Voices, Radical Ways: Articulating and Disseminating Radicalism in Seventeenth- and Eighteenth-Century Britain* (Manchester, 2018).
61. E. Higgs, *The Information State in England: The Central Collection of Information on Citizens, 1500–2000* (2004); P. Lawrence (ed.), *The Making of the Modern Police, 1780–1914* (2014).
62. E.C. Black, *The Association: British Extra-Parliamentary Political Organisation, 1769–1793* (Cambridge, MA, 1963).
63. Goodwin, *Friends of Liberty*, pp. 307–58.
64. S.H. Palmer, *Police and Protest in England and Ireland, 1780–1850* (Cambridge, 1988); Goodwin, *Friends of Liberty*, pp. 236, 309–10, 313.
65. Unlawful Societies Act (1799), 39 Geo. III, cap. 79; and for context, see K.R. Johnston, *Unusual Suspects: Pitt's Reign of Alarm and the Lost Generation of the 1790s* (Oxford, 2013).
66. 39 Geo. III, cap. 8 (1799).
67. J. Belchem, *Orator Henry Hunt and English Working-Class Radicalism* (Oxford, 1985); R. Poole *Peterloo: The English Uprising* (Oxford, 2019).
68. D. Thompson, *The Chartists: Popular Politics in the Industrial Revolution* (1984; 1987); J. Saville, *1848: The British State and the Chartist Movement* (Cambridge, 1987); W.H. Fraser, *Chartism in Scotland* (Pontypool, 2010); M. Chase, *Chartism: A New History* (Manchester, 2007).
69. H.U. Faulkner, *Chartism and the Churches: A Study in Democracy* (New York, 1968); A.M. Hadfield, *The Chartist Land Company* (Newton Abbot, 1970); D. Poole, *The Last Chartist Land Settlement: Great Dodford, 1819* (Dodford, 1999).
70. D.V.J. Jones, *The Last Rising: The Newport Chartist Insurrection of 1839* (Oxford, 1985; Cardiff, 1999).
71. R. Tyrrell, *Joseph Sturge and the Moral Radical Party in Victorian Britain* (1987).
72. Hayter, *The Army and the Crowd in Mid-Georgian Politics*.
73. A. Morgan, *Ballads and Songs of Peterloo* (Manchester, 2018).
74. S. Rossteutscher (ed.), *Democracy and the Role of Associations: Political, Organisational and Social Contexts* (2005).
75. R. Postgate, *That Devil Wilkes* (1930; 1956; 2001); J. Sainsbury, *John Wilkes: The Lives of a Libertine* (2017).
76. N.B. Lasson, *The History and Development of the Fourth Amendment of the United States Constitution* (Baltimore, 1937).
77. T. Bingham, *The Rule of Law* (2010), p. 4.
78. Green, Corfield and Harvey, *Elections in Metropolitan London*, vol. 1, pp. 26, 63.
79. Q. Skinner and R. Bourke (eds), *Popular Sovereignty in Historical Context* (Cambridge, 2016); R. Tuck, *The Sleeping Sovereign: The Invention of Modern Democracy* (Cambridge, 2016).
80. See e.g. 'A Well-Wisher to the Good People of Great Britain' [M. Decker], *Serious Considerations on the . . . High Duties which the Nation . . . Labours Under . . .* (1743).

Chapter 11: Seeking Social Solutions at Home

1. L. Davison, T. Hitchcock, T. Keirn and R.B. Shoemaker (eds), *Stilling the Grumbling Hive: The Response to Social and Economic Problems in England, 1689–1750* (1992); Innes, *Inferior Politics*.
2. B. de Mandeville, *The Grumbling Hive: Or, Knaves Turned Honest* (1705); expanded as *The Fable of the Bees* (1714).

3. Mandeville, *Grumbling Hive*, lines 425–6.
4. A. Kitch, *Political Economy and the States of Literature in Early Modern England* (Farnham, 2016).
5. A. Bonnett and K. Armstrong (eds), *Thomas Spence: The Poor Man's Revolutionary* (2014).
6. G. Claeys, *Searching for Utopia: The History of an Idea* (2011).
7. S. Dickie, *Cruelty and Laughter: Forgotten Comic Literature and the Unsentimental Eighteenth Century* (Chicago, 2011).
8. W. Motooka, *The Age of Reasons: Quixotism, Sentimentalism, and Political Economy in Eighteenth-Century Britain* (2013).
9. P.K. Leaver, *The History of Moorfields Eye Hospital* (2004).
10. M.W. Royden, *Pioneers and Perseverance: A History of the Royal School for the Blind, Liverpool 1791–1991* (1991).
11. J. Goodricke [also Goodridge], *The Phoenix: An Essay, [on] History and Astronomical Calculations...* (1781).
12. D. Rockey, *Speech Disorder in Nineteenth-Century Britain: The History of Stuttering* (1980), esp. pp. 46–7, 86–9, 174, 240.
13. R. Black (ed.), *To the Hebrides: Samuel Johnson's Journey to the Western Islands of Scotland ...* (Edinburgh, 2018), p. 428.
14. C. Hawes, *Mania and Literary Style: The Rhetoric of Enthusiasm from the Ranters to Christopher Smart* (Cambridge, 1996); C. Mounsey, *Christopher Smart: Clown of God* (2001).
15. J.P. Eigen, *Witnessing Insanity: Madness and Mad-Doctors in the English Court* (New Haven, 1995).
16. R. Porter, *Mind-Forg'd Manacles: A History of Madness in England from the Restoration to the Regency* (1987); M. Foucault, *Madness and Civilisation: A History of Insanity in the Age of Reason*, trans. J. Murphy and J. Khalfa (2006); R.A. Houston, *Madness and Society in Eighteenth-Century Scotland* (Oxford, 2000); W.L. Parry-Jones, *The Trade in Lunacy: A Study of Private Madhouses in England in the Eighteenth and Nineteenth Centuries* (2007).
17. A. Bennett, *The Madness of George III* (1992); A.R. Rushton, *Royal Maladies: Inherited Diseases in the Royal Houses of Europe* (2008).
18. A. Digby, *Madness, Morality and Medicine: A Study of the York Retreat, 1796–1914* (Cambridge, 1985).
19. A. Scull, C. MacKenzie and N. Hervey, *Masters of Bedlam: The Transformation of the Mad-Doctoring Trade* (Princeton, 2014).
20. P. Fennell, *Treatment without Consent: Law, Psychiatry and the Treatment of Mentally Disordered People since 1845* (2015).
21. M. Byrd, *Visits to Bedlam: Madness and Literature in the Eighteenth Century* (Columbia, 1974).
22. S. Braidwood, *Black Poor and White Philanthropists: London's Blacks and the Foundation of the Sierra Leone Settlement, 1786–91* (Liverpool, 1984).
23. D.T. Andrew, *Philanthropy and Police: London Charity in the Eighteenth Century* (Princeton, 1989).
24. Anon., *An Abstract of the Charter Granted in the Year 1741...* (Norwich, 1771).
25. Anon., *The State of the Charity for... Widows, Orphans and Distressed Families... within the... County of Nottingham...* (Nottingham, 1776).
26. G.B. Risse, *Hospital Life in Enlightenment Scotland: Care and Teaching at the Royal Infirmary of Edinburgh* (Cambridge, 1986); S.C. Lawrence, *Charitable Knowledge: Hospital Pupils and Practitioners in Eighteenth-Century London* (Cambridge, 1996); J. Reinarz, *Health Care in Birmingham: The Birmingham Teaching Hospitals, 1779–1939* (Woodbridge, 2009).

27. S. King, *Poverty and Welfare in England, 1700–1850: A Regional Perspective* (Manchester, 2000); idem and A. Tomkins (eds), *The Poor in England: An Economy of Makeshifts* (Manchester, 2003).
28. P. King, P. Sharpe and T. Hitchcock (eds), *Chronicling Poverty: The Voices and Strategies of the English Poor, 1640–1840* (Basingstoke, 1997); A. Levene et al. (eds), *Narratives of the Poor in Eighteenth-Century Britain, Vol. 1* (2006).
29. R.A. Houston, *Peasant Petitions: Social Relationships and Economic Life on Landed Estates, 1600–1850* (Basingstoke, 2014).
30. A. Eccles, *Vagrancy in Law and Practice under the Old Poor Law* (2016).
31. T. Hitchcock, *Down and Out in Eighteenth-Century London* (2004), pp. 75–9, 97–123.
32. L. McKay, 'The Mendicity Society and Its Clients: A Cautionary Tale', *Left History* 5 (1997), pp. 39–64.
33. R. Mitchison, *The Old Poor Law in Scotland: The Experience of Poverty, 1574–1845* (Edinburgh, 2000), pp. 84–5, 97–102, 135–53, 156–82.
34. J. Robins, *Lost Children: A Study of Charity Children in Ireland, 1700–1900* (Dublin, 1980); K. Sonnelitter, *Charity Movements in Eighteenth-Century Ireland: Philanthropy and Improvement* (Martlesham, 2016).
35. V. Crossman and P. Gray (eds), *Poverty and Welfare in Ireland, 1838–1948* (Dublin, 2011).
36. D. Green, *Pauper Capital: London and the Poor Law, 1790–1870* (2016).
37. Vaisey (ed.), *Diary of Thomas Turner*, p. 267.
38. N. Tadmor, 'The Settlement of the Poor and the Rise of the Form in England, c. 1662–1780', *Past & Present* 262 (2017), pp. 43–97.
39. J. Clare, *The Parish: A Satire* (1820–24), ed. E. Robinson (Harmondsworth, 1986), p. 57.
40. N. Landau, 'Who Was Subjected to the Laws of Settlement? Procedure under the Settlement Laws in Eighteenth-Century England', *Agricultural History Review* 43 (1996), pp. 139–59; L. Charlesworth, *Welfare's Forgotten Past: A Socio-Legal History of the Poor Law* (Abingdon, 2010); A. Winter and T. Lambrecht, 'Migration, Poor Relief and Local Autonomy: Settlement Policies in England and the Southern Low Countries in the Eighteenth-Century', *Past & Present* 218 (2013), pp. 91–126.
41. S. Hindle, 'Dependency, Shame and Belonging: Badging the Deserving Poor, c. 1550–1750', *Continuity and Change* 1 (2004), pp. 6–35.
42. S. Fowler, *Workhouse: The People, the Places, the Life behind Closed Doors* (2007).
43. S.R. Ottoway, *The Decline of Life: Old Age in Eighteenth-Century England* (Cambridge, 2004), p. 237.
44. K. Honeyman, *Child Workers in England, 1780–1820: Parish Apprentices and the Making of the Early Industrial Workforce* (2016).
45. Mitchison, *Old Poor Law in Scotland*, p. 70.
46. P. Thane, 'Old People and Their Families in the English Past', in M. Daunton, (ed.), *Charity, Self Interest and Welfare in Britain: 1550 to the Present* (1996), pp. 88–9.
47. M. Blaug, 'The Myth of the Old Poor Law and the Making of the New', *Journal of Economic History* 23 (1963), pp. 151–84; G.R. Boyer, *Economic History of the English Poor Law, 1750–1850* (Cambridge, 1990); Mitchison, *Old Poor Law in Scotland*, pp. 118–32, 135–53.
48. King, *Poverty and Welfare*, pp. 247, 249–50, 257–69.
49. Mitchison, *Old Poor Law in Scotland*, pp. 185–215.
50. J.W. Knott, *Popular Opposition to the 1834 Poor Law* (1986); F. Driver, *Power and Pauperism: The Workhouse System 1834–84* (1993).
51. King, *Poverty and Welfare*, pp. 227–51; D. Fraser (ed.), *The New Poor Law in the Nineteenth Century* (Basingstoke, 1976).
52. A. Brundage, *The English Poor Laws, 1700–1930* (Basingstoke, 2002), p. 7.
53. T.P. O'Neill, 'Famine Evictions', in C. King (ed.), *Famine, Land and Culture in Ireland* (Dublin, 2000), pp. 29–70.

54. T. Hitchcock and R.B. Shoemaker, *London Lives: Poverty, Crime and the Making of a Modern City, 1690–1800* (Cambridge, 2015), pp. 27–9, 42–52, 68–9.

55. Anon., *The Civil and Religious Rights of the Poor* . . . (1766); and context in S. Lloyd, *Charity and Poverty in England, c. 1680–1820: Wild and Visionary Schemes* (Manchester, 2009).

56. T. Paine, *Agrarian Justice* (1797); P. van Parijs and Y. Vanderborght, *Basic Income: A Radical Proposal for Free Society and a Sane Economy* (Cambridge, MA, 2017).

57. S. Tickell, *Shoplifting in Eighteenth-Century England* (Woodbridge, 2018).

58. C. Coleman and J. Moynihan, *Understanding Crime Data: Haunted by the Dark Figure* (Buckingham, 1996).

59. *Inverness Journal* (14 March 1817).

60. R. Cavendish, 'Daniel Defoe Put in the Pillory', *History Today* 53 (July 2003); T. Keymer, *Poetics of the Pillory: English Literature and Seditious Libel* (Oxford, 2019).

61. 7 William IV and 1 Victoria, cap. 23 (1837).

62. D. Hay et al., *Albion's Fatal Tree: Crime and Society in Eighteenth-Century England* (1977; 2011); P. Linebaugh, *The London Hanged: Crime and Civil Society in the Eighteenth Century* (1991); V. Gatrell, *The Hanging Tree: Execution and the English People, 1770–1868* (Oxford, 1994); T. Hitchcock and R. Shoemaker, *Tales from the Hanging Court* (2007).

63. N. Clifford, *Women and the Gallows, 1797–1837: Unfortunate Wretches* (Barnsley, 2017).

64. J. Kelly, *Gallows Speeches from Eighteenth-Century Ireland* (Dublin, 2001); J.A. Sharpe, *Crime and the Law in English Satirical Prints, 1600–1832* (Cambridge, 1986).

65. See https://www.undiscoveredscotland.co.uk/usbiography/d/maggiedickson.html (accessed 10 March 2021). Today a pub in Grassmarket bears her name, overlooking the site where the gibbet once stood.

66. See https://pasttenseblog.wordpress.com/2017/02/14/today-in-londons-medical-history -rioting-tyburn-crowd-tries-to-rescue-body-of-executed-soldier-from-dissection-1770/ (accessed 10 March 2021).

67. P. King and R. Ward, 'Rethinking the Bloody Code in Eighteenth-Century Britain: Capital Punishment at the Centre and on the Periphery', *Past & Present* 228 (2015), pp. 159–205.

68. S. Devereaux and P. Griffiths (eds), *Penal Practice and Culture, 1500–1900: Punishing the English* (Houndmills, 2004).

69. C. Campbell, *The Intolerable Hulks: British Shipboard Confinement, 1776–1857* (Tucson, 2001).

70. See variously G. Morgan and P. Rushton, *Banishment in the Early Atlantic World: Convicts, Rebels and Slaves* (2013); R. Hughes, *The Fatal Shore: A History of the Transportation of Convicts to Australia, 1787–1868* (1986); M. Bogle, *Convicts: Transportation and Australia* (Sydney, 2008).

71. *The Proceedings of the Old Bailey, 1674–1913*, April 1745, trial of Hannah Rosse (t17450424-2); online at https://www.oldbaileyonline.org (accessed 21 January 2021).

72. *Diary of Thomas Lloyd, Kept in Newgate Prison, 1794–6* online at http://digital.library. villanova.edu/Item/vudl%3A253901 (accessed 10 March 2021); and context in S. Halliday, *Newgate: London's Prototype of Hell* (Stroud, 2006).

73. J. Innes, 'The King's Bench Prison in the Later Eighteenth Century: Law, Authority and Order in a London Debtors' Prison', in idem, *Inferior Politics*, p. 267.

74. J. Beattie, *Policing and Punishment in London, 1660–1750: Urban Crime and the Limits of Terror* (Oxford, 2001).

75. J. White, *Mansions of Misery: A Biography of the Marshalsea Debtors Prison* (2016).

76. T. West, *The Curious Mr Howard: Legendary Prison Reformer* (Hook, 2011).

77. S. Devereaux, 'The Making of the Penitentiary Act, 1775–1779', *Historical Journal* 42 (1999), pp. 405–33; L. Throness, *A Protestant Purgatory: The Theological Origins of the Penitentiary Act, 1779* (2016).

78. R. Evans, *The Fabrication of Virtue: English Prison Architecture, 1750–1840* (Cambridge, 1982); J. Semple, *Bentham's Prison: A Study of the Panopticon Penitentiary* (Oxford, 1993).
79. U.R.Q. Henriques, 'The Rise and Decline of the Separate System of Prison Discipline', *Past & Present* 54 (1972), pp. 61–93; M. Foucault, *Discipline and Punish: The Birth of the Prison*, trans. A. Sheridan (1977; 1995); A. Brunon-Ernst, *Beyond Foucault: New Perspectives on Bentham's Panopticon* (Farnham, 2012; 2016).
80. J. Hatton, *Betsy: The Dramatic Biography of Prison Reformer Elizabeth Fry* (Oxford, 2005).
81. D. Garland, *Punishment and Modern Society: A Study in Social Theory* (Oxford, 1990); U.V. Bondeson, *Alternatives to Imprisonment: Intentions and Reality* (2017).
82. Anon., *A Speech without Doors . . . : With Some Remarks on the Present State of Gaol-Archy* (1729).
83. J. Demmers, *Theories of Violent Conflict: An Introduction* (2016).
84. H.F. Dahms and L Hazelrigg (eds), *Theorising Modern Society as a Dynamic Process* (Bingley, 2012).
85. Ferguson, *Essay on . . . Civil Society*, pp. 101–2.

Chapter 12: Encountering the World and Its People

1. T. Severin, *Seeking Robinson Crusoe* (Leicester, 2002).
2. Anon., *The Comical Pilgrim: Or, Travels of a Cynick Philosopher . . .* (1722).
3. J. Black, *The British Abroad: The Grand Tour in the Eighteenth Century* (Stroud, 2003); B. Dolan, *Ladies of the Grand Tour* (2001).
4. J. Taylor, *The India Guide . . .* (1801); E. Archer, *Tours in Upper India and in Parts of the Himalaya Mountains . . .* (1833); J. Blackburn, *The Overland Traveller: Or, Guide to Persons Proceeding to Europe . . . from India* (Calcutta, 1838).
5. M. Keevak, *The Pretended Asian: George Psalmanazar's Eighteenth-Century Formosan Hoax* (Detroit, 2004).
6. S. Lamb, *Bringing Travel Home to England: Tourism, Gender and Imaginative Literature in the Eighteenth Century* (Newark, DE, 2009); J.T. Boulton and T.O. McLoughlin (eds), *News from Abroad: Letters Written by British Travellers on the Grand Tour, 1728–71* (Liverpool, 2012).
7. K. Fullagar, *The Savage Visit: New World People and Popular Imperial Culture in Britain, 1710–95* (Berkeley, 2012), pp. 88–93. See also M. Daunton and R. Halpern (eds), *Empire and Others: British Encounters with Indigenous Peoples, 1600–1850* (1999; 2020).
8. Scrivener, *Cosmopolitan Ideal*; A.M. Thell, *Minds in Motion: Imagining Empiricism in Eighteenth-Century British Travel Literature* (Lewisburg, 2017).
9. S. Rudy, *Literature and Encyclopedism in Enlightenment Britain: The Pursuit of Complete Knowledge* (Edinburgh, 2007).
10. P. Blom, *To Have and to Hold: An Intimate History of Collectors and Collecting* (2002).
11. R.G.W. Anderson et al. (eds), *Enlightening the British: Knowledge, Discovery and the Museum in the Eighteenth Century* (2003).
12. T. Ito, *London Zoo and the Victorians, 1828–59* (Woodbridge, 2014), pp. 36–7.
13. S. Moore, *Paradise of the Pacific: Approaching Hawaii* (New York, 2015).
14. S.R. Bown, *Madness, Betrayal and the Lash: The Epic Voyage of Captain George Vancouver* (Vancouver, 2008).
15. See e.g. D. McBride, *An Historical Account of a New Method of Treating the Scurvy at Sea* (1767).
16. Benjamin, *Europeans, Africans, Indians and Their Shared History*; J. Scott, *When the Waves Ruled Britannia: Geography and Political Identities, 1500–1800* (Cambridge, 2011).
17. T. Ballantyne, *Science, Empire and the European Exploration of the Pacific* (2020).
18. J.R. Seeley, *The Expansion of England* (1883), ed. J. Cross (Chicago, 1971), p. 12.

19. P.J. Marshall (ed.), *The Oxford History of the British Empire, Vol. 2: The Eighteenth Century* (Oxford, 1998); D. Armitage, *The Ideological Origins of the British Empire* (Cambridge, 2000); B. Porter, *British Imperial: What the Empire Wasn't* (2016).
20. G. Berkeley, *On the Prospect of Planting Arts and Learning in the Americas* (1726).
21. P. Colquhoun, A *Treatise on the Wealth, Power and Resources of the British Empire . . .* (1814; 1815).
22. J. Summerson, *The Life and Work of John Nash, Architect* (1980), pp. 160–9; J.M.F. Rutherford, *A Prince's Passion: The Life of the Royal Pavilion* (2003).
23. O.M. Dickerson, *The Navigation Acts and the American Revolution* (New York, 1951; 1963); W. Ashworth, *The Industrial Revolution: The State, Knowledge and Global Trade* (2017).
24. D. Hall, *A Brief History of the West India Committee* (Kingston, 1971).
25. N.A.M. Rodger, *The Command of the Ocean: A Naval History of Britain, 1649–1815* (2004); S. Willis, *Fighting at Sea in the Eighteenth Century: The Art of Sailing Warfare* (Woodbridge, 2008).
26. W.A. Mozart, *Bardengesang auf Gibraltar!* (K. Anh. 25 / 386d; 1782); R.A. Adkins, *Gibraltar: The Greatest Siege in British History* (2017).
27. P.J. Corfield, 'Eighteenth-Century Britain and Spain: Do Their Imperial Histories Fit into a Common Grand Narrative?', *International Comparative Literature* 3 (2020), pp. 3–24.
28. A.G. Olson, *Making the Empire Work: London and American Interest Groups, 1690–1790* (Cambridge, MA, 1992); T.H. Breen and T. Hall, *Colonial America in an Atlantic World: From Colonies to Revolution* (Boston, MA, 2017).
29. Anon., *An Apology for the Times: A Poem* (1778), pp. 22–3.
30. J. Black, *The War of 1812: In the Age of Napoleon* (2009); T.O. Bickham, *The Weight of Vengeance: The US, the British Empire and the War of 1812* (Oxford, 2012).
31. G. Heuman, 'The Social Structure of the Slave Societies in the Caribbean', in F.W. Knight (ed.), *General History of the Caribbean, Vol. 3: The Slave Societies of the Caribbean* (New York, 2003), pp. 138–68.
32. H. Cavendish (ed.), *Debates in the House of Commons in . . . 1774* (1839).
33. R.M. Calhoon, *The Loyalists in Revolutionary America, 1760–81* (New York, 1973); M. Jasanoff, *Liberty's Exiles: The Loss of America and the Remaking of the British Empire* (2011).
34. P.A. Buckner, *The Transition to Responsible Government: British Policy in British North America, 1815–50* (1985).
35. K. Lalvani, *The Making of India: The Untold Story of British Enterprise* (2016); Gilmour, *The British in India*.
36. S. Massey, *Christian Missionaries in India* (New Delhi, 2007); A.J. May, *Welsh Missionaries and British Imperialism: The Empire of Clouds in North-East India* (Manchester, 2012); S. Dutta, *British Women Missionaries in Bengal, 1793–1861* (2017).
37. P.J. Stern, *The Company-State: Corporate Sovereignty and the Early Modern Foundation of the British Empire in India* (New York, 2007); J. Keay, *The Honourable Company: A History of the English East India Company* (2010).
38. T.A. Heathcote, *The Military in British India: The Development of British Land Forces in South Asia, 1600–1947* (Manchester, 1995); R. Holmes, *Sahib: The British Soldier in India, 1750–1914* (2005).
39. I.J. Barrow, *Making History, Drawing Territory: British Mapping in India, 1756–1905* (New Delhi, 2003).
40. M. Jasanoff, *Edge of Empire: Lives, Culture and Conquest in the East, 1750–1850* (New York, 2005), pp. 81–114, 149–96; K. Rüdiger, *The UK and India: The Other 'Special Relationship'?* (2008); F. Mount, *The Tears of the Rajas: Mutiny, Money and Marriage in India, 1805–1905* (2015).
41. Anon. [Price], *The Saddle Put on the Right Horse*; Nechtman, *Nabobs*; C. Williams, *The Nabobs of Berkshire* (Purley, 2010).

42. R. Harvey, *Clive: The Life and Death of a British Emperor* (1998).
43. F.G. Whelan, *Edmund Burke and India: Political Morality and Empire* (1996); N.B. Dirks, *The Scandal of Empire: India and the Creation of Imperial Britain* (Cambridge, MA, 2004); R. Bourke, *Empire and Revolution: The Political Life of Edmund Burke* (Princeton, 2015).
44. A. Dow, *A History of Hindostan . . .*, 2 vols (1770–72).
45. M.J. Franklin, *'Orientalist Jones': Sir William Jones, Poet, Lawyer and Linguist, 1746–94* (Oxford, 2011).
46. E.W. Said, *Orientalism* (1978); I. Warraq, *Defending the West: A Critique of Edward Said's Orientalism* (Amherst, NY, 2007); S. Makdisi, *Making England Western: Occidentalism, Race and Imperial Culture* (Chicago, 2014).
47. K. Brittlebank, *Tipu Sultan's Search for Legitimacy: Islam and Kingship in a Hindu Domain* (New Delhi, 1997); K. Sanderson, *The First Freedom Fighter: Tipu Sultan, the Tiger of Mysore* (2011).
48. C.A. Bayly, *Indian Society and the Making of the British Empire* (Cambridge, 1990); D. Judd, *The Lion and the Tiger: The Rise and Fall of the British Raj, 1600–1947* (Oxford, 2004).
49. C. Dewey, *Anglo-Indian Attitudes: The Mind of the Indian Civil Service* (1993; 2003); M. McLaren, *British India and British Scotland, 1780–1830: Career Building, Empire Building, and a Scottish School of Thought on Indian Governance* (Akron, 2001).
50. A. Bain, *James Mill: A Biography* (1882; New York, 1967).
51. A. Major, *Sovereignty and Social Reform in India: British Colonialism and the Campaign against Sati, 1830–60* (2010); J. Meenakshi, *Sati: Evangelicals, Baptist Missionaries and the Changing Colonial Discourse* (2016).
52. H.D. Sharma, *Raja Ram Mohan Roy: The Renaissance Man* (2002); R. Humari, *Women, Social Customs and Raja Ram Mohan Roy* (Patna, 2013).
53. C.E. Trevelyan, *On the Education of the People of India* (1838; 2011); B.B. Kachru, *The Indianisation of English: The English Language in India* (New Delhi and Oxford, 1983); B. Moor-Gilbert, *Writing India, 1757–1990: The Literature of British India* (1996).
54. D. Cannadine, *Ornamentalism: How the British Saw Their Empire* (2001); G. Rand, 'Same Difference? Liberalism, Modernity and Governance in the Indian Empire', in S. Gunn and J. Vernon (eds), *The Peculiarities of Liberal Modernity in Imperial Britain* (2011), pp. 134–46.
55. B. Porter, *Critics of Empire: British Radicals and the Imperial Challenge* (2007).
56. P. Brendon, *The Decline and Fall of the British Empire, 1781–1997* (New York, 2008); S. Tharpoor, *Inglorious Empire: What the British Did to India* (2017); M. Taberi, *The Accounts of the British Empire: Capital Flows from 1799 to 1914*, trans. J. Turnbull (2018); T. Roy, *How British Rule Changed India's Economy: The Paradox of the Raj* (Cham, 2019).
57. W.L. Whitty, *The Yamasee War: A Study of Economy, Culture and Conflict in the Colonial South* (2008); J.C.H. King, *Blood and Land: The Story of Native North America* (2016).
58. Anon., *Old England for Ever: Or, Spanish Cruelty Displayed . . .* (1740); L.M. Stevens, *The Poor Indians: British Missionaries, Native Americans, and Colonial Sensibility* (Philadelphia, 2004); J.P. Greene (ed.), *Exclusionary Empire: English Liberty Overseas, 1600–1900* (Cambridge, 2010).
59. A. Aleiss, *Making the White Man's Indian: Native Americans and Hollywood Movies* (Oxford, 2005).
60. B. Elder, *Blood on the Wattle: Massacres and Maltreatments of Aboriginal Australians since 1788* (1998); S. Krichauff, *Memory, Place and Aboriginal-Settler History: Understanding Australians' Consciousness of the Colonial Past* (2015).
61. Evans, *Slave Wales*; M. Dresser and A. Hann (eds), *Slavery and the English Country House* (Swindon, 2013).
62. K.D. Kriz, *Slavery, Sugar and the Culture of Refinement: Picturing the British West Indies, 1700–1840* (New Haven, 2008).

63. See the Emory Center for Digital Scholarship (ECDS) Database: Slave Voyages; online at https://slavevoyages.org/; and the overview in Wikipedia, https://en.wikipedia.org/wiki/Atlantic_slave_trade (accessed 11 March 2021).

64. K. Kant and K. Kubetzek, *The Atlantic Slave Trade: Effects on Africa* (2012).

65. J. Walvin, *The Zong: A Massacre, the Law and the End of Slavery* (2011).

66. G. Hutchinson, *Fuller of Sussex: A Georgian Squire* (Brede, 1993).

67. W. Cowper, *Pity for Poor Africans* (1788), lines 5–6. Among the pointed polemics, see Anon. ['a Liverpool merchant'], *No Slaves, No Sugar: Containing New and Irresistible Arguments in Favour of the African Trade* (1804).

68. B. Carey, *British Abolitionism and the Rhetoric of Sensibility: Writing, Sentiment and Slavery, 1760–1807* (Basingstoke, 2005); Z. Gifford, *Thomas Clarkson and the Campaign against the Slave Trade* (2007); H. Meier, *Thomas Clarkson: Moral Steam Engine or False Prophet? A Critical Approach to Three of his Anti-Slavery Essays* (Stuttgart, 2007).

69. R. Wedderburn, *The Horrors of Slavery* (1824), ed. I. McCalman (Edinburgh, 1991).

70. M.B. Rediker, *The Slave Ship: A Human History* (2007); S. Drescher, *Abolition: A History of Slavery and Antislavery* (Cambridge, 2009); B. Carey, *From Peace to Freedom: Quaker Rhetoric and the Birth of American Antislavery, 1658–1761* (New Haven, 2012).

71. See e.g. A. Matsumoto, 'Priestley and Smith against Slavery', *Kyoto Economic Review* 80 (2011), pp. 119–31.

72. E.F. Hurwitz, *Politics and the Public Conscience: Slave Emancipation and the Abolitionist Movement* (1973); D. Turley, 'British Anti-Slavery Re-Assessed', in Burns and Innes (eds), *Rethinking the Age of Reform*, p. 188.

73. C. Midgley, *Women against Slavery: The British Campaigns, 1780–1870* (1992).

74. W. Wilberforce, *The Speech of William Wilberforce, Esq. . . . on the . . . . Abolition of the Slave Trade* (1789).

75. R. Blaufarb, *Inhuman Traffick: The International Struggle against the Transatlantic Slave Trade* (New York, 2015).

76. M. Turner, *Slaves and Missionaries: The Disintegration of Jamaican Slave Society, 1787–1834* (1982).

77. For economic variants, see D. Tomich (ed.), *Slavery and Historical Capitalism during the Nineteenth Century* (Lanham, MD, 2017).

78. J. Gratus, *The Great White Lie: Slavery, Emancipation and Changing Racial Attitudes* (1973).

79. C. Hall, N. Draper and K. McClelland (eds), *Emancipation and the Remaking of the British Imperial World* (Manchester, 2014); 'Legacies of British Slave-Ownership' database, UCL Department of History (2021): online at https://www.ucl.ac.uk/lbs (accessed 15 February 2021).

80. W.L. Lai, *Indentured Labour, Caribbean Sugar: Chinese and Indian Migrants to the British West Indies, 1838–1918* (Baltimore, 1993).

81. J.D. Leary, *Post Traumatic Slave Syndrome: America's Legacy of Enduring Injury and Healing* (Milwaukie, 2005); J.M. Jemmott, *Ties that Bind: The Black Family in Post-Slavery Jamaica, 1834–82* (Kingston, Jamaica, 2015).

82. H.O. Russell, *Samuel Sharpe and the Meaning of Freedom: Reflections on a Baptist National Hero of Jamaica* (Oxford, 2012).

83. D. de Guistino, *Conquest of Mind: Phrenology and Victorian Social Thought* (2016).

84. C. White, *An Account of the Regular Gradation in Man . . .* (1799).

85. P.J. Corfield, *Time and the Shape of History* (2007), pp. 40–1.

86. K.F. Dyer, *The Biology of Racial Integration* (Bristol, 1974); A. Montagu, *Man's Most Dangerous Myth: The Fallacy of Race* (New York, 2001); A. Saini, *Superior: The Return of Race Science* (2019).

87. L.L. Cavalli-Sforza and F. Cavalli-Sforza, *The Great Human Diasporas: The History of Diversity and Evolution,* trans. S. Thomas (Reading, MA, 1995).

88. M. Banton, 'UNESCO Statements on Race', in R.T. Schaefer (ed.), *Encyclopedia of Race, Ethnicity and Society* (2008).
89. Equiano, *The Interesting Narrative*, p. 110.

Chapter 13: Aristocrats, Plutocrats and Cross-Class Gentlemen

1. W. Penn, *The Christian Quaker: and his Divine Testimony Vindicated . . . against the Injurious Attempts . . . to Render him Odiously Inconsistent with Christianity and Civil Society* (1699).
2. Anon., *Reflections on the Management of Some Late Party-Disputes . . . Showing How Destructive it has been Both to Religion and Civil Society . . .* (1715).
3. J. Dwyer and R.B. Sher (eds), *Sociability and Society in Eighteenth-Century Scotland* (Edinburgh, 1993); D. Hay and N. Rogers, *Eighteenth-Century English Society: Shuttles and Swords* (Oxford, 1997); Livesey, *Civil Society and Empire*.
4. W.G. Runciman, *Very Different but Much the Same: The Evolution of English Society since 1714* (2014).
5. F. Grose, *A Classical Dictionary of the Vulgar Tongue* (1796).
6. P.J. Begent and H. Chessyre, *The Most Noble Order of the Garter: 650 Years* (1999); P. Galloway, *The Order of the Thistle* (2009).
7. J. Cannon, *Aristocratic Century: The Peerage of Eighteenth-Century England* (Cambridge, 1984), p. 32.
8. F.L. Ford, *Robe and Sword: The Regrouping of the French Aristocracy after Louis XIV* (Cambridge, MA, 1953).
9. Whiteley, *Lord North*.
10. Goodrich, *Debating England's Aristocracy*; idem, 'Understanding a Language of "Aristocracy", 1700–1850', *Historical Journal* 56 (2013), pp. 369–98.
11. Hutchinson, *Fuller of Sussex*, p. 64; R.G. Thorne (ed.), *The History of Parliament: The House of Commons, 1790–1820* (1976), p. 848.
12. Austen, *Emma*, p. 353.
13. J. Simon, 'Keith, George, styled tenth Earl Marischal (1692/3?–1778)', *Oxford Dictionary of National Biography* (2004); online at https://www.oxforddnb.com/view/10.1093/ref:odnb/9780198614128.001.0001/odnb-9780198614128-e-1004725 (accessed 16 February 2021).
14. 'Lord Great Chamberlain', *Encyclopaedia Britannica*, 29 vols (Chicago, 1911), vol. 17; online at https://en.wikisource.org/wiki/1911_Encyclop%C3%A6dia_Britannica/Lord_Great_Chamberlain (accessed 16 February 2021).
15. R. Bucholz (2008), 'Seymour, Charles, sixth duke of Somerset (1662–1748), politician and courtier', *Oxford Dictionary of National Biography*; online at https://www.oxforddnb.com/view/10.1093/ref:odnb/9780198614128.001.0001/odnb-9780198614128-e-25158 (accessed 16 February 2021).
16. J.L.M. Stewart, *The Story of the Atholl Highlanders* (1987).
17. H. Costley-White, *Mary Cole, Countess of Berkeley: A Biography* (1961).
18. Z. Jamoussi, *Primogeniture and Entail in England: A Survey of Their History and Representation in Literature* (Cambridge, 2001).
19. S. Richardson, *Clarissa: Or, the History of a Young Lady* (1748), ed. J.A. Burrell (New York, 1950); C. Hill, 'Clarissa Harlowe and Her Times', in idem, *Puritanism and Revolution: Studies in Interpretation of the English Revolution of the Seventeenth Century* (1938), pp. 367–94; esp. p. 367.
20. H.C. Shelley, *The Art of the Wallace Collection* (1913).
21. L. Stone and J.F. Stone, *An Open Elite? England, 1540–1880* (Oxford, 1984).
22. N. Gash, *Lord Liverpool: The Life and Political Career of Robert Banks Jenkinson, 2nd Earl of Liverpool, 1770–1828* (1984); Hay, *Lord Liverpool*.
23. T. Raybould, *The Economic Emergence of the Black Country: A Study of the Dudley Estate* (Newton Abbot, 1973).

24. Cannon, *Aristocratic Century*, p. 127.
25. For James Cecil, 6th earl of Salisbury (1713–80), see https://en.wikipedia.org/wiki/James_Cecil,_6th_Earl_of_Salisbury (accessed 11 March 2021).
26. C. Oman, *The Gascoyne Heiress: The Life and Diaries of Frances Mary Gascoyne-Cecil, 1802–39* (1968).
27. C.S. Sykes, *Private Palaces: Life in the Great London Houses* (1985); J. Stourton, *Great Houses of London* (2012).
28. J.D. Hunt, *The Genius of the Place: The English Landscape Garden, 1620–1820* (1975); S. Bending, *Green Retreats: Women, Gardens, and Eighteenth-Century Culture* (Cambridge, 2013).
29. R. Wilson and A. Mackley, *Creating Paradise: The Building of the English Country House, 1660–1880* (2000); J. Macaulay, *The Classical Country House in Scotland, 1660–1800* (1987); H. Montgomery-Massingberd and C.S. Sykes, *Great Houses of Ireland* (1999).
30. D. Guinness, *Georgian Dublin* (1979); Sykes, *Private Palaces*; Stourton, *Great Houses of London*; and the Georgian House, Edinburgh: see https://www.visitscotland.com/info/see-do/the-georgian-house-p246361 (accessed 16 February 2021).
31. Cannon, *Aristocratic Century*, p. 85: table 20.
32. F. Russell, *John, 3rd Earl of Bute: Patron and Collector* (2004).
33. M. Kilburn, 'William Henry, Prince, first duke of Gloucester and Edinburgh (1743–1805)', *Oxford Dictionary of National Biography* (2008); online at https://www.oxforddnb.com/view/10.1093/ref:odnb/9780198614128.001.0001/odnb-9780198614128-e-29456 (accessed 16 February 2021).
34. Pope, 'Essay on Man', p. 542, lines 215–16.
35. W.D. Rubinstein, *Men of Property: The Very Wealthy in Britain since the Industrial Revolution* (1981); T. Piketty, *Capital in the Twenty-First Century*, trans. A. Goldhammer (Cambridge, MA, 2014); W.D. Rubinstein, *Who Were the Rich? British Wealth-Holders, Vol. 1: 1809–24* (Brighton, 2017).
36. Anon. [L. Meriton], *Pecuniae Obediunt Omnia: Money Masters All Things – A Poem . . .* (York, 1696), p. 4.
37. Anon., *No Money, No Friend: A Ballad* (*c.* 1670).
38. J. Swift, in the *Examiner* 13 (2 November 1710).
39. J. Gay, *The Beggar's Opera* (1728), act 1, sc. 8.
40. Thompson, *Gentrification*, pp. 73–4.
41. Southey, *Letters from England*, pp. 362, 371.
42. Corfield, *Power and the Professions*, p. 11.
43. T. Carlyle, *The French Revolution: A History* (1837), part 2, book 7, ch. 7.
44. E. Chamberlayne (ed.), *Angliae Notitia: Or, the Present State of England* (20th edn, 1702), p. 301.
45. G. Miège, *The New State of England* (1691), part 2, p. 230.
46. J. Raven, *Judging New Wealth: Popular Publishing and Responses to Commerce in England, 1750–1800* (Oxford, 1997).
47. G.A. Mingay, *English Landed Society in the Eighteenth Century* (1963); Thompson, *Gentrification*, pp. 36, 43–4, 96–7, 121–2, 143.
48. Ibid., p. 70, refuting Rubinstein.
49. N. Ferguson, *The World's Banker: The History of the House of Rothschilds* (1998).
50. P. Lawrence, *The Rise and Fall of Wanstead House, 1667–1857* (2008).
51. W. Speck, 'Dunk, George Montagu, second earl of Halifax (1716–1771), politician', *Oxford Dictionary of National Biography* (2006); online at https://www.oxforddnb.com/view/10.1093/ref:odnb/9780198614128.001.0001/odnb-9780198614128-e-8266 (accessed 16 February 2021).
52. For Sarah Fane, countess of Westmorland (1764–93), see https://en.wikipedia.org/wiki/Sarah_Fane,_Countess_of_Westmorland (accessed 11 March 2021).

53. P. Clarke, *The First House in the City: An Excursion with the History of Child and Co.* (1973).
54. Cannon, *Aristocratic Century*, p. 32; P.J. Corfield, 'Class by Name and Number in Eighteenth-Century Britain', in idem (ed.), *Language, History and Class* (Oxford, 1991), pp. 101–30, esp. p. 129.
55. G.C. Richards, 'The Creation of Peers Recommended by the Younger Pitt', *American Historical Review* 34 (1928), pp. 47–54; M.W. McCahill, 'Peerage Creations and the Changing Character of the British Nobility, 1770–1830', *English Historical Review* 96 (1981), pp. 259–84; idem and E.A. Wasson, 'The New Peerage: Recruitment to the House of Lords, 1704–1847', *Historical Journal* 46 (2003), pp. 1–38.
56. For William Pole-Tylney-Long-Wellesley, 4th Earl of Mornington, see https://en.wikipedia.org/wiki/William_Pole-Tylney-Long-Wellesley,_4th_Earl_of_Mornington (accessed 11 March 2021).
57. W.T. Gibson, '"Withered Branches and Weighty Symbols": Surname Substitution in England, 1660–1880', *British Journal for Eighteenth-Century Studies* 15 (1992), pp. 17–33; G. Clark, *The Son Also Rises: Surnames and the History of Social Mobility* (Princeton, 2014).
58. P. Gauci, *William Beckford: The First Prime Minister of the London Empire* (New Haven, 2013).
59. A. Boyd, *England's Wealthiest Son: A Study of William Beckford* (1962); D.E. Ostergard (ed.), *William Beckford: An Eye for the Magnificent, 1760–1844* (2001).
60. E. Richards, *The Leviathan of Wealth: The Sutherland Fortune in the Industrial Revolution* (1972).
61. Idem, 'Gower, Elizabeth Leveson- [*née* Lady Elizabeth Sutherland], duchess of Sutherland and *suo jure* countess of Sutherland (1765–1839), landowner', *Oxford Dictionary of National Biography* (2004); online at https://www.oxforddnb.com/view/10.1093/ref:odnb/9780198614128.001.0001/odnb-9780198614128-e-42000 (accessed 16 February 2021).
62. A. Boyington, 'Maids, Wives, Widows: Female Architectural Patronage in Eighteenth-Century Britain' (PhD thesis, University of Cambridge, 2018).
63. H.L. Malchow, *Gentlemen Capitalists: The Social and Political World of the Victorian Businessman* (Stanford, 1992); J.M. Crook, *The Rise of the Nouveaux Riches: Style and Status in Victorian and Edwardian Architecture* (1999).
64. L. Ince, *The South Wales Iron Industry, 1750–1885* (1993); C. Evans, 'The Labyrinth of Flames': Work and Social Conflict in Early Industrial Merthyr Tydfil* (Cardiff, 1993); K. Strange, *Merthyr Tydfil, Iron Metropolis: Life in a Welsh Industrial Town* (Stroud, 2005).
65. Cyfarthfa Park and Castle: see https://www.visitmerthyr.co.uk/things-to-do/attractions/cyfarthfa-park-and-castle (accessed 16 February 2021).
66. Thompson, *Gentrification*, p. 99.
67. I.G. Wyllie, *The Self-Made Man in America* (1954); T. Mulligan, *Justice and the Meritocratic State* (Abingdon, 2018).
68. P.J. Corfield, 'The Rivals: Landed and Other Gentlemen', in N.B. Harte and R. Quinault (eds), *Land and Society in Britain, 1700–1914: Essays in Honour of F.M.L. Thompson* (Manchester, 1996), pp. 1–33, esp. pp. 21, 23.
69. Ibid.; Williamson, *British Masculinity in the Gentleman's Magazine*.
70. Sir Thomas Smith, *De republica Anglorum* (1583), as cited in Corfield, 'The Rivals', p. 5.
71. Idem, *Power and the Professions*, p. 80.
72. R. Steele, *Guardian* 34 (20 April 1713).
73. J. Austen, *Pride and Prejudice* (1813), pp. 222, 224, 376.
74. N. Bailey, *An Universal Etymological English Dictionary* (1721), *sub* 'Gentleman'.
75. V. Knox, *Essays, Moral and Literary*, 2 vols (1779), vol. 2, p. 231.

Chapter 14: Middlocrats

1. P. Earle, *The Making of the Middle Class: Business, Society and Family Life in London, 1660–1730* (Berkeley, 1989); J. Smail, *The Origins of Middle-Class Culture: Halifax, Yorkshire, 1660–1760* (1994); J. Barry and C. Brooks (eds), *The Middling Sort of People: Culture, Society and Politics in England, 1550–1800* (Basingstoke, 1994); S. Gunn, 'Class, Identity and the Urban: The Middle Class in England, c. 1790–1950', *Urban History* 31 (2004), pp. 29–35; H.R. French, *The Middle Sort of People in Provincial England, 1600–1750* (Oxford, 2007); L. Davidoff and C. Hall, *Family Fortunes: Men and Women of the English Middle Class, 1780–1850* (2002; 2018).
2. P.J. Corfield, 'Business Leaders and Town Gentry in Early Industrial Britain: Specialist Occupations and Shared Urbanism', *Urban History* 39 (2012), pp. 20–49.
3. K. Wrightson, 'Estates, Degrees and Sorts: Changing Perceptions of Society in Tudor and Stuart England', in Corfield (ed.), *Language, History and Class*, pp. 30–52; and idem, 'Class by Name and Number'.
4. D. Defoe, *The Life and Strange Adventures of Robinson Crusoe* (1719/20; 1840), vol. 1, p. 3.
5. Ibid.
6. D. Hume, *Of Refinement in the Arts* (1742), quoted in Copley and Edgar (eds), *David Hume*, p. 111.
7. O. Goldsmith, *The Vicar of Wakefield* (1766; in Harmondsworth, 1982), p. 116.
8. D. Mallet [Malloch], *Horace Epistle 13, Book 1, Imitated* (1784), in *London Magazine* (1784), p. 125.
9. J. Priestley, as cited in R.V. Holt, *The Unitarian Contribution to Social Progress in England* (1938), p. 86.
10. J. Shipley, *The Works . . .*, 2 vols (1792), vol. 2, pp. 143, 273.
11. Anon. [J. Larwood], *Erratics: By a Sailor . . .* (1800), p. 39.
12. R.V. Holt, *The Unitarian Contribution to Social Progress in England* (1938), p. 86.
13. 'What is Middle Class, Anyway?', *CNN Business* (2017); online at http://money.cnn.com/infographic/economy/what-is-middle-class-anyway/index.html (accessed 16 Feburary 2021).
14. J. Tucker, *Selections from His Economic and Political Writings* (New York, 1931), p. 264.
15. Anon., *The Protester, on Behalf of the People* 2 (9 June 1753), p. 10; A.H. Johnson, *The Disappearance of the Small Landowner* (Oxford, 1909; 1963).
16. J.R. Wordie, 'The Chronology of English Enclosure, 1500–1914', *Economic History Review*, 2nd ser. 36 (1983), pp. 483–505.
17. M. Wodhull, *The Equality of Mankind: A Poem* (Oxford, 1765); M. Vaulbert de Chantilly, 'Wodhull, Michael (1740–1816), book collector and poet', *Oxford Dictionary of National Biography* (2008); online at https://www.oxforddnb.com/view/10.1093/ref:odnb/9780198614128.001.0001/odnb-9780198614128-e-29818 (accessed 16 February 2021).
18. G. Clark, *Betting on Lives: The Culture of Life Insurance in England, 1695–1775* (Manchester, 1999).
19. D.R. Green, 'Tontines, Annuities and Civic Improvements in Georgian Britain', *Urban History* 46 (2019), pp. 649–94.
20. C. Meldrew, *The Economy of Obligation: The Culture of Credit and Social Relations in Early Modern England* (Basingstoke, 1997); M. Finn, *The Character of Credit: Personal Debt in English Culture, 1740–1914* (Cambridge, 2003); T. Paul, *The Poverty of Disaster: Debt and Insecurity in Eighteenth-Century Britain* (Cambridge, 2019).
21. J.C. Bennett, 'The English Anglican Practice of Pew-Renting, 1800–1960' (PhD thesis, University of Birmingham, 2011).
22. J. Hoppit, *Risk and Failure in English Business, 1700–1800* (Cambridge, 1987).
23. Austen, *Emma*, p. 368.

24. Hill, *Women Alone*.
25. *British Parliamentary Papers* (1852–53), vol. 85, report 5, SW Division, pp. 78–9.
26. K. Hughes, *The Victorian Governess* (1993); R. Brandon, *Other People's Daughters: The Life and Times of the Governess* (2008); M.E. Smith (ed.), *Diary of a Betley Governess in 1812* (Crewe, 2010).
27. J. Trusler, *The Way to Become Rich and Respectable* . . . (1755; and many later edns).
28. Thompson, *Gentrification*, p. 20; F. Crouzet, *The First Industrialists: The Problem of Origins* (Cambridge, 1985), tables 2–5.
29. P. Gauci, *Politics and Society in Great Yarmouth, 1660–1722* (Oxford, 1996).
30. Austen, *Emma*, p. 281.
31. J. Bisset (ed.), *A Poetic Survey round Birmingham* . . . (Birmingham, 1800), pp. 21–36, 61–2.
32. W. Parson and T. Bradshaw (eds), *Staffordshire General and Commercial Directory for 1818*, 3 vols (Manchester, 1818), vol. 1, p. xxix.
33. Austen, *Emma*, p. 310.
34. W. Hutton, *An History of Birmingham* (Birmingham, 1781), p. 24; J. Money, *Experience and Identity: Birmingham and the West Midlands, 1760–1800* (Manchester, 1977); Whyman, *Useful Knowledge of William Hutton*.
35. Anon., *The Hampshire Directory* (Winchester, 1784), p. 28.
36. M.L. Cioni, *Women and Law in Elizabethan England, with Particular Reference to the Court of Chancery* (1985); N. Phillips, *Women in Business, 1700–1850* (2006).
37. *Kent's Directory for the Year 1774 [for] the Cities of London and Westminster* . . . (42nd edn, 1774), p. 104; R. Porter, *Health for Sale: Quackery in England, 1660–1850* (Manchester, 1969), pp. 80–1.
38. Corfield, 'Business Leaders and Town Gentry', pp. 34–6.
39. M.R. Hunt, *The Middling Sort: Commerce, Gender and the Family in England, 1680–1780* (Berkeley, 1996), pp. 129–32, 185–8; H. Barker, *The Business of Women: Female Enterprise and Urban Development, 1760–1830* (Oxford, 2006), pp. 47–54; Phillips, *Women in Business*.
40. P. Sharpe, 'Gender in the Economy: Female Merchants and Family Businesses in the British Isles, 1600–1850', *Social History/Histoire sociale* 34 (2001), pp. 296–7.
41. J. Cleland, *Fanny Hill: Memoirs of a Woman of Pleasure* (1748; 1970), p. 115.
42. J. O'Keefe, *Man-Milliner* (1798).
43. H.-C. Mui and L. Mui, *Shops and Shopkeeping in Eighteenth-Century England* (1989); A. Bennett, *Shops, Shambles and the High Street: Retailing in Georgian Hull, 1770–1810* (Wetherby, 2005).
44. E. Abrahamson, 'Managerial Fads and Fashions: The Diffusion and Rejection of Innovations', *Academy of Management Review* 16 (1991), pp. 586–612; J. Styles, *The Dress of the People: Everyday Fashion in Eighteenth-Century England* (2007).
45. J. Turner, 'An Anatomy of a "Disorderly" Neighbourhood: Rosemary Lane and Rag Fair, *c.* 1690–1765' (PhD thesis, University of Hertfordshire, 2014).
46. N. Corbie, *Frost Fairs to Funfairs: A History of the English Fair* (Stroud, 2017).
47. Austen, *Pride and Prejudice*, p. 177.
48. Tickell, *Shoplifting*.
49. R.J. Bennett, *Local Business Voice: The History of Chambers of Commerce in Britain, Ireland and Revolutionary America, 1760–2011* (Oxford, 2011).
50. Idem, *The Voice of Liverpool Business: The First Chamber of Commerce and the Atlantic Economy, 1774–c. 1796* (Liverpool, 2010).
51. Money, *Experience and Identity*, p. 34.
52. W.J. Reader, *Professional Men: The Rise of the Professional Classes in Nineteenth-Century England* (1966); C.M. Cipolla, 'The Professions: The Long View', *Journal of European Economic History* 2 (1973), pp. 37–51; G. Holmes, *Augustan England: Professions, State and Society, 1680–1730* (1982); Corfield, *Power and the Professions*.

53. T.L. Haskell (ed.), *The Authority of Experts: Studies in History and Theory* (Bloomington, IN, 1984).
54. G. Colman the Younger, *New Hay at the Old Market . . .* (1795), p. 10.
55. Corfield, *Power and the Professions*, pp. 82, 91, 110, 120, 122, 128, 158.
56. A. Digby, *Making a Medical Living: Doctors and Patients in the English Market for Medicine, 1720–1911* (Cambridge, 1994).
57. R. Porter, *Quacks: Fakers and Charlatans in English Medicine* (Stroud, 2000).
58. Corfield, *Power and the Professions,* pp. 42–69.
59. Idem, 'Eighteenth-Century Lawyers and the Advent of the Modern Professional Ethos', in P. Chassaigne and J.-P. Genet (eds), *Droit et société en France et Grande Bretagne/Law and Society in France and England* (Paris, 2003), pp. 103–26.
60. D. Lemmings, *Professors of the Law: Barristers and English Legal Culture in the Eighteenth Century* (Oxford, 2000); idem (ed.), *Crime, Courtrooms and the Public Sphere in Britain, 1700–1850* (Farnham, 2012).
61. R. Robson, *The Attorney in Eighteenth-Century England* (Cambridge, 1959), p. 159.
62. Corfield, *Power and the Professions,* p. 52; C. Brooks, *'Pettifoggers and Vipers of the Commonwealth': The 'Lower Branch' of the Legal Profession in Early Modern England* (Cambridge, 1986).
63. A. Tropp, *The School Teachers: The Growth of the Teaching Profession in England and Wales from 1800 to the Present Day* (1957); A. Etzioni (ed.), *The Semi-Professions and Their Organisation: Teachers, Nurses, Social Workers* (New York, 1969).
64. Corfield, *Power and the Professions,* p. 180.
65. D. Lemmings, *Gentlemen and Barristers: The Inns of Court and the English Bar, 1680– 1730* (Oxford, 1990); C. Kenny, *King's Inns and the Kingdom of Ireland: The Irish 'Inn of Court', 1541–1800* (Dublin, 1992).
66. S. Shorvon and L. Luxon (eds), *500 Years of the Royal College of Physicians* (2018); W.S. Craig, *History of the Royal College of Physicians of Edinburgh* (Oxford, 1976).
67. Z. Cope, *The Royal College of Surgeons of England: A History* (1959).
68. H.M. Dingwall, *A Famous and Flourishing Society: The History of the Royal College of Surgeons of Edinburgh, 1505–2005* (Edinburgh, 2005).
69. J.G.L. Burnby, *A Study of the English Apothecary from 1660 to 1760: Medical History* (1983), suppl. 3, pp. 1–116; I. Loudon, *Medical Care and the General Practitioner, 1750– 1860* (Oxford, 1986).
70. I. Waddington, *The Medical Profession in the Industrial Revolution* (Dublin, 1984); P.J. Corfield, 'From Poison Peddlers to Civic Worthies: The Reputation of the Apothecaries in Georgian England', *Social History of Medicine* 22 (2009), pp. 1–21.
71. M.S. Larson, *The Rise of Professionalism: A Sociological Analysis* (Berkeley, 1977); R. Dingwall and P. Fenn, '"A Respectable Profession?" Sociological and Economic Perspectives on the Regulation of Professional Services', *International Review of Law and Economics* 7 (1987), pp. 51–64.
72. *The Lancet* 1 (October 1823), p. 2.
73. B.L.B. Kaye, *The Development of the Architectural Profession in England: A Sociological Study* (1960).
74. R. Buchanan, *Engineers: A History of the Engineering Profession in Britain, 1750–1914* (1989); G. Watson, *The Smeatonians: The Society of Civil Engineers* (1989); G. Cookson, *The Age of Machinery: Engineering in the Industrial Revolution, 1770–1850* (Woodbridge, 2018).
75. Corfield, *Power and the Professions,* pp. 181–4.
76. Ibid., pp. 1–17, 174–99, 223–42.
77. P. Fara, *Erasmus Darwin: Sex, Science and Serendipity* (Oxford, 2012).
78. J.C. Loudon, *Architectural Magazine* 2 (1835), p. 472.
79. Wahrman, *Imagining the Middle Class.*

80. *Hereford Independent* (1 January 1825); K. Kissack, *Monmouth: The Making of a County Town* (Chichester, 1975), pp. 56–64; B. Smith, '"Men of Monmouth" versus the "Huffing Braggart Puff'd Nobility": What Light Does the Monmouth Burgess Crisis of 1818–26 Throw upon Local Structures of Power and Resistance?' (MA dissertation, Royal Holloway, London University, 1994), pp. 10–12, 31–3.

81. M. Craven on male dress, cited in R.B. de Monvel, *Beau Brummell and His Times* (1908); P. Byrde, *The Male Image: The Men's Fashion in England, 1300–1970* (1979); N. Waugh, *The Cut of Men's Clothes, 1600–1900* (2013).

82. E.J. Lapsansky and A.A. Verplanck (eds), *Quaker Aesthetics: Reflections on a Quaker Ethic in American Design and Consumption, 1720–1920* (Philadelphia, 2002).

Chapter 15: The Advent of the Workers

1. R.S. Neale, *Class in English Society, 1680–1850* (Oxford, 1981); D. Cannadine, *The Rise and Fall of Class in Britain* (New York, 1999).

2. Thompson, *Making of the English Working Class*; Hitchcock and Shoemaker, *London Lives*.

3. Pottle (ed.), *Boswell's London Journal*, p. 72.

4. Hecht, *Domestic Servant Class*, p. 187.

5. F.M. Misson, *Memoirs and Observations in His Travels over England*, trans. J. Ozell (1719), p. 221.

6. Anon., *The Humour of the Age: A Comedy* (1701), p. 18.

7. B. Lemire, *Dress, Culture and Commerce: The British Clothing Trade before the Factory, 1660–1800* (Basingstoke, 1997).

8. T. Spence, *The Giant-Killer: Or, Anti-Landlord* 1 (6 August 1814).

9. Grose, *Classical Dictionary of the Vulgar Tongue*; idem, *A Provincial Glossary, with a Collection of Local Proverbs . . .* (1787); J. Sorensen, *Strange Vernaculars: How Eighteenth-Century Slang, Cant, Provincial Languages and Nautical Jargon became English* (Princeton, 2017).

10. Tucker, *Protean Shape*, p. 80.

11. *The World* (1755), cited in C.W. Cunnington and P. Cunnington, *A Handbook of English Costume in the Eighteenth Century* (1957), p. 21.

12. Mme van Muyden (ed. and trans.), *A Foreign View of England in the Reigns of George I and George II: The Letters of M. César de Saussure to His Family* (1902), p. 192.

13. Anon., *Low-Life: Or, One Half of the World Knows Not How the Other Half Live* (1752); and see above, p. 83.

14. T. Paine, *The Complete Writings . . .*, ed. P.S. Foner, 2 vols (New York, 1969), vol. 2, p. 478.

15. Corfield, 'Class by Name and Number', p. 119.

16. E.P. Thompson, 'The Patricians and the Plebs', in idem, *Customs in Common*, pp. 16–96.

17. Anon. [R. Steele], *The Plebeian* (1719); answered by Anon., *The Patrician* (1719).

18. J. Poole, *Patrician and Parvenu: Or, Confusion Worse Confounded – A Comedy* (1835).

19. G. Crossick, 'From Gentleman to the Residuum: Languages of Social Description in Victorian Britain', in Corfield (ed.), *Language, History and Class*, pp. 150–78, esp. pp. 161–2, 167–9, 171–2, 174.

20. D. Defoe, *A Review of the State of the British Nation* 6/36 (2 June 1709).

21. M.D. George, *England in Transition* (Harmondsworth, 1964), pp. 10–11.

22. *Monthly Review* 4 (January 1751), p. 229.

23. Norfolk Record Office, Case 16c, Corporation of Norwich: Petition for Bill to Regulate Burden of Poor Rate, 1763.

24. J. Gray, *Some Reflections intended to Promote the Success of the Said Society*, in G. Dempster, *A Discourse containing . . . Proceedings . . . of the Society for Extending the Fisheries and Improving the Sea Coasts of Great Britain* (1789), p. 50.

25. Bible, Luke 10:7.

26. Corfield, 'Class by Name and Number', p. 125.
27. Anon., *Earnestly Recommended to the Serious Attention of My Fellow Labourers and Fellow Townsmen, the Honest, Well-Meaning and Industrious Mechanics and Manufacturers of the Town of Birmingham . . .* (Birmingham, 1790).
28. Anon., 'Wholesome Advice to the Swinish Multitude' (1795), in J. Holloway and J. Black (eds), *Later English Broadside Ballads* (1975), pp. 278–9.
29. Burke, *Reflections*, p. 173.
30. G. Cruikshank, *The British Beehive* (1840; publ. 1867).
31. T. Gray, *Elegy, Written in a Country Churchyard* (1751), stanza 14.
32. J. Goodridge and B. Keegan (eds), *A History of British Working-Class Literature* (Cambridge, 2017).
33. J. Burnett, *Useful Toil: Autobiographies of Working People from the 1820s to the 1920s* (1974).
34. See variously R. Davis, *Stephen Duck, the Thresher Poet* (Orono, ME, 1926); A. Yearsley, *Poems on Several Occasions* (1785; 1994); R. Southey, *Lives of Uneducated Poets* (1836), pp. 125–34; K. Andrews, *Ann Yearsley and Hannah More, Patronage and Poetry: The Story of a Literary Relationship* (2015); Anon. [J. Woodhouse], *Poems on Sundry Occasions, by James Woodhouse a Journeyman Shoemaker* (1764); I. McIntyre, *Robert Burns: A Life* (1995; 2001); G.S. Wilkie, *Robert Burns: A Life in Letters* (Glasgow, 2011); J. Bate, *John Clare's New Life* (Cheltenham, 2004); S. Kövesi, *John Clare: Nature, Criticism and History* (2017).
35. J. G. Williamson, *Did British Capitalism Breed Inequality?* (1985; 2013); C. Feinstein, *Conjectures and Contrivances: Economic Growth and the Standard of Living in Britain during the Industrial Revolution* (Oxford, 1996); R. Floud and B. Harris, 'Health, Height and Welfare: Britain 1700–1980', in R.H. Stekel and R. Floud (eds), *Health and Welfare during Industrialisation* (Chicago, 1997), pp. 91–126; E. Griffin, 'Diets, Hunger and Living Standards during the British Industrial Revolution', *Past & Present* 239 (2018), pp. 71–111.
36. Thompson, *Making of the English Working Class*.
37. King and Tomkins (eds), *The Poor in England*, pp. 11, 120–34, 254–8.
38. M. Tebbutt, *Making Ends Meet: Pawnbroking and Working-Class Credit* (Leicester, 1983).
39. M. Thale, 'Introduction', in idem (ed.), *The Autobiography of Francis Place* (Cambridge, 1972), pp. xviii–xix, xxiv–xxvi, xxx; D. Miles, *Francis Place, 1771–1854: The Life of a Remarkable Radical* (Brighton, 1988).
40. J. Rule, *The Labouring Classes in Early Industrial England, 1750–1850* (2014).
41. E.H. Hunt, 'Industrialisation and Regional Inequality: Wages in Britain, 1760–1914', *Journal of Economic History* 46 (1986), pp. 935–66; idem, *Regional Wage Variations in Britain, 1850–1914* (Oxford, 1973).
42. S. Shave, *Poverty, Gender and Life-Cycle under the English Poor Law, 1760–1834* (2012).
43. Hitchcock, *Down and Out*; idem, 'Begging on the Streets of Eighteenth-Century London', *Journal of British Studies* 44 (2005), pp. 478–98.
44. H. Shore, *London's Criminal Underworlds, c. 1720–c. 1930: A Social and Cultural History* (Basingstoke, 2015).
45. J.A. James, 'Personal Wealth Distribution in Late-Eighteenth-Century Britain', *Economic History Review*, 2nd ser. 41 (1988), pp. 543–65; R.V. Jackson, 'Inequality of Incomes and Lifespans in England since 1688', *Economic History Review*, 2nd ser. 47 (1994), pp 508–24; Piketty, *Capital*, pp. 343–4, 377, 413–14.
46. R.Q. Gray, *The Labour Aristocracy in Victorian Edinburgh* (Oxford, 1976); T. Lummis, *The Labour Aristocracy, 1850–1914* (Aldershot, 1994).
47. S. Pollard, *A History of Labour in Sheffield* (Liverpool, 1959); D. Smith, *Conflict and Compromise: Class Formation in English Society, 1830–1914 – A Comparative Study of Birmingham and Sheffield* (1982); D. Hey, *The Fiery Blades of Hallamshire: Sheffield and Its Neighbourhood, 1660–1740* (Leicester, 1991).

48. Anon., *The Vicar of Bray* (1728), verse 5.
49. B.R. Mitchell, with P. Deane, *Abstract of British Historical Statistics* (Cambridge, 1971), pp. 468–73, 476.
50. B. Semmel, *The Rise of Free Trade Imperialism: Classical Political Economy, the Empire of Free Trade and the Rise of Imperialism, 1750–1850* (Cambridge, 1970; 2004); C. Schonhardt-Bailey (ed.), *Free Trade: The Repeal of the Corn Laws* (Bristol, 1996).
51. H.-J. Voth, *Time and Work in England, 1750–1830* (Oxford, 2001).
52. J. Lown, *Women and Industrialization: Gender and Work in Nineteenth-Century England* (Cambridge, 1990); S. Nicholas and D. Oxley, 'The Living Standards of Women during the Industrial Revolution, 1795–1820', *Economic History Review*, 2nd ser. 46 (1993), pp. 723–49; D. Valenze, *The First Industrial Woman* (Oxford, 1995); J. Humphries, *The Wages of Women in England, 1260–1850* (2014).
53. 'Sempronia' [M. Lamb], 'On Needlework', *New British Lady's Magazine* (April 1815); S. Burton, *A Double Life: A Biography of Charles and Mary Lamb* (2003).
54. For the long-term trend in earnings, see Mitchell, *Abstract of British Historical Statistics*, p. 343.
55. W. Cudworth, *Worstedopolis: A Sketch History of the Town and Trade of Bradford* (Bradford, 1888); G. Firth, *A History of Bradford* (Chichester, 1997).
56. R.G. Wilson, 'The Textile Industry' and P.J. Corfield, 'From Second City to Regional Capital', both in C. Rawcliffe and R.G. Wilson (eds), *Norwich since 1550* (2004), pp. 139–66 and 219–42.
57. R.J. Morris, *Class and Class Consciousness during the Industrial Revolution, 1780–1850* (1979); C. Calhoun, *The Question of Class Struggle: Tradition and Community in England Popular Radicalism, 1790–1830* (Chicago, 1981); Rule, *Labouring Classes*.
58. L.J. Colley, *Britons: Forging the Nation, 1707–1837* (1992; 2003); K. Navickas, *Loyalism and Radicalism in Lancashire, 1798–1815* (Oxford, 2009).
59. Anon., *The British Tocsin: Or, Proofs of National Ruin* (1795), pp. 8, 21.
60. G. Claeys, *Machinery, Money and the Millennium: From Moral Economy to Socialism, 1815–60* (Cambridge, 1987); E. Dell, *A Strange, Eventful History: Democratic Socialism in Britain* (2000); G. Claeys, *Owenite Socialism: Pamphlets and Correspondence* (2005).
61. Boswell, *Life of Johnson*, ed. Chapman, p. 423 (October 1769).
62. C. Cappe, *An Account of ... a Female Friendly Society in York ...* (York, 1800); E. Hopkins, *Working-Class Self-Help in Nineteenth-Century England: Responses to Industrialisation* (1995); S. Cordery, *British Friendly Societies, 1750–1914* (Basingstoke, 2003); B. Harris, *The Origins of the British Welfare State: Social Welfare in England and Wales, 1800–1945* (Basingstoke, 2004).
63. Paine, *Rights of Man*, p. 262.
64. C.R. Dobson, *Masters and Journeymen: A Prehistory of Industrial Relations, 1717–1800* (1980); J. Rule (ed.), *British Trade Unionism, 1750–1850: The Formative Years* (Harlow, 1988); A.J. Reid, *United We Stand: A History of Britain's Trade Unions* (2004); M. Chase, *Early Trade Unionism: Fraternity, Skill and the Politics of Labour* (2012).
65. K. Navickas, *Protest and the Politics of Space and Place, 1789–1848* (Manchester, 2015).
66. Colley, *In Defiance of Oligarchy*, p. 155.
67. *Oxford English Dictionary*, sub verb 'to strike', IV: 8; N. McCord, *Strikes* (1980).
68. *Gentleman's Magazine* 22 (October 1752), p. 476.
69. P. Mantoux, *The Industrial Revolution in the Eighteenth Century: An Outline of the Beginnings of the Modern Factory System in England* (1928), pp. 79–83.
70. A. Plummer, *The London Weavers' Company, 1600–1970* (1972), pp. 315–39.
71. A. Smith, *An Inquiry into the Nature and Causes of the Wealth of Nations*, 2 vols (1776; 1970), vol. 1, pp. 57–78.
72. G.E. Manwaring and B. Dobrée, *The Floating Republic: An Account of the Mutinies at Spithead and the Nore in 1797* (1935; Barnsley, 2004); A.V. Coats and P. MacDougall (eds), *The Naval Mutinies of 1797: Unity and Perseverance* (Woodbridge, 2011).

73. M.I. Thomis, *The Luddites: Machine-Breaking in Regency England* (Newton Abbot, 1970); J. Dinwiddy, 'Luddism and Politics in the Northern Counties', in idem, *Radicalism and Reform in Britain, 1780–1850* (1992), pp. 371–401; F. Peel, *The Risings of the Luddites, Chartists and Plug-Drawers* (2019).
74. W. Cobbett, *Political Register* (11 September 1819).
75. S.E. Jones, *Against Technology: From the Luddites to Neo-Luddism* (2006).
76. Caricature in J. Addy, *A Coal and Iron Community in the Industrial Revolution* (1969; 1971), p. 71.
77. U. Carpenter (ed.), *Trade Unions under the Combination Acts, 1799–1823* (New York, 1972); S. Mac A'Ghobhainn and P. Berresford Ellis, *The Scottish Insurrection of 1820* (Edinburgh, 2001).
78. Miles, *Francis Place*.
79. G.A. Williams, *The Merthyr Rising* (1978; Cardiff, 1988).
80. G.D.H. Cole, *Attempts at General Union: A Study in British Trade Union History, 1818–34* (1953).
81. N. Thompson and C. Williams (eds), *Robert Owen and His Legacy* (Cardiff, 2011).
82. H.V. Evatt, *The Tolpuddle Martyrs: Injustice within the Law* (Sydney, 2009).
83. R.M. Martin, *TUC: The Growth of a Pressure Group, 1868–1976* (Oxford, 1980).
84. R. King, *The Frauds of London Detected . . .* (1776).
85. G. Cruikshank, *A Comic Alphabet* (1836): letter E.

Chapter 16: The Allure of Celebrities and Meritocrats

1. Anon., *A Treatise on Merit: Calculated to Correct the Vain, Improve the Modest, and Encourage the Deserving*, trans. T. Branch (1748), p. 6.
2. G. Ballard, *Memoirs of Several Ladies of Great Britain . . .* (1752).
3. J.M. Stott, *The Pantomime Life of Joseph Grimaldi: Laughter, Madness and the Story of Britain's Greatest Comedian* (Edinburgh, 2009).
4. N. Parsons, *Reading Gossip in Early Eighteenth-Century England* (Basingstoke, 2009).
5. T. Mole (ed.), *Romanticism and Celebrity Culture, 1750–1850* (Cambridge, 2009); A. Lilti, *The Invention of Celebrity, 1750–1850*, trans. L. Jeffress (Cambridge, 2017).
6. H. Greig, *The Beau Monde: Fashionable Society in Georgian London* (Oxford, 2013).
7. Foreman, *Georgiana, Duchess of Devonshire*.
8. M. Waldron, *Lactilla, Milkwoman of Clifton: The Life and Writings of Ann Yearsley, 1753–1806* (Athens, GA, 1996); Andrews, *Ann Yearsley and Hannah More*.
9. Southey, *Uneducated Poets*.
10. M. Collier, *The Woman's Labour: An Epistle to Mr Stephen Duck . . .* (1739); D. Landry, *The Muses of Resistance: Labouring-Class Women's Poetry in Britain, 1739–96* (Cambridge, 1990).
11. I. McIntyre, *Joshua Reynolds: The Life and Times of the First President of the Royal Academy* (2003).
12. G. Perry, *The First Actresses: From Nell Gwynne to Sarah Siddons* (Ann Arbor, 2011).
13. S.M. Rosenfeld, *The Theatre of the London Fairs in the Eighteenth Century* (1960).
14. G. Hopkins, *Nell Gwynne: A Passionate Life* (2000).
15. L. Ritchie, *David Garrick and the Mediation of Celebrity* (Cambridge, 2019).
16. M. Jonson, *A Troubled Grandeur: The Story of England's Greatest Actress* (Boston, MA, 1972).
17. L.-J. Rosenthal, *Infamous Commerce: Prostitution in Eighteenth-Century British Literature and Culture* (2006); White, *Queen of the Courtesans*.
18. A. Hanham, 'Parsons, Anne [Nancy] [*married name* Anne Maynard, Viscountess Maynard] (*c.* 1735–1814/15), courtesan and political mistress', *Oxford Dictionary of National Biography* (2005); online at https://www.oxforddnb.com/view/10.1093/ref:odnb/9780198614128.001.0001/odnb-9780198614128-e-75617 (accessed 17 February 2021).

19. I.M. Davis, *The Harlot and the Statesman: The Story of Elizabeth Armistead and Charles James Fox* (Kensal, 1986).
20. Q. Colville (ed.), *Emma Hamilton: Seduction and Celebrity* (2016); E. Contogouris, *Emma Hamilton and Late Eighteenth-Century European Art: Agency, Performance and Representation* (2018).
21. Anon. [E. Thompson], *The Meretriciad* (1761); M. Pointon, 'The Lives of Kitty Fisher', *Journal for Eighteenth-Century Studies* 27 (2004), pp. 77–97.
22. H.J. Jackson, *Those who Write for Immortality: Romantic Reputations and the Dream of Lasting Fame* (2015).
23. T. Seccombe and D. Turner, 'Lewson [*née* Vaughan], Jane [*known as* Lady Lewson] (1699/1700?–1816), eccentric and centenarian', *Oxford Dictionary of National Biography* (2009); online at https://www.oxforddnb.com/view/10.1093/ref:odnb/978019861 4128.001.0001/odnb-9780198614128-e-16613 (accessed 17 February 2021).
24. D. Greene, *Samuel Johnson* (Boston, MA, 1989); J.C.D. Clark, *Samuel Johnson: Literature, Religion and English Cultural Politics from the Restoration to Romanticism* (Cambridge, 1994); P. Martin, *Samuel Johnson: A Biography* (Cambridge, MA, 2008).
25. N.F. Löwe, 'Sam's Love for Sam: Samuel Beckett, Samuel Johnson, and "Human Wishes"', *Samuel Beckett Today* 8 (1999), pp. 189–203.
26. In sequence: S. Beckett, *Endgame* (1958), p. 37; S. Johnson, cited in Boswell, *Life of Johnson*, ed. Chapman, p. 754 (May 1776).
27. J. Harris, *Satire, Celebrity and Politics in Jane Austen* (Lewisburg, 2017).
28. G. McDayter, *Byronmania and the Birth of Celebrity Culture* (Albany, 2009); C. Tuitte, *Lord Byron and Scandalous Celebrity* (New York, 2015).
29. O. Goldsmith, *The Life of Richard Nash of Bath, Esq.* (1762); J. Eglin, *The Imaginary Autocrat: Beau Nash and the Invention of Bath* (2005).
30. I. Kelly, *Beau Brummell: The Ultimate Dandy* (2005).
31. R. van Krieken, *Celebrity Society* (2012); B. Kahr, *Celebrity Mad: Why Otherwise Intelligent People Worship Fame* (2019).
32. M.D. Young, *The Rise of the Meritocracy, 1870–2033: An Essay on Education and Equality* (1958).
33. Pope, 'Essay on Man', p. 542, lines 215–16; F. Rosslyn, *Alexander Pope: A Literary Life* (Basingstoke, 1990).
34. R. Burns, 'For a' That, and a' That' (1795), in T. Burke (ed.), *The Collected Poems of Robert Burns* (Ware, Hertfordshire, 1994), pp. 330–1; P.S. Hogg, *Robert Burns: The Patriot Bard* (Edinburgh, 2008).
35. J. Wesley, *Sermons on Several Occasions*, 9 vols (1788–1800), vol. 7, p. 14.
36. Anon., *Treatise on Merit*, p. 46.
37. Anon, [W. Combe], *Original Love Letters between a Lady of Quality and a Person of Inferior Station* (1784; Dublin 1811), pp. 291–30: letter 33.
38. S.-Y. Teng, 'Chinese Influence on the Western Examination System ...', *Harvard Journal of Asiatic Studies* 7/4 (September 1943), pp. 267–312; J.W. Chaffee, *The Thorny Gates of Learning in Sung China: A Social History of Examinations* (Albany, 1995), esp. pp. 182–4.
39. Letter from B. Jowett, 18 August 1846, in E. Abbott and L. Campbell (eds), *The Life and Letters of Benjamin Jowett, MA ...*, 2 vols (New York, 1897), vol. 1, p. 151.
40. W. Playfair, *British Family Antiquity ...* (1809).
41. A. Goodrich, *Henry Redhead Yorke: Politics and Identity in the Atlantic World, 1771–1832* (2019).
42. Whyman, *Useful Knowledge of William Hutton*, pp. 34–55.
43. Gore-Browne, *Chancellor Thurlow*, pp. 2–3.
44. P. Durrant, 'FitzRoy, Augustus Henry, third duke of Grafton (1735–1811), prime minister', *Oxford Dictionary of National Biography* (2008); online at https://www.oxforddnb.com/

view/10.1093/ref:odnb/9780198614128.001.0001/odnb-9780198614128-e-9628 (accessed 17 February 2021).

45. Anon. [A. Polson], *Law and Lawyers: Sketches and Illustrations* . . ., 2 vols (1840), vol. 1, pp. 99–100.

46. W.R. Anson (ed.), *Autobiography and Political Correspondence of Augustus Henry, 3rd Duke of Grafton* (1898), pp. 228–9 n. 1.

47. J. Boswell (ed.), *The Celebrated Letter from Samuel Johnson, LLD, to Philip Dormer Stanhope, Earl of Chesterfield* . . . (1790), p. 4.

48. A. Goldgar, *Impolite Learning: Conduct and Community in the Republic of Letters, 1680–1750* (New Haven, 1995); P. Clark, 'Spaces, Circuits, and Short-Circuits in the European Enlightenment', *Special Issue: Enlightenment? De Achttiende Eeuw* 43 (2011), pp. 50–64; A. Prendergast, *Literary Salons across Britain and Ireland in the Long Eighteenth Century* (Basingstoke, 2015).

49. Field, *Kit-Kat Club*.

50. L. Damrosch, *The Club: Johnson, Boswell and the Friends who Shaped an Age* (2019).

51. S.H. Myers, *The Bluestocking Circle: Women, Friendship and the Life of the Mind in Eighteenth-Century England* (Oxford, 1990); E. Eger, *Bluestockings: Women of Reason from Enlightenment to Romanticism* (Basingstoke, 2010).

52. C.E. Vulliamy, *Mrs Thrale of Streatham* (1936); D'Ezio, *Hester Lynch Thrale Piozzi*.

53. Prendergast, *Literary Salons*, pp. 106–31.

54. E. Lynch, *The Life of Samuel Pepys* (Oxford, 2006); D. Dougan, *Samuel Pepys: Reading the Diaries* (Bury St Edmunds, 2013).

55. J. Hostettler and R. Braby, *Sir William Garrow: His Life, Times and Fight for Justice* (Hook, 2010).

56. R.A. Melikan, *John Scott, Lord Eldon, 1751–1838: The Duty of Loyalty* (Cambridge, 1999).

57. A. Konstam, *Horatio Nelson, Leadership, Strategy, Conflict* (Oxford, 2011).

58. R. Holmes, *Wellington: The Iron Duke* (2002); A. Roberts, *Napoleon and Wellington* (2002); H.J. Davies, *Wellington's Wars: The Making of a Military Genius* (2012).

59. L. Schiebinger, *The Mind Has No Sex? Women in the Origins of Modern Science* (Cambridge, MA, 1989); P. Fara, *Pandora's Breeches: Women, Science and Power in the Enlightenment* (2004).

60. R.E. Schofield, *The Lunar Society of Birmingham: A Social History of Provincial Science and Industry in Eighteenth-Century England* (Oxford, 1963); P.M. Jones, *Industrial Enlightenment: Science, Technology and Culture in Birmingham and the West Midlands, 1760–1820* (Manchester, 2008).

61. D.P. Miller, *James Watt, Chemist: Understanding the Origins of the Steam Age* (2015); M. Dick and C. Archer-Parré, *James Watt, 1736–1819: Culture, Innovation and Enlightenment* (Liverpool, 2020).

62. I.B. Cohen, *The Newtonian Revolution* (Cambridge, 1980); J. Gleich, *Isaac Newton* (2003); Iliffe, *Priest of Nature*.

63. Cantor, *Michael Faraday, Sandemanian and Scientist*; I.R. Morus, *Michael Faraday and the Electrical Century* (2017).

64. D. Robinson, 'The Nobility', in *Blackwood's Magazine* 18 (September 1825), p. 350.

65. A. Durden, *Measures of Genius: The Scientists who Gave Their Name to Units of Measure* (Bramber, 2014), pp. 266–94.

66. V. Coltman and S. Lloyd (eds), *Henry Raeburn: Context, Reception and Reputation* (Edinburgh, 2012).

67. J. Egerton, *George Stubbs, 1744–1806* (1984); M. Myrone, *George Stubbs* (2002).

68. A. Graciano, *Joseph Wright, Esq: Painter and Gentleman* (Cambridge, 2012).

69. T.G. Natter (ed.), *Angelica Kauffmann: A Woman of Immense Talent* (2007).

70. E. Bulwer-Lytton, *Richelieu: Or, the Conspiracy* (1839), act 2, sc. 2.

71. S. Gill, *William Wordsworth: A Life* (Oxford, 1989; 2020); J. Bate, *Radical Wordsworth: The Poet who Changed the World* (2020); J.A. Colmer, *Coleridge: Critic of Society* (Oxford, 1959); K. Cooke, *Coleridge* (2016); D. Weiss, *The Female Philosopher and Her Afterlives: Mary Wollstonecraft, the British Novel and the Transformations of Feminism, 1796–1811* (Basingstoke, 2017).
72. Corfield, *Power and the Professions*, p. 218.
73. W. Hazlitt, *The Spirit of the Age: Contemporary Portraits* (1825; Oxford, 1970), p. 39.
74. W. Scott, 'Song of Blondel: Fytte Second', in idem, *The Poetical Works of Sir Walter Scott* (Edinburgh, 1848), p. 710; R. Mayer, *Sir Walter Scott and Fame: Authors and Readers in the Romantic Age* (Oxford, 2017).
75. H. Martineau, *Autobiography*, ed. L.H. Peterson (2007), pp. 21, 120.
76. T. Carlyle, *Latter-Day Pamphlets* (1850), no. 4, 'The New Downing Street', p. 4.
77. F.E. Mineka (ed.), *The Collected Works of John Stuart Mill, Vol. 12: The Earlier Letters . . . 1812–48* (1963), pp. 27–8.
78. S. Johnson, 'London: A Poem, in Imitation of . . . Juvenal' (written 1738), line 177, in *A Collection of Poems by Several Hands* (1784).
79. F. Rosen (ed.), *Jeremy Bentham* (Aldershot, 2007).
80. N.B. Harte and J. North, *The World of University College London, 1823–1978* (1989).
81. M.D. Sahlins, *How 'Natives' Think: About Captain Cook, for Example* (Chicago, 1995); G. Obeyesekere, *The Apotheosis of Captain Cook: European Myth-Making in the Pacific* (Princeton, 1997); B. Richardson, *Longitude and Empire: How Captain Cook's Voyages Changed the World* (2005); J. McAleer and N. Rigby (eds), *Captain Cook and the Pacific: Art, Exploration and Empire* (New Haven, 2017).
82. Lee, *George Canning and Liberal Toryism*.
83. Burns, 'For a' That and a' That', in Burke (ed.), *Collected Poems*, p. 331.

Chapter 17: Georgians in an Age of Experimentation

1. Z. Biener and E. Schliesser (eds), *Newton and Empiricism* (Oxford, 2014); N. Maxwell, *Understanding Empiricism: Aim-Oriented Empiricism* (2017).
2. P.C. Myers, *Our Only Star and Compass: Locke and the Struggle for Political Rationality* (Oxford, 1998); P.R. Anstey, *John Locke and Natural Philosophy* (Oxford, 2011); R.W. Grant. 'John Locke on Custom's Power and Reason's Authority', *Review of Politics* 74 (2012), pp. 607–29.
3. R. Porter, *Enlightenment: Britain and the Creation of the Modern World* (2001); P.A. Elliott, *Enlightenment, Modernity and Science: Geographies of Scientific Culture and Improvement in Georgian England* (2010); J. Israel, *Democratic Enlightenment: Philosophy, Revolution and Human Rights, 1750–90* (Oxford, 2011); R. Robertson, *The Enlightenment: The Pursuit of Happiness, 1680–1790* (2020).
4. R. Boyle, *Certain Physiological Essays . . .* (1661), in idem, *The Works of the Hon. Robert Boyle in Six Volumes* (1772), vol. 1, 299; M. Hunter, *Boyle: Between God and Science* (New Haven, 2009).
5. I. Newton, *Opticks* (1704), book 1, part 1, p. 1; N. Guicciardini, *Isaac Newton and Natural Philosophy* (2018).
6. W.H. Cropper, *Great Physicists: The Life and Times of the Leading Physicists from Galileo to Hawking* (Oxford, 2001), p. 145.
7. W. Blake, 'Jerusalem' (*c.* 1804), plate 15, in D.V. Erdman (ed.), *The Complete Poetry and Prose of William Blake* (1982), p. 158; Thompson, *Witness against the Beast*; M.K. Schuchard, *Why Mrs Blake Cried: William Blake and the Erotic Imagination* (2013).
8. Quotation from W. Blake's illuminated manuscript 'All Religions are One' (etched *c.* 1788), plate 3, cited in G. Keynes (ed.), *Poetry and Prose of William Blake* (1961), p. 148.
9. Malthus, *Essay on the Principle of Population*, p. 69.

10. Austen, *Pride and Prejudice*, p. 1; Maioli, *Empiricism and the Early Theory of the Novel*; J. Wharton, *Material Enlightenment: Women Writers and the Science of Mind, 1770–1830* (Woodbridge, 2018).
11. Austen, *Persuasion*, p. 46; W.S. Jones, *Jane on the Brain: Exploring the Science of Social Intelligence with Jane Austen* (New York, 2017).
12. Anon. [W. Whewell], *Quarterly Review* 58 (1834), pp. 58-61; and context in S. Ross, 'Scientist: The Story of a Word', *Annals of Science*,18 (1962), pp. 65–85.
13. A. Coppola, *The Theatre of Experiment: Staging Natural Philosophy in Eighteenth-Century Britain* (New York, 2016).
14. Goldgar, *Impolite Learning*; D. Wootton, *The Invention of Science: A New History of the Scientific Revolution* (2015).
15. C. Brock, *The Comet Sweeper: Caroline Herschel's Astronomical Ambition* (2007).
16. R. Lamont-Brown, *Humphry Davy: Life beyond the Lamp* (Stroud, 2004).
17. C. Ludwig, *Michael Faraday: Father of Electronics* (Scottdale, PA, 1978).
18. R. Holmes, *The Age of Wonder: How the Romantic Generation Discovered the Beauty and Terror of Science* (2008); A.J. Meadows, *The Victorian Scientist: The Growth of a Profession* (2004).
19. J.H. White, *The History of Phlogiston Theory* (New York, 1973).
20. R. DeSalle and I. Tattersall, *Troublesome Science: The Misuse of Genetics and Genomics in Understanding Race* (New York, 2018); E. Kolbert 'There's No Scientific Basis for Race: It's a Made-Up Label', *National Geographic* (12 March 2018); online at https://www.nationalgeographic.com/magazine/article/race-genetics-science-africa (accessed 17 March 2021).
21. P. Razzell, *The Conquest of Smallpox: The Impact of Inoculation on Smallpox Mortality in Eighteenth-Century Britain* (Firle, 1977); J. Smith, *'The Speckled Monster': Smallpox in England, 1670–1970, with Particular Reference to Essex* (Chelmsford, 1987); I. Grundy, *Lady Mary Wortley Montagu* (Oxford, 1999); G. Weightman, *The Great Inoculator: The Untold Story of Daniel Sutton and his Medical Revolution* (New Haven, 2020).
22. R. Boddice, *Edward Jenner* (Stroud, 2015).
23. Smith, *'Speckled Monster'*, pp. 54–5; S. Bhattacharya (ed.), *The Global Eradication of Smallpox* (New Delhi, 2010).
24. See variously https://en.wikipedia.org/wiki/Newtonian_telescope and https://en.wikipedia.org/wiki/Electrostatic_generator (accessed 14 March 2021).
25. A. Cook, *Edmond Halley: Charting the Heavens and the Seas* (Oxford, 1998).
26. Tucker, *Instructions for Travellers*, p. 21.
27. D.M. Knight, *Humphry Davy: Science and Power* (Cambridge, 1992); J. Golinski, *The Experimental Self: Humphry Davy and the Making of a Man of Science* (Chicago, 2016).
28. B. Duckham and H. Duckham, *Great Pit Disasters: Great Britain 1700 to the Present Day* (Newton Abbot, 1973).
29. M.W. Flinn and D. Stoker, *The History of the British Coal Industry, Vol. 2: The Industrial Revolution, 1700–1830* (1984).
30. C. Evans and L. Miskell, *Swansea Copper* (Baltimore, MD, 2020).
31. R. Burt et al, *Mining in Cornwall and Devon: Mines and Men* (Exeter, 2014); W. Graham, *Poldark's Cornwall* (2015).
32. Therry (ed.), *Speeches of the Right Honourable George Canning*, vol. 6, pp. 404–5.
33. T. Preston, *Thomas Newcomen of Dartmouth and the Engine that Changed the World* (Dartmouth, 2012).
34. B. Trinder, *The Darbys of Coalbrookdale* (Chichester, 1974); C.K. Hyde, *Technological Change and the British Iron Industry, 1700–1870* (Princeton, 1977).
35. W. Rosen, *The Most Powerful Idea in the World: A Story of Steam, Industry and Invention* (Chicago, 2013); Dick and Archer-Parré, *James Watt*.
36. D.S. Landes, *The Unbound Prometheus: Technological Change and Industrial Development in Western Europe from 1750 to the Present* (Cambridge, 1969); K. Pomeranz, *The Great*

Divergence: China, Europe and the Making of the Modern World Economy (Princeton, 2000); J. Mokyr, *The Enlightened Economy: An Economic History of Britain, 1700–1850* (New Haven, 2010); E.A. Wrigley, *The Path to Sustained Growth: England's Transition from an Organic Economy to an Industrial Revolution* (New York, 2016).

37. Smith, *Wealth of Nations*, vol. 1, pp. 4–5; Corfield, 'Business Leaders and Town Gentry'.

38. R.S. Fitton and A.P. Wadsworth, *The Strutts and the Arkwrights, 1758–1830: A Study of the Early Factory System* (Matlock, 2012).

39. S. Chapman (ed.), *The Cotton Trade: Its Growth and Impact, 1600–1935* (Bristol, 1999); G. Riello, *Cotton: The Fabric which Made the Modern World* (Cambridge, 2013).

40. Corfield, *Impact of English Towns*, p. 98.

41. W. Cobbett, *Rural Rides* (1830): 31 January 1830; D. Hey, *Historic Hallamshire* (Ashbourne, 2002).

42. E.L. Golding, *A History of Technology and Environment: From Stone Tools to Ecological Crisis* (2016).

43. H.S. Homer, *An Enquiry into the Means of Preserving and Improving the Publick Roads of this Kingdom . . .* (Oxford, 1767), p. 8; C. Hadfield, *British Canals: Inland Waterways of Britain and Ireland* (Stroud, 1998).

44. N. Corble, *James Brindley: The First Canal Builder* (Stroud, 2005).

45. P.A. Lynn, *World Heritage Canal: Thomas Telford and the Pontcysyllte* (Dunbeath, Caithness, 2019).

46. A.D. Cameron, *The Caledonian Canal* (Lavenham, 1972); J. Glover, *Man of Iron: Thomas Telford and the Building of Britain* (2018).

47. S. Smiles, *Lives of the Engineers . . . Comprising Also a History of Inland Communication in Britain*, 5 vols (1861–62).

48. H. Davies, *George Stephenson: The Remarkable Life of the Founder of Railways* (Stroud, 2004); S. Hylton, *Early Pioneers of Steam: The Inspiration behind George Stephenson* (2019).

49. T. Coleman, *The Railway Navvies: A History of the Men who Made the Railways* (1965; 2015).

50. M.R. Bailey (ed.), *Robert Stephenson: The Eminent Engineer* (Aldershot, 2003).

51. C. Maggs, *Isambard Kingdom Brunel: The Life of an Engineering Genius* (Stroud, 2016).

52. A.K.B. Evans (ed.), *The Impact of the Railway on Society in Britain* (Aldershot, 2002).

53. L.T.C. Rolt, *The Aeronauts: A History of Ballooning, 1783–1903* (1966).

54. 'Tullamore', in *Wikipedia*; online at https://en.wikipedia.org/wiki/Tullamore (accessed 17 February 2021).

55. R. Dee, *The Man who Discovered Flight: George Cayley and the First Airplane* (Toronto, 2007).

56. J. Priestley, *Experiments and Observations . . .*, 3 vols (1774), vol. 1, p. vii.

57. For a knockabout exposition of this concept, see J. Gimpel, *The End of the Future: The Waning of the High-Tech World*, trans. H. McPhail (1995). See also D. Sahal, *Patterns of Technological Innovation* (Reading, MA, 1981); B.H. Bunch and A. Hellemans, *The Timetables of Technology: A Chronology of the Most Important People and Events in the History of Technology* (1994).

58. M. Faraday, 'Notes for a Friday Discourse at the Royal Institution' (1858), quoted in B. Jones, *The Life and Letters of Faraday*, 2 vols (1870), vol. 2, p. 404.

59. C.L. Harbo, *Frankenstein's Monster and Scientific Methods* (2014); D. Hay, *The Making of Mary Shelley's Frankenstein* (Oxford, 2019).

60. J.A. Etzler, *The Paradise within the Reach of All Men, Without Labour, by Powers of Nature and Machinery . . .* (Pittsburgh, 1833; 1836), part 2, p. 212.

61. S. Smiles, *Lives of the Engineers, Vol. 5: The Locomotive* (1862; 1879), p. 7.

62. Franklin lodged for long periods at 36 Craven Street, just off the Strand in central London, the residence being opened in 2006 as the admirable Benjamin Franklin House Museum, complete with immersive tours: see https://benjaminfranklinhouse.org (accessed 17 February 2021).

63. Franklin, *Autobiography*, ed. P. Shaw, p. 151; also quoted above, p. 60. See for context M.B. Schiffer, *Draw the Lightning Down: Benjamin Franklin and Electrical Technology in the Age of Enlightenment* (2006).

Chapter 18: Georgians in an Age of Urbanisation

1. P.J. Corfield, 'Walking the City Streets: The Urban Odyssey in the Eighteenth-Century', *Journal of Urban History* 16 (1990), pp. 132–74; idem, 'Songs, Satire and City Life: Pro-Urban Popular Traditions in Eighteenth-Century Britain', in R.-E. Mohrmann (ed.), *Städtische Volkskultur im 18 Jahrhundert/Popular Culture in Eighteenth-Century European Towns* (Cologne, 2001), pp. 143–56
2. M. Falkus, 'Lighting in the Dark Ages of English Economic History: Town Streets before the Industrial Revolution', in D.C. Coleman and A.H. John (eds), *Trade, Government and Economy in Pre-Industrial England* (1976), pp. 248–73; J. Griffiths, *Third Man: The Life and Times of William Murdoch, 1754–1839 – The Inventor of Gas Lighting* (1992).
3. N.C. Smith (ed.), *Selected Letters of Sydney Smith* (Oxford, 1981), p. 170, letter dated July 1838; and ibid., p. 17, similar sentiments in June 1801.
4. For helpful overviews, see Butlin (ed.), *Development of the Irish Town*; R. Sweet, *The English Town, 1680–1840: Government, Society and Culture* (Harlow, 1999); B. Harris, *The Scottish Town in the Age of the Enlightenment, 1740–1820* (Edinburgh, 2014).
5. Whyman, *Pen and the People*; Browne, *Getting the Message*; M.J. Daunton, *Royal Mail: The Post Office since 1840* (2015).
6. B.F. Ronalds, *Sir Francis Ronalds: Father of the Electric Telegraph* (2016), p. 142; idem, 'Sir Francis Ronalds and the Electric Telegraph', *International Journal for the History of Engineering and Technology* 86 (2016), pp. 42–55.
7. J.P. Bowen, *British Lighthouses* (1947).
8. See https://en.wikipedia.org/wiki/1782_Central_Atlantic_hurricane (accessed 15 March 2021).
9. Maritime Memorials database, Royal Museums Greenwich: online at https://www.rmg.co.uk/discover/maritime-memorials-database (accessed 17 February 2021).
10. D. Ormrod, *The Rise of Commercial Empires: England and the Netherlands in the Age of Mercantilism* (Cambridge, 2003), p. 295; M. Berg et al. (eds), *Goods from the East, 1600–1800: Trading Eurasia* (Basingstoke, 2015); B. Lemire, *Global Trade and the Transformation of Consumer Culture: The Material World Remade* (Cambridge, 2018).
11. B. Gough, *The War against the Pirates: British and American Suppression of Caribbean Piracy in the Early Nineteenth Century* (Basingstoke, 2018).
12. M.J. Trebilcock, *The Regulation of International Trade* (2012); O. Suttle, *Distributive Justice and World Trade Law: A Political Theory of International Trade Regulation* (Cambridge, 2018).
13. S. Barton (ed.), *Travel and Tourism in Britain, 1700–1914* (2014); P. Clark and R.A. Houston, 'Culture and Leisure, 1700–1840', in P. Clark (ed.), *The Cambridge Urban History of Britain, Vol. 2: 1540–1840* (Cambridge, 2000), pp. 575–613; M. Huggins, *Horse Racing and British Society in the Long Eighteenth Century* (Woodbridge, 2018).
14. W. Cowper, *The Diverting History of John Gilpin* (1782).
15. R. Malcolmson, '"A Set of Ungovernable People": The Kingswood Colliers in the Eighteenth Century', in J. Brewer and J. Styles (eds), *An Ungovernable People: The English and Their Laws in the Eighteenth and Nineteenth Centuries* (New Brunswick, 1980), pp. 82–127.
16. See his own account, in Anon. [J. Metcalf], *The Life of J. M., Commonly Called Blind Jack of Knaresborough* (York, 1795).
17. R. Devereux [M.R.R. Pember-Devereux], *John Loudon McAdam: Chapters in the History of Highways* (1936).

18. J. Rickman (ed.), *Life of Thomas Telford, Civil Engineer: Written by Himself* (Brore, Sunderland, 2019); Glover, *Man of Iron*.
19. W. Albert, *The Turnpike Road System in England, 1663–1840* (Cambridge, 1972).
20. W. Taylor, *The Military Roads of Scotland* (Newton Abbot, 1976).
21. D. Gerhold (ed.), *Road Transport in the Horse-Drawn Era* (Aldershot, 1996).
22. A.L. Murphy, *The Origins of English Financial Markets: Investment and Speculation before the South Sea Bubble* (Cambridge, 2009); P. Walsh, *The South Sea Bubble and Ireland: Money, Banking and Investment, 1690–1721* (Woodbridge, 2014).
23. D. Kynaston, *Till Time's Last Sand: A History of the Bank of England, 1694–2013* (2017).
24. B.L. Anderson and P.L. Cottrell, *Money and Banking in England: The Development of the Banking System, 1694–1914* (Newton Abbot, 1974); S.G. Checkland, *Scottish Banking: A History, 1695–1973* (1975).
25. L. Neal (ed.), *The Rise of Financial Capitalism: International Capital Markets in the Age of Reason* (Cambridge, 1993), pp. 170–1; Ashton, *Economic Fluctuations*, pp. 103–37, esp. pp. 128–9.
26. J. Israel, *The Dutch Republic: Its Rise, Greatness and Fall, 1477–1806* (Oxford, 1995).
27. L.S. Pressnell, 'The Rate of Interest in the Eighteenth Century', in idem (ed.), *Studies in the Industrial Revolution*, pp. 178–214.
28. Corfield, *Time and the Shape of History*, pp. 180–2; I. Szelenyi, *Varieties of Post-Communist Capitalism: A Comparative Analysis of Russia, Eastern Europe and China* (Leiden, 2020).
29. See cognate discussions by R. Harris, 'Government and the Economy, 1688–1850', in R. Floud and P. Johnson (eds), *The Cambridge Economic History of Modern Britain*, vol. 1: *Industrialisation,1700–1850* (Cambridge, 2003), pp. 204–37; and essays in J. Guldi (ed.), *Roads to Power: Britain Invents the Infrastructure State* (2012).
30. J. Anderson, 'Urban Development as a Component of Government Policy in the Aftermath of the Napoleonic War', *Construction History* 15 (1999), pp. 23–37.
31. J.D. Chambers and G. Mingay, *The Agricultural Revolution, 1750–1880* (1966); D.R. Mills (ed.), *English Rural Communities: The Impact of a Specialised Economy* (1973); M. Overton, *Agricultural Revolution in England: The Transformation of the Agrarian Economy, 1500–1850* (Cambridge, 1996).
32. Anon., *The Rational Farmer and Practical Husbandman* (1743).
33. E.P. Thompson [with E.E. Dodd], 'The Crime of Anonymity', in Hay et al., *Albion's Fatal Tree*, pp. 255–344.
34. P.B. Munsche, *Gentleman and Poachers: The English Game Laws, 1671–1931* (Cambridge, 1981).
35. J.M. Neeson, *Commoners: Common Right, Enclosure and Social Change in England, 1700–1820* (Cambridge, 1993).
36. S. Rutherford, *Capability Brown and His Landscape Gardens* (2016).
37. J. Barrell, *The Dark Side of the Landscape: The Rural Poor in English Painting, 1730–1850* (Cambridge, 1983); P. Horn, *The Rural World, 1780–1850: Social Change in the English Countryside* (Basingstoke, 2017).
38. Corfield, *Impact of English Towns*, pp. 6–16; J. de Vries, *European Urbanisation, 1500–1800* (1984), pp. 167–72, 270–1.
39. P. Clark (ed.), *Oxford Handbook of Cities in World History* (Oxford, 2013).
40. Corfield, *Impact of English Towns*; P. Borsay, *The English Urban Renaissance: Culture and Society in the Provincial Town, 1660–1760* (Oxford, 1989); Sweet, *English Town, 1680–1840*; Harris, *Scottish Town in the Age of the Enlightenment*.
41. F.H. Spencer, *Municipal Origins: An Account of English Private Bill Legislation relating to Local Government, 1740–1835* (1911); Corfield, *Impact of English Towns*, pp. 157–8, 175–6.
42. A. Borg and D. Coke, *Vauxhall Gardens: A History* (2011); P.J. Corfield, *Vauxhall, Sex and Entertainment: London's Pioneering Pleasure Garden* (2012).
43. S. Gater and D. Vincent, *The Factory in a Garden: Wedgwood from Etruria to Barlaston – The Transitional Years* (1988).

44. A. Kenny, *Staffordshire Spaniels: A Collectors' Guide* . . . (1997).
45. N.B. Harte, 'State Control of Dress and Social Change in Pre-Industrial England', in Coleman and John (eds), *Trade, Government and Economy*, pp. 132–65, esp. pp. 151–3.
46. P. Langford, *A Polite and Commercial People: England, 1727–83* (Oxford, 1989), pp. 59–121; Klein, 'Politeness and the Interpretation of the British Eighteenth Century'.
47. P.D. Stanhope (ed.), *The Works of the Earl of Chesterfield, Including His Letters to His Son* (New York, 1838), p. 160: letter 129 (1747).
48. Tucker, *Protean Shape*, p. 75.
49. Stanhope (ed.), *Works*, p. 177: letter 142 (1748).
50. J. Hawkins, *The Life of Samuel Johnson, LLD* (1787), p. 191.
51. H. Waters, *Racism on the Victorian Stage: Representations of Slavery and the Black Character* (Cambridge, 2007); P. Panayi, *An Immigration History of Britain: Multicultural Racism since 1800* (Harlow, 2010); R. Hanley, 'Slavery and the Birth of Working-Class Racism in England, 1814–33', *Transactions of the Royal Historical Society* 26 (2016), pp. 103–23.
52. D. Livesay, *Children of Uncertain Fortune: Mixed-Race Jamaicans in Britain and the Atlantic Family, 1733–1833* (2017).
53. P. Byrne, *Belle: The True Story of Dido Belle* (2014).
54. P.J. Corfield, 'Dress for Deference and Dissent: Hats and the Decline of Hat Honour', *Costume: Journal of the Costume Society* 23 (1989), pp. 64–85; idem, 'From Hat Honour to the Handshake: Changing Styles of Communication in the Eighteenth Century', in idem and Hannan (eds), *Hats Off, Gentlemen!*, pp. 11–30.
55. D. Newell, 'Masculinity and the Plebeian Honour Fight: Dispute Resolution in Georgian England' (PhD thesis, Oxford Brookes University, 2017).
56. M.C. Jacob, *The Origins of Freemasonry: Facts and Fictions* (Philadelphia, 2006).
57. Anon. [M. Hake], *Something New on Men and Manners: A Critique of the Follies and Vices of the Age* . . . (Hailsham, 1828), p. 174.
58. P. Ward, *The Clean Body: A Modern History* (Montreal, 2019), esp. pp. 18–29, 107–12.
59. R. Vaughan, *The Age of Great Cities: Or, Modern Society Viewed in Its Relation to Intelligence, Morals and Religion* (1843).
60. P. Manning and T. Trimmer, *Migration in World History* (2020); S. Shah, *The Next Great Migration: The Story of Movement on a Changing Planet* (2020).

Chapter 19: Georgian Deeds and Misdeeds

1. P. Henry, 'Speech on the Stamp Act at the Virginia Convention' (1775); see also J.A, Ragosta, *Patrick Henry: Proclaiming a Revolution* (2016).
2. D.P. Womersley, *Gibbon and the 'Watchman of the Holy City': The Historian and His Reputation, 1776–1815* (Oxford, 2002).
3. See J. Ebsworth, 'Davis, William (1627–1690)', *Oxford Dictionary of National Biography* (1888); online at https://www.oxforddnb.com/view/10.1093/odnb/9780192683120.001.0001/odnb-9780192683120-e-7295 (accessed 17 February 2021). But note that there are also other candidates for the Golden Farmer's real-life identity. See e.g. B. White, 'Bennet [Bennett], John [*alias* William Freeman or Hill; *called* the Golden Farmer] (d. 1690), thief', *Oxford Dictionary of National Biography* (2018); online at https://www.oxforddnb.com/view/10.1093/ref:odnb/9780198614128.001.0001/odnb-9780198614128-e-76838 (accessed 17 February 2021).
4. W.H. Ainsworth, *Rookwood: A Romance* (1834); J.A. Sharpe, *Dick Turpin: The Myth of the English Highwayman* (2005).
5. 'Paget [formerly Bayly], Henry William, first Marquess of Anglesey (1768–1854), army officer and politician', *Oxford Dictionary of National Biography* (2008); online at https://www.oxforddnb.com/view/10.1093/ref:odnb/9780198614128.001.0001/odnb-9780198614128-e-21112 (accessed 17 February 2021).

6. T. Dixon, *Weeping Britannia: Portrait of a Nation in Tears* (Oxford, 2015); I. Hislop, *Stiff Upper Lip: An Emotional History of Britain* (TV series, 3 pts: 2012).

7. S. Dugan, *Baroness Orczy's Scarlet Pimpernel: A Publishing History* (2016); S. Parson and J.L. Schatz (eds), *Superheroes and Masculinity: Unmasking the Gender Performance of Heroism* (Lanham, MD, 2020).

8. W. Churchill, *Marlborough: His Life and Times* (1933–38).

9. C.C. Lloyd, *Lord Cochrane: Seaman – Radical – Liberator* ... (1947); D. Cordingly, *Cochrane the Dauntless: The Life and Adventures of Admiral Thomas Cochrane, 1775–1860* (2007).

10. A.E. Navarrete, *Lord Cochrane en Chile: toma de Valdivia* (Santiago, Chile, 1992); B. Vale, *Cochrane in the Pacific: Fortune and Freedom in Spanish America* (2007).

11. D. Redford (ed.), *Maritime History and Identity: The Sea and Culture in the Modern World* (2014).

12. T.L. Peacock, *Melincourt* (1817).

13. S. Bae, *When the State No Longer Kills: International Human Rights Norms and Abolition of Capital Punishment* (Albany, 2007).

14. See e.g. B. Zachariah, 'Responses to Empire: "Indian" Perspectives from the Twentieth Century', in *Zeithistorische Forschungen/Studies in Contemporary History*, Online-Ausgabe, 3 (2006): https://zeithistorische-forschungen.de/1-2006/4766, DOI: https://doi.org/10.14765/zzf.dok-1980 (accessed 17 March 2021); J.T. Ducker, *Beyond Empire: The End of Britain's Colonial Encounter* (2020); S. Sanghera, *Empireland: How Imperialism Has Shaped Modern Britain* (2021).

15. B. Simms and D.J.B. Trim (eds), *Humanitarian Intervention: A History* (2011); M. Sinha, *The Slave's Cause: A History of Abolition* (New Haven, 2016); F. Klose, *'In the Cause of Humanity': Eine Geschichte der humanitären Intervention im langen 19 Jahrhundert* (Göttingen, 2019).

16. P. Manning (ed.), *Slave Trades, 1500–1800: Globalisation of Forced Labour* (2016); L. Marques, *The United States and the Transatlantic Slave Trade to the Americas, 1776–1867* (2016); and the Trans-Atlantic Slave Trade database, online at https://www.slavevoyages.org/voyage/database (accessed 17 February 2021).

17. See Anti-Slavery International, online at https://www.antislavery.org (accessed 17 February 2021); as well as P. Kotiswaran (ed.), *Revisiting the Law and Governance of Trafficking, Forced Labour and Modern Slavery* (Cambridge, 2017); J. Nolan and M. Boersma, *Addressing Modern Slavery* (Sydney, 2019); H. Kenway, *The Truth about Modern Slavery* (2021).

18. Located in Boston Memorial Park, between Washington and School Streets, Boston, MA 02108.

19. G. Jacques, *Beyond Impunity: An Ecumenical Approach to Truth, Justice and Reconciliation* (Geneva, 2000); D.T. Green, *Truth and Reconciliation* (2011).

20. J. Waldron (ed.), *Theories of Rights* (Oxford, 1984).

21. W.H. Bond, *Thomas Hollis of Lincoln's Inn: A Whig and His Books* (Cambridge, 1990).

22. S.M. Wise, *'Though the Heavens May Fall': The Landmark Trial* ... (2006); N.S. Poser, *Lord Mansfield, Justice in the Age of Reason* (Montreal, 2013).

23. Paine, *Rights of Man*, p. 136; Lamb, *Thomas Paine and the Idea of Human Rights*; S. Edwards and M. Morris (eds), *The Legacy of Thomas Paine in the Transatlantic World* (2017).

24. M. Wollstonecraft, *A Vindication of the Rights of Woman* (1792); J. Spence, *The Rights of Infants* (1796); Anon., *The Rights of British Slaves* (*c.* 1796); W.H. Drummond, *The Rights of Animals: And Man's Obligation to Treat Them with Humanity* (1838).

25. G. Brown (ed.), *The Universal Declaration of Human Rights in the Twenty-First Century: A Living Document in a Changing World* ... (2016).

26. E.g. Anon., *The Duties of Man in Connection with His Rights: Or, Rights and Duties Inseparable* (1793); Anon., *The Catechism of Man: Pointing Out from Sound Principles and*

Acknowledged Facts the Rights and Duties of Every Rational Being (1793); and see E.R. Boot, *Human Duties and the Limits of Human Rights Discourse* (2017).

27. R. Holmes, *'African Queen': The Real Life of the Hottentot Venus* (2007); S. Qureshi, *Peoples on Parade: Exhibitions, Empire and Anthropology in Nineteenth-Century Britain* (Chicago, 2011).

28. T.J. Hunt, *The Politics of Bones* (Toronto, 2005); C. Quigley, *Dissection on Display: Cadavers, Anatomists and Public Spectacle* (Jefferson, NC, 2012).

29. W.O. Henderson, *The Industrial Revolution on the Continent: Germany, France, Russia, 1800–1914* (1967); N.F.R. Crafts, *Industrial Revolution in England and France: Some Thoughts on the Question, 'Why Was England First?'* (Warwick, 1975); K. Bruland (ed.), *Essays on Industrialisation in France, Norway, and Spain* (Oslo, 2005); J. Horn, *The Path Not Taken: French Industrialisation in the Age of Revolution, 1750–1830* (2006); D.R. Meyer, *The Roots of American Industrialisation* (Baltimore, 2003).

30. A. Burton, *The Railway Empire: How the British Gave Railways to the World* (Barnsley, 2018).

31. Anon., *Treatise on Merit*, p. 6.

32. J. Littler, *Against Meritocracy: Culture, Power and Myths of Mobility* (2017); S.J. McNamee, *The Meritocracy Myth* (Lanham, MD, 2018).

33. The Adam Smith Institute, based in London SW1: see https://www.adamsmith.org (accessed 17 February 2021); the American Association of Private Enterprise Education (APEE), based in Lubbock, TX: see https://www.apee.org (accessed 17 February 2021).

34. Burke, *Reflections*, p. 135.

35. See also K. Yamamoto, *Taming Capitalism before Its Triumph: Public Service, Distrust and 'Projecting' in Early Modern England* (Oxford, 2018).

36. Corfield, *Power and the Professions*, pp. 180–4; and see above, p. 281.

37. I. Clark, *Governance, the State, Regulation and Industrial Relations* (2000); P.L. Rousseau and P. Wachtel (eds), *Financial Systems and Economic Growth: Credit, Crises and Regulation from the Nineteenth Century to the Present* (Cambridge, 2017).

38. A. Smith, *A Theory of Moral Sentiments* (1759); J.R. Otteson, *Adam Smith's Marketplace of Life* (Cambridge, 2002); C.J. Berry, *The Idea of Commercial Society in the Scottish Enlightenment* (Edinburgh, 2015).

39. Smith, *Wealth of Nations*, vol. 1, p. 400.

40. Corfield, *Time and the Shape of History*, pp. 122–49.

41. Z. Bauman, *Liquid Modernity* (Cambridge, 2008).

42. U. Volz (ed.), *Regional Integration, Economic Development and Global Governance* (Cheltenham, 2011); C. Dejung and N.P. Petersson (eds), *The Foundations of Worldwide Economic Integration: Power, Institutions and Global Markets, 1850–1930* (Cambridge, 2013); S. Malamud and A. Malkhozov, *Market Integration and Global Crashes* (2016).

43. P. Goldstein, *Copyright's Highway: From the Printing Press to the Cloud* (Stanford, 2019).

44. But see e.g. A. Ciampi (ed.), *History and International Law: An Intertwined Relationship* (Cheltenham, 2019); N. Ryder and L. Pasculli, *Corruption, Integrity and the Law: Global Regulatory Challenges* (2020).

45. H.H. Lamb, *Climate: Present, Past and Future* (2011); C. Figueres and T. Rivett-Carnac, *The Future We Choose: Surviving the Climate Crisis* (2020).

46. Burns, 'Man was Made to Mourn: A Dirge' (1784), in Burke (ed.), *Collected Poems*, p. 112.

SELECT BIBLIOGRAPHY

Introducing the 'exploding galaxy' of eighteenth-century studies, for which detailed references are provided in the endnotes. The place of publication is London unless otherwise indicated.

Allan, D. *Scotland in the Eighteenth Century: Union and Enlightenment* (Harlow, 2002).

Allen, R.C. *The British Industrial Revolution in Global Perspective* (Cambridge, 2009).

Black, J. *Britain as a Military Power, 1688–1815* (Abingdon, 1999).

Cannadine, D. *Class in Britain* (New Haven, 2000).

Clark, P.A. *British Clubs and Societies, 1580–1800: The Origins of an Associational World* (Oxford, 2000).

Colley, L. *The Gun, the Ship and the Pen: Warfare, Constitutions and the Making of the Modern World* (2021).

Drescher, S. *Abolition: A History of Slavery and Ant-Slavery* (Cambridge, 2009).

Hay, D. and N. Rogers. *Eighteenth-Century English Society: Shuttles and Swords* (Oxford, 1997).

Jones, C. (ed.). *A Short History of Parliament: England, Great Britain, the United Kingdom, Ireland and Scotland* (Woodbridge, 2009).

Lemire, B. *Global Trade and the Transformation of Consumer Culture: The Material World Remade* (Cambridge, 2018).

Manning, P. (ed.). *Slave Trades, 1500–1800: Globalisation of Forced Labour* (2016).

Marshall, P.J. (ed.). *The Oxford History of the British Empire, Vol. 2: The Eighteenth Century* (Oxford, 1998).

McBride, I. *Eighteenth-Century Ireland: The Isle of Slaves* (Dublin, 2014).

O'Gorman, F. *The Long Eighteenth Century: British Political and Social History, 1688–1832* (1998).

Porter, R. *Enlightenment: Britain and the Creation of the Modern World* (2001).

Prest, W. *Albion Ascendant: English History, 1660–1815* (Oxford, 1998).

Taylor, M.E. *The Interest: How the British Establishment Resisted the Abolition of Slavery* (2020).

Thompson, E.P. *The Making of the English Working Class* (Harmondsworth, 1968).

Wrigley, E.A. and R.S. Schofield, *The Population History of England, 1541–1871: A Reconstruction* (Cambridge, 1981).

Yates, N. *Eighteenth-Century Britain: Religion and Politics, 1713–1915* (Harlow, 2008).

INDEX